T0322468

'The product of Marc Millon's lifelong passion for Italy, this fascinating account of the place of wine in Italian life over the centuries is an utterly absorbing read. Enjoy it with a good glass of vino to hand!'

Fiona Beckett, wine writer, *The Guardian*

'Marc Millon has blended history with wine in a highly original format. This is a scholarly yet accessible work imbued with love for its subjects—a truly excellent book and a must-read for any lover of Italy or wine in general.'

Susy Atkins, Wine and Drinks Correspondent, *The Daily Telegraph*

'What a brilliant idea! Marc Millon takes us on a breezy, boozy tour through Italy's past, serving up bite-sized historical summaries with wine pairings to reveal how wine flavours history, and history flavours wine. Bring your corkscrew!'

Tom Standage, author of *A History of the World in 6 Glasses*

'It's not often that a wine writer can engross and enthrall you with the history of a culture where wine merely plays its part along with many other players. Marc Millon does this absorbingly and impressively, telling the intriguing, exasperating, but ultimately optimistic story of Italy and its wines.'

Oz Clarke, broadcaster, wine writer and author of
The History of Wine in 100 Bottles and *Wine by the Glass*

'Marc Millon has a gift for blending wine and travel together, bringing to life the history and sense of place, and revealing where these wines' characteristics originated. I've shared that passion over many a meal, often cooked by Marc and frequently accompanied by wines from Italy, all served up with his incredible depth of knowledge. Bravo, Marc.'

Michael Caines MBE, Michelin-starred chef

'An extraordinary and breathtaking book, *Italy in Wine Glass* is a crowning achievement! Not only is it an enthralling journey with an exceptional guide, it is also an irresistible invitation by a great host to taste 8,000 years of Italian wine history and culture, bottle by bottle, glass by glass.'

Rachel Roddy, food writer and author of *An A–Z of Pasta* and *My Kitchen in Rome*

'Marc Millon is a true Italian wine ambassador, and no one is better equipped to tell this story. His mouth-watering history had me drooling from the very first chapter! Packed full of personal observations and insights, it is essential reading for anyone interested in Italian wine, its past, present and future.'

Stevie Kim, Managing Director, Vinitaly International

'Appreciation of wine is always enriched with a story and Marc Millon is a master storyteller. In pairing fascinating histories with expertly chosen bottles, he takes on a unique journey through Italy's cultural past. Here, you get to share a glass with Ancient Greek philosophers, sip with Roman legionnaires and make a toast with intellectual revolutionaries. This is a book in which you really can taste a place and its history.'

Dan Saladino, broadcaster and author of *Eating to Extinction*

'Millon is a great storyteller with decades of experience of Italy's wines, wineries and winemakers. Read it for an insider's view of the Italian winemaking tradition, and a richly entertaining account of the country's history seen through the bottom of a wine glass.'

Helena Attlee, author of *Lev's Violin: An Italian Adventure* and *The Land Where Lemons Grow*

'It is no negligible task to wander through the meanders of Italian culture, with which wine is so intertwined, and to grasp such an extensive history of radical transformations. Marc Millon juggles this venture with enviable mastery.'

Piero Mastroberardino, President, Mastroberardino winery

'An intriguing and clever way to view Italy's history. *Italy in a Wineglass* is full of curious facts and historical diversions. Best of all it helps me to make sense of the wine aisle in my local supermarket here in Genoa.'

Nicholas Walton, author of *Genoa, 'La Superba'*

'A delectable, Epicurean celebration of the profound role wine has played, and continues to play, in Italian society. Millon's history is hedonistic and thought-provoking in equal measure.'

Jamie Mackay, author of *The Invention of Sicily*

'*Italy in a Wineglass* gathers a multitude of small stories and anecdotes from which the enchantment of the richest land of vineyards arises. An excellent literary work, an innovative contribution to wine writing.'

Sandro Boscaini, President, Masi Agricola winery

'This beautiful book tells the story of wine and at the same time the history of human civilisation, two stories that have been intertwined for about 8,000 years, especially in Italy. Wine was a story initially only for men, but today women are increasingly playing a leading role.'

Donatella Cinelli Colombini, Casato Prime Donne, and founding member and former president, Le Donne Del Vino national association

'An insightful journey through time, unveiling Italy's rich wine heritage and its importance and presence in the country's history and culture. Delivering a unique overview of Italy's past and future, Millon's seamless blend of fascinating history and engaging storytelling makes this an exciting read for those who want a better understanding of Italy through the lens of wine.'

Claudio Povero, Trade Analyst (Wine), Italian Trade Agency

ITALY IN A WINEGLASS

MARC MILLON

Italy in a Wineglass

The Taste of History

HURST & COMPANY, LONDON

First published in the United Kingdom in 2024 by
C. Hurst & Co. (Publishers) Ltd.,
New Wing, Somerset House, Strand, London WC2R 1LA
Copyright © Marc Millon, 2024
All rights reserved.

A Cataloguing-in-Publication data record for this book
is available from the British Library.

ISBN: 9781911723073

This book is printed using paper from registered sustainable
and managed sources.

www.hurstpublishers.com

Printed in Great Britain by Bell & Bain Ltd, Glasgow

To Kim
Guy and Hannah
Bella and Michael
and Sol

CONTENTS

CONTENTS

N

Aosta

Milan
Pavia
Turin
Alba
Barolo
Parma

Bolzano
Bressanone
Trento
Cividale del Friuli
Cormòns
Lake Iseo
Venice
Verona
Trieste

Genoa
Cinque Terre
Pisa
Gorgona
Carmignano
Florence
San Gimignano
Siena
Montalcino
Bologna
Forlimpopoli
Elba
Spoleto
Orvieto
Ancona
Loreto
Ascoli Piceno
Pescara
Tarquinia
Montefiascone
Gran Sasso
ROME
Frascati
Anagni
Campobasso
Montecassino
Castel del Monte
Naples
Caserta
Avellino
Monte Vulture
Brindisi
Vesuvius
Pompeii
Matera
Lecce
Salerno
Potenza
Taranto
Paestum
Mamoiada
Oristano
Cagliari
Cirò
Lipari
Reggio Calabria
Palermo
Mozia
Marsala
Selinunte
Etna
Vittoria
Syracuse
Pantelleria

© S.Ballard (2024)

INTRODUCTION

The story of Italy has been entwined, since its earliest days, with the story of wine. From 6,000 years ago—and possibly earlier—when indigenous Italians were known to have used wine in funeral rituals, to the present day, wine has been an ever-present element on the Italian Peninsula and its islands. Throughout centuries and millennia, it has been a celebratory libation at great events in Italian history; it has lubricated moments of triumph and offered solace in times of despair; and it has been a constant feature of quotidian life for tyrants, emperors, kings, popes, Holy Roman emperors, aristocrats, nobles, abbots and monks, as well as for the common man and woman. In short, wine has been and continues to be an essential element of Italian civilisation. It seems an obvious and enjoyable pursuit, then, to explore the story of Italy through its wines, naturally with a glass in hand.

Where to begin? I pour myself a measure of Pithos Rosso from a short, squat bottle. The wine has a distinctive, slightly sour nose and an earthy, stone taste. I roll the wine around in my mouth, chewing it, savouring it, and consider how wine, uniquely, has the power to transport us through space and time. Within a bottle of wine, good wine, real wine, there is a precise place contained, that spot where grapes were grown, cared for, harvested, then pressed and fermented to produce the liquid that we are now enjoying. Wine can encapsulate time, too, not only the year when those grapes were grown, harvested and pressed—the vintage date on the bottle—but even further back, connecting us in myriad ways to long-ago eras, movements, personalities and great moments in history. Italian wine, perhaps more than wine from anywhere else, holds within it such a rich concentration of stories and connections that link us directly to the past, whether to ancient times or to yesteryear. This wine, Pithos Rosso, for example, has been fermented on the skin in terracotta vessels buried underground, as wine was made thousands of years ago; as wine was made in south-east Sicily after the Greeks came to settle in Italy and Sicily in the eighth and seventh centuries BCE in what came to be known as Magna Graecia; and as wine is once again being made today.

To the ancients, wine was a sophisticated product that had the capacity to approach the divine. Copious libations were offered to the gods, and indeed there were deities dedicated to wine: Dionysus, Fufluns, Liber, Bacchus. Wine's mythic power continued with the story of Christianity, that at the Last Supper Jesus Christ urged his disciples to drink wine and eat bread in memory of him through the miracle of the Eucharist, the transubstantiation of wine into the blood of Christ and bread into the body. From the ancient world to the present day, myths, stories, legends, all intimately linked to wines, have helped define and shape an ever-evolving narrative that is the story of culture and civilisation on the Italian Peninsula and its islands.

These stories intertwine and overlap in some cases but often mainly stand alone, linked to specific times, places or areas, people, moments and movements. Because Italy from the fall of the Roman Empire was never a single nation until it was unified in 1861, there is not necessarily a unifying and clear narrative that connects everything neatly. Indeed, this is perhaps why so many regions and localities are still able to maintain such strong identities and personalities that distinguish them from anywhere else, the *campanilismo* whereby everyone's loyalty lies first to the precise neighbourhood where they were born. If this is the case with history and identity, so it is with Italy's wines, their incredibly rich diversity of styles, types, grape varieties often limited to very specific regions or even tiny locales for any number of reasons, sometimes historical, or sometimes, it seems, simply because it has always been so, that these grapes are here, or there, and always have been. If we are what we eat, what we drink, then Italy's wines, like its rich gastronomy, culture and history, proudly define who Italians are and often very precisely where they come from. Indeed, most Italians given a choice would still mainly prefer the foods and the wines of their home locality or region. It's a question of tradition and habit, sure, but it is also their histories, which continue to go hand in hand with wine and wine-drinking habits, regional and local taste memories seemingly embedded in one's own very DNA.

Why is it important to understand Italy's richly complex and often confusing history, and to connect it to its wines? Because Italians themselves do and because learning about the past helps us to understand and appreciate the present. Speak to most Italians, and it is remarkable how closely they feel connected to the past, their own past. I was on a bus to Vinitaly—Italy's most important annual wine fair, which takes place each year in Verona—and sat down next to an elderly lady, a wine producer from Calabria, from a remote and minor wine zone that I hadn't heard of before. 'Our town has a castle built by Frederick II', she told me, 'You should come and visit. Did you know that he was called "Lo Stupor Mundi"—the wonder of the world', she added, as proudly as if she were talking about her own son. On another occasion, my wife Kim and I were on a walking holiday in Alto Adige in the company of a mountain guide named Alboin. I said to him that I had never heard the name before. 'Alboin was the first king of the Lombards who conquered almost all of Italy. It is why many of us here in the north have blond hair and blue eyes', he explained patiently, and as if he himself were a direct royal descendant of that warrior king.

Italians are deeply knowledgeable and immensely proud of their own histories: they will talk of Roman or Greek ruins in their locality with detailed knowledge, or of a beautiful Mannerist painting in their local church with sensitivity and pride. Or they might point out, casually and in passing, that when Napoleon passed through their town this now-deconsecrated church was used by French soldiers as a stable—'look, you can still see on the wooden door where the horses' hooves scraped and scratched', they'll say, as if it happened just yesterday.

Wine is always a reflection of society and culture. In the medieval period, a form of sharecropping known as the *mezzadria* was in place across much of Central and Northern Italy, whereby in return for a farmhouse and land, tenant farmers were entitled to keep half of what they produced, with the other half going to the *padrone*, the landowner. This agrarian contract between worker and landowner was considered a model of self-sufficiency based on obligations, rights and tasks, ensuring (when not abused) that landowner and tenant alike shared produce, whether grapes for wine, olives for oil, vegetables and grain, or the slaughter and curing of a pig. This feudal system continued in parts of Italy until as late as the 1970s and defined the countryside.

The history of Italy from the sixteenth century until unification is in part characterised by foreign domination. The Spanish, first under the Habsburgs and later under Bourbons, controlled Southern Italy and Sicily for centuries. Sardinia was from the fourteenth century under the Spanish Aragonese until it was taken over by the Piedmontese House of Savoy in 1718. During the Napoleonic era, French influence extended across large parts of Italy, exerted through compliant client states and sister republics, while after Napoleon's demise the Austrian Habsburgs controlled all of North-East Italy, their influence encompassing the *terraferma* lands of the former Venetian Republic and from the Brenner Pass across Lombardy. These foreign occupations left a profound mark on Italy culturally as well as gastronomically.

The story of the Risorgimento and Italy's unification is also linked to wine. Giuseppe Garibaldi and his 'Thousand' landed in the small wine town of Marsala in May 1860 and from there began a march that was to eventually drive the Spanish Bourbons from Sicily and Southern Italy and pave the way for the creation of a new nation. The Savoia, whose Kingdom of Sardinia oversaw not only much of North West Italy but also extended over the Alps into what is now France, helped to create the Kingdom of Italy and became its first rulers. They themselves were particularly fond of a wine called Barolo, which was proclaimed 'the king of wines, the wine of kings'. King Carlo Alberto I, the father of Italy's first king, was so fond of it that he purchased a castle with a vineyard in Verduno. Count Camillo Benso Cavour, an aristocrat who was to become Italy's first prime minister, helped to improve the quality of Barolo from his estate based around the Castello di Grinzane by bringing in French winemaking expertise. Vittorio Emanuele II, Italy's first king, installed the love of his life, Rosa Vercellana, in a sumptuous villa amid a Barolo wine estate that grew to be one of the area's most renowned and that continues to produce great wine today. Barolo then was most certainly 'a wine fit for kings'—and so Barolo remains today, though fortunately we don't have to have royal or aristocratic blood to enjoy it. Just a little bit of money.

Over the centuries, countless wars have been waged on the Italian Peninsula and its islands. In the twentieth century, some of the country's most idyllic and beautiful wine country was turned into killing fields. In both the First and Second World Wars, the north-east corner of the country, the region that became Friuli–Venezia Giulia and was once part of the Austro-Hungarian Empire, was particularly ravaged. In the north-west, meanwhile, the peaceful wine hills of Barolo were the scene of fierce fighting between partisans, fascists and Germans. The Gothic Line in the vine-covered hills of Romagna above Bologna witnessed unspeakable tragedies and atrocities. Today, Italy is at peace, its wine country recuperated and cultivated once more. Yet it is important to remember those dark times when we enjoy glasses of Friulano, Langhe Nebbiolo and Sangiovese di Romagna. The Vigna del Mondo is a unique vineyard located in Friuli's Cormòns, planted with some 550 different vines from all over the world, which are blended to produce 'Il Vino della Pace'—the 'wine of peace'—bottles of which, decorated with labels by eminent artists, have been sent to every head of state in the world.

If wine has long reflected Italian society, then it would be remiss not to cast a glance at some of the darker elements of this complex nation. The murky origins of the Mafia can be traced back to the land, to the 'guardians' hired by absentee landlords to look after their agricultural affairs, thugs who exploited the peasants cruelly as well as stealing from the landowners when they could, in the process amassing huge power and influence for themselves. While the Mafia has gone on to involve itself in extortion, construction, drugs, money laundering, trafficking and just about everything else, in recent years there has been a return to the land, as Italy's organised crime families reap rich rewards by infiltrating Italy's famous food and wine industries. But there are organisations that are fighting back. Libera Terra seeks to restore dignity to territories with a strong Mafia presence through the creation of cooperative farms utilising lands confiscated from the Mafia.

The story or stories of Italy—in large or small part—are contained within almost every single bottle of Italian wine. For here, more than perhaps anywhere else, wine is never just an alcoholic liquid. There is always a larger context and a story, sometimes deeply personal (a winemaker whose great-grandparents were *mezzadri* or sharecropping peasant farmers to the great maestro Giuseppe Verdi); sometimes linked directly to historic events—a wine that Roman soldiers drank in quantity on the eve of a famous battle against the Carthaginians, or a winery located in the hunting lodge of an aristocratic family from the time when the Spanish Bourbons ruled the south of Italy. Even wines that seemingly have no compelling story to tell still have their own narratives. A wine produced industrially by the literal millions of bottles tells of Italy's post-war 'economic miracle', when Italian wines conquered the world. Wines that come from factory-like cooperative wineries are an enduring and important testament to a social movement that today accounts for some 60 per cent of all Italian wine production, including wines that are now consistently winning the highest awards and accolades.

This book broadly tells the story of Italy through its wines in chronological order. It makes no claim to be comprehensive, and the historical narrative is presented with a light brush. I hope that historians will not judge this too harshly, and I fully understand and acknowledge that Italy's history is infinitely richer, more complex and nuanced than I have been able to cover here. Moreover, this is *my* story of Italy through its wines, based on research that goes back more than forty years to places I have visited, people I have met, wines I have tasted and learned from, plates of food I have enjoyed, conversations shared. There may be many wines not included here that well deserve to be. I look forward to tasting them, learning their stories, too.

Italy in a Wineglass comes up to the present moment, to an Italy that, like the rest of the world, had to endure the miseries and uncertainties of COVID-19 and lockdown. It is a restless time in history, with people on the move, desperate to cross borders by sea and land in search of a better life, as happens from time to time across centuries and millennia, a dangerous time, too, when the dark forces of extreme nationalism in Italy and elsewhere have gained power. It is also a frightening moment for our planet, with the world almost literally on fire. In the heatwave summer of 2023, there were red alert heat emergencies in place across twenty-three Italian cities, and record temperatures were exceeded in Sicily and Sardinia. Climate change is happening quickly and presents an immense challenge to all Italians, not least to its wine producers. Can solutions be found? Let us hope so. Meanwhile, Italian wines have been sent into outer space to spend up to a year on the International Space Station to find out what effect this will have on the ageing of wines and vines in zero gravity. As has ever been the case, from antiquity to the present moment, the compelling and intoxicating story of Italy—yesterday, today and tomorrow—continues to be intimately entwined with the story of Italian wines.

It is my sincere hope that this dip into Italian history and wine will give you a thirst to explore, to taste, to learn, to enjoy, to drink deeply and to delve further. So please, without further ado, let me urge you to pour yourself a glass of good Italian wine and let our journey begin!

Marc Millon
Topsham, Devon
October 2023

1

ACROSS WINE-DARK SEAS

Selinunte, founded in Sicily in 628 BCE on the north-west coast of the island over-looking the pounding surf of the Sicilian Channel, was once one of the most powerful Greek colonies in Italy. Today it is a magnificent, jumbled ruin. Temple E is the only one of Selinunte's numerous temples to have been partially reconstructed, its fluted Doric columns made of local sandstone glowing warmly, golden in the late afternoon sun. For me, the ruins of the adjacent Temples F and G are perhaps even more impressive and poignant, a confused heap of haphazard pieces of broken stone, cylinders of immense bits of columns, shards of capitals, pediments, entablatures, metopes sprawled out over such vast superficial areas: the monumental discard of a great civilisation long gone. How to piece together the past, to make any sense of it at all? I reach into my backpack and take out a half bottle of a wine called Ben Ryé. I carefully cut the foil, extract the cork, pour a glass of a deep amber liquid as dark as the sea before me. I should be tasting this gently sweet elixir from a beautifully decorated earthenware kylix rather than a stout tumbler, but even still, it exudes its heady and dreamlike perfume that is redolent of sweet honey, fresh figs, dried apricots, perhaps a touch of balsamic medicinal herbs. I roll the wine around my tongue, close my eyes, and imagine when the stone streets of this once great city were thronged with people simply going about their daily lives.

The History

In Homer's *Odyssey*, the hero Odysseus, at sea and lost on his wanderings as he attempts to return home to the island of Ithaca after the Trojan War, finds himself and his men in the land of the Cyclops, which scholars generally agree was the island of Sicily. Here, they encounter Polyphemus, a one-eyed giant

7

who welcomes them by picking up a couple of men, dashing their heads against the floor, tearing them from limb to limb and eating them up, bones, entrails and all. Despite such behaviour, Polyphemus was not entirely uncivilised. He treats his ewes tenderly, milking them to make ricotta cheese in a manner not dissimilar to how it is still made in Sicily and Southern Italy today. And when Odysseus offers him a wondrously special wine given to him as a gift by Maron, son of Euanthes, the priest of Apollo, the behemoth says, 'We Cyclops have wine of our own made from the grapes that our rich soil and timely rains produce. But this vintage of yours is nectar and ambrosia distilled' (trans. E.V. Rieu). Needless to say, he drinks his fill of the neat, undiluted vintage, 'ruby-coloured and honey-smooth', falls into a drunken stupor, and thus the crafty Odysseus and his men are able to bore out his single eye and make their escape.

An indication that Sicily was a land rich in vines from its earliest days even before the Greeks came was demonstrated by the discovery in 2012 of evidence of winemaking dating back 6,000 years ago, far longer ago than anyone had ever assumed for this part of the Mediterranean. Deep within the bowels of an underground network of caves under Monte Kronio, in the province of Agrigento, archaeologists discovered the remains of large terracotta storage jars that had an organic residue within them. Using chemical analysis techniques, they were able to identify the residue as coming from pure grape wine dating back to the Copper Age. The evidence of such early, systematic winemaking, an activity that possibly required the domestication of the grape vine, *Vitis vinifera*, as well as the technology and knowledge to produce a stable fermented beverage capable of being stored without spoilage, sheds new light on these ancient, indigenous communities, their economies, methods of living as well as dying. Moreover, it would also seem to indicate that wine, far from being a gift introduced to Italy by seafaring traders who spread viticulture across the Mediterranean, was developed here possibly independently far earlier than previously thought.

Indeed, when the ancient Greeks came to the Southern Italian Peninsula and to Sicily sometime around the eighth century BCE, they found themselves in a land already rich in vineyards to such an extent that they called it Oenotria—the land of vines, or to be more precise, the land of trained or staked vines (in contrast to the Greeks' preferred method of freestanding bush training with no additional vine supports). Over the following centuries, Greek colonies were established in Sicily as well as in the present-day regions of Calabria, Basilicata, Campania, Apulia. Cumae was possibly the earliest, founded around 740 BCE. Sybaris became a city famous for its wealth and excessive luxury. Crotone was the home of the mathematician Pythagoras and the famous wrestler Milo, who won no fewer than six victories in the ancient Olympic Games. Tarentum was founded by the Spartans and was blessed with a fine natural harbour, important strategically in an era of Mediterranean trade across countries and cultures. Syracuse, Selinunte and Agrigento were all important Greek colonies in Sicily. So prevalent were Greek settlements and so extensive was Greek culture in Southern Italy and Sicily that the Romans referred to all the south as Magna Graecia—Greater Greece.

Why did the Greeks choose to settle in the Southern Italian Peninsula and its islands? It seems that there were probably a variety of motives, from possible demographic and political crises, to simply the ever-curious quest of a maritime trading people for new commercial outlets and ports. The land was fertile and productive, and the position of these lands formed the meeting point between the Phoenician, Etruscan and Greek worlds. Though the colonies shared Greek culture with common influences in art, architecture, religion, literature, philosophy and a uniquely Pan-Hellenic way of living, they were small, usually fiercely independent city-states, often at war among themselves, forming alliances and leagues in times of need, abandoning them to form rival pacts with former enemies if and when it suited them.

It is quite probable that much of the economic wealth of these colonies was based in no small measure on the production of wine and olive oil, two elements fundamental to Greek civilisation. In Southern Italy and its islands, the Greeks had found a land more than well suited to the quality production of both. Wine, however, was more than just a commodity. It was a cornerstone of Hellenic civilisation and indeed a central element to what the Greeks considered to be the civilised life.

Competition, a part of the Greek ethos

The desire to compete was central to the Greek character, something that classical scholar Nigel Spivey calls 'a fetish ... a pervasive, abrasive, eagerness for outdoing the opposition in any field of human endeavour'.

The Grecian ideal of the male form was based on a physical culture whereby regular attendance at the gymnasium was a means of perfecting the body, maintaining physical and mental health. Regimes of exercise and diet were followed rigorously by the most devoted, and the various sporting disciplines and events were practised and honed to perfection to be able to compete at the various Pan-Hellenic games that took place across the Greek world. The games held at Olympia were the most important and famous, at once a religious festival to honour Zeus, king of the Greek gods, as well as an opportunity for Greek males to demonstrate sporting prowess, strength, agility, wit and more, earning glory and ever-lasting fame in the process.

Naturally, competitors came from Italy's Magna Graecia, and it seems that at different periods they enjoyed considerable success. The most famous athlete in classical antiquity was Milo the wrestler from Crotone, a small and today remote southern outpost in present-day Calabria. Milo was a colossus, a giant of a man, huge and gluttonous, able to carry an ox on his back to bring to sacrifice at the temple of Zeus at the start of the Games. He was victorious at games that took place across the Hellenic world, but it was at Olympia that his fame was most celebrated.

This sense of competition extended beyond athletics to cultural achievements, too. Literary festivals took place where playwrights and poets competed against one another. At musical festivals, instrumentalists and choruses contested for honour and prizes.

Even the simple and convivial act of gathering with friends to drink wine could be turned into a competition of sorts. For rich, educated Greeks, a sophisticated wine culture centred on the symposium, the Greek name for an all-male drinking party. This was a formal social event where men reclined on sofas to dine and to drink wine, sometimes while being entertained by pipe girls and dancing girls.

One of the most vivid descriptions of such a gathering comes from Plato's *Symposium*, wherein a group of Athenian men of high standing get together at the playwright Agathon's to celebrate the tragedian's latest victory in one of Athens' dramatic festivals. Other participants include the comic playwright Aristophanes, the philosopher Socrates, Alcibiades, Socrates' lover and reputedly the best-looking man in Athens, and other prominent Athenians. After dining, they perform the necessary libations and hymns to Zeus and then set about the serious business of drinking and competing. Their host challenges them all to present an *encomium* in praise of Love. One by one, they make their considered arguments, using the rules of classical rhetoric, with references to Homer, Hesiod and other great writers and thinkers, each admiring the others' arguments. Socrates presents a brilliant discourse on the relation between love and immortality, and the drunken Alcibiades declares him to be the winner.

Clearly, the symposium, even one as serious and as illustrious as that which Plato describes, was an opportunity to compete among each other, as well as to drink and drink in quantity. The wine, drawn from a *krater*—a two-handled, often beautifully decorated earthenware vessel—was usually carefully diluted with water before being served in a *kylix* or shallow drinking vessel, the best of which were beautifully decorated with depictions of Dionysus, the god of wine, or of scenes of drinking, acts of a sexual nature or gods or mortals playing games.

The symposium was much enjoyed throughout Magna Graecia even long after it had declined in Athens. Was this because of the popularity of a drinking game that apparently developed in Sicily in the sixth century BCE called *kottabos*? Writers such as Pindar, Aeschylus, Sophocles, Euripides and Aristophanes wrote about this pursuit, while depictions on the sides of drinking vessels illustrate various ways that it was played. Considering that ancient wine was unfiltered and would have necessarily contained a sediment, it seems that once a sufficient amount of wine dregs had settled to the bottom of a *kylix*, the aim was to dextrously flick the contents to hit a target balanced on a special *kottabos* stand, so dislodging the target (called a *plastinx*) so that it would fall on to a lower target (the *manes*) that when struck would make a melodious tone. So popular was this messy after-dinner parlour game that in Sicily special rooms were even constructed for it to be played.

The cult of Dionysus

In 1998, fishermen from Mazara del Vallo, working in the narrow Sicilian Channel that separates south-western Sicily from the north coast of Africa, pulled up in their nets a remarkable rediscovery: the bronze torso and head of a dancing satyr. It had been scooped from the seabed some 500 metres below sea level where it had lain for more than 2,000 years. Amazingly, the same fishermen had a year earlier pulled up in their nets the left leg of the same statue. In a film about the discovery and restoration of this important work of Greek art—possibly an original by the famous sculptor Praxiteles dating back to the fourth century BCE—the fishermen describe their immense excitement when they found the statue in their nets: with his face tilted up to the sky, the whites of his alabaster eyes seemingly gazing at the fishermen, they noted that 'it was as if he had been waiting all these years to be rescued!'

It took five years of painstaking restoration at the Istituto Superiore per la Conservazione ed il Restauro in Rome before the Dancing Satyr was ready to be displayed. When it appeared in Italy's parliament building in 2003, it caused a sensation, universally hailed as the most important discovery since the Riace bronzes had been found in the sea off Calabria in 1972.

What is most striking about this beautiful piece of art is its energy and vivacity; head with pointed satyr ears flung back and flying hair cascading horizontally behind him, the figure is caught in an orgiastic frenzy, whirling round and round in an endless Dionysian dance.

The rites and rituals associated with Dionysus varied between regions and areas and evolved over the course of centuries. The god who came from afar—Dionysus was considered the eternal outsider—perhaps had his origins in that fertile cradle of humanity that was one of the earliest places that wine and the culture of wine emerged, Mesopotamia. Though unpredictable, as a god Dionysus was held in high esteem within the Greek pantheon, considered the deity of not only the grape harvest, winemaking and wine but also of fertility, ritual madness, religious ecstasy and theatre.

The Greeks left a lasting and powerful legacy of wine and the culture of wine drinking across Southern Italy. Ancient grape varieties introduced by the Greeks are still in production today. Methods of viticulture, such as the low-lying, free-standing *albarello* form of training, are found in vineyards across Southern Italy, Sicily and the islands. Wines are still made today, as they were thousands of years ago, even once again fermented in terracotta amphora. The format of the symposium encouraged the consumption of wine as a catalyst for civilised philosophical discourse, the recitation of literature, poetry or drama, and a cultured appreciation of the arts that to this day remains a vital part of Italian life and way of living.

The Wines

Pithos Rosso IGT, Azienda Agricola COS, Vittoria, Sicily

It is usually difficult for us to imagine what ancient wine tasted like. Pithos Rosso is a rare exception that gives us just such an insight. The wine comes from the far tip of south-east Sicily, a land settled by the Greeks and never far from the Sicilian Channel that separates Italy from North Africa. Here Giambattista Cilia, Giusto Occhipinti and Cirino Strano founded their wine estate—the company is an acronym of their surnames—in 1980 with the aim of making wines that express the stories of their ancestral lands. Fascinated by ancient winemaking practices, they decided in 2000 to work with terracotta receptacles, installing some 150 clay vessels to replace former oak vats to produce wines in the same clay wine jars that were once used on these lands by ancient Greek winemakers more than 2,500 years ago. As in the ancient past, the terracotta fermentation vessels are buried below the earth to keep the conditions stable. To see row after row of these in the COS cellar all at ground level with just the necks of the vessels visible is to view how an ancient Greek or Roman wine cellar once looked.

The wines themselves are produced today much as they would have been in the ancient past. To produce Pithos Rosso, Nero d'Avola grapes cultivated biodynamically—a complex system of organic viticulture based on the ideas of Rudolf Steiner—are harvested towards the end of September or into early October. The grapes are lightly crushed then simply added to the terracotta vessels. Fermentation occurs spontaneously with the indigenous yeasts present on the grape skins feeding on the grape sugars to transform into alcohol. After fermentation is complete, the wine is racked to clean terracotta vessels where it continues to age for up to a year, followed by further ageing in the bottle.

The wine that results is fascinating, vivid, pure and totally unlike wines that have fermented and aged in either stainless-steel or oak barrel. Terracotta seems to bring out a crystalline brilliance that enhances the fruit while leaving a cold and stony aftertaste. If the stated aim of the COS winery founders has been to make wines that express the character of their ancestral lands, then they have certainly succeeded.

Ripe del Falco Cirò Rosso Classico Superiore Riserva DOC, Ippolito 1845, Cirò Marina, Calabria

This is a wine, quite simply, that makes me feel like wrestling! It is powerful and uncompromising, a wine that comes from a harshly beautiful land, supple, sinewy and not without considerable grace and elegance.

Was it because so many victors of the Olympic Games were from this area that they came to be traditionally fêted with the wine of Krimisa, produced near Crotone? Or was it perhaps because Milo, the greatest and most renowned Olympian that ever lived, was a connoisseur of it? Maybe it was thought that through drinking such a wondrous vintage, Milo's strength and prowess would be conveyed to others? More likely, the wine of Krimisa became a traditional libation for the victors at the ancient games of Olympia simply due to its excellence.

The vineyards for Krimisa are located where the vineyards for modern Cirò are situated today, and thus Cirò can rightly lay claim to an ancient vinous heritage that harks back to those famous moments of celebration and victory, and such prestigious antecedents should by no means be sniffed at. Yet though renowned in ancient times, today wines from this faraway outpost, located in the extreme south of Italy on the instep of the 'boot' overlooking the beautiful and little visited Ionian coastline, remain one of Italy's best kept secrets. Few wine lovers may have encountered Cirò, unless you happened to be an athlete on the 1968 Italian Olympic team—in a neat nod to the history of the modern Olympic Games, Cirò from Ippolito 1845 was the official wine of the Italian national team at the Mexico City Olympics.

'Ripe del Falco' means the hillsides of the hawk, and there is savageness in the countryside here that translates into this massive, well-structured heavy-weight. The wine is a true expression of the Ippolito family's long wine tradition, utilising only the finest selection of Gaglioppo grapes from vines that are more than forty years old. Though in some cases this uncompromising southern grape can ripen to huge sugar levels to produce wines that are rustic and rarely subtle, in this high-quality example, care in both the vineyard and the wine cellar results in an exceptional wine: surprisingly light in colour, rich in acidity that enables it to age, with a huge and immensely powerful character that is totally uncompromising. Ripe del Falco Cirò Rosso has the capacity, through ageing in the bottle, to evolve and mellow, revealing extraordinary complexity and intensity, with a bouquet of dried cherries, wild berries, liquorice, spices and tannins that with age begin to soften from their youthful mouth-drying astringency to a finish that is long, complex and persistent.

980 Contrada Carrana Etna Rosso DOC, Azienda Agricola Sciara, Randazzo, Sicily

Etna, the ever-smoking volcano, remains today an ancient land of myth and legend. Indeed, the coastline below Etna, just to the south of Taormina, is known as the Riviera dei Ciclopi because at Aci Trezza, a small, timeless fishing village, three rocks stand prominently in the sea, said to be the very same rocks tossed in anger and rage by Polyphemus after he was taunted by Odysseus. Etna is also, since time immemorial, an ancient land of wine. Wine has certainly been made here since antiquity, and so it has continued to be made down the ages, the grapes cultivated on lava-and-lapilli-rich soil of differing eras, depending on the dates of the eruptions, whether centuries or millennia ago, with the passing of time the determinant of the breakdown and gradual erosion of the *sciare*—the lava-flows that scar and shape the mountainside. Traditionally the grapes were harvested from high-altitude vineyards and pressed directly in primitive *palmenti*, ancient stone buildings where the wine was made *come una volta*, as it always had been.

Stef Yim is no giant, but he has a volcanic energy that drives him fiercely, determined to make great wine from grapes grown on this still highly active volcano and at high altitudes that reach up towards the skies where perhaps the gods of the mountain continue to reside. Each of the wines from the Sciara winery is identified by the altitude of the vineyard. Old vines, high altitude and volcanic soil are a potent combination that can yield extraordinary results. Sciara 980 is one of Stef's flagships, produced from ancient, ungrafted Nerello Mascalese grapes grown on gritty volcanic sand at up to 1,000 metres above sea level in Contrada Carrana. This is a wholly natural wine, a wine made as wine has always been made on Etna, with no irrigation, no fertiliser, no pesticides, no herbicides, fermented using the indigenous yeasts present on the grape skins. Afterwards, the wine ages in various containers, wooden barrel, amphora, concrete egg. What is most striking is the purity, the sheerness and transparency of this high-altitude wine, with its invigorating freshness and acidity, balanced tannins, notes of black fruits, mountain herbs and a shimmering, ethereal quality that belies its underlying power: a wine for men and women, giants and gods.

Pian di Stio, Paestum IGP, San Salvatore 19.88, Giungano, Campania

The extensive archaeological sites of the ancient Greeks across Southern Italy are a reminder of the important contribution they made to Italian culture and society, not least the culture of wine. Poseidonia—later renamed Paestum by the Romans—was one of the most important early colonies on the Italian mainland. Today, on the Campanian coast of the Tyrrhenian Sea within the Cilento National Park, the considerable and impressive excavations stand witness to a sophisticated ancient civilisation, including three of the best-preserved Greek temples found anywhere in the world, dating from 550 to 450 BCE. It is impossible not to be deeply moved when you see these incredibly beautiful and impressive Doric structures, dedicated to ancient gods, standing proudly and perfectly in the Campanian countryside by the sea.

Archaeology provides a vivid testimony to the past; it can also provide inspiration for the present and the future. Grapevines certainly would have been cultivated on the mineral-rich soil behind Poseidonia, leading up into the higher hills. And so it is today once more, since Giuseppe Pagano, a visionary entrepreneur and successful hotelier, decided in 2003 to return to his agricultural roots to create an extensive estate that links wine, healthy organic food, ancient history and the people of Cilento. Thus San Salvatore 19.88 was born, a project inspired from faith that this ancient, fertile land could once again produce great things, including great wines and foods.

Pian di Stio is a majestic wine that does justice to a majestic and historic land where the past lies all around. The vineyard is located 25 kilometres from Paestum in the high hills at an altitude of 550–650 metres above sea level. Here, Fiano, one of the great grape varieties of antiquity, is cultivated, and grapes from select small parcels are transported to the winery at harvest to undergo cryomaceration—a winemaking technique where the grapes are held at low temperature for a time in order to extract greater aroma and structure—for six hours before fermentation in stainless-steel followed by ageing on the lees for six months. The lees are the yeast remains after fermentation, and prolonged contact, sometimes with *bâtonnage* or lees stirring, adds more complex flavours and texture to the finished wine. The wine that results is a beautiful expression of grape variety and terroir (that 'sense of place' that can be expressed in a wine): delicate notes of white flowers and white peach, mountain herbs, fresh in the mouth, invigorating yet with an intriguing richness, opulence and body, a wine to sip and think, perhaps pondering on the greatness of the past.

Ben Ryè Passito di Pantelleria DOC, Donnafugata, Pantelleria, Sicily

In Hesiod's *Works and Days*, the poet, writing in the eighth century BCE, gives instruction to his brother Perses not only on how to conduct himself but also on how to manage their estate. He does this by writing a sort of farmer's almanac, explaining the agricultural activities required throughout the year. In September, for example, Hesiod advises:

> But when Orion and Sirius come into mid-heaven, and rosy-fingered Dawn sees Arcturus, then cut off all the grape-clusters, Perses, and bring them home. Show them to the sun ten days and ten nights: then cover them over for five, and on the sixth day draw off into vessels the gifts of joyful Dionysus. (trans. Evelyn White)

One of the greatest examples of a wine made in a broadly similar manner to that described by Hesiod comes from Pantelleria. Pantelleria is a tiny volcanic island located in the Sicilian Channel between mainland Sicily and the coast of North Africa. Its history of habitation mirrors that of Sicily, the native peoples taken over successively by Carthaginians, Romans, Byzantines, Arabs, Normans, Aragonese and more. It is a harsh and windswept land with severe climatic conditions. Yet here, as they have for millennia, the people of Pantelleria still struggle to cultivate the grape vine to produce a rare wine that has been enjoyed and savoured since antiquity.

Such are the conditions of intense heat and wind that a particular form of labour-intensive cultivation used by the Greeks and Romans is still carried out today, a practice known as *vite ad alberello*, designated by UNESCO as an 'Intangible Cultural Heritage of Humanity'. This accolade recognises a unique form of viticulture that has been passed down through oral and practical instruction through the generations, centuries and millennia. To protect the vines from the near-constant wind that sweeps through the Sicilian Channel, a hollow is prepared in the volcanic, mineral-rich soil into which a single Zibibbo vine is planted. The main stem of the vine is then carefully pruned to form a low, freestanding bush with a radial arrangement. The fragrant grapes thus ripen in a sheltered, hot-house environment.

By sometimes as early as late July, more usually into the first half of August, the grapes are ready to be harvested manually. For the creation of Ben Ryè, a proportion of the earliest-harvested grapes are laid out exactly as Hesiod advised, to wither in the direct and intense near-African sunshine of high summer usually for about a fortnight. A second harvest then takes place in early September, and the freshly pressed must is fermented in stainless-steel with temperature control. The dried grapes are then added to the fresh, fermenting must in several batches. During maceration, the dried grapes contribute an extraordinary character: sweetness allied with freshness, acidity and unique, persistent aromas. After fermentation is complete, ageing takes place in stainless-steel for a further seven months, followed by at least a year in the bottle prior to release.

The wine that eventually emerges is a glorious, wondrous expression of the fermented grape: at once concentrated and complex, yet at the same time fresh and exhilarating. The bouquet is intensely fragrant, with aromas of dried apricots, candied citrus zest and notes of Mediterranean thyme and rosemary. The considerable sweetness that comes from the dried grapes is balanced by fresh acidity and minerality. The finish is long and persistent, truly a *vino da meditazione*.

2

THE MYSTERIOUS ETRUSCANS

We are in southern Tuscany, wandering along an ancient, sunken road, a via cava *hand-carved into the earth more than 2,000 years ago. High walls of soft, volcanic tuff tower over us, sometimes by as high as 15 metres. We are in an extraordinary, hidden corner of Tuscany known as the Maremma that was once a vital and thriving centre of Etruscan civilisation. Remains from that period, as well as from medieval times, lend the landscape a rare, faded beauty and grandeur. Though it is high summer and baking hot, it is more bearable within this hidden, sunken byway, and we enjoy the shade that the cool, steep, stone channel we are walking in provides. But it's hot work all the same, so we pause for refreshment. I saw off chunks of saltless Tuscan bread and wedges of fresh young* pecorino, *creamy and salty. We wash down this simple repast with an extraordinary wine, Vie Cave, produced from vineyards around the tiny town of Sovana that are criss-crossed by these mysterious sunken lanes. The wine, a deep red with an intense nose of ripe red fruits and a spicy finish, is intriguing, Tuscan in character, yet strangely exotic as though from afar. A mystery.*

The History

The Etruscans flourished from roughly the eighth century to the fifth century BCE before they were conquered and eventually subsumed by the Romans around the third century BCE. Who were they, and where did they come from? There are no definitive answers to these and many other questions.

Though they had their own written language, it appears that it came from non-Indo-European roots and is only partly understood. There are no known texts revealing the history, religion, literature or philosophy of the Etruscans, and much of what we do know comes from accounts written by Greek or

Roman historians. According to Herodotus, writing in the fifth century BCE, the Etruscans were Lydians who came from Anatolia. Dionysius of Halicarnassus, writing in the first century BCE, considered them to be Pelasgians, pre-Hellenic people indigenous to the Aegean who were driven out by the Greeks, eventually arriving on the Ionian gulf to settle in the country they called Tyrrhenia. The Roman historian Livy, by contrast, writing about the early history of Rome, said that the Etruscans were already in Italy by the time of Aeneas, the Trojan who is considered the founder of Rome. Virgil's *Aeneid* also describes the Etruscans as native to Italy. While the narratives of Livy and Virgil can be seen in the light of their attempt to legitimise the origins of Rome, what is certain is that the Romans, even as they destroyed it, admired Etruscan culture and civilisation and attempted to emulate and absorb essential elements of that culture into their own.

The English novelist D. H. Lawrence, writing *Etruscan Places*, is perhaps no less inaccurate than the ancient historians:

> The Etruscans sailed the seas. They are even said to have come by sea, from Lydia in Asia Minor, at some date far back in the dim mists before the eighth century BC. But that a whole people, even a whole host, sailed in the tiny ships of those days, all at once, to people a sparsely peopled central Italy, seems hard to imagine. Probably ships did come—even before Ulysses. Probably men landed on the strange flat coast, and made camps, and then treated with the natives. Whether the newcomers were Lydians or Hittites with hair curled in a roll behind, or men from Mycenae or Crete, who knows. Perhaps men of all these sorts came, in batches. For in Homeric days a restlessness seems to have possessed the Mediterranean basin, and ancient races began shaking ships like seeds over the sea. More people than Greeks, or Hellenes, or Indo-Germanic groups, were on the move.

Wherever they came from, at its height, by the sixth and fifth centuries BCE, the Etruscans were loosely organised into a League that consisted of twelve independent settlements or city-states. It seems this grouping served mostly as an economic alliance rather than a militaristic one. Their wealth came from a rich and fecund land based on agriculture, especially the production of wine and olive oil, as well as the mining of ample reserves of precious metal ore, and the manufacture of goods from such natural resources, all commodities that could be traded, mainly by sea across the Mediterranean. Such wealth resulted in an aristocratic class that clearly lived well and even died well.

Much of what we can glean of the Etruscans, their way of life and their society comes from the art they left behind. Their artisans and artists were highly proficient in terracotta work, creating beautiful figurative models that adorned temples and the elaborate sarcophagi found in tombs and necropolises.

Drinking and other everyday vessels as well as funerary and votive ware were created from a shiny black earthenware known as *bucchero*. This fine ware, black from surface to core, was created by skilled potters who utilised a finely ground clay fired in an oxygen-restricted kiln. The result was beautiful and sophisticated not only in shape but also in design, with early examples thin and delicate, bearing finely incised depictions, and later ware much thicker with elaborate pictorial scenes in low relief. It appears that the art of creating such beautiful *bucchero* ware was unique to the Etruscan civilisation, the process not seen again after its demise.

Such ware has been discovered mainly in excavations in Etruscan tombs found throughout Central Italy. Drinking vessels, mixing bowls and splendid ceremonial artefacts demonstrate the sophistication and skills of Etruscan potters as well as indicate the importance of wine in the daily scheme of life, and indeed death. It is in Etruscan tombs that we gain a glimpse into a society that was at once tender and intimate as well as deeply connected to the joys of living: through the liberal consumption of wine, through dancing, music and revelry. We might even go so far as to imagine, perhaps, that this was a society where death itself held little fear, for the life afterwards was assumed to be a seeming continuation of a long and never-ending party.

Etruscan wine culture

Wine was clearly central to Etruscan culture. It was also central to the Etruscan economy as a product that could be transported and traded, within Italy and beyond. Indeed, the Etruscans traded wine, oil and metal ore such as tin, copper and iron extensively, to areas within Magna Graecia as well as across the Tyrrhenian, establishing colonies in what are now Sardinia, Corsica, Spain and Southern France.

Orvieto, a small town in Umbria, is built over what was once the ancient Etruscan city-state of Velzna. It rises dramatically from the plain below, built on a butt of tuff (*tufo* in Italian)—a bedrock of soft stone formed by heat from compacted volcanic ash and debris (confusingly different from *tufa*, which is a limestone sedimentary deposit). Orvieto's elevated, strategic position was common to many Etruscan towns, sited on high and with fortified walls for protection from invaders and enemies. The tuff butt on which the city was built is a soft rock that can easily be tunnelled into. Over the centuries, from the time of the Etruscans more than 2,500 years ago, through the Roman era and across the Middle Ages and the Renaissance to the present time, tunnels, galleries and cellars were carved out of this soft bedrock to serve as refuge in times of strife and invasion, to create escape routes, as well as to use as storage areas and working cellars for the production of both wine and olive oil. In just such historic cellars that can still be visited we can gain a fascinating insight into the production of wine in antiquity.

With a commodity so central to Etruscan culture and identity, as well as so valuable as a commodity to trade, the Etruscans perfected sophisticated systems of production to ensure the quality of their wines, carefully husbanding the cultivation of the vine by pruning, as well as by training the vines up trees or other living supports, a method known as *arbustum* or *maritate*, in contrast to the *alberello* or low bush training favoured by the Greeks. So successful was the Etruscans' high training method that it was not only adopted by the Romans but carried on across Central Italy, especially in Tuscany, through the Middle Ages, and even until the time when the *mezzadria* was abolished as late as the 1970s. Indeed, the high pergola system of training whereby the vines form canopies, still favoured in the vineyards of Verona—an area once influenced by the Etruscans who traded with northern tribes—is further evidence of the enduring influence of the Etruscan way of viticulture.

The Etruscans were clearly sophisticated when it came to wine, for they also made considerable improvements in the process of vinification. Indeed, winemaking methods perfected by the Etruscans were later adopted by the Romans as they developed their own culture of wine and wine drinking. In Orvieto, they excavated deep into the soft tuff bedrock, extending down for 3 stories or even more to create galleries that provided the perfect conditions for the production of wine, conditions that may be equalled but not bettered even in the most modern cellars that make use of temperature-controlled stainless-steel fermentation vats. They perfected a so-called 'three-floor' system of vinification, bringing the freshly harvested grapes from the vineyards below up to the town, where they were crushed probably by human foot on the floor closest to ground level and where the temperature in autumn was probably around 25 degrees C. The *mosto* or unfermented grape juice then ran down stone channels by gravity to the second underground level, which maintained a constant temperature of around 15 degrees C, ideal for fermentation to take place in terracotta vessels. Once fermentation was complete, the wine was racked off its lees—removed from its sediment of dead yeast—to new vessels, again by gravity, flowing along stone channels for storage in an even deeper subterranean level where it was left to age in a cool, constant temperature that was perfect for the conservation of wine even for lengthy periods.

The quality of the fruit grown in surrounding vineyards together with these ideal conditions for the production of wine resulted in wines from Orvieto gaining great fame and renown, not only during the times of the Etruscans and the Romans but throughout the Middle Ages, Renaissance and to the present day. In fact, these same underground cellars carved out by the Etruscans and expanded by the Romans were still in use for commercial wine production by the Barberani family (one of Orvieto's leading producers) until the mid-1980s, when they transferred from the picturesque if inconvenient *centro storico* to a new purpose-built eco-winery above the shores of nearby Lake Corbara.

Tarquinia and its painted tombs

Tarquinia, located in the province of Viterbo near the present-day border between Lazio and Tuscany, was inhabited from the ninth century BCE and grew into one of the most important city-states in the loosely formed Etruscan League. Its economic prosperity was based on its proximity to the sea, making it an important centre for maritime trade across the Tyrrhenian, as well as on its rich mineral and ore deposits, which gave the raw material for the manufacture of bronze and gold objects by talented craftsmen. Tarquinia grew in prosperity through the sixth and fifth centuries BCE, its wealth and importance in part demonstrated by the existence of more than 2,000 tombs, some simple, others elaborate and monumental. Some of the most important display beautifully painted frescoes depicting scenes of everyday life—banquets, dancing, hunting, fishing, wrestling or making love—as well as depictions of animals and fantastical creatures such as the hippocampus, a mythical sea horse. What is most striking about Etruscan art is its sheer vitality, its joyous depiction of a society where, for the rich at least, life is to be enjoyed to the fullest.

The Tomb of the Lionesses, for example, depicts a large drinking party scene. In the gable above, there are two lionesses (or spotted leopards) facing one another, while below, both men and women are sprawled out luxuriously, a naked slave brandishing a great wine vase to refill cups, while dancers and musicians play. Below and all around is the rippling sea, where dolphins frolic and leap in the deep. Consider that these tombs most probably also contained beautiful objects, dining sets, *bucchero* drinking vessels and mixing bowls, jewellery and gold: clearly there was the expectation that life, happy life, would continue in much the same way after death, come what may.

The Tomb of the Painted Vases depicts a man holding a large wine vessel, intimately caressing his female companion gently under the chin. If for the Greeks the wine symposium was entirely a male affair—women were only ever part of the entertainment—it seems that for the Etruscans, the civilised enjoyment of wine was something to be shared equally between man and woman. Indeed, women feature in many of the painted tombs as prominently as men. In the Tomb of the Baron, a woman is depicted fondly saying farewell, presumably to the tomb's occupant. In the Tomb of the Bulls, there are erotic frescoes of couples making love, heterosexual, homosexual, moments of passion, of human love, captured, immortalised forever. The enjoyment, the pleasure that comes from drinking wine, the Etruscans taught us, is a universal right, something for us all.

Vie cave—*hidden Etruscan byways*

The *vie cave*, or sunken roads, of Tuscany's Maremma are among the most intriguing of all man-made natural phenomena in Italy, a network of excavated lanes that are sometimes little more than narrow trenches dug out of soft volcanic tuff, deeply sunken byways with stone walls that tower high above. They can be explored and traversed on foot, connecting Etruscan settlements between Pitigliano, Sorano and Sovana. The effort taken to construct them would have been considerable, and their purpose remains, like so much relating to the Etruscans, a mystery. Were they channels to direct and collect precious rainwater? Were they hidden byways that linked those in the land of the living to subterranean necropoli where departed ancestors resided? Were they secret escape routes, necessary in a war-prone era when attacks could come suddenly and unexpectedly? Or were they simply normal thoroughfares connecting different settlements with each other, and if so, why the need to sink them underground? We simply don't know.

Pitigliano, a small hill town in southern Tuscany perched on a clifftop, has the appearance of a claustrophobic medieval conglomeration, its narrow and moody streets lined with *palazzi* that were once homes to the noble and aristocratic families who ruled over the surrounding countryside. Prior to the unification of Italy, this was the frontier between the Grand Duchy of Tuscany and the Papal States. It was also home to a flourishing Jewish community, and the quarter of the town that housed the ghetto was known as Little Jerusalem. Underneath the cliffs upon which the town was built, the soft volcanic tuff is riddled with caves, some originally used by the Etruscans, while radiating out from the base of the town there is a fascinating network of *vie cave* that can be explored on foot. Wandering these ancient byways is one of the best ways to immerse ourselves in the ancient and mysterious world of the Etruscans.

The Via Cava del Gradone traces its way through Pitigliano's archaeological park to the *città dei morti*—the city of the dead. Along the way, an Etruscan tomb has been completely reconstructed to demonstrate how these tombs were furnished, adorned and decorated with personal objects, plates, wine cups, jewellery and more. The Via Cava del Gradone soon reaches the Necropoli del Gradone, where a number of excavated Etruscan tombs can be explored. From time to time, the museum puts on re-enactments of Etruscan funerary rites and rituals. Given that the Etruscan civilisation remains so little known compared to the great classical civilisations of the Romans, Greeks and Phoenicians, this is one important way to gain greater insight into a culture and civilisation that helped to shape the very character of Italy and the Italians.

Numerous other *vie cave* extend to the west and north of Pitigliano. Some are wholly accessible; others cannot be explored in their entirety. It is fascinating to strike out into these secret and hidden byways, cool in the heat of summer, dense with an overgrowth of green vegetation, a reminder of the fertility of this ancient land.

The Etruscans loved wine, and it was fundamental to their culture and way of life and death. Their heartland extended across a large central area of Italy, including the present-day regions of Tuscany, Umbria and Lazio. Today, good and sometimes great wine continues to be produced throughout these regions in every single one of their provinces. Indeed, the cultured appreciation and enjoyment of the fruits of the vine, together with the everyday pleasures of wine, food, music, dance and love—enjoyed by women as well as men—are all a direct and enduring link between Italians today and their Etruscan ancestors.

The Wines

Luigi e Giovanna Orvieto Classico DOC, Azienda Agricola Barberani, Baschi, Umbria

Technology has always played a vital part in winemaking, in the ancient past as it does today. When Luigi and Giovanna Barberani took the decision to move out of the historic cellars in the *centro storico* to a new purpose-built winery, they knew that the challenge would be to match those near perfect conditions in the caves of Orvieto where wines had been made for more than 2,500 years. They therefore set out to create a sustainable, state-of-the art eco-winery that would enable them to transform their grapes cultivated entirely organically on their own vineyards into a range of wines that could match in excellence and reputation those that have given fame to Orvieto, from antiquity, through the Middle Ages and the Renaissance, to the present day.

This wine, Luigi e Giovanna, pays homage to the visionary founders of this forward-thinking modern family winery, a glorious expression that demonstrates just how great—and how unique—the wines of Orvieto can be. Grechetto (primarily) and Procanico grapes are cultivated biodynamically on marine sedimentary soils rich in fossils, pebbles and chalky accumulations. Each year, a small proportion of the grapes are naturally affected by *muffa nobile* or noble rot, adding complexity to the bouquet and texture. The grapes are harvested and fermented in the modern eco-winery at Baschi in stainless-steel using only the native, indigenous yeasts. The wine that results, though dry, is seductively rich in the mouth, concentrated and beautifully balanced, redolent of dried apricots, honey and tropical notes that give that gentle, sweet roundness for which Orvieto wines have always been renowned. This is simply a gorgeous, beautiful wine. Taste it and you will immediately understand why, across the ages, the wines of Orvieto have been so highly prized.

Pourriture Noble, Orvieto Classico Muffa Nobile DOC, Decugnano dei Barbi, Orvieto, Umbria

Whoever would have first thought that making wine from rotten grapes, covered in an ugly veil of mould, could result in such exquisitely textured and luscious, sweet wines that are some of the greatest and most exalted expressions of the fermented grape? The ancients, almost certainly, for we believe that the honeyed sweetness and texture that results from making wine from such grapes was one reason for the popularity and success of wines from the timeless vineyards of Orvieto even as far back as the time of the Etruscans.

Not all rot is by any means beneficial. Consistently wet, humid, damp conditions can provide the conditions for a host of maladies, from powdery mildew on both leaf and grape to black rot, which destroys the crop. But one special fungus thrives on misty, humid and warm conditions, especially in well-ventilated vineyards where late morning autumn sunshine drives away the damp. The grey mould that results looks every bit as unpromising as detrimental versions of rot, leaving an ash-like covering over the fruit. Yet grapes that have been attacked by this form of decay, *Botrytis cinerea*, can be simply magical.

In ancient times as well as today, Orvieto was one of very few places in Italy where these favourable conditions could and still can be depended upon to happen with any regularity, providing the perfect conditions for the formation of this special type of noble rot. *Muffa nobile* not only concentrates grape sugars; it also has the capacity to impart exotic, honeyed, luscious, tropical flavours and textures to the resulting wine while retaining vibrant and refreshing acidity. Such wines have an almost indefinite capacity to age and evolve with time in the bottle. For this reason, it is probable that the rare and treasured wines produced here, combined with the ease of transport from Orvieto along the Tiber to the sea, made them as highly prized in antiquity as they are today, wines that could not only be enjoyed but traded too.

Pourriture Noble, produced by the Barbi family of Tenuta Decugnano dei Barbi, is one of Italy's greatest dessert wines, made from Grechetto and Procanico (60 per cent) and Semillon and Sauvignon Blanc (40 per cent). The vineyards extend over terroir that was once underneath an ancient sea, the soil rich in oyster shells and marine fossils. Only individual grapes that have been attacked by *muffa nobile* are harvested and used to produce this rare wine, so the harvest takes place over several passes through the vineyard, selecting bunch or berry by berry. *Muffa nobile* has the effect of shrivelling the grapes while still on the vine. Through this natural process, the yield is considerably reduced, since the liquid content is diminished, but what remains is rich in sugar, as well as concentrated acidity, flavour and above all persistent and unique aromas. Pourriture Noble—the name means 'noble rot' in French—is an incredibly complex wine that is simply astonishing. We marvel that such a golden, concentrated elixir can be created by grapes alone, left to rot on the vine, transformed by the skill of man to result in a nectar that is richly textured in the mouth, with notes of honey, tropical fruit, bitter orange and a luscious, creamy and incredibly persistent aftertaste. Pourriture Noble is a wine to sip, wonder and enjoy and perhaps to consider those ancient and mysterious civilisations who gave us the gift of wine.

Vie Cave Toscana IGT, Fattoria Aldobrandesca, Antinori, Sovana, Tuscany

The Etruscans not only planted vineyards across Etruria, primarily over the modern regions of Tuscany, Umbria and Latium; as skilled maritime traders, they also carried Etruscan wine with them on voyages across the Mediterranean. Maritime archaeologists discovered an ancient shipwreck carrying Etruscan wine vessels off the coast of Cap d'Antibes on the French Riviera dating from 575 to 550 BCE. Etruscan amphorae have been discovered in excavations along the Rhône and Saône river valleys.

This wine is called 'Vie Cave' in recognition of its Etruscan past and because the vineyards around Sovana are surrounded by *vie cave*. The vineyards rise on the slopes of a spur of tuff surrounded by a timeless landscape of natural beauty. Here at the Fattoria Aldobrandesca, named after a powerful medieval family who ruled this corner of Tuscany, an almost equally old family, the Antinori, undertook careful geological and vinous research, taking the decision to cultivate Malbec, which they deemed able to thrive in the Maremma's mineral-rich volcanic soil. The thin-skinned grapes are manually harvested usually in mid-September, de-stemmed and macerated at low temperature to extract the fullest aromatic components. Fermentation then takes place at a temperature of 30 degrees C for about a week, before the wine is transferred for ageing in French oak *barriques* (225 litres) for around ten months, followed by a further year of ageing in the bottle prior to release.

The result is extraordinary and unique. Malbec is known to make full, rather tough and chewy red wines in Cahors in south-west France as well as in Argentina, where the grape reigns supreme. Here, however, it produces a wine that is wholly Tuscan, or rather southern Tuscan, in character, full of deep red fruit overlayered with spices, cloves, wild herbs and a touch of vanilla. On the finish, there is an intense note of dark chocolate. This is a modern wine from an ancient wine land, at once quietly elegant and understated. With roots that extend deep into the tuff subsoil, it runs straight and true like the *vie cave* themselves, directly connecting the vinous heritage of Tuscany today with that of the mysterious Etruscans who were so instrumental in the development of a sophisticated culture of wine: a sacred beverage to enjoy in this world, as well as perhaps (might we all hope?) in some afterworld, too.

3

WINE, SALT AND IMPERIAL PURPLE

It is a bright, windy day just off the coast of western Sicily. I have taken a short ferry ride across the Stagnone lagoon to the small island of Mozia (known also as San Pantaleo). As the ferry makes its way across the shallow waters, we pass a chequerboard of salt ponds, each separated from the others by low dry-stone walls. This is a compli-cated and precious eco-system whereby through a system of pumps that utilise an Archimedes' screw, the waters are lifted and moved so that they continually increase in salinity, leading to an eventual manual harvest of sea salt, an activity carried out here continuously since the time of the Phoenicians.

Once ashore on the island, I visit the archaeological site of the once powerful city of Motya, founded around the eighth century BCE and a key colony of the Carthaginians in their struggles against both the Greeks and the Romans. Afterwards, I sit out by the kiosk near the ferry jetty and enjoy a glass of golden Grillo di Mozia, produced from Grillo grapes bush-trained on this windswept island and, after harvest, taken by boat to the mainland to be transformed into wine. The Grillo di Mozia is exquisite, lemon yellow in colour, rich in flavour, spicy, complex, with a long and deliciously salty finish.

The History

Though the wild grapevine *Vitis vinifera sylvestris* most certainly grew haphaz-ardly across the Italian Peninsula and islands in ancient times, archaeological evidence points to the spread of the domesticated grape vine and subsequent systematic viticulture by way of traders and seafarers who came from the Eastern Mediterranean. The most intrepid of such seafaring peoples were the Phoenicians. The proliferation of dense cedar forests in their homeland of

Phoenicia—present-day Lebanon and southern Syria—gave them the raw material to build sturdy seafaring craft that could roam far and wide. They developed sophisticated ships with heavy keels that enabled them to carry large amounts of cargo and made innovations such as caulking ships with pitch to ensure that they remained watertight. The Phoenicians mastered the skills of navigation, which allowed them to sail out of sight of land so that they were able to make longer sea passages than others had previously attempted, their maritime expertise enabling them to establish colonies and settlements far and wide across the Mediterranean. It seems that for the Phoenicians, their aim, at least originally, was not primarily military conquest and domination: they were essentially intrepid and enterprising entrepreneurial traders and merchants, plying the high seas for economic gain and well-being.

Evidence from the findings of marine archaeologists indicates that Phoenicians were certainly trading in wine as early as the eighth century BCE and probably long before. The discovery in 1997 and subsequent recovery of two sunken vessels of Phoenician origin off the coast of Gaza revealed that they were carrying some 400 amphorae each. Analysis of the remains of the clay containers indicates that the amphorae were lined with pine-resin and had been filled with grape wine. These two vessels alone, each carrying some 15,000 litres of wine, would have represented a considerable investment for the entrepreneurial shipowners, and a considerable economic loss when they went down.

Trade across the seas in those ancient days was significant, and the Phoenicians were the masters, their laden ships carrying wine—possibly from the Beqaa Valley, still the source of outstanding Lebanese vintages—as well as such valuable commodities as incense, gold, camels, tin, silver, slaves and more.

Imperial purple

One special commodity, however, stands out as linked to Phoenician economic and trading activity and prosperity. The Phoenicians discovered as early as 1500 BCE the art of extracting a rare and precious substance that became highly sought after throughout the ancient world: the so-called Tyrian purple dye, so precious and expensive to produce that it became a highly valuable trading commodity. According to legend, this was first discovered by divine providence: apparently a god was strolling on his beach with his pet dog somewhere along the coast in Tyre. The dog ran ahead, found a sea mollusk, bit into it, and came back with his muzzle stained a deep and vivid purple. The compound that resulted in the purple colour was found to exist only in a particular species of sea snail, the Murex, and only in specific areas of the Mediterranean. The Phoenicians perfected the complex art of extracting a single vein from each mollusk that contained a tiny quantity of the dye and found a way to do so in sufficient quantity to make it commercially viable. Amphorae recovered from shipwrecks, their shattered remains stained an intense and deep purple colouration, indicate that this trade was carried out far and wide. And why not: so precious, so rare was the Tyrian purple dye that its worth was more than its weight in gold. Its value and scarcity made it the prerogative of the ruling classes, priests, even emperors.

Tyrian purple thus became one of the most valuable trading commodities for the Phoenicians, who created a loose confederation of merchant and trading communities across the Mediterranean, from Crete to the shores of North Africa, and from the Balearic Islands to beyond the Straits of Gibraltar, where they established settlements on the Atlantic coast of Africa, even heading up to Cornwall.

In North Africa, the Phoenician settlement of Carthage, located on the site of what is now present-day Tunis, grew to be the strongest and most influential of all Phoenician colonies in the Mediterranean, its influence extending far beyond its North African home. Indeed, so mighty did Carthage become in the centuries following its foundation in the ninth century BCE that it grew into a powerful independent city-state in its own right and name. It was the Carthaginians who created settlements in Sicily, notably at Motya on the island of Mozia, at Solunto below Cape Zafferano, and at Panormus (present-day Palermo). Indeed, Carthaginian influence spread further all along the North African coast and well into the Iberian Peninsula.

In Sicily, the Carthaginians were able to carry on the valuable industry of extracting Tyrian purple, and in this regard the settlement on the island of Mozia was significant. For the shallow Stagnone lagoon was not only a source of the rare and prized sea mollusk, the Murex, but also proved to be a propitious habitat for the harvesting of salt from the sea. Salt was particularly valued for many commercial reasons, not least as it was the necessary component required to extract the precious Tyrian purple.

Thus, more than 2,500 years ago, the Phoenicians began the commercial harvesting of salt through the creation of a complex patchwork of salt pans that have been in virtually continuous use since those ancient days. Salt was and has always been a vital and valuable commodity for peoples across the world. Its use for the extraction of Tyrian purple dye, transported in amphorae across the seas, made it even more valuable, a commodity worth protecting, safeguarding, fighting for. The settlement of Motya, located just a short distance from the mainland of western Sicily, thus grew in importance, its position influential both economically and militarily.

The Punic Wars

The Punic Wars were a series of three encounters between Carthage and Rome, waged from 264 to 146 BCE. They were the largest and most sophisticated military encounters the world had ever seen, fought furiously on land and at sea, and the outcome determined the course of Italian history.

The Carthaginians, as heirs to Phoenician maritime expertise, possessed one of the largest and most sophisticated military fleets in the ancient world, far larger than that of the Romans. Initially they prevailed, but the Romans soon built up their fleet to more than 100 warships. Some of the fiercest maritime battles took place in the channel between the mainland of Sicily and the Aegadian islands just to the west of Mozia and what was then the Roman city of Lilybaeum (present-day Marsala).

Imagine what these great naval battles must have been like, the speed and power of such sleek and beautiful vessels attacking each other, the tremendous noise and judder when wooden boats propelled by the collective power of human oarsmen thudded against their foe, the splintering of wood, the cries as free men or slaves were thrown from their thwarts, the stench of fear, blood and death flowing down the wooden planking of the decks, and all of this taking place on this timelessly beautiful and now peaceful stretch of water. The Romans, though inferior at maritime warfare at the start of the First Punic War, eventually prevailed through superior military strategy. Realising that they did not have the sailing skills to defeat the Carthaginian fleet, they decided that rather than attempting to ram and sink their opponents' crafts, they would manoeuvre alongside instead, swing hinged bridges on to the enemy vessels to secure the ships together, then board with their superior infantry to engage in bloody hand-to-hand combat.

The discovery in 1969 of a Punic warship just off the coast of Mozia gives a vivid sense of the scale of the ferocious sea battles. Known as the 'Marsala ship', carbon dating indicates that it may have gone down in the last naval battle of the First Punic War in 241 BCE. The remains of the hull are now displayed in the Baglio Anselmi Archaeological Museum in Marsala. The hull's long, narrow and sweeping proportions indicate a vessel built for speed, while the Punic alphabet carved and painted into the planking gives clues to its construction. At 35 metres long and less than 5 metres wide, it would have been propelled by thirty-four oars powered by slaves or mercenaries, the beak-like ram of the prow a fearful weapon in naval warfare. That this was a warship was ascertained not only by the shape and proportions but by the lack of any room for cargo; rather, provisions for the crew were contained within a variety of amphorae found on the seabed, including vessels containing the remains of butchered meat.

After Rome's victory in the First Punic War, a fragile peace prevailed. The Carthaginians had to give up their colonies in Sicily and pay Rome substantial war indemnities. Their expansionist ambitions, however, continued on the Iberian Peninsula, where Rome also had interests. This inevitably led to further conflict.

The Second Punic War of 218–201 BCE is best remembered for the great Carthaginian commander Hannibal coming from Hispania to cross the Alps with a vast army of more than 20,000 troops, calvary and of course his African war elephants. Once in Italy, Hannibal won a succession of victories in Rome's own backyard, leaving Rome itself seemingly at the great warrior's mercy. Hannibal's equally fierce younger brother Hasdrubal Barca was tasked with bringing reinforcements to enable them to sack the city. Hasdrubal successfully crossed the still-snow-covered mountains with an army almost as large his brother's and with his own fleet of war elephants. The plan was for the two of them to meet up in Umbria and from there plan their assault on Rome.

The Romans, meanwhile, fearing the enormous threat of their joint forces, dispatched two consuls, Claudius Nero and Marcus Livius, to engage the two brothers, the former with a force of some 40,000 men set to take on Hannibal, while Livius was sent north to meet Hasdrubal. An intercepted message from Hasdrubal to Hannibal, however, caused Nero to turn north to support Livius, joining forces with him by the banks of the Metaurus River, near the Roman garrison of Fanum on the Adriatic coast, in the region today known as Le Marche.

Hasdrubal's troops consisted of a vast army supported by legions of Ligurians and Gauls, a mighty cavalry force, and the terrifying war elephants that could cause sheer panic when they charged. The Roman troops thus spent an uneasy night in anticipation of the mighty battle that would befall them. But, according to legend, they spent their time wisely, fortifying themselves by drinking copious quantities of the local wine, the precursor to today's modern Bianchello del Metauro. This potent beverage, it is claimed, gave the troops belief and immense courage. Through the superior fighting skill of the Roman legions combined with the astute military strategy of Nero and Livius that allowed them to outflank their opposing armies, the Romans were able to win a decisive battle that proved to be pivotal in the war between Rome and Carthage.

Hasdrubal was killed in battle, and his head, unceremoniously severed from the body, was taken by the Romans and thrown contemptuously into Hannibal's camp, a demonstration of the might of Rome. Hannibal and his troops eventually left the Italian Peninsula having never achieved the goal of sacking Rome. On his return to Carthage, he and his army suffered a humiliating defeat at the Battle of Zama at the hands of the great Roman general Scipio Africanus. With Roman supremacy established and Carthage mortally weakened, Rome nonetheless remained wary of its longstanding traditional foe. When the Carthaginians had discharged themselves of the onerous payments of indemnities levied after the Second Punic War and began to assert themselves as an independent power once again, the mood in Rome hardened, with Cato the Elder vehemently and repeatedly denouncing Carthage and concluding 'Carthago delenda est'—'Carthage must be destroyed.' And so it came to pass: the Third Punic War (149–146 BCE) involved a brutal siege of Carthage and the eventual destruction of this once proud city-state and civilisation. So utter was the destruction that the scorched earth, says legend, was even scattered with salt, perhaps from those very same Phoenician salt works that had been established centuries earlier in Sicily.

Carthaginian and Phoenician influence across the Mediterranean was no more; the supremacy of Rome was complete. But in a sense, the entrepreneurial Phoenicians and Carthaginians, with their intrepid maritime skills that allowed them to establish outposts, settlements and colonies far and wide, trading goods such as wine, Tyrian purple, silver, gold, tin and so much more, inspired the Romans to enlarge their commercial as well as military ambitions. Indeed, the completion of the Punic Wars marked a period of Roman expansion across the Mediterranean, with new provinces created in Iberia, much of the Balkans, as well as throughout the Italian Peninsula. Rome was growing in influence and importance, on its way to becoming one of the world's earliest and greatest superpowers.

The Wines

Grillo di Mozia Sicilia DOC, Tenuta Whitaker, Mozia, Sicily

The colony of Motya, located on the small island known as Mozia, off the west coast of Sicily, was in its time one of the most important of all

Carthaginian settlements, the rich source of two products vital to its commercial activities: sea salt and Tyrian purple dye. It was probably founded sometime in the eighth century BCE, that is, about a century after the founding of Carthage itself. Due to its economic activity and strategic position, it grew in affluence and influence. This proud city-state, however, was destroyed by the Greek tyrant Dionysius I from Syracuse in the fourth century BCE and the inhabitants either slaughtered or moved to the mainland. There is no documentation of what happened afterwards, though excavations on the island from 2007 to 2009 would indicate that there may have been a thriving Carthaginian population who returned after the Greek destruction.

During the Middle Ages, it appears that the island was occupied by Basilian monks who renamed it San Pantaleo. However, after they left, the island lay abandoned until the end of the nineteenth century. At that time, Joseph Whitaker, a British amateur ornithologist, and heir to a lucrative Marsala wine business, came to settle in the area and set about excavating the Phoenician ruins. At the same time, he noted the potential for the island to support viticulture, as it no doubt had done during the time of the Phoenicians as well as under the monks. And so it was that he planted a vineyard with Grillo grapes, the principal grape for the production of Marsala wine. Whitaker's excavations literally put ancient Motya and the Phoenician civilisation in this part of Italy on the map. He purchased Mozia in 1902, continued his excavations, wrote a book about his findings and founded a museum on the island.

Today, the Whitaker Foundation still owns Mozia, oversees the museum that holds some important works (most notably 'The Youth of Mozia', a beautiful Greek statue) and remains dedicated to researching and preserving the ruins. Part of the Whitaker Foundation project today also involves the reconstruction of the vineyard that Whitaker himself had established when he purchased the island. This is being done in partnership with one of Sicily's leading wine producers, the Tasca d'Almerita family who have been one of Sicily's leading wine producers since 1830. Together they established Tenuta Whitaker, restoring the vineyard along historical lines using procedures that would have been carried out centuries ago, long before modern interventionist viticulture was in place. This means that the vines are cultivated as they probably would have been in the time of the Phoenicians, bush-trained, free-standing and low, to protect them from the ferocious salt winds that almost constantly sweep across the island from the sea. The vineyard is farmed organically without irrigation, and all harvesting is carried out by hand.

Once the grapes are harvested, they are placed in small plastic crates and taken to the island's jetty, where they are taken by boat the short distance across the lagoon to the mainland. From there, they are transported in refrigerated lorry to the Tasca d'Almerita's family Regaleali winery. Here, the Grillo grapes from this historic and ancient vineyard are transformed by the most modern winemaking technology, using temperature-controlled fermentation in stainless-steel tanks, while at the same time following tradition. For example, the Grillo grapes macerate on the skin for upwards of two weeks to gain in character and fullness, and afterwards the wine remains on the lees for a further five months to add complexity and richness. The result is a wine of both immense character and historic significance: Grillo grapes cultivated within this enclosed maritime eco-system emerge with a character quite different from Grillo grapes grown on the mainland, resulting in wine that is deeper in colour, with a depth of flavour and a long, persistent aftertaste that is rich in minerals and tastes of the salt-laden Phoenician island from which it hails.

'Rocho' Bianchello del Metauro DOC Superiore, Roberto Lucarelli, Cartoceto, Le Marche

One of the great and constant pleasures about Italian wine is the surprise that comes from encountering little-known, obscure vintages that have deep and profound historical antecedents. Bianchello del Metauro is one such example, a wine that is inextricably linked to one of the pivotal moments in ancient history: the Battle of the Metaurus.

So, what of this special wine that was able to give courage and strength to the Roman legions? The countryside around Cartoceto and all along the Metauro Valley inland from Fano and the coast has been noted since antiquity for the quality of both its wines and olive oil. And so it continues today. This gently soft, rolling countryside is typical of Le Marche, where the influences of sea breezes from the Adriatic combine with the drier air from the mountains. Here, the Bianchello grape, a local variety cultivated only in this area, ripens well especially in vineyards exposed to the south-west to produce a white wine of structure and power. 'Rocho' Bianchello del Metauro from Roberto Lucarelli is an impressive example, produced from grapes grown on vines with an average age of at least half a century, vinified mainly in stainless-steel tank with a part in wooden *tonneau*. The wine has the characteristic stone fruit flavour of Bianchello allied with more delicate floral undertones and a salty minerality. There is a richness and power, too, as well as a hefty hit of alcohol—generally between 13 and 14 per cent, just the level needed to fortify and give courage at those pivotal and perhaps combative moments in life that we all must battle through from time to time.

4

SLAKING THE THIRST OF AN EMPIRE

I am standing on a terrace below Cape Miseno, at the north-western limit of the Gulf of Naples, looking across the glistening waters. The island of Capri lies ahead of me, the Amalfi Peninsula stretching out to hug it; to the west, beyond Cape Miseno, rise the island shapes of Procida and Ischia, like the backs of looming prehistoric monsters; to the east, I can make out the urban sprawl of Naples that now spreads over almost the whole bay. And further around still, dominating both sea and land is the broad, gently sloping shape of Mount Vesuvius, a somma stratovolcano located less than 10 kilometres from Italy's third largest city, casting its immense shadow over not only Campania's capital city but also over coastal towns such as Portici, Torre di Greco, Torre Annunziata and over the ruins of Herculaneum and Pompeii.

Miseno was once the Roman port of Misenum, home of the Roman naval fleet. In 79 CE, it was under the command of the great Roman naturalist and philosopher Gaius Plinius Secundus, known as Pliny the Elder. It was from near this very point that the great commander and historian watched in horror and fascination on that fateful day when Vesuvius erupted with such maleficent force and catastrophic power. Pliny himself, ever curious to witness natural phenomena as well as desperate to help those in need, commandeered the Roman navy to embark on a rescue mission and himself sailed with one of his ships from Misenum across the Bay of Naples towards Pompeii. The details of what happened are not clear, but what is certain is that the great Roman perished, as noted in letters written by his nephew, Pliny the Younger, who described the sky blackened with ash like a dense black cloud.

Today, it is bright, and a gentle and warm sea breeze is blowing as I look across the Bay of Naples. White flecks of foam appear among the boats—pleasure craft and small fishing trawlers—which weave and bob on the waters. On such a calm and beautiful day, it's hard to imagine the horror of that cataclysmic time nearly 2,000 years ago. I connect to that ancient past with a tumbler of wine, rich ruby in colour, redolent of forest fruits, deep and satisfying, with an earthy vegetal finish. It has been made from an ancient grape variety, Piedirosso, first introduced by the Greeks. This vine has grown and been nourished on the mineral-rich volcanic soil of the Campi Flegrei—the Phlegraean Fields—that lie just behind Miseno seemingly almost forever. It makes no claim to historic greatness; it is not the modern derivative of one of Rome's famous and most prized 'grand crus' of ancient fame. I prefer to imagine that this Piedirosso from the Campi Flegrei that I am drinking now—sound, relatively inexpensive and eminently drinkable—is not entirely dissimilar to the wines that were once purchased, drunk and enjoyed copiously by the ordinary people in the many taverns that once lined the hectic streets of Pompeii and Herculaneum, until that fateful day when life was so suddenly, cruelly and catastrophically wiped out.

The History

The rise of Rome is a remarkable story—how a small Italian city with a population of only a few thousand grew over the centuries, continuing to expand its territory and influence until it eventually held sway over most of the countries of the Mediterranean, including much of North Africa, the Levant and the Eastern Mediterranean, as well as Britannia, Germania and Gaul. This was achieved not only by military might but also by encompassing all the lands conquered within the orb of Roman civilisation and culture. Technology—the building of roads to connect areas with one another, aqueducts to bring fresh water to urban areas, the construction of theatres and amphitheatres to entertain and astonish—all helped to establish Roman hegemony as diverse peoples were given the gift of Roman civilisation. And wine lay at the very heart of this uniquely Roman way of life.

According to legend, the story of Rome begins when two twin baby boys were found floating down the Tiber by the foot of the Palatine hill where a she-wolf rescued them, suckling the hungry duo with her own teats. These divine twins, Romulus and Remus, were reputed to be descendants of the great Trojan hero Aeneas himself. The twins quarrelled; Romulus killed his brother and subsequently went on to found the greatest empire the world had ever known.

Notwithstanding such divine origins, the history of Rome in its early period is one of almost constant warfare and conquest, as the Romans, just one of many competing tribes on the Italian Peninsula, fought relentlessly to subdue and conquer all others: Sabines, Umbrians, Oscans, Volsci, Samnites, Picenes, as well as the dominant cultures and civilisations that we have already encountered, the Etruscans, mainly to the north and east, and the Greeks, mainly to the south. In this way, a small city-state built on seven hills that rise from the Tiber was able to subdue all of Italy.

The Roman Republic commenced in 509 BCE when the monarchy was replaced with rule by elected senators. By 146 BCE, with the completion of the Third Punic War and the destruction of Carthage, Rome had grown to be the greatest power across the entire Mediterranean, and the foundation was laid for the creation of an empire that would stretch across most of the known world.

The Romans were never averse to borrowing from the cultures and civilisations they subdued. Their pantheon, for example, was based on the Greek, with influences also coming from the Etruscans. The Greeks' Aphrodite, beautiful goddess of love, became Venus to the Romans; Athena, goddess of wisdom, was the Roman goddess Minerva; Hades, god of the underworld, Pluto; Hera, wife of Zeus, Juno; Hermes, messenger of the gods, Mercury; Poseidon, god of the oceans, Neptune; Zeus, king of the gods, Jupiter. Dionysus, the Greek god of wine, became Bacchus, while the Etruscan god of fertility and wine, Fufluns, became the Roman Liber.

If the Romans were not originally that at home on the sea, they learned the art of naval warfare from their foes the Carthaginians, while from the Etruscans they learned that mastery of the seas through naval trade was a sea route to riches. Indeed, from the lightweight triremes and quadriremes used so effectively in naval battles off the western coast of Sicily, to the sturdy cargo ships and freighters that were the super-tankers of the ancient world, carrying massive loads of goods to and from the empire, Roman ships came to rule the waves.

A sophisticated culture of wine drinking was another important element that the Romans had learned from both the Greeks and the Etruscans. If the Romans modelled their banquets and drinking parties on the all-male *symposia* of the Greeks, they learned from the Etruscans that the pleasures that come from wine were something to be shared equally between man and woman. Wine became a drink that cut across all classes and strata of society, available to aristocratic patricians, men and women alike, even peasants and slaves.

Wine was soon one of the most important commodities traded across the Mediterranean. The evidence of shipwrecked Roman vessels that went down laden with their cargos of thousands of amphorae filled with quantities of wine, as well as olive oil and garum—fermented fish sauce—are testimony to lucrative commercial activities, with wine not only flowing out from Roman ports but also returning, brought in from vineyards across the Roman provinces to slake the near unquenchable thirst of the people of Rome.

To be able to produce wine in sufficient quantity to have surplus to trade required a systematic approach to viticulture and winemaking. By the second century BCE, the cultivation of a vineyard had become an important agricultural activity, and, if a vineyard was tended well, and careful winemaking practices were followed, then fortunes could be made through the production of this valuable product. Marcus Porcius Cato, known as Cato the Censor, was devoted to agriculture and to finding ways to systematically run a farm to its most productive for it to be economically profitable. In his manual *De agri cultura* (On Agriculture), he outlines the most important methods of cultivating a vineyard in order to get the best commercial results. Many of the principles this early treatise advocated are still just as relevant today as then: how to train vines for optimum results; the necessity of allowing grapes to become as ripe as possible; the importance of hygiene in the vineyard and cellar. Cato advocated training vines up trees and other living supports to allow the grapes to reach higher levels, exposing them to more sunlight, a practice that persisted in parts of Central Italy under the *mezzadria* and beyond.

A later work, *De re rustica* (On Country Matters), was written by Lucius Junius Moderatus Columella and built on Cato's practical manual. Columella's was a comprehensive twelve-volume manual on all matters related to agriculture, including two volumes dedicated to viticulture. Columella, like Cato, was brutally direct, advising even on how best to treat slaves in order to get the most out of them. He described which sites were best suited to a vineyard, examined such factors as soil types, exposure and elevation; he considered the best grape varieties to plant, how to space and train the vines, when to prune; and an entire volume was devoted to winemaking practices, boiling down grape must, for example, to serve as a sweetener or to add extra sugar to result in a stronger wine, practices that are still carried out in parts of Italy today.

Pliny the Elder was another prolific writer. His *Naturalis historia* (Natural History) was a vastly important and ambitious work that purported to impart all the known knowledge of the ancient natural world, covering such topics as astronomy, meteorology, zoology, mineralogy and of course botany, including agriculture. Wine is an important subject for Pliny, who states that there are at least 185 different qualities of wine. He was a keen and curious observer, and it was Pliny who first noted and wrote about the importance of terroir, that the specific site itself was the most important determinant of quality in wine: 'Indeed some vines have so great an attachment to certain localities that their reputation is indissolubly linked to them and they cannot be transplanted anywhere else without inferior results' (trans. John Healey).

Pliny also identified and catalogued superior grape varieties. Aminea was considered the top quality, prized because of its strength and body as well as ability to undergo lengthy ageing in amphora. Aminea was the variety apparently used to produce Rome's most famous wine, Falernum. The Appian vine was another that he extolled, writing:

> it acquired its name because bees are especially greedy for it. There are two kinds, both covered with down when young. The difference is that one ripens more quickly, although the other is not slow to ripen. These vines do not object to cold locations, but no others rot more quickly in the rain.

Ampelographers have tried to correlate these ancient varieties with varieties still extant today, in some cases successfully: it would appear that Aminea may be the Falanghina grape, while Appia is Fiano, both varieties that were in the last century on the verge of extinction but through the assiduous work of viticultural archaeologists have now been safeguarded for posterity and are producing some of Campania's best and most distinctive wines.

Wine and empire

It seems that the genius of the Romans, in large measure, was their ability to conquer militarily, then absorb and adapt to the existing cultures, traditions and mores of those whom they had subdued, bringing the benefits of Roman civilisation to the conquered while at the same time learning from them and allowing indigenous culture to continue and even flourish.

When Julius Caesar conquered Gaul (58–50 BCE), the grapevine had already established deep roots, brought to Southern France first by the Greeks, who arrived here as early as the seventh century BCE. The Provincia Romana grew in importance as a major strategic thoroughfare, with Roman roads leading to the north as well as along the Mediterranean coast to Hispania, the Iberian Peninsula and across all of Gallia, Aquitania and even up to Britannia. The grapevine was carried along all these ancient byways, with some of the greatest wine regions in Europe established nearly two millennia ago by the Romans: the vineyards of the Rhône Valley, Burgundy, Bordeaux, Alsace, Germany's Rhine and Mosel Valleys, and all along the Danube. If the Phoenicians had originally brought the grapevine to Southern Spain, the Romans brought viticulture to most other corners of the Iberian Peninsula, even mainly arid and treeless La Mancha. There, where clay was abundant, Roman expertise led to the creation of giant earthenware fermentation vessels, the *dolia* of antiquity translated to *tinajas*, magnificent clay vessels that were still being produced locally and widely in use in Valdepeñas as recently as just a few decades ago. Meanwhile, across the Thracian Plain to the Eastern Mediterranean where a new capital was eventually established at Constantinople, and all along the coast of North Africa, Roman viticulture thrived, and wines were made, sold, traded, drunk and enjoyed.

Pompeii

Our knowledge of everyday life in ancient Rome has been infinitely enriched and enhanced by the haphazard chance of a terrible natural event: the eruption of Mount Vesuvius in 79 CE. The power and force of this phenomenon was utterly beyond anything previously experienced in known European history, lasting for two days and spewing volcanic matter, debris and super-heated gases to a height of some 33 kilometres, blocking out the sun, making day darker than night, then raining ash deposits, pumice stone and other solid matter on the surrounding communities, completely burying the thriving and populous towns of Pompeii and Herculaneum. Many escaped, but thousands, probably tens of thousands, perished. Those who were not buried or stoned to death were killed by the intense heat of the massive and multiple pyroclastic surges that followed. So intense were these blasts that death would have been immediate through inhalation of the super-heated air. Ash continued to rain down, covering the inert bodies of the victims, which eventually decomposed, leaving voids under the layers of hardened volcanic ash. Centuries later, these voids, when filled with plaster of Paris, revealed in remarkable and terrifying detail those final, frantic moments of flight when death came to the people of Pompeii and Herculaneum. For almost 1,700 years, the secrets of both these important cities lay buried, hidden underground. It was only in the eighteenth century that excavations began to reveal the everyday details of life during the early years of the Roman Empire.

That Pompeii in its heyday was a busy city of commercial activity is evident from the excavation of at least 600 *tabernae*, a term that refers to any type of business, usually located in relatively small shops, sometimes with accommodation above, and facing directly on to the streets. These shops sold anything from hardware goods—oil lamps, oil for the lamps—to bread and wine; or the *tabernae* might have housed bankers, barbers, doctors, pawnbrokers or prostitutes.

It is estimated that there were perhaps as many as 150 places selling wine and food, a remarkably high number for a city with a population of just 12,000. Of course, in addition to the city's residents, there were many travellers and merchants who passed through Pompeii, and these itinerant visitors would certainly have needed places to frequent not only for sustenance but also for pleasure and entertainment. Scenes of tavern life on the painted walls of such establishments demonstrate that customers came not only for wine and food but also for pleasure and more. Indeed, the lines between bar and brothel are sometimes difficult to establish: were there barmaids who offered additional services, or prostitutes who were also skilful in the service of wine and food to their appreciative and hungry clients?

What is certain is that wine was an important feature of establishments throughout the city. In the remains of a bar owned by a landlady named Hedone, for example, there is a sign that says 'you can drink wine for an *as* [a Roman coin of small value]. For two you can drink better. For four, you can drink Falernum.' Amphorae discovered in the taverns and bars of Pompeii give further indication that the wine on offer was varied. Some amphorae have inscriptions painted on them giving either addresses for delivery or else origin and vintage, with some coming from afar, demonstrating that wines came from local sources as well as being imported from abroad. The shape of the amphorae was also an important clue to the origins of the contents, an example from the Greek island of Rhodes identifiable by its distinctive, hipped handles.

Such establishments were not only Pompeii's equivalent to our bars and nightclubs but also served as the city's street food stalls, purveyors of fast foods, perhaps to eat standing up (some, but not all, such places had interior rooms) or with the hands: dried fruit, beans, chickpeas and the like while supping on measures of wine drawn from the bar-top receptacles with a ladle. As such, they provided sustenance for a hungry and busy peripatetic population, seemingly always on the move.

Dining in wealthy homes was quite another and altogether more leisurely affair. From the archaeological remains of patrician houses and villas, we gain a vivid glimpse of another world where those with money lived. In beautifully frescoed *triclinia* dining rooms, the well heeled were able to recline on sofas to be offered titbits of delicious foods, their wine cups never empty, as they were waited on by slaves who were at their every beck and call. Dining in such style was probably never an everyday occurrence except perhaps for the most powerful and indolent. More likely, people usually ate more informally, perhaps seated at tables, perhaps grabbing a bite on the run, as we ourselves do today. But for big set-piece feasts, for entertaining friends on special occasions and for being able to show off one's wealth and abundance, then dining formally was an important part of Roman life. In the House of the Triclinium, so named because of the splendour of its dining room, there are scenes that depict just such get-togethers, men and women sprawled on their luxurious sofas, some much the worse for wear, captured for eternity, being served and generally looked after by diminutive slaves.

Roman farms—*villae rusticae*—were spread out across the hinterland outside the urban areas of Pompeii, Stabiae, Oplontis and Herculaneum. Archaeologists have excavated a small farm just a kilometre outside Pompeii, the so-called Villa Regina at Boscoreale, and this gives us insight into the rural enterprises that in great measure fuelled the Roman economy. Villa Regina was a small and productive working farm of modest dimension, with wine the principal but by no means only agricultural product. The working *cantina* has been reconstructed just as it was in 79 CE. Grapes from the surrounding vineyard would have been harvested, brought to the estate and deposited in large vats, stems and all, where they were trodden by slaves to release the grape must. The juice flowed down stone channels directly into large fermentation *dolia*—terracotta urns buried almost entirely underground, each with a capacity of 500 to 700 litres. On this small farm alone, some eighteen such vessels have been excavated and are still exactly in place today. Though a small farm, it nonetheless had a by no means insubstantial capacity to produce and store upwards of 10,000 litres of wine.

Once the grape must had run into the *dolia*, the juicy mass of grape skins, stems, pulp and seeds would have been transferred to the press area, where, using a large wooden beam press, the last drops of juice were extracted. Fermentation would have occurred naturally, the yeast present on the bloom of the grapes feeding on the sugar-rich must, producing alcohol as well as carbon dioxide as by-products. Though the placing of the *dolia* underground helped to keep the temperatures stable, the intense heat of early autumn in the Campania Felix would have caused the fermentation to take place relatively swiftly, the *dolia* kept uncovered for the initial phase. The result was probably an oxidised style of wine, which appears to have been a style the Romans favoured. Once fermentation was complete, the *dolia* were sealed shut, and a second lid was placed over the first to protect from rain and frost. Thus, the wine would rest and evolve until at least the spring of the following year, when it was ready to be transported in great ox-skin receptacles directly to bars and customers in Pompeii, wine that was never destined for lengthy ageing but to be consumed young, probably as quickly as possible.

The 'grands crus' of the Roman world

Can we ever really know what Roman wine was like? Of course not, but what seems certain is that the best was more than likely sweet, strong and aged, reserved for connoisseurs and the very rich or *nouveau riche*. For the everyday man and woman in the street, wines were altogether simpler as well as most probably from the latest vintage.

The Romans made wine in as many styles as are made even today. Winemaking techniques were outlined in the treatises by Cato, Columella and Pliny. The pressing need, in antiquity as today, was to be able to produce a stable beverage that was capable of being stored, whether for a few months after the harvest or even for upwards of decades and even centuries. To achieve this, a certain level of alcohol would need to be reached, possible only if the vines had been carefully tended and pruned to reduce quantity and increase quality and fermentable sugar levels, fundamental practices still carried out today.

Virgil advised that winegrowers should be the first to till the ground and the last to harvest, stressing the need to give the vine sufficient growing season for the grapes to reach their full degree of ripeness and potential alcohol. Sometimes other methods were used to boost sugar levels. Grapes could be laid out to dry to a semi-raisined state to increase the sugar levels, a process still carried out today throughout Italy to produce any number of *passito* wines. Grapes were sometimes submerged under the sea for a period of days to wash the natural bloom from their surface before being left out to dry in the sun, this pre-process apparently helping the grapes to raisin more quickly prior to fermentation. Another method was to boil down fresh grape must to a sugar-rich syrup to boost fermentable sugars during fermentation, as well as to add sweetness to the finished wines.

Columella believed that the best wines should be able to be conserved without any preservatives and with no additional ingredients added to obscure the natural taste. This is as relevant today as it was 2,000 years ago and gives an insight into the world and taste of Roman wine. Yet at the same time, Columella notes that numerous additives can be added to wine, including boiled must; chalk or marble dust (possibly added to temper wines that were overly acidic); seawater or salt during fermentation; pitch or resin, either directly to the wine, or else as a coating for fermentation and storage vessels, the resin adding flavours one assumes not unlike that of modern Greek *retsina*. Wines were rarely served undiluted and were often mixed with water or seawater together with other ingredients, including honey, boiled grape must and/or spices.

The fifth-century CE author of *De re coquinaria* (On Cookery), attributed as Apicius, starts his treatise with a recipe for an extraordinary, spiced wine, flavoured with honey, pepper, saffron, cinnamon and mastic resin. He furthermore advises how an ordinary wine can be transformed into a stimulating spiced beverage with the addition of ingredients such as wormwood, mastic, costmary (a perennial herb native to Southern Europe and Western Asia) and saffron to produce a sort of Roman absinthe. He gives recipes for other titillating beverages made by infusing wine with rose and violet petals, palm branches and leaves of the citron tree.

Every last bit of fermentable and commercially valuable residue from the winemaking process was used. A sort of 'after wine' was made from the cake of the first pressing of wine-drenched skins, cut up and then pressed again to extract even more must. Farm labourers, according to Cato, were not even given this beverage. Rather, a 'sharp' wine was made from inferior or underripe grapes mixed with vinegar, boiled must, fresh water and old seawater, a potation that reputedly could last through the winter. Other potations—it is hardly fair to call them wine—were *lora*, made from the dry grape pomace left over after winemaking mixed with water, and *faecatum*, made out of the lees, or solid residue left over in the fermentation vessels after the wines were racked or transferred. Such beverages were available to the lowest in society, for even the poor as well as slaves, it seems, had the basic right to enjoy a wine of sorts.

Pliny estimated that there were at least eighty wines of note in the Roman world, with most of these produced in Italy. His *grand crus* or great growths included Falernum, from vineyards between Rome and Naples; Caecuban, grown on marshy ground north of the Falernum vineyards; Alba, referring to wines from the Colli Albani, south of Rome, incorporating the modern wine zones of Frascati and Marino ('mostly very sweet but occasionally dry' said Pliny); and Surrentinum from the Sorrento Peninsula, 'recommended for persons recovering from illness because of their thinness and health-giving properties'. He also rated wines from Mamertinum, a favourite of Julius Caesar from Messina in Sicily; Praetutian from Ancona, where vines had first been planted by the Greeks; Rhaetic from Verona's Valpolicella wine hills; Luna from Tuscany; Trebellian from Naples; and Cauline from Capua. The 'wines of Pompeii', however, were given faint praise for being 'best within ten years and gain nothing from greater maturity. They are also observed to be injurious because of the hangover they cause, which persists until noon on the following day.'

Not only were wines from certain superior terroirs identified, but Pliny also noted that there were great variations in quality from one year to the next. He drew particular attention to the year when Lucius Opimius was consul (121 BCE) as a vintage that surpassed all others. 'The weather was hot and sunny: men called it "good ripening weather". Wines from that year still survive today—nearly 200 years later—although they have now evaporated to the consistency of honey and have a rough taste. Such is the nature of wines when old' (trans. John Healey).

Falernum

Falernum was the most famous and prized of all Roman wines, a wine that could even claim divine origins: according to Silius Italicus, the Roman orator and poet, it was linked to the god of wine himself, Bacchus, who had given it as a gift to an old man, Falernus, who had offered him hospitality. The vineyard area where Falernum was reputedly produced has been identified as lying along the southern slopes of Monte Massico, in the heart of what was the Romans' fertile Campania Felix, in the modern province of Caserta extending across the Phlegraean Fields. Just as in quality vineyards today, the area for the cultivation of Falernum was divided into specified *crus* areas that produced wines with different qualities and characteristics: Caucinium from vineyards on the hilltops, Faustianum from the slopes and Falernum from the plain.

Falernum was so highly valued partly because of its high natural strength, a wine that was powerful and full-bodied (*firmissima*) and so high in alcohol that it could be ignited with a flame. Like all the best Roman vintages, Falernum was a wine for connoisseurs, most appreciated after between ten and twenty years of ageing in amphora. Pliny the Elder in his *Naturalis historia* distinguished three styles of Falernum: *austerum* (dry and tannic), *dulce* (sweet) and *tenue* (light). The famous Opimian vintage that this naturalist and historian cited is an indication that in the best years it was a wine that could live almost forever. It cannot be known for certain the grape variety or varieties that were used to produce Falernum, though scholarly archaeologists of the vine have endeavoured to link grapes still being cultivated today with this most famous wine of antiquity. It is conjectured that it was made in both *niger* (red) and *xanthos* (amber) styles.

So much of modern Italy and indeed modern Europe owes a debt to the intrepid and tireless empire-builders that were the Romans, not least for their gift to European culture of the cultivation of vineyards across Italy and the continent. Above all, the Romans spread the art of civilised wine drinking throughout Italy and beyond as an enduring and essential way of life and good living. I raise a glass to them.

The Wines

Colle Rotondella, Campi Flegrei DOP, Cantine Astroni, Napoli, Campania

Few places in Italy are more closely and intimately linked to the ancient world than the Phlegraean Fields, or Campi Flegrei. According to mythology, Lake Avernus was the gateway to the Underworld, and the whole area is a still-active volcanic landscape of 'burning land' located to the west of Naples. There are waves of steep volcanic hills rising from the coast with fertile, mineral-rich volcanic soil. Calderas, depressions left after a volcano erupts and collapses, have filled up with water to form lakes. Fumaroles emit pungent gaseous emissions, leaving a stinky, sulphurous cloud that sometimes hangs over the coastal towns. Thermal springs, sinkholes and boreholes abound, so it is no surprise that the Romans loved the area for the therapeutic powers of its waters.

Yet, though the Phlegraean Fields are one of Italy's most ancient wine lands, cultivated first by the Greeks then the Romans, as happened elsewhere, an ancient patrimony that should have been treasured had almost become lost as viticulture was mainly abandoned, particularly in the last century. Indeed, it is only since the mid-1990s that there has been a significant revival, making the Phlegraean Fields at once one of Italy's most ancient wine areas as well as one of its newest and most exciting. For example, the Varchetta family have been growing grapes and making wine in the Phlegraean Fields for well over 100 years and at least four generations. Yet it was only in 1999 that the Cantine Astroni was founded with the express aim to revalue this ancient patrimony by making wines that truly reflect the unique volcanic terroir of the area, using the fruit from ungrafted, ancient pre-phylloxera native vines that had almost been abandoned: Falanghina for white and sparkling wines and Piedirosso for red and *rosato*.

Colle Rotondella Piedirosso Campi Flegrei is an example of how good such wines from this only recently rediscovered wine zone can be. Piedirosso, known in dialect as 'Per 'e Palummo' ('pigeon leg', because of its red stem), makes juicy, fresh reds with moderate tannins that are simply beautiful wines to drink. Colle Rotondella is a modern wine made from an ancient grape, vibrant, bright and vivid, holding within it something of the powerful yet controlled energy of the 'burnt lands' that give it birth. Is it fanciful to suggest that this would be just the sort of wine that Gaius Plinius Secundus himself (possibly Italy's first wine critic?) would have wholeheartedly enjoyed, though perhaps not so much on that fateful day in 79 CE?

SLAKING THE THIRST OF AN EMPIRE

Naturalis Historia, Taurasi DOCG, Mastroberardino, Atripalda, Campania

How to choose a wine to pay homage to the mighty Romans, who not only forged an empire that extended across the entire Mediterranean, through all of Europe and across northern Africa as well as into Asia Minor but were also so instrumental in making wine a central feature of European culture? It must be a mighty wine, a wine of historic pedigree, a great wine that does justice to the enduring legacy of the Romans.

Naturalis Historia Taurasi Riserva is just such a wine, the product of a historic grape variety, Aglianico, cultivated on a select single vineyard on the Tenuta Mirabella Eclano in the province of Avellino, an ancient land that the poet Virgil defined as 'terra gelosa dei suoi tanti misteri'—'a land that holds its mysteries dearly'. The name of the wine also pays homage to that great naturalist and historian, Pliny the Elder.

Our knowledge of and pleasure from Italian wines made from grape varieties with ancient antecedents is in no small measure due to the vision and considerable efforts of pioneering producers such as the Mastroberardinos. This family winery, located in Atripalda in the heart of inland Irpinia, is now in its eleventh generation and can trace its history back to 1720, with the current company established in 1878. Though international markets had already been established in the early nineteenth century, the company lost almost everything in the aftermath of the Second World War. At that time, the visionary head of the family, Antonio Mastroberardino, took the far-sighted decision to rebuild the company, not by adapting to international tastes but by basing its future firmly on the ancient, deep-rooted vinous patrimony of viticulture in the region that could trace its origins directly back to the Romans and indeed to the Greeks before them.

The Aglianico grape can produce wines that are tough and formidable and require time and patience: but indeed, were not the greatest Roman wines just like this, too, revealing themselves most fully only after lengthy periods of ageing? Naturalis Historia is produced from ancient vines in some cases a half-century old or more. Once harvested, usually in October and even sometimes as late as November, they are destemmed, crushed and vinified in the traditional manner with lengthy maceration on the skins to fully extract aromas and sufficient tannins to enable the wine to continue to evolve and develop for literally decades. The wine then ages in French oak *barriques* for a period of not less than two years followed by a further thirty months ageing in the bottle before release. Naturalis Historia Taurasi is powerful and important, dense in structure, rich in tannin, with a complex and persistent bou-

49

quet that offers tantalising aromas of flowers, herbs, Mediterranean undergrowth, tobacco, chocolate and much more: a truly great wine and a fitting
heir to the greatest Roman wines of the ancient world.

Villa dei Misteri, Rosso Pompeiano IGT, Mastroberardino, Atripalda, Campania

The Villa dei Misteri project began in 1996, a collaboration between the
Soprintendenza Archeologica di Pompeii (Pompeii's archaeological authority)
and the Azienda Vinicola Mastroberardino winery. The project, which continued until 2021, brought the world's attention to Pompeii and to the long
continuity of wine produced and enjoyed in the Campania Felix.

'The project was born from the dream of Antonio Mastroberardino, my
father,' explained Piero Mastroberardino, the present CEO of the company:

> In the 1970s he tried to imagine how the origins of the wines of the ancient
> Campania Felix could be presented to the world. In 1996, we began planting
> a vineyard within the walls of Pompeii, divided into lots of different parcels
> within the gardens of the houses of the city.

The aim was to replicate vineyards in ancient Pompeii using the same grape
varieties cultivated and trained in the same manner as in antiquity. DNA
analysis was carried out on grape seeds recovered from the volcanic ash, and
it was deemed that the most likely grapes to have been cultivated were
Piedirosso and Sciascinoso, varieties still cultivated widely on the volcanic
slopes of Vesuvius today. Thus, about a hectare of vines was planted originally across four different sites within Pompeii: the House of the Ship
Europa, the Inn of the Gladiators, the Foro Boario and the House of the
Summer Dining Room.

The first harvest was in 2001, with the production of 1,721 bottles of Villa
dei Misteri Rosso Pompeiano, made from about 90 per cent Piedirosso and
10 per cent Sciascinoso. The production of wine from Pompeii for the first
time in almost 2,000 years was an achievement that captured the imagination
of wine lovers from all around the world. Many of the bottles were sold by
auction and the proceeds used to excavate the ancient winery of the Foro
Boario, revealing ten *dolia* that had once been used to produce and store
Pompeiian wine.

In 2007, new sites within Pompeii were identified as possible former vineyards, and thus the authorities granted a further concession to Mastroberardino
that permitted the expansion of the plantation across ten further small sites.
This allowed for additional experimentation with grape varieties such as
Aglianico, as well as to try out various methods of training as well as pruning.

The Villa dei Misteri 2011 vintage was produced from a blend of 40 per cent Aglianico, 40 per cent Piedirosso and 20 per cent Sciascinoso, and it is this blend that more or less continued until the project ceased in 2021.

This is a wine I long dreamed of tasting, a wine, I imagined, that would be truly 'the taste of history'. However, I must report that the wine, though perfectly sound with juicy, crunchy fruit and aromas of cherries and raspberries, was surprisingly underwhelming. 'There is no reason why it should be extraordinary', explained Piero, as we sipped the wine together in the Mastroberardino cellars in Atripalda. 'Pompeii is on the coast and the vineyards are mainly flat. This is not where great wine ever comes from, neither now nor in the past.' It is further noteworthy, explained Piero, that the vineyards were mainly sited near the Arena, the Roman amphitheatre where crowds would have gathered to watch the spectacle of men fighting to the death against other men or wild beasts. There were wine stalls in the streets leading to this ancient stadium as well as stalls set up within the walls of the Arena itself, so it is probable that wines just such as this, produced in Pompeii nearly 2,000 years ago, were always intended to be sold and drunk young, within the city itself, to slake the thirst of spectators whose throats had become parched through roaring on their heroes.

The Villa dei Misteri project and the wine produced has helped to connect us vividly and directly to the literal ancient roots of the past and has brought us even closer to the time when Pompeii was vibrant, exciting, noisy, alive. Tasting this special wine was therefore a deeply emotional experience that went far beyond the taste of the liquid in the glass. Every time I visit Pompeii, I cannot help but feel uneasy and deeply uncomfortable, for it connects to a precise moment in time when lives were suddenly and catastrophically wiped out through the random and frightening force of nature. We stroll the rutted, basalt-paved streets, marvel at how the people lived; see the street stalls from where they purchased food, bought wine; like voyeurs we peek into rooms where they slept, ate, made love. As I sipped that extraordinary everyday wine from the past, I could not also help but feel deeply and emotionally their panic, their fear, their pain, their absolute choking terror.

Vigna Caracci, Falerno del Massico Bianco DOP, Villa Matilde Avallone, Cellole, Campania

If no wine was ever more famous in antiquity than Falernum, the truth is that its origins, after centuries and millennia of neglect, had been all but lost in the midst of time and legend. In the 1960s, however, Dr Francesco Avallone, a lawyer and classical scholar from Naples, became curious to try to rediscover the wine that had been so extolled by the great Roman writers. Working with a group of friends, including professors from the Faculty of Agriculture at the University of Naples, over the course of many years, Dr Avallone undertook extensive research into the wine Falernum, looking at possible grape varieties and methods of production. It seems that, like for wines today, there were strict rules that defined the way it had to be produced. When pressing the grapes by human foot, slaves had to dance to sacred music, keeping to a regular rhythm. Once pressed, the juice flowed from the pressing tank down stone channels directly into fermentation *dolia* made from terracotta and buried underground. Because the juice ran off from the tank, the wine did not ferment on the skins, which is what gives wine its colour and tannin. Therefore, it seems that both white and red grapes could have been used to produce Falernum. For wines destined for lengthy ageing, the terracotta receptacles were sometimes placed in a fumarium or smoke house, the smoke helping to preserve the wine as smoking preserves food while at the same time lending the wine a characteristic smoky aroma and flavour.

Villa Matilde Avallone is a winery that was conceived and created out of sheer passion and dedication to the ancient past. Today Dr Avallone's children, daughter Maria Ida and son Salvatore, together with their respective children Maria Cristina and Francesco Paolo, continue the Villa Matilde Avallone project. They have expanded the estate to other areas to produce wines that express the full personality and strong identity of the ancient Campania Felix, while always respecting the past and the work that their father did to further knowledge of viticulture and wines, in antiquity as well as today.

Dr Avallone identified a wine grape that he believed to have been one of the main varieties used to produce Falernum. In Roman times, it may have been called *uva della falanga* or *uva falanghina* because the vines were trained on a pole (*falanga*) rather than left free-standing, which was the Greek way. The grape variety thus came to be called Falanghina, and Dr Avallone worked tirelessly to save it from extinction after it had been mainly abandoned after phylloxera. Today, the Falanghina grape, nearly extinct just fifty years ago, is widely planted throughout Campania to produce white wines of real distinction and character.

Vigna Caracci Falerno del Massico Bianco is a white wine able to combine character, structure and elegance and is thus worthy of the exalted esteem in which Falernum was once held. Today at Villa Matilde Avallone it is vinified by both modern methods and ancient. Once harvested, the grapes undergo a period of cryomaceration. The grapes are then lightly crushed to extract the must, which undergoes fermentation in stainless-steel as well as in terracotta amphora. The wine is not released until five years after its harvest. This is a well-structured white wine, with a concentration of almost exotic aromas, including pear, pineapple, peach. There is weight and body in the mouth, and the wine finishes cleanly with a well-balanced persistence and a tension that comes from its high natural acidity and concentrated minerality. Of course, this wine is completely different from the vintages drunk by the Romans, yet nonetheless, it is a fitting tribute that connects us through wine to the ancient past and to the grandeur that was ancient Rome.

Nesos 'vino marino', Arrighi Vini, Isola d'Elba, Tuscany

The elusive search for ancient wine—the flavours of the past—is also being carried out on the island of Elba. Here winemaker Antonio Arrighi is making a fascinating wine using an ancient process documented by Pliny the Elder and carried out by the Romans more than 2,000 years ago. To make *vino marino*, said to have been favoured by Julius Caesar, Arrighi takes Ansonica grapes, cultivated and harvested on Elba, places them in handwoven baskets holding about 25 kilograms, and immerses them 10 metres deep in the crystalline waters of the Tyrrhenian Sea for a period of five days. It is a process he first learned about from Professor Attilio Scienza, Vinitaly International Academy's chief scientist and Italy's leading vine geneticist. After the baskets are retrieved from the sea, the grapes are then laid out to undergo a brief period of two days of *appassimento* outdoors in direct sunlight. The time spent under the sea results in an osmosis, with saltwater penetrating into the grapes without breaking the skin (Ansonica has a very tough and resistant skin). This helps to preserve the grapes from oxidation while at the same time removing much of the bloom on the skins, and so allowing the drying process in the sun to happen more speedily while at the same time preserving the aroma of Ansonica. The lightly dried grapes are then crushed by foot and fermented on the skins in terracotta amphorae containing just 25 litres. Only the tiniest quantity of this very special *vino marino* is being produced—somewhere between just 240 and 400 bottles per year.

Nesos is the product of the land in which the grapes grow, the sea into which they have been plunged and the sun that dries them afterwards. The wine is pale gold in colour, made in a slightly oxidative style that nevertheless retains its freshness with notes of beeswax, honey, herbs, sea vegetables, resin and a beautiful, marked saline finish that recalls the grapes' sojourn underwater. The finish is remarkable, the briny aftertaste lingering long in the mouth and memory. Arrighi explained to me that he began the project out of curiosity and strictly as an experimental project. The unique character and extraordinary quality of this *vino marino* is a clear demonstration to the world that winemaking techniques from antiquity were certainly able to result in wines every bit as wondrous, as beautiful and as astonishing as anything we can produce today.

5

THE TRIUMPH OF CHRISTIANITY

Since the thirteenth century, millions of pilgrims have made their way to the Basilica della Santa Casa, one of the holiest shrines in Italy—indeed in all of Christendom. It is in Loreto, in Le Marche, a region that until the unification of Italy was part of the Papal States. The Basilica della Santa Casa is so named and so widely visited because within its grandiose and monumental edifice, expanded over the years and centuries by successive popes, is a humble stone house that is purported to be the abode where the Virgin Mary lived in Judaea. Pious legend says that the Holy House miraculously arrived in Loreto propelled by the strong wings of angels, who carried it over the seas to deposit it where it can now be found (more or less, since it has apparently been moved on more than one occasion). Other more pragmatic believers think it was more likely to have been transported here by Crusaders after the Holy Lands were conquered by the so-called infidel. Recent investigations have scientifically proven that the stones really have come from Judaea. Across the ages and even still today, the Basilica della Santa Casa has been and continues to be a shrine of great significance for the devout, attracting pilgrims and those seeking divine assistance or healing, with people coming not only from across all of Italy but also the world. Even for those of us who do not believe, it is humbling to be in the presence of such devout faith: some have travelled here literally on their hands and knees (grooves have been worn in the stone floor from centuries of shuffling devotion). The intensity of emotion within the Santa Casa is tangible, undeniable, deeply moving, even overwhelming.

Such faith is exhausting. I sense this as I exit from the darkness of the basilica into the light of day. Believers and tourists alike immediately repair to the bars and restaurants that line the town, me included. I sit outside and ask for a glass of the local wine, Verdicchio, which has quenched the thirst of millions of pilgrims over the years and centuries. I don't want the breezy, light version served on the beaches of Le Marche. I'm in need of something bigger, fuller in body. The barman suggests a local wine from Loreto, from the Garofoli winery just down the road. It is astounding, uplifting, invigo-

rating, unadulterated by oak, rich in flavour, powerful and persistent, a wine that has the power to make you believe. But in what? The power of the Catholic Church? Or the power of wine?

The History

By the fourth century CE, the Roman Empire was in serious decline. Too unwieldy and top-heavy due to the huge extent of its territory, it had already been split in two in 286 CE by Emperor Diocletian, who appointed Maximian as co-emperor to oversee the east from its capital at Byzantium, while he himself continued to rule over the west from Rome. Even this could not save the empire from retreat, as barbarian threats continued across the provinces and even into Italy itself. Constantine took over as Augustus, or senior Western emperor, in 306 and eventually named himself sole emperor in 324, ruling over the remnants of both east and west until his death in 337. He enacted financial, social and military reforms to strengthen the empire and built a new imperial palace in Byzantium, renaming it Constantinople, a city that remained the capital of what later became the Byzantine Empire for more than 1,000 years.

Even under this great ruler, Rome continued its irreparable decline. At the same time, a new and powerful force was rising that would not be denied: Christianity. The empire may have been crumbling, but this new religion gave hope to the poor and the downtrodden, the belief that through the mercy of God the Father there was the chance of redemption and eternal life. Roman society had always been pantheistic, and the emperors had even allowed themselves to be worshipped as divine entities, with their effigies and statues placed everywhere. Christianity, however, believed in just a single god, an anathema that the Romans tried to stamp out through continual persecution, martyring the believers by torture and brutal death. Yet still the faith continued to grow, at first underground, then increasingly in the open.

Its popularity and importance meant that the continued persecution of the Christians that had been carried out so brutally by Constantine's predecessor Diocletian was never going to succeed in stamping out the religion. Belief in Jesus Christ the Saviour had by now established itself in the hearts and minds of much of the populace, and Constantine recognised this by declaring tolerance for Christianity and even converting to the religion himself on his death-bed, thus making him the first Christian Roman emperor. The significance of

Constantine's conversion was considerable, for Christianity and the ever-growing power of the Church came to define the course of Italian, and indeed world, history.

The triumph of the Catholic Church

As the Western Empire disintegrated further, Christianity continued to grow in both the west and east. The Edict of Milan, issued by Constantine in 313, gave freedom of religion to all faiths, and in 380 the Edict of Thessalonica declared Nicene Christianity to be the official faith of the Roman Empire (as opposed to other creeds that were deemed heretical). Those who accepted this faith became known as Catholic Christians. Thus, in both east and west, Christianity was now the official religion. Christians no longer had to worship underground. Grand churches began to be constructed, and the cross became the symbol of suffering and redemption, as well as of a growing temporal and spiritual force.

Those who held the seats of power in the Church became important dignitaries with not only spiritual but also, increasingly, political and economic power. The leader of the Church was the bishop of Rome, who became known also as supreme pontiff or pope, a vital spiritual role that according to Catholics could trace itself back to when Peter was granted authority directly from Jesus, who referred to him as the rock of the Church. 'I will give you the keys of the Kingdom of Heaven, and whatever you bind on earth will be bound in heaven, and whatever you loose on earth will be loosed in heaven' (Matthew 16:18–19). Through his teachings, Peter undoubtedly rallied Christians when they were most at risk of persecution, and he was instrumental in the formation of the Catholic Church. The first basilica in Rome dedicated to St Peter was constructed during Constantine's reign, and from this seat the bishops of Rome could thus claim their role as the head of the Church.

The Western Empire fell to the barbarians in 476, but even through times of turmoil the pope was able to maintain spiritual and ecclesiastical power. Indeed, in no small measure, the Church became the most cohesive institution as the remnants of the Roman Empire fractured and disintegrated. The first great medieval pope of this era was Gregory I, known also as Pope Gregory the Great, who came from an ancient Roman senatorial family. At a time when stability and continuity were required, Pope Gregory worked tirelessly to improve and reform the administration of the Church and to deal with the political and social challenges of the day. Not only was this a time of great change and uncertainty but a plague was also ravishing the land, and there was famine as well as threats from both the Byzantines who controlled the Eastern Empire and from the new invaders, the Lombards, whom Pope Gregory helped to convert from pagan beliefs and Arianism to Catholic Christianity.

Though those 'Dark Age' centuries remained unstable, Gregory's successors thus helped to establish the Church as the third major force in the Italy of this period, lending support to the exarch of Ravenna, the Byzantine emperor's representative in Italy, when expedient, while reaching a relatively stable equilibrium with the occupying Germanic invaders. Christianity spread throughout Italy through the efforts of the papacy, the Byzantines and the increasingly devout Lombards, who oversaw the construction of a vast number of churches and monasteries.

Christianity and wine

The sacrament of the Eucharist is fundamental to Catholic belief. At the Last Supper, Jesus instructed his disciples that the bread is his body and the wine his blood and that they should eat and drink in remembrance of him: 'Whoever eats my flesh and drinks my blood lives in me and I live in that person' (John 6:53–6). The sacrament of the Eucharist thus became the principal act for the Christian faithful, the partaking of the consecrated bread and wine a sacred covenant of redemption and resurrection.

With the Eucharist a central element of daily worship, it can be argued that the spread of viticulture across Europe—and later the New World—can be allied directly with the spread of Christianity in no small measure because of the pressing need to have wine on hand to celebrate Mass. In the early centuries of Christianity, churches would not have had the manpower or the land to cultivate and care for a vineyard, nor necessarily the knowledge to make wine. What is more likely is that wealthy donors were more than willing to contribute wine to the Church as a mark of faith as well as a means of gaining favoured entrance into the Kingdom of Heaven. From there, it was only a short step from giving donations of wine to donating land for a vineyard. Monasteries across Italy, endowed with land that could be converted into vineyards, were therefore able to devote themselves to viticulture and the production of wine.

By the eighth century, the Church already had extensive holdings of land, and this was to form the base that gave it increasingly immense wealth, as well as economic and political strength. As the Byzantines began turning their attention away from Italy to more pressing threats in the east, the papacy was able to assert not only greater spiritual but also temporal power.

And so it continued as the next foreign military force rose to power on the Italian Peninsula, the Franks. The Lombards had continuously tried to expand into papal and Byzantine territory, and when they threatened Rome and Central Italy around 750, Pope Stephen II fled to the Frankish kingdom and appealed to Pepin the Short, the first Carolingian king of the Franks. Pepin waged a successful campaign against the Lombards and secured several cities that he then granted to the pope. These lands formed the legal basis for the creation of the Papal States, or Stati Pontifici, in 756 through what came to be known as the Donation of Pepin. This political entity managed to remain intact, holding out even during the unification of Italy until as late as 1870.

Around this same time, an important early medieval forgery of an imperial Roman decree was created and then 'discovered', possibly to assist Pope Stephen II in his negotiations with Pepin. Known as the Donation of Constantine, this decree purportedly granted authority from Constantine the Great to the pope and his successors over Rome and the western part of the Roman Empire, including that part of Italy under the Byzantines, thus confirming by right the Papal States as not only a spiritual but also a temporal power. Other territories were granted to the Church by the Treaty of Pavia, while Charlemagne gave further grants of land to the papacy, as did later Carolingian rulers. Thus the Church and its leader the pope came to rule over a vast territory that ran from Rome across Central Italy to the Adriatic and up the coast as far as Ravenna.

Holy Roman Empire

The vital relationship between the papacy and the Church and Frankish and later German rulers was firmly cemented on Christmas Day, 800, when Pope Leo III crowned Charlemagne, king of the Franks, to be 'Charles, most serene Augustus, crowned by God, great and pacific emperor, governing the Roman Empire'. In so doing, the Church established its position as the supreme spiritual leader, while the coronation of Charlemagne marked the creation of the first Holy Roman Emperor and the making of a new political entity and force that was to dominate all of Europe and last for 1,000 years until its dissolution in 1806.

If the Church can rightly be credited with encouraging and promoting wine production, Charlemagne, too, demonstrated that temporal powers also had a stake in ensuring a continuous flow of good wine. During his rule, he issued directives that called for improvements in agriculture, farming and viticulture. In the *Capitulare de villis* (On Managing the Royal Estates), winemakers were instructed that 'winepresses be kept in good order, and no one dare crush the grapes with their feet, that everything is clean and decent … and that wine be put in good barrels bound with iron'.

Wine and the Church; wine and empire: the story of wine in Italy became ever more intertwined with the story of medieval and Renaissance Italy, defined in large measure by the near constant struggle between popes and Holy Roman emperors. Popes held the extreme and ultimate power of excommunication, while the emperors continually sought to assert their supremacy over the pope even over such crucial ecclesiastic matters as the right to investiture. The conflict between the papacy and the Holy Roman Empire was a near constant back and forth tussle, with incessant power struggles and quarrels over the succeeding centuries. Through it all, wine, good Italian wine, continued to flow and to be enjoyed by popes and emperors alike as well as by all, from nobles and the clergy right down to the common man.

The Wines

I Portali di Pietra, Cesanese del Piglio Superiore DOCG, Casale della Ioria, Acuto, Lazio

Wine is intimately linked to the story of Christianity, so it stands to reason that there are wines that have direct links with the Church and the papacy. The French have long been the masters at drawing such connections, a papal seal of approval a huge boost to marketing their wines. Witness the fact that the papacy was only moved to Avignon from 1309 until 1377 (see Chapter 12), but this brief period was enough to result in two great wines that proudly assert their blessed links. Château Pape Clément is a *grand cru classé* of Graves from the family vineyard of Clement V, who, with the connivance of Philip IV of France, was invested as pope in 1305 and immediately decided to relocate the papacy from Rome to Avignon. His successor, Pope John XXII, then went on to build a new château in the stony wine hills above Avignon. Today, wines made from grapes grown on vineyards around that ancient ruin give France and the world one of its greatest wines, its renown in no small measure partly because of its evocative name: Châteauneuf-du-Pape.

Cesanese del Piglio DOCG may not have the same resonance or renown, yet this is nonetheless an outstanding red wine from Lazio that is most certainly fitting to commemorate its direct papal links. The area for its production is Ciociaria, south-west of Rome and close to Anagni, a medieval hill town in the province of Frosinone. Anagni, the birthplace of no fewer than four popes, was the scene of some of the most momentous events in Italian history concerning the power struggle between the papacy, Holy Roman Empire and temporal powers such as the king of France. It was at the Papal Palace at Anagni that popes received imperial legates and excommunicated emperors, including Frederick Barbarossa by Pope Alexander III in 1176, as well as his grandson Frederick II by Gregory IX in 1227 (the latter duo were later reconciled in Anagni Cathedral in 1230).

The Casale della Ioria wine estate extends over former ecclesiastical lands that were more than likely cultivated with vines to supply wine to the papal delegations at Anagni. Certainly, no prelate would turn their nose up at this wine: I Portali di Pietra, Cesanese del Piglio Superiore DOCG, produced by the Perinelli family winery from Cesanese d'Affile grapes cultivated organically at about 400 metres above sea level. After the harvest, about two-thirds of the grapes are vinified in stainless-steel, while the remaining third undergoes a period of *appassimento* whereby the grapes are carefully laid out on cane mats to dry and shrivel for a period of a couple of months. These partially raisined grapes are then added to the previously fermented wine to provoke a further secondary fermentation, adding about half a degree or so of alcohol, but most of all rich dried-fruit aromas and texture, as well as complexity and structure. The colour is not unlike the deep scarlet of a cardinal's robe, and the wine is quite simply opulent, powerful, complex, intriguing.

Poggio Verde, Frascati Superiore DOCG, Principe Pallavicini, Monte Compatri, Lazio

The Colli Albani or Alban Hills lie along a gentle volcanic ridge to the south of Rome. For well over two millennia, this higher area has served as a retreat, an escape from the city in times of turmoil or summer heat, and a refuge for the wealthy and the privileged. When Rome was at risk of being sacked by barbarian tribes from the north, popes and their entourages often had to take refuge in this beautiful and strategic vine-covered hill country. The Colli Albani proved to be a salubrious retreat in times of malarial outbreaks, and perhaps it was for this reason that in the sixteenth century an official summer residence was constructed for the popes at Castel Gandolfo, near Frascati.

Due to the papal connection at Castel Gandolfo as well as its proximity to Rome and the Vatican, Frascati has long been called 'the wine of the popes'. Over the centuries, it is probable that the pontiffs have drunk more than their fair share of it. Pope Paul III, the first pope of the Counter Reformation, specified that Frascati was the wine to be served for daily meals at the Vatican. In the seventeenth century, under both Popes Innocent X and Clement X, Frascati wine was said to have flowed from the fountains for their inaugural celebrations, the people of Rome rushing to capture with cups or flagons quantities of good Frascati wine sprouting from the nostrils of Marcus Aurelius's horse.

The noble Principe Pallavicini family can trace their presence in the Lazio region back for centuries and can boast a pope in the family, Pope Clement IX, as well as various cardinals, including Giovanni Battista Pallavicini and Lazzaro Pallavicini. Historical documents in the family archives of Palazzo Pallavicini show that they have long supplied wine to the Vatican. It is fitting today that they remain one of the best producers of Frascati, a wine that can otherwise be much derided for the oceans of bland and indifferent bottles that have long been produced on a near semi-industrial scale to slake the unquenchable thirst of Rome and its millions of visitors, as well as to find a place on the red checkered tablecloths of Italian restaurants and trattorias around the world.

Poggio Verde is a benchmark Frascati with genuine character and personality, produced mainly from the superior Malvasia Puntinata grape with some Greco and Bombino Bianco, all grown to restricted yields. The grapes undergo cryomaceration to extract flavour and aroma and are then gently pressed before fermentation at controlled temperature in stainless-steel. The wine is kept on the lees for four to five months with *bâtonnage* (stirring the lees to add a creamy texture and flavour). This is a full white wine, with a bright and vivid yellow colour with tints of gold, an intense bouquet of wildflowers, yellow fruit, ripe melon and with structure, balance and a herbal balsamic persistence that lingers in the mouth and in the memory.

Podium, Verdicchio dei Castelli di Jesi, Garofoli, Loreto, Le Marche

Pilgrims who visit shrines need accommodation, food and drink, and the town of Loreto that sprawls around the giant Basilica has benefitted over the centuries as a result. So it continues today. After visiting this great holy shrine to worship the Santa Casa, visitors and pilgrims alike emerge with, perhaps, their spiritual needs somewhat assuaged but with their fleshly appetites more ravenous than ever. Bars and restaurants therefore do a brisk business, while wine producers from the surrounding Castelli di Jesi and Conèro have long found a ready and thirsty market for their products.

The Garofoli family, located in Loreto, readily acknowledge their debt to the millions of thirsty pilgrims who have come to the area to visit the Basilica of the Santa Casa, sometimes stayed for a while, or else who, on returning home, have found that they have gained a taste for the zesty Verdicchio whites of the Castelli di Jesi and the chunky, crunchy reds of the Conèro. The family business dates to 1871 and is now in its fifth generation; over that time, it has established itself as one of the area's leading producers of wines at all levels.

While the Garofolis make easy-drinking Verdicchio to enjoy by the seaside with a plate of *spaghetti coi moscioli*—spaghetti with a sauce made from the wild mussels of Portonovo—Podium is one of its flagship standard-bearers, a Verdicchio dei Castelli di Jesi that is serious and full-structured. To produce Podium, Verdicchio grapes are allowed to reach full ripeness on a single vineyard in Montecarotto, harvested and full-bunch pressed, with fermentation in stainless-steel at low temperature. Afterwards, the wine rests on its lees for fifteen months followed by a minimum of four months further ageing in the bottle before release. This is a big, unoaked white wine of immense character, with notes of yellow fruits, rich in the mouth with a salty sapidity that makes it an excellent accompaniment to full-flavoured foods. It is a wine to sip and savour, a wine perhaps even to heal the body and the soul.

Campolongo di Torbe, Amarone della Valpolicella Classico DOCG, Masi Agricola, Sant'Ambrogio di Valpolicella, Veneto

When seeking to discover the best historical vineyards of the Valpolicella, Dr Sandro Boscaini of Masi Agricola believed that the archives of the Church could reveal vital information of use to the winegrower today. The Church, he surmised, would always have known where the wine was best, and if historical records could indicate that one vineyard was rated superior over others, then it was probably a sound basis for excellence that could still be valid in present times. Thus, he delved into historic records, including medieval Church documents, to discover where in the past the Church's most valued vineyard holdings were specified. Through these means, he discovered that as long ago as 1194, the San Zeno Monastery had leased some of its land to one Musio di Panego in return for a rent to be paid with a certain quantity of grapes from hillside sites in the high Negrar Valley of the Valpolicella, identified as both Mazzano and Campolongo di Torbe. Boscaini's Masi winery managed to acquire both sites, which today produce two of Masi's greatest cru Amarone, wines that by any definition are simply world class.

The process of harvesting and then drying grapes to concentrate their sugars has been practised since antiquity. In many cases, the result is a sweet dessert wine since the high level of sugar may not fully ferment out, leaving behind a raisiny residual sweetness. However, in the case of Amarone—'the big bitter'—a particular strain of indigenous yeast is robust enough to convert all the sugar into alcohol, thus resulting in a full, powerful, dry red wine. At Masi Agricola, the Boscaini family have tirelessly researched the best way to undergo the *appassimento* and the subsequent fermentation.

Because it is produced from semi-raisined grapes, not fresh fruit, the wine that results, though high in alcohol—usually around 16 per cent—is a 'gentle giant', with softly rounded tannins and a wealth of tertiary flavours and aromas that makes this one of the most concentrated and complex of all Italy's greatest red wines.

Campolongo di Torbe was rediscovered through the careful historical research of Dr Boscaini. It is a testament to the diligence and hard work of monks and clergymen of ancient times as well as to the Boscaini family, who had the foresight and the curiosity to look to the past in their tireless search for excellence.

Vino per la Santa Messa, Liquoroso Rosso, Pomilia Calamia Vini, Sicily

The Code of Canon Law (Canon 924, paragraph 3) states that wine used for the Eucharist 'must be natural, from the fruit of the vine, and not altered'. Further stipulations indicate that the wine can be fortified with the addition of grape spirit up to a level of 18 per cent (fortification is one important means of making a wine that remains stable in all climatic conditions, even once opened). No additives can be used, and utmost care must be taken to ensure that the wine is kept in good condition and does not turn into vinegar. In the celebration of the Mass itself, the wine can be mixed with a modest amount of water. Until 1880, it was stipulated that sacramental wine was always to be red in colour for the symbolic importance of it being the blood of Christ. However, since then, white or amber sacramental wines have also been permitted.

In medieval times, such wines would have been produced in monastic wineries. Today, sacramental wines may be the main product of wineries that specialise in their production, or they can be a sideline to wineries making other table or fortified wines. Pomilia Calamia is one such company that specialises in the production of Vino per la Santa Messa. Located in western Sicily, Pomilia Calamia use local grape varieties, including Zibibbo, Catarratto and Inzolia, to produce white or amber wine, and Nero d'Avola for red. The grapes are pressed, lightly fermented, then fermentation is stopped with the addition of grape brandy to bring the alcohol level up to 18 per cent while maintaining the natural residual sugar that gives the wine its characteristic sweetness. To ensure the wines are made to the highest standard and in accordance with the Code of Canon Law, they are tested and granted a certificate of authorisation by the bishop of Mazara del Vallo.

The finished wines are virtually indestructible, made completely naturally and without the use of any preservatives. These robust products can therefore be sent to dioceses not only throughout Italy but also abroad to allow the daily miracle of Holy Communion to be celebrated by Catholics around the world. Though sacramental wine may not be one that we normally consider when discussing the great wines of Italy, it is nonetheless of considerable importance historically, spiritually, symbolically and economically.

6

DARK AGE ILLUMINATION

I'm in a simple osteria in Cividale del Friuli and ask for a tajut, *a small measure or 'cut' of white wine, served together with a plate of local smoked* prosciutto d'Osvaldo *and a hunk of Montasio cheese. In Friuli, to have a* tajut *is not merely to enjoy a drink of wine; it is a communal ritual, a convivial invitation to sit down with the people of this area to toast, to laugh, to eat and drink. The* tajut *is poured from a 2-litre unlabelled bottle, probably a Friulano or a Ribolla Gialla. It goes perfectly with the* prosciutto *from Cormòns, chewy and only slightly smoky in flavour. The cheese is redolent of the* malga, *made with fragrant milk from high alpine meadows where cows are transported during summer months for the transhumance. The flavours of all three are a mix of cultures and peoples that reflect a land that has for centuries and millennia been a crossroads, traversed by visitors and invaders who have come and gone yet always left their footprints.*

The History

As Rome declined towards the end of the fourth century CE, Europe and the Mediterranean were in turmoil as Vandals swept across North Africa, Saxons invaded Britain, and Franks, Alamanni and Burgundians occupied Gaul and parts of former Roman territory. The void left after the disintegration of the Roman world encouraged wave after wave of so-called barbarians, mainly from the Germanic lands and Northern Europe, to migrate over the mountains to attempt to seize and populate the precious prize of Italy. In 401, the Visigoths invaded, capturing Rome in 410. The Vandals sacked the city in 455. Finally, in 476, Romulus Augustulus, the last Roman emperor, was deposed by the German Odoacer, probably a member of the Sciri tribe, who thus became the first barbarian king of Italy, nominally at the behest of the Byzantine Emperor Zeno. When Odoacer got too big for his boots and crossed the Danube to threaten Zeno in his own territory, the ruler of the Eastern Empire appointed another barbarian, Theodoric the Ostrogoth, as king of Italy. Theodoric the Great, as he came to be known, invaded in 489, forcing Odoacer to take refuge in Ravenna, where he held out until 493. Eventually, Theodoric entered Ravenna in triumph, invited Odoacer to a banquet, and there promptly had him murdered.

Such bloody tales reinforce the popular image of the invaders as uncouth, hairy barbarians who did nothing but rape, pillage and kill. It was a violent age, no doubt, but probably no more violent than the eras that had preceded it. The Romans, after all, were only able to create an empire by force and subjugation, while across the Mediterranean, disputes were settled by might of arms, the strongest emerging victorious.

Theodoric the Great not only proved to be a great warrior; he was also an enlightened ruler. Under the Ostrogoths who ruled Italy for sixty years, there was mainly peace and stability across almost all the Italian Peninsula. Wine culture was appreciated and extolled even during these so-called Dark Ages. Cassiodorus, Theodoric's chronicler, wrote of a wine called Acinaticum that was particularly prized as a 'meaty liquid or edible drink'. It seems that this wine was produced by the process of *appassimento*, making it a possible precursor to the Amarone and Recioto wines of Valpolicella that are today still produced from semi-dried grapes.

Through the sixth century CE, the Ostrogoths continued to come to Italy to settle and make their homes and lives. Cities such as Pavia, Verona, Ravenna and Rome were renewed and reinvigorated by this influx. The Goths were great builders, constructing important monuments and palaces such as Theodoric's magnificent unfinished tomb at Ravenna.

Meanwhile, however, while the remnants of the Western Empire may have been in tatters, the Eastern Empire remained very much an important force across the Mediterranean. In 535, Emperor Justinian appointed the great Byzantine commander Belisarius to take on the Ostrogoths in an attempt to re-establish the Western Empire on Italian soil. Moving up from Sicily through the southern mainland, he was gradually able to enter and occupy Rome, successfully defending it against a much larger Ostrogoth army. Bit by bit, the Byzantines worked their way up the peninsula, defeating the Franks who had settled north of the Po River, and eventually taking Ravenna in the name of Emperor Justinian. Thus began the reconquest of Italy by the Byzantines: the Goths had been wiped out utterly, and the Western Empire re-established as a province of the Eastern Empire, with the reinstatement of many Roman institutions and property returned to the old Roman ruling elite. Justinian is further remembered for his codification of Roman law. But almost as soon as he died in 565, Italy was under threat from a new set of barbarian invaders, the Lombards.

The Longobards or Lombards

The Longobards—Longbeards—or Lombards were already known to Strabo, the Greek philosopher, geographer and historian. Writing in the first century CE, he noted their nomadic lifestyle, carrying their possessions including livestock with them and moving from place to place on their wagons. Where precisely they came from is not entirely clear. Paul the Deacon, who wrote *Historia Langobardorum* (History of the Lombards) in the late eighth century CE, believed they descended from a small tribe in what is today northern Germany. Others believe they may have originated from Scandinavia.

By the middle of the sixth century CE, the Lombards had descended from the north to occupy Pannonia (a former Roman province encompassing modern day Hungary). Their wanderlust continued, for from there, led by Alboin, they came over the Julian Alps into Northern Italy in 568. Their arrival should not necessarily be seen as an invasion but rather as part of a mass migration of peoples as has happened since the dawn of time and as is still happening today. Then as now, people were compelled to leave their homes for many reasons: to escape threat or danger, out of economic necessity or else simply in search of a better life in a more promising land.

The Lombards were able to conquer and dominate the new land with extraordinary speed and with a minimum of bloodshed, an indication that they probably encountered little organised opposition. For the void left after the fall of Rome had disrupted civilian life in every aspect, with agriculture and trade reduced and lawlessness and pillaging rife. Moreover, the late Roman defensive belt across the north-east mountains, the Claustra Alpium Iuliarum, had been shifted rearwards, so there was no adequate resistance to the Lombards.

The first step was the capture of the important Roman garrison town of Forum Iulii (Cividale del Friuli), which would remain a Lombard stronghold and duchy for the next 200 years. They then moved westwards across Friuli and Veneto, taking Aquileia, parlaying with the bishop of Treviso to enter the city without the loss of blood and then pushing into the heart of the fertile Po Plain, capturing Vicenza, Verona and eventually Milan. By 572, Pavia, to the south, had also fallen, and this was to become the new capital of the Kingdom of the Lombards. Thus, within a shockingly brief time—just four years—the Lombards had taken control of what is now Lombardy—the region to which they gave their name—Friuli and Veneto, and they eventually spread even further out into Liguria and Tuscany.

This was a bloody age and rulers came and went. Alboin, who had forced his wife Rosamund to follow Lombard custom by taking a drink from the skull of her father whom he himself had slain, eventually got what he deserved: his wife, biding her time, plotted her revenge and had him murdered in his palace in Verona, with the apparent assistance and connivance of the Byzantines. His immediate successors were also killed, and it seems it was difficult for a strong ruler to emerge who would be able to hold the new kingdom together.

The Byzantine Exarchate, meanwhile, weakened from its lengthy struggles during the Gothic wars, and with one eye cast over events happening in the Balkans and Persia, was unable ever to completely subdue the new invaders. Even so, ruling from its seat at Ravenna, it managed to retain power over an important belt of the country that extended from the Adriatic to Rome as well as parts of the south. This was achieved with the support of the papacy, which by now was a growing political power in its own right that held large swathes of land and gave some support to the local populace. It was in the papacy's interests to ally with the Christian Byzantines against the militaristic Arian Lombards, who initially at least were anything but god fearing. Yet while the Church helped to muster resistance against the incursions of the barbarians and to keep this territory intact, the Lombards eventually managed to by-pass the holdings of the exarchate and the papacy to take control over much of the centre and south, establishing the powerful Duchies of Spoleto and Benevento.

Dark Age brilliance

Thus, the Lombards were set to rule much of Italy for more than 200 years. Indeed, without the Church propping up the Byzantine Empire, they almost certainly would have succeeded in uniting all of Italy. If the Ostrogoths mainly adopted Roman systems of government, the Lombards by contrast brought Germanic traditions and customs to their rule. Rather than trying to govern centrally, which had already proved to be difficult, Lombard realms were semi-devolved, broken into dukedoms ruled by independent nobles, warriors or *gastaldi* who controlled their own localities while at the same time owing loose allegiance to the king. This form of confederate governance may have contributed to the independent development of self-contained and self-ruled cities and regions with boundaries that in some cases survived for centuries, even lasting up until the time of unification in 1861.

The Lombards on their arrival in Italy were originally pagans and Arian heretics, but they eventually adopted the Catholic faith and became devout Christian rulers, overseeing the construction of many monasteries, convents and churches across the kingdom. They also built fortresses and splendid palaces, developing their own specific culture, a synthesis of architectural styles that encompassed the classical heritage of ancient Rome, Christian spirituality, the influence of the Byzantines and elements from their Germanic origins in Northern Europe. Indeed, the splendid monuments that survive today are testimony of the contribution of the Lombards to the spiritual and cultural development of medieval Italy, evidence that the so-called Dark Ages were in fact already quite enlightened.

The cultural contribution of the Lombards in Italy is evident in sites across the country. Cividale del Friuli today has within its city walls a Lombard monument that is considered one of the most significant in Italy, the Gastaldaga area and the Episcopal complex, recognised as part of the UNESCO World Heritage list that pays homage to the 'Longobards in Italy: Places of Power AD 568–774'. The *gastald* was the administrator of the royal demesne and the Duchy of Friuli, so the Gastaldaga was the administrative and political centre of power for this corner of Italy. Within the complex, there is a beautiful *tempietto* dedicated to Santa Maria in Valle that is considered one of the best preserved of all such monuments dating from the Lombard era, classic in form yet combining elements from the Roman era with that of the Middle Ages. The decor within the *tempietto* includes sculpture and the remains of murals, and around the altar there is a finely detailed depiction of a grapevine laden with grapes. While symbolic of Christ, this is an indication that even at this early age the grapevine was prevalent in these lands, wine an important feature for the Lombards. Other monumental Lombard achievements include the monastic complex of San Salvatore–Santa Giulia at Brescia in Lombardy; the *castrum* at Castelseprio-Torba, which served as a high-altitude fortress for the defence of Pavia, also in Lombardy; the monumental Basilica of San Salvatore in Spoleto, Umbria; Campello sul Clitunno with its tetrastyle Corinthian *tempietto*, also in Umbria; the beautifully preserved Church of Santa Sofia in Benevento, Campania; and the Sanctuary of Monte Sant'Angelo in Apulia's Gargano, testament to the Lombards' worship of the Archangel Michael.

The cult of the pig

If the significant cultural contribution of the Lombards has been recognised, little is known of their way of life and society. Much of what we can glean of their history comes from Paul the Deacon's *Historia Langobardorum*. Paul was a Benedictine monk from Cividale del Friuli, the Lombard capital of the Duchy of Friuli. He was writing at the time when the Franks had already overthrown his native Lombard nation, and he wanted to chronicle his people and their origins, history and contributions. His work is based on that of other contemporary historians as well as on legend, first-hand research, oral memory and recollection. Paul describes the regions of Italy, recounts the legendary origins of the Lombards and faithfully chronicles the Lombards in Italy, detailing their struggles, battles and the various leaders who played a part in their history over the previous 200 years. He gives graphic accounts of what it was like during the plague, and a great flood 'such as is believed not to have existed since the time of Noah' that inundated Verona and all the Veneto as well as the city of Rome.

The Lombards were quite happy to integrate with the Italians and adopt elements of Italian and Roman culture, intermarrying with the local populace, converting to the prevailing Catholic religion, even taking up the Italian language. In short, the Lombards were almost completely integrated into Italy while at the same time leaving their own mark on Italian culture by the time Charlemagne was created the first Holy Roman Emperor on Christmas Day, 800.

One important way the Lombards influenced Italian culture was through bringing their native pig with them from Northern Europe. While Romans had enjoyed fresh pork and to a lesser degree cured meat, the great wealth of *salume*—the generic term for cured pork and meat products—that we associate with the cuisine of Italy is not generally considered to have been a significant feature in Roman life. What is certain is that the lands occupied by the Lombards developed a rich and sophisticated culture of curing as well as smoking meats. Indeed, the keeping of a pig as part of a smallholding remained a feature of life from the Dark Ages into the Middle Ages and well beyond, even into the last century. In those northern regions occupied by the Lombards, sea salt was readily available from Cervia, while rock salt came from the Roman salt mines of Salsomaggiore. Home smoking took place over the home hearth. Thus, preserved pork became an essential part of the domestic diet of the peasantry (the rich nobility could afford fresh meat, and of course the hunt was both sport and source of food).

In Friuli, the first region settled by the Lombards, this culture of the pig remains well defined today. Salted and air-dried *prosciutto di San Daniele* is one of the sweetest and most highly prized of all the world's air-cured hams. The taste for preservation through smoking, a characteristic method common to Germanic tradition, remains evident in the delicious *prosciutto di Sauris* and *prosciutto d'Osvaldo* from Cormòns. In the South Tyrol (Südtirol), the region on the Italian side of the Brenner Pass that leads to Austria and Bavaria, smoked *speck* is still widely enjoyed today. Meanwhile, down on the rich and fertile flatlands of the Po Valley where the Lombards also resided, the variety and production of cured and preserved pork products has been developed into an art form—and an industry: *prosciutto di Parma*, *salame di Felino*, *coppa Piacentina*, *culatello di Zibello*, *mortadella di Bologna*, *zampone di Modena* and much more. Though international breeds of pig such as the Large White were brought into Italy towards the end of the nineteenth century, the smaller native breeds can still be found such as the Nero di Parma. Is this tasty black pig, which bears similarities to the Ibérico of Spanish fame, a direct descendant of the pigs brought to Italy by the Lombards?

We cannot say for sure. What is certain is that the Lombards during their 200-year sojourn in Italy left a legacy that has shaped and formed the Italian character, culture and gastronomy.

The Wines

Pignolo, Friuli Colli Orientali DOC, Dorigo, Premariacco, Friuli–Venezia Giulia

If wine was part of Lombard culture, as demonstrated by the richly carved grapevines on the altar of the *tempietto* in Cividale del Friuli, so it is still a vital part of culture and life in Friuli today. Though a relatively tiny region, this is one of Italy's most productive when it comes to high-quality wine, the source of outstanding whites as well as less well-known but still notable reds from native as well as international grape varieties.

The rarely encountered Pignolo grape is an ancient variety. It was first documented in 1333 CE but may well have been cultivated in the region for much longer, perhaps even in the time of the Lombards. Pignolo is difficult to cultivate, producing small, hard berries that make wine that can be intensely tannic but has long been valued for the quality that can result. Girolamo Dorigo is credited with saving this distinctive grape from extinction, and today his son Alessio continues to produce a totally singular wine. Alessio prefers to leave the Pignolo grapes on the vine until very ripe. The selected, hand-harvested grapes are then vinified in stainless-steel at controlled temperature, with a lengthy maceration involving at least once-a-day *rimontaggio*—pumping the juice back over the mass of grape skins to extract colour and softer tannins. The wine that results has such immense structure, extract and mouth-filling tannins that it must subsequently spend the next thirty months in French oak barrels (a mixture of new and used), followed by at least a further six months in bottle prior to release. Even then, it is an immense wine that might take upwards of a decade to mellow, soften and lose some of its fierce aggression.

Yet come around it eventually will. Dorigo's expression is a truly triumphant and glorious wine that must be sampled by all who believe that great wine comes to those with patience. It is a wine that seems to me not unlike the Lombards, barbarians whose character was eventually shaped, perhaps even tamed, by the beautiful lands they made their home over the course of some 200 years and the society into which they integrated so thoroughly. Pignolo's initially harsh and mightily bellicose tannins undergo something of a similar metamorphosis through the patient passing of time to reveal a wine that is austere and powerful, yet with refinement, a tribute to the indelible legacy that the Lombards left not only on this north-eastern corner of Italy but across the whole country.

Rosso frizzante naturale, Colli di Parma DOC, Azienda Agricola Lamoretti, Langhirano, Emilia-Romagna

The present-day division of Italy into twenty regions sometimes brings together areas that developed from separate histories. German-speaking Südtirol is aligned with Italian-speaking Trentino in Trentino–Alto Adige, but the regions are quite different historically, culturally and gastronomically. Lombard-influenced Friuli combines with Venetian-influenced Venezia Giulia, the latter a historic area that extends into present-day Slovenia and Croatia. Yet both Friuli and Venezia Giulia maintain their own traditions, influences, even languages. Emilia-Romagna is another example, a divide that goes back to the Dark Ages, to when the Lombards, from their capital at Pavia, came to dominate the Po Valley along the Roman Via Emilia, encompassing the territories of Piacenza, Parma, Reggio Emilia, Modena and Bologna. Romagna, by contrast, was under the Byzantines who ruled from the Exarchate of Ravenna and controlled the Adriatic seaboard.

If the Lombards can take credit in part for the development of Italy's rich heritage of *salumi*, then there may also be a corresponding link to a style of wine that developed in their heartland. For, though the fertile Po Valley is the source of some of Italy's greatest food products, this stretch across Emilia has never been considered one of its great wine regions. It's too flat, too hot, too humid. However, the wines in this area are produced in a unique style that is perfectly suited to be enjoyed with the cured meats of the region: light, wildly foaming, semi-sparkling red wines that are low in alcohol, high in acidity and naturally *frizzante*, or sparkling. Romagna, by contrast, did not have a tradition of cured pork *salumi* to anywhere near the same degree. There, in the hill country that extends down from the higher mountains, sheep were and continue to be farmed on fields that also support the cultivation of vines and olives. To accompany grilled lamb or mutton, a fuller style of red was preferred, made from the more well-structured Sangiovese grape. This simple example demonstrates how history, culture and geography shape foods as well as wines and how across Italy areas in such proximity can have such divergent gastronomic traditions.

The hill country of Langhirano, sited in the province of Parma at the foot of the Apennine mountains, has become a centre for the production of world-renowned *prosciutto di Parma*. Immense ham-curing lofts are sited with their windows facing the mountains to take advantage of the natural conditions. When dry, scented winds descend from the mountains, the windows are opened so that this gentle breeze promotes the careful air-drying of hams that have been only lightly salted to keep the meat at its sweetest. If, on the other hand, hot, humid winds come up from the Po Valley, then the windows are shut to keep the hams from spoiling. With such careful attention, the hams slowly age for a minimum of twelve months and often for much longer to result in the world's most famous, sweetest and most delicate of all cured raw hams.

Such a delicacy is best matched with a wine that comes from these same lands. At the Azienda Agricola Lamoretti, you can sit outdoors overlooking the Castle of Torrechiara, a magnificent medieval fortress in a commanding position overlooking the Parma River, a reminder that this part of Italy was once ruled by powerful warlords, a legacy of the Lombards. Torrechiara was not only a mighty defensive fortress but also an elegant residence decorated with beautiful frescoes where the *condottiere* Pier Maria II de' Rossi installed his beautiful mistress Bianca Pellegrini d'Arluno. From Lamoretti, enjoy the view over the vineyards to the castle while feasting on platters of exquisite *prosciutto di Parma* sliced so thinly that it is transparent, alongside other cured local *salumi*. The platters of meat are best paired with Lamoretti's Rosso Colli di Parma, a simple wine made from Barbera and Bonarda grapes in the *frizzante naturale* style. The high acidity of Barbera and Bonarda combined with the natural secondary fermentation make this a perfect wine to accompany *salumi*—deep in colour, with an effervescence that is vigorous on pouring but not persistent, and a dry freshness that cleans the palate. We know little of the dining customs of the Lombards, but it is not improbable to conjecture that simple, no-nonsense wines like this accompanied by meats eaten with the hands would have satisfied the appetites of warlords and their mistresses alike.

Spoletino, Trebbiano Spoletino DOC, Cantina Fratelli Pardi, Montefalco, Umbria

The Lombards' influence was not just limited to the north of the country but extended right through the Italian Peninsula. The city of Spoleto, a UNESCO World Heritage site strategically located in central Umbria along the Roman Via Flaminia that connected Rome with the Adriatic, was a centre of considerable power under the militaristic Lombards. Yet the Basilica of San Salvatore, built in a Romanesque architectural style unique to the Lombards, also demonstrates the rich cultural sophistication of the Lombards. Spoleto went on to become an important and fought-over city-state through the Middle Ages and eventually came under the jurisdiction of the Papal States.

   This wine, Spoletino, is produced from a rare native grape variety that thrives only in vineyards around Spoleto and Montefalco. The grape is Trebbiano Spoletino, capable of producing white wine of great character, far superior to wines produced from lesser Trebbiano varieties that are not genetically related to it. Cantina Fratelli Pardi produces a notable example from grapes cultivated on sedimentary clay at an altitude of 220 metres above sea level. The grapes are harvested in October, and the *mosto fiore* or free-run juice is used with only the lightest pressing for fermentation at 18 degrees C and then aged on the lees for eight months. After bottling, the wine rests for a minimum of a further nine months before release. This is a big, solid white wine: powerful, well structured, with a strong foundation that comes from an alcohol level of 14 per cent. The bottle itself is solid and heavy, with a deep rounded punt, somewhat reminiscent of the vaulted nave of a Lombard Romanesque church. If Lombard architecture was noted for its fortress-like strength and simplicity while at the same time revealing within more complex and delicate features such as rhythmic ornamental arches, cupolas, vaulted ceilings, squinches and fine carvings, so does this powerful and well-structured wine open up to reveal surprisingly intricate and sophisticated aromas and flavours of both complexity and delicacy, with an acidity that pierces like a shaft of light entering from a high window, intense and persistent with underlying notes of white peach, floral almond blossom and exotic tropical fruit.

7

THE MONASTIC TRADITION

The Brenner Pass that leads from Austria's Tirol into Italy's Südtirol has been a natural corridor connecting Italy with Northern Europe since the time of the Romans and earlier. We had flown to Innsbruck and were now driving from Austria into Italy. With the border open, it hardly seems that we have even passed a frontier: though we are now in Italy, all the road signs are bilingual, the half-timbered architecture is distinctly Tirolese, older women are walking around in dirndl dresses, the men in characteristic blue cotton aprons. As we approach Brixen (or Bressanone as it is called by Italians in this German-speaking autonomous region), we decide to stop, have a light bite, taste and purchase some wine from the twelfth-century Kloster Neustift. This is one of the great historic monasteries of Italy, its circular fortified Chapel of St Michael, reconsecrated in 1198, modelled on the Church of the Holy Sepulchre in Jerusalem. Since its foundation, this Augustinian monastery has served as an important hospice, a place of refuge for pilgrims en route to Rome as well as a place to stop for thirsty and hungry travellers. We relax in the atmospheric, vaulted tap room and enjoy a platter of crunchy schuttelbrot, *smoked* speck, *and* local *cheese while sampling a glass of Kerner, redolent of ripe peaches and orange peel, brightly concentrated, a vivid and beautiful white that connects us to the centuries-old monastic traditions of wine and hospitality.*

The History

From its early origins, Christianity held within it a tantalising choice for the truly devout: whether to embrace the faith within the temporal world or whether to retreat from that world into splendid isolation or even solitude. Those who chose the latter course in some cases became hermits, removing themselves from the world for years at a time.

One such faithful individual was Benedict of Nursia, born in 480 CE only four years after Romulus Augustulus, the last Roman emperor of the Western Empire, had been deposed. Benedict came from a wealthy patrician family and was sent to Rome to study at a time when the Eternal City was in a period of upheaval and moral uncertainty. Though Theodoric, the Ostrogoth crowned king of Italy, was considered something of an enlightened ruler who tried to maintain former Roman institutions, a new age had clearly dawned. Roman life and civilisation was dissolving, and German 'barbarians' were now in charge. Benedict, perhaps shocked by the licentiousness of this new era, perhaps simply seeking solitude in which to contemplate and pray, chose to retire to the foothills of the rugged Abruzzo near Subiaco, some 70 kilometres east of Rome. There he lived as a hermit for three years, furnished only with food and clothing left for him by monks from nearby monasteries.

When he finally emerged from his self-imposed isolation, Benedict's piety was recognised by the monks who had assisted him, and they invited him to be their abbot. Benedict, however, demanded obedience and piety beyond the monks' own way of life, his reforming zeal deemed to be so severe that his disciples tried to kill him by poisoning his wine. However, when the adulterated chalice was brought to him to be blessed, the vessel containing the toxic potion apparently shattered in his presence. Dismayed by how his fellow brothers had treated him, Benedict retreated to his cave for another period of self-imposed solitude, before eventually being persuaded to return to the world by those who recognised his exceptional piety and leadership. He went on to found twelve monastic communities, each with twelve monks, all under his overall control. The most important was the Abbey of Montecassino, founded in 529 and located on the hilltop of Cassino, about 130 kilometres south of Rome. It consisted of a simple building that included an oratory, refectory, dormitory and reading room. Here Benedict lived the rest of his saintly life, refining and writing what came to be known as the Benedictine Rule, a code that was to define Western monasticism for centuries.

What is most significant about the Benedictine Rule was that it found a way for monks to live that was moderate, humane and practical. This detailed document was carefully copied out by scholastic monks over subsequent centuries to define in detail such matters as the structure of a monastery; the practical affairs of its community such as the number of Psalms to be recited and when; rules of hospitality for guests and travellers; punishments for different sins and faults; ways of behaviour, especially humility, in order to ascend the steps that lead to heaven, and much more. Rule 40 for example regulated the quantity of wine that monks were to be allowed:

> Each man has his own gift from God, one this and another that. We are therefore hesitant in deciding how much others should eat or drink. Keeping in mind the weakness of the less robust, we consider that a quarter of a litre of wine a day is sufficient for everyone. But in a case where the locality or the work or the heat of summer may make a larger allowance necessary, the abbot must decide, taking care that there is no excess or drunkenness.

This example demonstrates the practical flexibility of Benedict's strictures: each abbot could decide for himself on such matters, and it is probable that in many abbeys this meagre allowance was often deemed pitifully insufficient.

Benedict thus established the basic rhythms of monastic life, built around the canonical hours and consisting of *ora, lege et labora*—prayer, study and work—which became the motto of the Benedictine order. The day was thus divided into five hours devoted to liturgical and other prayer, five hours to manual labour and four hours to study, including reading the scriptures and spiritual writings. Monasteries thus became repositories of knowledge.

Following the Benedictine Rule, the cultivation of vineyards became one of the most significant tasks of manual labour, carried out in monasteries not only across Italy but all of Europe. Tending vineyards was suitable manual toil to satisfy the Benedictine Rule and necessary to produce sufficient wine for the monastery's own needs—both to celebrate the Eucharist and to serve as a daily beverage. Wine was, wine is, a precious commodity after all, sacred and fundamental to Christianity: 'Wine that maketh glad the heart of man.'

Monks and wine

So prevalent was viticulture in monasteries across Italy and elsewhere that it has been claimed that monks were responsible for safeguarding winemaking and wine after the fall of the Roman Empire. Certainly, the Germanic tribes that descended into Italy were not always interested in preserving either Roman culture and its way of life or indeed the emergence of Christianity and its traditions and institutions. The Lombards, for example, sacked and destroyed the Abbey of Montecassino in 570, less than thirty years after Benedict's death. But there is little evidence that the Ostrogoths, Lombards, Franks and other 'barbarian invaders' were at all hostile to the culture of wine. On the contrary, with wealth rooted deeply in agriculture, and wine one of the most valuable commodities, as well as one of its most pleasurable, it is more than probable that viticulture continued and even expanded under the various occupiers.

Nonetheless, wine lovers owe a great debt to the work carried out in monasteries across Italy and Europe. As monasteries continued to grow from the sixth and seventh centuries and beyond, they expanded in size, importance and influence, attracting men (and later women) from all strata of society and eventually growing into communities that numbered in the hundreds or more, including lay brethren. The Abbey of San Colombano (known also as Bobbio Abbey), for example, was founded in 614. As early as 643, it already had under its jurisdiction some twenty-eight farms worked by 150 monks and producing 800 amphorae of wine per annum. With an amphora containing roughly 40 litres, this represents a production of around 32,000 litres of wine, a by no means inconsiderable amount.

Charlemagne, as first Holy Roman Emperor, saw wine as an important agricultural activity and laid down strict laws relating to methods of production and granted rights to winegrowers, for example the right to sell the new year's wine direct from their premises at certain times without being subject to taxation. Meanwhile, under the Franks, the construction of monasteries was carried out at pace as wealthy benefactors continued to donate tracts of land to the Church, seeking in return the gift of eternal salvation, a fair bargain. Sometimes these tracts of land were in uninhabited areas perhaps deemed of little worth as they were heavily forested, or steep or rocky. But once reclaimed, the monks set to work, inevitably planting a vineyard wherever it was suitable (and sometimes where it was not). The plantation of a vineyard was a long-term task that did not give easy returns: it required investment, skill and knowledge, as well as intensive manual labour, all of which monasteries could supply. The reward was wine in abundance, enough to slake the thirst of the monks themselves and the communities that had grown around them. By the ninth century, many abbeys had grown immensely powerful and wealthy, and some were almost like small towns inhabited by hundreds or even thousands of souls. A monastery needed to be able to support a population of not just the monks themselves but of laymen, too, including craftsmen, artisans, serfs and their families. That they were able to do so is testament to their immense economic prosperity, in many cases based on their agricultural and viticultural patrimony.

As centres of learning, monasteries had the wherewithal to practise and perfect the complicated science of viticulture, charting annual variations in the growing season, weather, treatments to cure vine maladies and how to prune and care for the vines throughout the year. Through close observation, they learned that certain grape varieties fared better in some areas than others and that certain vineyards consistently produced grapes with more sugar or flavour or which usually ripened earlier. Thus, they were able to differentiate between the mediocre, the good and the truly great, helping to create the concept of fine wine that had existed during the times of the Romans but that had perhaps been waylaid during the Dark Age centuries. This can be documented historically through examination of Church and monastic tithes that specified the supply of wines from particular and specific vineyards, the reasoning being that the monks would always know where the wine was best.

Large monasteries built great wine cellars and invested in the necessary equipment and technology to produce wine efficiently and carefully, including massive beam presses and large wooden fermentation and storage vats where wines could be matured in the best conditions, resources that would have been far beyond anything most individual landowners might have been able to achieve. Thus, by the Middle Ages, monasteries had become the greatest wine producers in the Western world, not only in Italy but also in Burgundy, where they owned great tracts of land in the fabled Côte d'Or, and as far afield as Germany's Rhineland and well beyond.

Monastic communities grew ever larger and became rich beyond belief. Over the centuries, many thousands of monasteries were built and populated, many following the Benedictine Rule that had mainly defined monasticism for hundreds of years across all of Europe. The very form and shapes of monasteries themselves were laid down by the Benedictines, usually built with features such as the abbey itself, cloister, chapterhouse, refectory, library, scriptorium and dormitory as well as such practical buildings as a wine cellar, stables, infirmary and workrooms. In such communities, the Benedictines prospered and enjoyed the ample fruits and wealth that their labours brought, sometimes to considerable excess.

If St Benedict originally founded an order based on piety and strict adherence to the Benedictine Rule, it is perhaps not surprising that as they grew in size and wealth, many monasteries began to drift away from those lofty ideals, becoming ever more attached to the pleasures and riches of the world. At the same time, the Church itself had become more fully involved in temporal affairs, and indeed some monasteries grew not only into economic powerhouses but also became involved and entwined in the great political affairs of their time.

It is understandable, then, that new reformed orders emerged that sought to return to a purer way of life and worship. They rejected the worldly wealth of the Benedictines and sought to reclaim the poverty that Christ professed.

The Franciscans followed the teaching of St Francis, born in Assisi in 1181, and became a powerful and influential mendicant order eschewing the acquisition of wealth and property. The Dominicans and Augustinians were also mendicant orders. Other orders grew in popularity and influence too. But from the point of view of their contributions to wine, its production, as well as its civilised enjoyment, it was the Benedictines and related orders such as the Cistercians and Vallombrosans who were most influential.

Monasteries in Italy

The suppression and dissolution of Italy's monasteries began in 1789 under Napoleon with the suppression of religious orders and the confiscation of their properties. Though the Congress of Vienna restored territories to their former rulers and allowed the Church to resume some of its former activities after Napoleon's demise, many monastic buildings, lands and treasured property were lost forever. The unification of Italy under King Vittorio Emanuele II brought further conflicts between Church and state, not least because the Papal States were in direct conflict and resisted unification until as late as 1870 when the Vatican was finally forced to concede its remaining territories of Lazio and Rome.

Monastic life in Italy today is much diminished, but some monasteries that can trace their histories to the early years of Christianity in Italy remain active. In Tuscany, numerous former abbeys and the remains of abbeys are connected to wine. The Badia di Passignano is a Benedictine abbey founded during the time of the Lombards that in the eleventh century became part of the newly formed Vallombrosan order that spread throughout this central region. Evidence that this fortified monastic complex in the heart of the Chianti Classico zone has cultivated the vine since its foundation was confirmed when in 1983 a 1,000-year-old *Vitis vinifera* plant was discovered on the lands surrounding the Badia. Today, these vineyards are cultivated by one of Italy's oldest aristocratic winemaking families, the Marchesi Antinori.

Another well-known Tuscan wine estate with monastic origins is the Badia a Coltibuono, located near Gaiole-in-Chianti along the high route through the Monte dei Chianti that led from Florence to Siena. Founded by Vallombrosan monks in 1051, the name comes from *cultus boni*—or good harvest, an indication of the fecundity of the estate, cultivated with the vine and olive, as well as with other produce and the raising of livestock in order to be a self-sufficient community. The abbey prospered as lands were bestowed by rich benefactors and more modest citizens alike, and a hospice was established to give shelter, food and drink to travellers and pilgrims passing through. A monk's document from Coltibuono, dating from the twelfth century, refers for the first time to this area as 'Chianti'. Today, outstanding Chianti and other wines, as well as extra-virgin olive oil, are produced on the estate by the Stucchi Prinetti family who have re-established hospitality for weary travellers once more at Badia a Coltibuono.

Some monasteries have been in existence for upwards of hundreds of years, as spiritual homes to their communities and as places where the vine has been and continues to be cultivated. The Abbazia di Monte Oliveto Maggiore, located in the province of Siena, for example, was founded in 1313 by a nobleman Giovanni Tolomei and grew in importance to become almost a virtually self-contained city. The territory that it owned and controlled made it one of the wealthiest and most influential landowners in the Siena countryside, and it literally shaped and modified the starkly beautiful landscape of the Crete Senesi, cultivating wherever possible vineyards, olive groves, mixed farming and woods. Today, as it has over the past nearly seven centuries, the Benedictine monks of Monte Oliveto Maggiore live a strict life that revolves around *ora, lege et labora*, spending their time between Opus Dei (choral prayer), Lectio Divina (study of the word of God) and manual labour, which involves work on the farm's 850 hectares of property, tending vines, olives and other crops, as well as toiling in the cellar. Wine and extra-virgin olive oil have been produced here almost since the monastery's foundation, and the extensive abbey cellar dates from its earliest days. It comprises two parts, one for the vinification and wine production, the other lined with large numbers of wooden barrels for the storage of wine. The size and number of barrels is testimony to the former extent and importance of the abbey, the vinification and storage facility not only used for the monks' own harvest of grapes but also to make wine for the small peasant winegrowers of the community.

Another example of more than 900 years of devotion, to God as well as to the production of wine, is Kloster Neustift, known also as the Abbazia di Novacella, located just below the Brenner Pass that leads into Italy from Austria's Tirol. Kloster Neustift was founded in 1142 following the teaching of St Augustine. Its strategic position along an ancient and well-travelled route that connects Northern Europe with Italy meant that it was perfectly positioned to offer hospitality to pilgrims en route to the Holy See at Rome. As has been the case with monasteries throughout Italy and abroad, wealthy benefactors left Kloster Neustift considerable donations of land, and the abbey grew in influence, overseeing parishes throughout the South Tyrol.

This is winegrowing country par excellence, and the abbey continues to work vineyards that produce an outstanding and highly regarded range of wines that can be sampled in its welcoming tap room.

Christian monasteries and the communities they serve have co-existed for more than 1,500 years. As society transitioned from the 'Dark Ages' into the medieval era, then the Renaissance, and even up to the present day, monastic devotion to prayer, study and manual labour allied with their locations often in areas suitable for the cultivation of the vine has meant that they have been able to cultivate vineyards and make wine over this long period: wine to serve for the celebration of the Eucharist, to enjoy as part of their allotted daily ration and to share with visitors, pilgrims and those who have passed by and continue to pass by their walls.

The Wines

Praepositus Kerner, Alto Adige Valle d'Isarco DOC, Kloster Neustift, Brixen, Südtirol

The period of secularisation that followed Napoleon's occupation saw monasteries stripped of much of their lands and wealth. Today, Kloster Neustift, though considerably diminished from what it once was, is still home to nineteen Augustinian monks and continues to hold tracts of vineyards across this part of Südtirol, while the grapes from former monastic vineyards still find their way into the Kloster Neustift cellar as the monastery works for local farmers and landowners to transform their grapes into wine. In this manner, Kloster Neustift continues to be one of the oldest active wineries in the world.

Terraced vineyards surround the abbey and extend from the monastic complex on the steep hills at an altitude between 600 and 900 metres above sea level. Growing vines at such high altitude is only possible in the best exposed sites, and the fruit that ripens in this rarefied atmosphere can yield wines that are pure and intense in fruity aroma and flavour. Aromatic grape varieties thrive at this more extreme limit of the vine's viability: Sylvaner, Müller-Thurgau, Kerner and Riesling, and the monastery is best known for its acclaimed range of white wines. If monasteries have long been at the vanguard of winemaking technologies, this remains the case at Kloster Neustift. Its glistening, modern cellar is equipped with the latest technology, enabling it to produce wines of the highest quality that consistently win awards.

The best wines are reserved for the Praepositus range. Since its foundation, there have been fifty-nine abbots, and these special wines are dedicated to them. Praepositus Kerner is a superlative example. This grape variety, widely planted in Germany, is a cross between Riesling and Vernatsch (Schiava, a red grape variety that grows well in Südtirol). It was originally developed for its resistance to frost as well as for its abundant yield, yet it was soon discovered that in the Etsch/Isarco Valley it can express itself most fully and magnificently, capable of creating a truly great white wine of structure, elegance and complexity. This outstanding Praepositus example offers pure, intense aromas of ripe peaches, dried apricots, orange peel, richly textured in the mouth with a finish that is clean, concentrated and powerful. In its purity and simplicity, it is a wine that pays homage to the dedication, diligence and toil of generations of hardworking monks in monasteries across Italy and over the centuries.

Grance Senesi DOC, Azienda Agricola Abbazia di Monte Oliveto Maggiore, Asciano, Tuscany

The farm of the Abbey of Monte Oliveto Maggiore remains extensive and productive today, the source of good wines, outstanding extra virgin olive oil, cereals, honey, fresh vegetables, a range of herbal products, special liqueurs and own-brewed beers. In short, the monastery has for centuries been virtually self-sufficient in many of the products needed to support its community and so it remains today.

The importance of wine at Monte Oliveto Maggiore is clearly demonstrated by the extensive and vast abbey cellars, parts of which date back to the first half of the 1300s, testament to its importance as a landowner that produced wines not only for itself but also for up to twenty-four sharecropping farms belonging to the abbey that worked under the *mezzadria*. Today, good table wines are still produced to serve on the daily table of the refectory as well as Sanctus, a wine to celebrate the Holy Mass, produced and bottled *ex genimine vitis* in accordance with Canon 924 of the Code of Canon Law.

Grance Senesi DOC is the classic red wine of this part of Tuscany, primarily produced from Sangiovese grapes fermented then aged in large wooden barrels. It represents something of the soul of the monastery, for traditional wines such as this have been produced literally for hundreds of years, from grapes grown on vineyards extending across the bare and majestic hills of the Crete Senesi, vinified and aged in these same ancient cellars. The Grance Senesi DOC refers to the *grance* that are typical of this area: large, fortified farms, granaries and storage warehouses that served the vast agricultural estates, such as the Abbazia di Monte Oliveto Maggiore as well as the Spedale Santa Maria della Scala.

This and all the wines of the Abbazia di Monte Oliveto Maggiore, are certified 'Prodotto di Origine Monastico', which guarantees that the production and processing is carried out completely by monks and nuns within the cellars of the monastery. It is wine that is truly testimony to centuries of faith and devotion. As Padre Antonio Braon, the administrator of the abbey farm, says: '*Ora et labora*—work helps spirituality.'

Cultus Boni Chianti Classico Riserva DOCG, Badia a Coltibuono, Gaiole-in-Chianti, Tuscany

If the former Vallombrosan abbey of Badia a Coltibuono, in the hands of the Stucchi Prinetti family since 1846, is no longer an ecclesiastical institution, you can still gain an insight into how a self-sufficient monastic smallholding served to support not only its own religious community but also to give hospitality to guests and travellers who passed along this way. The fine abbey still stands at the heart of the property, now transformed into an elegant family villa with cloister, corridors, frescoed rooms, as well as accommodation for guests in restored apartments and individual bedrooms transformed from the former cells of the monks. The restaurant, located in the former stables, is highly regarded for its traditional Tuscan *cucina* (cuisine). Vegetables and herbs come from the garden, pasta is made by hand daily, traditional local meats including lamb, rabbit and Chianina beef are grilled over an open fire. Cheeses are local, made from the milk of sheep and goats, and everything is well lubricated with the outstanding extra virgin olive oil of the estate. It is no wonder that the place was named *coltibuono*—the place of good harvest—for the Badia today as in the past is an abundant and fertile source of good things to eat and drink. Its wines are simply outstanding, examples of how Chianti Classico has transformed itself from something sold in wicker flasks a few decades ago to one of the greatest red wines in Italy. Roberto Stucchi Prinetti was one of the first in Chianti to transform the family's 74 hectares of vineyards to certified organic. The vineyards are mostly located in the prized sub-zone of Monti in Chianti, and the family is rightly proud of its stock of ancient and historic clones of Sangiovese, which they can utilise to replant when necessary.

Cultus Boni Chianti Classico Riserva is a flagship wine that gives the fullest expression to this magnificent land and to the history of the Badia. Primarily Sangiovese grapes are blended with the traditional native varieties of Chianti such as Ciliegiolo, Colorino, Canaiolo, Mammolo, Fogliatonda, Malvasia Nera, Sanforte, Pugnitello. Some of these varieties have been virtually abandoned elsewhere but are here valued for the complexity they bring to the finished wine. A long and slow fermentation occurs naturally using the autochthonous yeasts present on the grapes, with the regular punching down of the cap of skins to extract greater colour and tannin, followed by ageing in casks of various sizes including some French *barrique* as well as ageing in the bottle before release.

The wine that results is simply glorious in its purity and fresh intensity. Chianti Classico at best is never a heavy wine—medium in colour and body, with notes of wild berries, a touch of spice and smooth, well-knit tannins—a wine above all to enjoy with the generous and ample foods of the Badia, the place of the good harvest.

8

'LO STUPOR MUNDI'

I am at a bird-of-prey centre, wearing a thick leather gauntlet. A peregrine falcon is perched on my protected hand. When it spreads its beautiful, pointed wings, it is enormous. With its shaped feathers and long claws, this raptor is built to fly fast and would have been trained to hunt, capable of striking and capturing mammals such as large rodents and rabbits. The bird's head swings left, right, keenly attentive. It is a powerful and independent force of nature, and I feel frankly uneasy. I pass it to its trainer and take off the heavy gauntlet. Later, I calm myself with a large goblet of red wine, Il Falcone, from the Castel del Monte region of Apulia, a wine produced in homage to Frederick II. Frederick by all accounts was also a force of nature, known as 'lo Stupor Mundi'. While staying at Castel del Monte, his beloved octagonal castle that he had built to his own architectural design in 1246, he found the time to write De arte venandi cum avibus *(The Art of Hunting with Birds), a book that even today is still considered the best treatise ever written about the art of falconry. Il Falcone, the wine, is rich and virile yet also supple and vibrant, a fitting toast to this 'wonder of the world' who was at once warrior, scholar, writer, poet.*

The History

The story of Italy is sometimes also the story of great men—usually men, but also occasionally women—who have come to embody their age and through their sheer force of personality have helped to shape and change the course of history. One such *personaggio* was Frederick II of Hohenstaufen.

Frederick was grandson of two of the most famous and influential rulers in Europe: Holy Roman Emperor Frederick Barbarossa and Norman King Roger II of Sicily. His arrival on earth was apparently a very public event, according to contemporary chroniclers: his mother Constance de Hauteville, daughter of King Roger II, gave birth to him in a tent set up in a public square in Jesi, a town in the present-day region of Le Marche. Constance had come out of confinement in a convent to marry Barbarossa's heir Henry VI, duke of Swabia, later himself to be crowned Holy Roman Emperor. She was travelling to join Henry in Palermo when on 26 December 1194 she had to pause her journey in Jesi. Constance was by then considered an 'old woman': some contemporary reports said she was fifty years old, but it is more likely that she was in her forties, considered in that era an advanced age to give birth. It was important that there should be no doubts about the legitimacy of her offspring, hence the public nature of the delivery. Even still, rumours abounded: the pregnancy was a sham, and Frederick was said to be the offspring of a physician, a miller, a falconer or even a Jesi butcher. Less generous if more colourful legends related that his mother had lain with a serpent, with Frederick the demonical result. Some prophets foresaw Frederick as the Antichrist; others, however, were more favourable. Godfrey of Viterbo told Henry VI that his son would be a future Caesar who would unite the Holy Roman Empire and the Kingdom of Sicily. What seems certain is that a special fate was destined for Frederick almost from the moment he was born.

As a two-year-old, Frederick was elected king of the Romans and thus successor to the German throne. When Henry VI died in 1197, Frederick also became king of Sicily at the tender age of just three. His mother appealed to Pope Innocent III to be the boy's guardian and assumed the role of queen regent of Sicily. Constance, however, died later that year, and, while turmoil and struggle took place as pretenders tried to seize the rich prize of Sicily, Frederick was left, according to chroniclers, to grow up 'on the streets' of Palermo. Certainly, Pope Innocent III, nominally the boy's guardian but far away in Rome, had little interest in helping the infant to come to maturity.

As an adult, Frederick was a polyglot, fluent in Latin, Sicilian, Arabic, Greek, German and French, and there was not a subject that did not interest him. Michael Scot, a Scottish mathematician and polymath who was also the court astrologer, became Frederick's tutor, mentor and friend. The two of them would spend hours in study and disputation on subjects as diverse as law, religion, philosophy, mathematics, astronomy, music and literature. When only thirteen, a contemporary wrote of him: 'He is never idle but passes the whole day in some occupation or other, and so that his vigour may increase with practice he strengthens his agile body with every kind of exercise and practice of arms.'

In 1208, this precocious mental and physical specimen was declared of age at just fourteen years old and assumed the role of king of Sicily. Almost immediately, he proved to be a more than capable and ambitious ruler. When Otto of Brunswick, the elected Holy Roman Emperor, was excommunicated by Pope Innocent III, Frederick assumed the imperial title in 1220. He also became the king of Jerusalem in 1225 through marriage as well as through waging the Fifth and Sixth Crusades. He thus ruled over a vast territory encompassing the Holy Lands, the Kingdom of Sicily (Sicily and Southern Italy), much of Northern Italy and through Burgundy and Alsace all the way up through the Germanic lands. Much of his life was subsequently devoted to trying to hold these lands together and to unite the Holy Roman Empire with the wealthy Kingdom of Sicily. But the lands of the Papal States under the rule and jurisdiction of the pope were always standing in the way. He was excommunicated no fewer than four times, and his papal opponents, believing that the earlier prophecy had come true, called him the Antichrist. In one sense, part of Frederick's legacy was an ongoing and near constant struggle between papacy and Holy Roman Empire, which would later manifest itself in the Guelph and Ghibelline conflicts that were to emerge across medieval Italy.

Though much of his life was spent in war and conflict, Frederick is also known and acclaimed for his pursuit of humanist ideals, his constant thirst for knowledge, learning and scientific and empirical enquiry. His grandfathers, Frederick Barbarossa and Roger II, had both been disposed to granting scholars special privileges, and his Norman heritage led him to be not only tolerant of different religions and cultures but also to be deeply curious and interested in them. In many ways, he can be seen as a forerunner of the Renaissance, neither Norman nor German but a true European, open to embracing the best from all cultures. He was a patron of the arts and himself proficient in the fields of painting, sculpture, architecture, literature and science. He encouraged the Sicilian School of Poetry and promoted the use of the Sicilian language in written form, something later acknowledged by Dante Alighieri, himself considered the father of Italian literature. Frederick's treatise on falconry was illustrated with his own meticulous sketches based on close observation. He apparently understood the migrations of birds at a time when such things remained mainly a mystery.

By any standard, this colossus of his age was wholly unorthodox. He was a religious sceptic, unusual for his era. His grandfather Roger II had claimed to be anointed king of Sicily not by the pope but by divine intervention of Christ himself as depicted in a mosaic showing the 'Divine Coronation of

King Roger II' in the Church of Santa Maria dell'Ammiraglio in Palermo. But Frederick himself had no need for such proof of legitimacy, and his humanistic vision allowed for multiple interpretations of the divine. He was in a sense oriental in outlook. He loved richly embroidered clothing and was able to indulge in this through the still operating, Arab-influenced court of the Palermo palace (silkworms and silk production were just one of the many innovations the Arabs had introduced into Sicily, and production continued under Arab expertise in the Norman kingdom).

Castel del Monte

As an architect, Frederick brought innovative features to the castles, residential palaces and triumphal bridge-towers he designed, while always keeping an eye on the classical past. His most striking achievement, and apparently his own personal favourite, was Castel del Monte, which sits in a commanding position on a high plateau in Apulia's Murgia. Why did he choose this seemingly remote place in a far-flung outpost of Southern Italy on which to build his *capolavoro*? It must be remembered that Apulia had long served as a bridge between the Western and Eastern Mediterranean. The Greeks first came here and probably brought the grape vine with them. Brindisi was a vital Roman port for voyages to all points east, while in Frederick's time it remained a launchpad for the Crusades to the Holy Lands.

Castel del Monte is unique. There is nothing like it in military architecture. Designed as an octagon, with an octagonal tower at each of the corners of the main structure, it was built out of cream-coloured limestone, the individual stones cut with such precision that the joints must have been barely noticeable. The huge main portal is one of the most significant features, the design harking back to antiquity yet at the same time wholly of the Gothic age, with the pointed arch of the doorway and its unmistakable decorations of the Hohenstaufen lions. Each of the seven remaining walls between the octagonal towers has Gothic windows, and the overall effect is of a construction that has overtones of the classical, Gothic and Apulian Romanesque. Though austere from the exterior, the eight rooms of the upper floor give a hint of Frederick's taste for interior decor and his love of creature comforts: it would have been decorated with once colourful marble columns, richly inlaid mosaic floors, walls of white marble. The complex embroidered fabrics so beloved by the Norman rulers combined with Frederick's known love of oriental finery and Arab splendour would have made this sumptuous building spectacularly fitting for the greatest ruler of his age.

Wine was clearly important to Frederick II. Born in a tent in the wine town of Jesi, baptised in Assisi, he discovered the small wine town of Coccorone and renamed it Montefalco, a place he particularly loved for he could study the birds of prey who inhabited that part of Umbria. Did he enjoy the wines from Montefalco while he stayed there? Almost certainly. At Castel del Monte, he introduced new grape varieties, for example bringing Fiano to the limestone hill vineyards of the Murgia plateau. From time to time, it is known that he placed orders for wines from certain areas or of certain types, such as 'Galop' (or Gaglioppo) from Calabria, while a citation dating from 1240 relates to a purchase of Greco wines.

The Wines

'Il Falcone', Castel del Monte Rosso Riserva DOCG, Azienda Vinicola Rivera, Andria, Apulia

The Murgia extends across a high plateau in northern Apulia, a complex geological area primarily consisting of a bedrock of karst limestone. If Frederick chose to build his Castel del Monte on a high, commanding position, there are also equally stunning places of refuge to be found underground, such as the extensive karst caves of Castellana Grotte. Limestone and tuffaceous chalk are almost always propitious habitats for *Vitis vinifera*, and this area is no exception. Indeed, here the porous, mineral-rich sub-soil is perfect for the cultivation of ancient native grape varieties such as Nero di Troia, Bombino Nero and Aglianico.

The Azienda Vinicola Rivera was founded in the 1940s with vineyards cultivated at an altitude of between 200 and 350 metres above sea level. Though we are in Italy's deep south, nights here are positively cool, especially compared to the soaring daytime temperatures, and this thermal contrast allows the grapes to ripen well while the karst limestone terrain helps to retain freshness, acidity and aroma. 'Il Falcone' is the company's flagship wine, named in homage of Frederick's love of falconry and because falcons and other raptors still live in this protected natural habitat. The wine is a blend of 70 per cent Nero di Troia and 30 per cent Montepulciano. Harvest is usually in mid-October, relatively late in this far southern vineyard. The grapes are destemmed and crushed, then vinified traditionally, with *rimontaggio*, that is, pumping of the must over the skins to extract colour and softer tannins, before ageing in oak cask and *barrique* for fourteen months followed by at least a further year in bottle before release.

The wine that eventually emerges is capable of further ageing for at least a decade or more. Nero di Troia, one of the great grapes of the south, combines particularly well with Montepulciano in this wine, the former lending structure and tannin, the latter a lovely soft, juicy roundness. Garnet-red in colour, the bouquet displays wild fruit, spice, leather, and on the palate the tannins are well balanced and integrated, making this a wine of great power combined with delicacy and a beautiful, cedary finesse. Frederick was considered the first truly modern man of his era yet was at the same time an undoubted product of his Norman and German heritage. This sleek and sophisticated wine is similarly modern, yet its roots extend profoundly deep into the limestone soil and history of an ancient land.

'Puer Apuliae', Castel del Monte Nero di Troia Riserva DOCG, Azienda Vinicola Rivera, Andria, Apulia

'Puer Apuliae' was a derogatory nickname that the German barons gave to Frederick II. The moniker means 'son of Apulia' because he spent so much time in Apulia rather than in the Germanic lands. It became a nickname that Frederick wore with pride. At the Rivera winery, the name refers to the Murgia's most impressive and important native grape variety, Nero di Troia. In the past, this variety was usually cultivated in the same vineyard together with Montepulciano, perhaps a couple of rows of the former then a single row of the latter, the grapes all harvested to make a sort of 'field blend'. Nero di Troia, a true 'son of Apulia' on its own, can be a difficult grape variety to vinify successfully because of its leanness and the forthright nature of its tannins. However, this special cru wine is produced from an almost forgotten, small-berried clone of Nero di Troia from Rivera's oldest vineyard, Tafuri. It is only produced in the best years. The wine that results, aged in new *barriques* for fourteen months, is simply imperial in character: deep in colour, with aromas of fresh blue and blackberry fruits, violets, medicinal herbs and well-knit soft tannins.

Montefalco Sagrantino Passito DOCG, Azienda Agricola Giampaolo Tabarrini, Montefalco, Umbria

The grapevine had long been cultivated since antiquity in vineyards that surround Montefalco—the town in Umbria that Frederick renamed due to the large number of birds of prey—though it is probable that here as elsewhere during the Middle Ages, viticulture continued to be kept alive mainly by the religious orders. Indeed, the zone's most distinctive grape variety, Sagrantino, possibly took its name from a corruption of *sacramentino*, indicating a wine that was used for sacramental purposes. Originally, wines from this distinctive native grape variety were exclusively produced in the *passito* style from grapes harvested then laid out to dry on cane mats for a period of some weeks or months. Sagrantino is a grape that is deeply rich in colour with dense, chewy tannins, and with an intense and persistent bouquet of blackberries. The production of a sweeter *passito* style of wine served to soften a wine that can be tough and utterly uncompromising.

Many producers now eschew this ancient style of wine, preferring instead to produce powerful, dry red wines, either Montefalco Sagrantino from 100 per cent Sagrantino or Rosso di Montefalco from primarily Sangiovese with about 15 per cent Sagrantino. Giampaolo Tabarrini makes outstanding, full-on, uncompromising Montefalco Sagrantino: austere, tooth-stainingly rich in colour and tannin, with an underlying thicket of brambly fruit. Much less well known (perhaps because produced in the most minute quantity) is Giampaolo's magnificent Sagrantino *passito*, handcrafted entirely from the estate's own Sagrantino grapes, grown on a south-east-facing hill composed of sand, clay and river stones. The grapes are harvested late then laid out carefully to dry on racks for a period of at least three months followed by pressing and fermentation. The result is simply glorious, at once powerful at 15 per cent alcohol and intriguingly complex, with a background residual sweetness that is not immediately apparent due to the severity of the wine's tannins. It is a true *vino da meditazione*, a thoughtful, almost philosophic wine. Frederick II was himself intriguing and complex, a warrior who took on the might of the papacy on more than one occasion, yet someone who was also sensitive, a poet, a lover of the arts and of the sweeter things in life. I'm certain that this is just the sort of wine that *lo Stupor Mundi* would have delighted in sipping, particularly after pursuing his favourite sport, falconry.

9

PILGRIMS' PROGRESS

The Via Francigena enters Italy at the Great St Bernard Pass in the high Alps and runs for 1,000 kilometres to Rome. Established in the Middle Ages, today it remains an important pedestrian thoroughfare. Of course, it is nowhere near as crowded as it was in its medieval heyday when a pilgrimage to Rome was the adventure of a lifetime as well as a means to salvation. But it is still busy all the same. As we walk, we pass and are passed by others, some simply out for a day's hike, others clearly making an important spiritual journey. Long-distance walking is thirsty work, and from time to time we stop for refreshment. That evening, we lodge in a simple and basic ostello pellegrino, *a pilgrim's hostel. There is no refectory, so we make our way into town to find somewhere to eat. At a humble, local* osteria, *we order a plate of* pici—*handmade pasta—served with a* ragù di cinghiale *made from wild boar. The wine is* sfuso—*drawn from a plastic-covered demi-john—and served in a litre carafe. Sometimes such offerings are just about drinkable, sometimes they can be shockingly bad, made all the worse when the proprietor beats himself on the chest and proudly declares, 'L'ho fatto io!'—'I made it myself.' But this wine is good, good, good!!!*

The History

In the year 990, Sigeric, newly appointed archbishop of Canterbury, made his way from there to Dover, crossed the English Channel, and walked all the way across Northern France and Switzerland, crossing the Alps at the Great St Bernard Pass, then travelled through Piedmont, Lombardy, Emilia-Romagna, Tuscany and Latium eventually to reach Rome, a foot journey of some 2,000 kilometres. There he was invested by Pope John XV with the pallium, a white woollen stole with six black crosses that was the official seal of office. After his papal investiture, the archbishop spent the next three days visiting churches in and around Rome, before beginning the long trek back to Britain. Sigeric's journey home took seventy-nine days and was documented by the archbishop's secretary who accompanied him. This work, *De Roma ad usque mare* (Journey on the Via Francigena), written in Latin (the original manuscript is held in the British Library), became the first 'guide' for pilgrims from Britain who wanted to journey to the Holy See at Rome along a route that came to be known as the Via Francigena, 'the road that comes from France'.

The tradition of making a pilgrimage to Rome had started centuries earlier, indeed probably not long after Constantine issued the Edict of Milan in 313 that granted religious freedom to Christians. Devout believers were anxious to worship at the tombs of Saints Peter and Paul, as well as those of other early Christian martyrs, and this led to a steady stream of visitors, travelling along well-maintained Roman roads to reach the Holy See. As the numbers grew, a network of facilities was established along the way, in some cases in *mansiones*—inns for pilgrims and other travellers—which served to offer accommodation, food and drink to the tired, hungry and thirsty. But during the Dark Ages, the Lombards and the Byzantines had control over most of the Italian Peninsula, and life for pilgrims became far more precarious. Once well-maintained Roman roads and bridges fell into disrepair, accommodation along the way was no longer secure, and pilgrims were at risk of being robbed by thieves in a world that seemed mainly lawless.

There was therefore a pressing need to establish a route that was safe and relatively secure, leading from the Alps via Pavia, the capital of the Lombards, to Rome. Moving away from the main roads, and avoiding Byzantine territory, a well-trodden path gradually came to be the favoured route for pilgrims, climbing over the Apennines by way of the Cisa Pass, then descending into Tuscany's Valle del Magra, through Lucca, San Gimignano, Siena and the Val d'Orcia, before entering Latium to join with the ancient Roman Via Cassia that led to the Eternal City. It was this route that came to be called the Via Francigena and that Sigeric, archbishop of Canterbury, chose to follow in 990.

Over the years and subsequent centuries, a pilgrimage to one of Christendom's most holy sites—Rome, Santiago de Compostela, Canterbury or to the Holy Lands themselves—came to be a rite of passage that many Christians endeavoured to undertake at least once in their lives. It is estimated that in medieval times, as much as a fifth of Europe's entire population would have made a pilgrimage at some point in their lives. Why, I wonder, did people—archbishops, nobles, ordinary folk alike—feel compelled to make such arduous and massively challenging journeys? In the Christian medieval paradigm, in a world lit only by fire, where violent death, illness, famine and plague repeatedly thinned the population, and where illiteracy was the norm across all classes, not just the poor; where knowledge of the Bible came not from sermons uttered in the obscure language of Latin but from visual clues carved in stone or painted on canvas or on the walls of a church, it is no surprise that the fear of eternal damnation was a horrifying reality. Surely any hardship could be endured if it were to help to save one's soul from the fires and horrors of eternal damnation in the frightening bowels of hell, or from an interminable period spent in the limbo of purgatory.

There would have been other motivations, too. For those who had offended not only God but also their fellow man, punishment for crimes could be atoned by ordering the offender to make a pilgrimage, perhaps walking all the way barefoot, carrying a pilgrim's testimonium signed by the clergy that specified whatever crimes or offences had been committed. In other cases, those who had lived lives that had been anything but pure and unblemished might choose voluntarily to pay penance in search of absolution and forgiveness through the act of going on a pilgrimage, sometimes making the journey as arduous and even torturous as possible.

For most, however, it is probable that pilgrimage was at once widely accepted as one of the most important spiritual practices to demonstrate devotion to Christianity and help secure one's place in paradise, as well as at the same time an opportunity to leave behind the humdrum of everyday existence and experience the adventure of a lifetime. Indeed, in that dimly lit world where daily life was often repetitive, manually taxing and precarious, the chance to leave one's daily toil behind and simply concentrate on putting one foot in front of another would have been compelling, especially if there was the surety of salvation.

A cultural crossroads

The great age of pilgrimage lasted from the eleventh to the sixteenth century. Pilgrimage to Rome received a vital impetus in 1300 when Pope Boniface VIII declared that year to be a Jubilee or Holy Year, meaning that pilgrims would receive plenary indulgence, that is, complete remission of all sins. In that single year alone, it is estimated that some 2 million pilgrims made their way to Rome, resulting in an economic boom for the city and Church alike, with pilgrims' donations swelling the coffers of the Vatican, and businesses and monasteries along the way all benefitting. Not surprisingly, Jubilee Years continued to be declared every quarter of a century or so, but even in normal years, the numbers of pilgrims making their way to Rome continued to grow.

What an extraordinary cultural crossroads the Francigena must have been, what an important thoroughfare of international interchange! Indeed, the Francigena became not only a religious byway but a strategic route for the transport of wares from the north of Europe, with damask linen, for example, coming from Flanders, silk and spices from the East, and much more. Imagine the international toing-and-froing along this medieval byway: people travelling back and forth from Rome, all from different countries, walks of life, speaking different languages, carrying their own foods, singing their own songs. Nobles, peasants, clerics, bishops, monks, nuns, traders and commercial travellers, vagabonds, thieves, rogues, rascals, murderers, entertainers and charlatans: what a diverse and fascinating gathering of humanity from across Europe walked these ancient stone byways. And they would have had all the time in the world, the precious time that today we lack, to talk, to share, to exchange stories and human experiences, to meet, dispute religion, maybe make love, certainly eat and drink. Some who stumbled along were gravely ill, hoping perhaps to be granted a miraculous cure; many died along the way, a passage that was at least considered meritorious by the Church, sufficient to earn a shorter term in that dreadful state of spiritual limbo, purgatory.

The Via Francigena was never conceived as a route that connected city to city but rather one that meandered through the countryside, in many cases leading from one monastery or pilgrim's hospital or hostel to the next. Such establishments offered the pilgrims' basics: *lectum* (bed), *panem* (bread), *vinum* (wine). No doubt there were levels of comfort for nobles and the rich, and something rather less for the poor. Even so, there was wine, good wine, almost everywhere, from the rarefied, high-altitude vineyards of Aosta, below the Great St Bernard Pass, down through Piedmont to Lombardy's Oltrepò Pavese. In Tuscany, wines that watered pilgrims continue to rank among some of Italy's finest, including the whites of San Gimignano, reds from Lucca, Siena and Montalcino, and in Latium, wines from vineyards around the volcanic-rich soil of Viterbo and Montefiascone.

The tradition of walking from England to Rome that had begun with Sigeric in 990 came to an abrupt end in 1538 when Henry VIII and Thomas Cromwell banned pilgrimages to Rome. But the Counter Reformation that addressed practical and doctrinal issues relating to the Catholic Church allowed it to reclaim many of its European followers, and the necessity and desire to make pilgrimages to Rome was soon revived. So it has continued through the ages and the centuries. Perhaps in the twenty-first century, the advent of easy mass transport by rail, air or car has made the concept of a peripatetic pilgrimage appear less relevant. But new interest and awareness has undoubtedly come back in recent times, as people living in the fast lane of life, today just as in the medieval past, are rediscovering the importance of taking a sabbatical from one's everyday cares and occupations to make a journey on foot, whether for physical, spiritual, emotional or religious motivations. Indeed, the value of this ancient route as a historic byway that connects cultural identities, peoples and heritage was recognised when the Council of Europe granted the Via Francigena status as a 'Cultural Route of the Council of Europe'. So today's pilgrims can continue to walk the Francigena and continue to tell stories, laugh, sing, stop to sleep, eat and of course to refresh themselves with the many wonderful wines they encounter along the way.

The Wines

Petite Arvine, Valle d'Aosta DOP, Les Crêtes, Aymavilles, Valle d'Aosta

For a pilgrim walking from Canterbury—or from anywhere in Northern Europe—to Rome, a watershed moment would have been the crossing of the Alps from Switzerland via the Colle Gran San Bernardo to enter an entirely new world: Italy. Down, down, down, the road would now seem to lie, though it was still a trek of 1,000 kilometres to reach the Eternal City. Even so, I'm sure it would have been an exciting moment to descend from the snow-covered peaks of the high Alps to the Aosta Valley, the path sometimes following stone roads that had been built by the Romans more than 2,000 years ago and crossing and recrossing the mighty Dora Baltea River over beautiful Romanesque arched bridges. The Francigena passes through Aosta itself (an ancient Roman town named after Emperor Augustus) into more fertile lower stretches where vines are still often trained on low-lying pergolas with stone supports on terraced vineyards, the vines fanned out to catch the rays of alpine sunshine that can be surprisingly intense.

This alpine corridor running down from the high mountains was a great thoroughfare even in antiquity, and the millions of pilgrims who walked and continue to walk along the Via Francigena would certainly have brought an international exchange of ideas as well as goods, even plants. The Petite Arvine grape variety is an example, widely planted in Switzerland's Valais wine region, possibly brought over the mountains into Italy by settlers or maybe even carried over by pilgrims travelling down this well-trodden route.

Whatever the exact origins, I consider Petite Arvine a perfect wine for the thirsty pilgrim (or wine pilgrim), and there is no better place to sample it than in the beautiful, warmly welcoming Rifugio del Vino of the Les Crêtes winery. A modern interpretation of an alpine mountain hut, this is a place where visitors can sit, read books on wine and the Valle d'Aosta, taste and enjoy the range of Les Crêtes wines, and just admire a stunningly beautiful alpine panorama. As for the wine itself, Petite Arvine has delicate aromas of mountain wildflowers, a backbone of fresh acidity and a quenching drinkability in a wine of surprising structure and body. If I were a pilgrim with 1,000 kilometres still ahead of me, I would stop to enjoy a glass (or perhaps just two at most, given its strength) then continue on my way; if I were a wine pilgrim in search of the genuine, the authentic and the hard-to-find, then Petite Arvine is a great starting point to discover the little known and wonderful wines of Valle d'Aosta.

Moscadello di Montalcino DOC, Tenuta Caparzo, Montalcino, Tuscany

As the Via Francigena extends down from the Valle d'Aosta, through Piedmont and Lombardy, across Emilia-Romagna and over the Apennines into Tuscany before dropping down into Latium and Rome, it leads through countryside that is often carpeted with vines: from the Alta Piemonte vineyards around Vercelli to the wine hills of the Colli Piacentini; and in Tuscany from Lucca down to San Gimignano, and through Siena to the Val d'Orcia vineyards of Montalcino. Romanesque churches, chapels, hospitals and monasteries make this a particularly beautiful wine countryside to discover on foot.

Today, the vineyards of Montalcino are among the most prestigious and famous in Italy, above all for the production of Brunello di Montalcino, one of Italy's greatest red wines, made from 100 per cent Sangiovese grapes, a richly textured wine that is complex and elegant. But Brunello di Montalcino is a wine that was only created in the nineteenth century when Clemente Santi identified the Sangiovese Grosso clone—known locally as Brunello 'the big brown one'—as capable of producing wines that are full, robust, rich in tannin.

If for medieval pilgrims travelling along the Via Francigena, Brunello di Montalcino did not yet exist, nonetheless grapes were most certainly being grown and wine made in this fertile corner of Tuscany. Indeed, the wine associated historically with Montalcino is a gently sweet wine made from the Moscato Bianco grape known here as Moscadello di Montalcino. From the 1990s, as the Brunello di Montalcino boom gathered pace, vineyards planted with this varietal had mainly been grubbed up in the rush to plant Sangiovese for the production of Brunello and Rosso di Montefalco wines, but today there has been a return to its historic cultivation.

Tenuta Caparzo is an estate that is actually located directly along the Via Francigena. It is well known above all for its sleek red wines that rank among the finest expressions of Brunello di Montalcino. However, less well known but no less exquisite is its Moscadello di Montalcino, a wine that Francesco Redi, writing in 1685 in his verse *Bacco in Toscana*—'Bacchus in Tuscany'— extolled: 'That so divine and light Moscadello di Montalcino.' At Tenuta Caparzo, the Moscadello grapes are not harvested until the beginning of October, allowing them to undergo a partial drying on the vine to concentrate sugar and aroma. Once harvested, the grapes are pressed, and fermentation takes place in French oak *barriques*. The wine that results is gently sweet yet retains a backbone of acidity that keeps it fresh, vigorous and well balanced, floral, spicy and absolutely gorgeous. I wonder, does a luscious and special wine like this have the power to alleviate the pain of swollen knees or blisters on blisters? Perhaps. Indeed, if I had been walking for 1,000 kilometres or more, for days or weeks, then a taste of a sweet nectar such as this would be welcomed as something truly wondrous and miraculous.

Le Pòggere, Est! Est!! Est!!! di Montefiascone DOP, Falesco, Montefiascone, Latium

Montefiascone is so close to Rome that it's hard to imagine a peripatetic journey that reaches the virtual outskirts of one's destination but never quite arrives. Apparently, such a fate befell one wine-loving bibulous bishop. The story goes that in the twelfth century a German prelate named Bishop Johannes Fugger was making his way down the Via Francigena to Rome. A man of impeccable taste, he did not want to waste his noble tastebuds on inferior vintages, so he sent his trusted servant Martin ahead of him to scout out those inns along the way that served the best wine. Martin presumably was also a man of irreproachable taste, and his brief was simple: to visit each inn along the way and sample the local tipple. If the wine was good, he was to mark the door of the tavern with the Latin word 'Est' ('it is', indicating that the wine was up to scratch). By such means, Bishop Fugger travelled through Italy in a pleasant haze, trusting in Martin's unfailing judgements that led him from one *osteria* or *ostello* to the next, confident that he would not waste his superior, ecclesiastic tastebuds on inferior *vinum*. Having made it all the way from Germany through Piedmont, Lombardy, Tuscany and finally into Latium, the gates of Rome were almost in sight, as the bishop made his way around Lake Bolsena and across the volcanic, vine-covered hills that led to Montefiascone, just north of Viterbo. However, here in this charming medieval town, the bishop's trusted servant Martin excelled himself, finding an inn that served such utterly exquisite wine that he scrawled on its door the triple superlative *Est! Est!! Est!!!* before presumably falling asleep in an inebriated stupor. Bishop Fugger clearly must have shared his servant's enthusiasm. The wine of Montefiascone was so close to divine that he never made it to Rome, preferring instead to stay in that town enjoying the local tipple until his death (history does not record whether this was untimely or from overindulgence). Ever faithful to the end, Martin erected a tombstone that can still be seen in the churchyard of the town's Romanesque Chiesa di San Flaviano. The poignant epithet reads:

Est. Est. Propter Nimium
Est Hic. Jo. Defuk Dominus
Meus Mortuus Est.

Roughly translated, Martin's lamentation is as follows: 'Because of too much Est! Est!! Est!!! my master, Johannes Fugger, died here.'

If truth be told, the story is probably tastier than most examples of the wine that recalls the tale of the bishop in its name, Est! Est!! Est!!! di Montefiascone, for indeed much of what is produced is nothing to write home or books about. However, one of Latium's leading family estates, Famiglia Cotarella, produces a version that is considerably more than passingly good. Riccardo Cotarella is considered one of Italy's greatest winemakers, known as 'Il Mago'—the wizard—for his skill in producing great wines not only from his own family estate but also as a consultant on any number of exciting projects throughout the country. It is not surprising, then, that the Cotarella 'Le Pòggere' Est! Est!! Est!!! di Montefiascone is a considerable cut above most other examples. It is produced from Trebbiano and Malvasia grapes blended with a high proportion of Rossetto, an intriguing local grape variety that is rarely encountered. It is the Rossetto, cultivated on volcanic soil at 400 metres above sea level, that particularly adds real character and class to this otherwise sometimes ordinary wine. Cold maceration on the skin draws out its unique aroma, followed by fermentation at 13–15 degrees. The wine that results is fresh and impeccably clean, with floral as well as ripe tropical fruit notes, a beautiful glass that could well make you forget where your journey was even headed to. On retasting this wonderful old favourite, I'm sure the bishop—or perhaps more to the point, his faithful and diligent servant Martin—would have approved.

10

THE MEZZADRIA

It became our evening ritual: the careful construction of a wood fire in the huge hearth of our small farmhouse—first a scrunch of newspaper, then the smallest twigs to make a pyramid, then larger bits of kindling, light the match, blow gently, add a little more wood. After a while, there would be sufficient embers to rake out and place an iron grate over them. I would then saw off two and a half slabs of unsalted Tuscan bread (for me, Kim and our two-year-old son Guy), and I would toast the bread on the grate over the embers. Once toasted, I'd take a clove of garlic, cut on the slant and scrape it over the charred, scratchy bread, place it on a platter and generously drizzle over some gorgeous, green-gold olio extra-vergine d'oliva. *We'd rub the oil in with our fingers, add a pinch of coarse sea salt, a turn of freshly ground black pepper. Nothing else. This was* fettunta, *made with 'our olio' from the estate we were living on, and we would enjoy this simple repast together with a tumbler of* vino rosso *poured from an unlabelled bottle. I remember that wine so fondly, not because it was the best wine that we'd ever had. It wasn't but it was a* vino genuino *and, more importantly, like that exquisite oil, it tasted all the better because it was 'our wine'.*

The History

The rise and rise of cities and city-states, particularly in Tuscany, Umbria and Central Italy, had by the thirteenth century created a new class of professional and artisanal city-dwellers: bankers, lawyers, clergymen, merchants, tradesmen, wool entrepreneurs, artisans, artists and more. Food from the countryside was needed to be able to sustain the growing urban population. As in Roman times, vast quantities of 'industrially produced' food still came up from the south, from vast estates that were the legacy of *latifundium*, whereby great tracts of land in Southern Italy and Sicily had been granted originally to victorious Roman consuls and legionnaires, later to aristocratic and wealthy landowners whose descendants had exploited the land and the workers for centuries, taking substantial profits in some cases without ever stepping foot on the estate.

Central Italy differed from southern regions in that there was less of a legacy of *latifundium* and far fewer vast agricultural estates. In Tuscany, Umbria and Le Marche, this was partly determined by the landscape itself. Hill country, often with stony, poor soil, would not have been so well suited to any form of intensive agriculture. Even so, newly rich urban dwellers who had made their money through trade, banking or other means began to accumulate land, acquiring pieces here and there that would not only give them a place in the country but that would also be a source of food for their families, as well as providing income from any surplus that could be sold in the cities. The tendency was to organise their holdings into *poderi* or small farms. A wealthy landowner, for example, might acquire as many as twenty or thirty *poderi* or more, either located around a central country villa or dotted around the surrounding countryside.

With no source of coerced labour available any longer, a system of land tenure developed that became known as the *mezzadria*. Basically, a landowner would divide his terrain into different *poderi*, each contractually assigned to a *mezzadro* or sharecropping farmer and his family. The family would be granted not only a piece of land but also a house—a *casa colonica*. Each family of *mezzadri* worked the land and in return shared *la metà* with the landowner—half of everything produced, whether grapes, olives, livestock, fruit, grain or other produce. For example, they would take half the eggs their chickens laid to the *padrone*, and when they killed a pig and salted it to make *salumi*, they would take half to the master, always giving him the best bits of course—*prosciutto*, *culatello*, *coppa* and the like. And so it was with everything that was grown or raised.

With time and little by little, the nature of the contractual relationship inevitably changed. Those astute Florentine and Sienese aristocrats and wealthy merchants brought their legal knowledge and financial acumen to bear on the contractual arrangement, imposing fees for the use or upgrade of equipment or rental of communal facilities or for making the wine or oil so that the relationship inevitably became more skewed in favour of the landowner. Yet nonetheless, it was a system that mainly worked and, remarkably, that continued to be in place for centuries, even into the modern era.

The *mezzadria* not only came to define social relationships between worker and landowner for some 800 years but also shaped and defined the very countryside itself. As each *podere* had to be self-sufficient to support the *mezzadro* and his family, a system of mixed farming was carried out that was known as *cultura promiscua*—promiscuous cultivation. Each smallholding was divided up into sections, perhaps a few rows of olive trees, a patch of grain, a vegetable garden, three or four rows of vines, an area to keep the chickens or the pig, and so on, depending on whatever was being cultivated. Vines were sometimes trained on to trees or other living supports to free the land below for other crops, a method that had been used since Roman times. When the grapes were harvested, they were taken to the landowner's cellar, where each *mezzadro* had his own *tino* or vat. One load of grapes was to be tipped into the vat of the *padrone*, one load for the *mezzadro*, a fifty-fifty sharing of the harvest. Similarly, when the olives were harvested, these, too, went to the *frantoio*— olive mill—with half the resulting *olio extra-vergine d'oliva* going to the *padrone*, half to the *mezzadro*. No wages were paid; instead, after the crops had been brought in, the fruit, olives or grain processed, the *mezzadro* would receive a certain number of *barile* of wine or oil, or a number of *staia* of grain in exchange for his family's labours, minus of course any expenses imposed by the landowner. The old measuring containers, sometimes stamped with the insignia of the landowner's family, can still be seen on many farms and estates even today, piled up in a corner or used as planters for geraniums.

The *mezzadria* gave the landowner a ready source of labour to work his lands to enable him to bring in produce with a market value; and it gave the *mezzadro* a modicum of contractual security, self-sufficiency to provide food and wine for his family and the ability to pass on the contract of land tenure to his children.

It is remarkable that this system of land tenure worked so successfully that it lasted for more than 800 years. It was only in 1964 that a law was passed that forbade the granting of new contracts. In practice, the *mezzadria* was not completely abolished until as late as the 1970s. Even after that date, many *mezzadri* chose to continue to work for their landowner—after all, in many cases they had spent their whole lives living and working the same land that their ancestors had also worked, and this tie was deep and strong and enduring. Though no longer entitled to a share of the crops they had always considered their own, they were now paid a weekly wage and gained benefits such as health care and old age pensions. But the land they had felt so intimately tied to for generations was no longer their own (even if it never really had been), and there was inevitably a sense of loss on both sides. Indeed, I have heard many people—admittedly mostly the landowners themselves—still bemoaning the demise of a land tenure system that had existed for such a long period of time.

The economic crisis of the 1950s and 1960s combined with the legal demise of the *mezzadria* led to a mass exodus from the land as people moved from country to city, where work could be more easily found in the newly emerging post-war economy. Whole estates and even entire multi-family hamlets or *borghi* were abandoned, and much of rural Central Italy went into considerable decline. The hilly country between Florence and Siena was an area particularly dependent on the *mezzadria* and suffered greatly. The charming, simple, whitewashed houses of the tenant farmers were abandoned, while lands cultivated by the promiscuous system of mixed agriculture were left overgrown and untended.

Yet the demise of the *mezzadria* turned out, in fact, to be a watershed moment in the history of modern Italian wine. For generations, families of *mezzadri* had shaped and husbanded Italy's landscape, especially in central and northern areas through a system of agriculture that was not only effective for self-sufficient farming but also aesthetically pleasing. The families and generations of these sharecropping farmers had also been, perhaps unwittingly, effective guardians for Italy's astonishingly rich biodiversity, cultivating the native indigenous grape varieties because these were the varieties that their fathers had cultivated, and their grandfathers and great-grandfathers before them. They rotated their crops, and the mixed agriculture under the *cultura promiscua* encouraged a type of regenerative cultivation that many estates are actually returning to today.

On the other hand, under the *mezzadria*, grapes were viewed as just another agricultural commodity, and the goal was always to try to produce as large a crop as possible: there was no incentive whatsoever for quality. So, the demise of the *mezzadria* in a sense can also be seen as the beginning of the renaissance of modern Italian wine, especially across Central Italy.

Chianti at that time, we should recall, was never known as a great wine but rather a beverage to be drunk young, bottled in a squat, wicker-covered *fiasco* that became the enduring image not just for Chianti but for Italian wine the world over. Yet if the wine was not all that great, the countryside most definitely was, its rolling and majestic hills the backdrop of a Renaissance painting. Italians who had made their fortunes in other sectors, as well as foreigners—English, Germans, Dutch, Swiss, Americans—purchased these charming houses that had once housed humble sharecropping farmers, brought in architects to convert them tastefully and stylishly or tore them down altogether and constructed new houses in their place. In other cases, whole *borghi* were converted into holiday rentals and a new industry—*agriturismo*, or farmhouse tourism—was created. Tourists began to flock to the area as a holiday destination, and the English discovered a new playground: 'Chiantishire'.

The demise of the *mezzadria* had a profound effect in changing not only the shape of the land but also the mentalities of winegrowers. Only since then has Italy, with its long and beautiful vinous patrimony, been able to emerge on the global stage as the source of some of the greatest, most individual and unique wines in the world. A whole generation of new wines was soon to emerge, produced from native as well as international grape varieties. But that is all another story.

The Wines

'Benefizio', Pomino Bianco Riserva DOC, Castello Pomino, Frescobaldi, Tuscany

In the fourteenth century, the aristocratic Frescobaldi family were influential bankers, earning the title of treasurers to the English crown. During the Renaissance, they were patrons of the arts and of major works in Florence, including the construction of the Santa Trinità bridge and the Basilica of Santo Spirito. Throughout this long period, from at least the 1300s to the present day, the family have been major landowners in Florence and its surrounds as well as producers of wine. Today, the Frescobaldi family has seven estates across Tuscany.

For the social historian as well as the lover of fine wine, Castello Pomino is among the most interesting. The wine region of Pomino is a tiny and separate *denominazione* within the Chianti Rufina, in the wine hills to the east of Florence. It was singled out for its exceptional wines when it was included in the Medici Granduca Cosimo III's 'Il Bando' in 1716, an important grand-ducal decree that identified the exact zones for the production of Tuscany's most important wines. The Castello Pomino estate had once supported some forty *mezzadri* families who each had their own house and plot of land. Here you can still see and feel how this age-old system of sharecropping worked in practice, for the large wooden *tini* (open-topped fermentation vessels) are still in place, one for each sharecropper's family. The grapes would have been carried to the wine *cantina* in cylindrical wooden tubs known as *bigonce*, which could be strapped to a man's back. Each *tino* could hold some ninety *bigonce* at a time, one vessel to be tipped into the vat of the landowner, the next into that of the *mezzadro*. Then, once the wine was made, it was measured out into small wooden barrels known as *barili*. For each *barile* of wine measured out and poured through an opening in the floor beneath the vat that led to the *padrone*'s underground *cantina*, a *barile* was given in turn to the *mezzadro* to take back home for his own family use. In reality, the system was more complex and sophisticated than this simplification, but the sharing of the fruits of the land between landowner and *mezzadro* was absolutely fundamental to how it worked and why it survived for some 800 years.

Chardonnay grapes were planted on the Castello Pomino estate as long ago as 1855, so this seemingly international grape has adapted to its unique mountain environment over the course of more than 165 years. The Benefizio vineyard is situated at an altitude of over 700 metres above sea level, which means that it stays relatively cool in summer and suffers the bitter cold of winter, conditions that challenge this variety and that can result in exceptional wine. Benefizio was the first Italian white wine to be fermented in small wooden French oak *barriques* that are 50 per cent new each year. The style is Burgundian, not New World, with the oak well integrated, giving the wine a toasted, creamy texture balanced by a fresh, lemony streak of acidity that keeps it fresh.

Benefizio Pomino Bianco Riserva, first produced in 1973 at a time when Tuscany's timeless system of land tenure was in transition, demonstrates that, whatever the system, world-class wine can be made provided there is vision and cooperation.

Vin Santo di Carmignano DOC, Fattoria di Calavria, Comeana, Tuscany

This is a homage to a wine and a wine estate that no longer exists. Our wine. The Villa Calavria is in the small hamlet of Comeana, a *frazione* of Carmignano. It dates to 1550, when it was acquired by the aristocratic Pecori family. The Michon Pecori could thus trace their family roots as *proprietari-viticoltori* back to the 1500s. However, when we rented our little *casa colonica* from them in 1989, we found ourselves living on the property just after a moment of profound change and transition. The *mezzadria* had been abolished a good decade or more earlier, and former sharecroppers had by now moved away from the land to work in factories in nearby Prato, Pistoia and Florence, causing an exodus from the country, as was happening all across Central Italy (as well as Northern Italy, though to a lesser extent). With the workers gone, Count Michon Pecori and his elderly sisters who also lived in the villa had to undertake all the cellar work themselves, an enormous task. Nonetheless, grapes and olives continued to be cultivated, wine and *olio extra-vergine d'oliva* produced, as it had for centuries, and life carried on as best it could.

114

If truth be told, the Fattoria di Calavria Carmignano wine was just about drinkable, but it was nowhere near the level of wines being produced elsewhere, notably at neighbouring Capezzana and Fattoria di Artimino, the zone's leading producers. However, the Vin Santo di Carmignano that the count and his sisters laboured to make, entirely by ancient hand-methods, was utterly exquisite. To produce this special and unique wine, Trebbiano Toscano and Malvasia grapes were carefully selected at harvest and laid out to dry on cane mats to form a *castello* five layers high in the attic of the villa's winery. Here the grapes were left to dry and shrivel for a period of at least three or four months. When the weather was conducive, the count would open the windows to assist in the drying process, but when it was damp or humid, as it often could be during a damp, cold Tuscan winter, the windows were shut to keep out moisture, which would have led to rot. By February, the semi-raisined grapes were shrivelled and rich in sugar. They were then pressed and the sweet must added to small wooden barrels of no more than 100 litres called *caratelli*. The *caratelli* would still contain some of the *madre*, the dregs and lees of preceding vintages, and they were not filled to the top, thus allowing the wine to oxidise. The bungs of the barrels were sealed with concrete and left to age in the attic for upwards of seven years, suffering both the stifling heat of a Tuscan summer and the bitterly damp cold of winter. The wine that would eventually emerge was utterly extraordinary and complex, the intense sweetness balanced with a concentration of flavour and nutty, dried fruit and caramelly aromas that were truly remarkable.

Fattoria di Calavria Vinsanto di Carmignano is a wine that no longer exists from a wine estate that no longer exists. Eventually, the backbreaking labour was too much for the elderly count and his sisters. The wine activities ceased, and the vineyards were sold. Even so, Fattoria di Calavria Vinsanto di Carmignano is a wine that continues to live long in our memories. We have just two bottles of this extraordinary wine left from the 1983 vintage, a precious memento to our time in Tuscany with our then baby son, and a memento, too, to a vanished estate and a vanished way of life.

Carlo Verdi Rosso, Antica Corte Pallavicino, Polesine Parmense, Emilia-Romagna

A recurring story I encounter is of younger generations doing well in their chosen activity but never losing sight of the hard work and dedication of the generations that had preceded them. Winegrowers today are proud to declare that their grandparents or great-grandparents had been *mezzadri*.

The Spigaroli family, for example, were originally *mezzadri* to Maestro Giuseppe Verdi, arguably Italy's greatest composer. The maestro himself had been born in humble circumstances, at Roncole, in the Bassa Parmense or lowlands of the Po Valley north of Parma where his father had a smallholding and ran an *osteria*. Though Verdi's musical talent was spotted at an early age, and he was to go on to great things and travel all around the world, he never lost sight of his origins and still loved the countryside where he had been born and raised. Indeed, later in life, once successful and established, he took over the family villa at nearby Sant'Agata in 1851 and eventually moved there with Giuseppina Strepponi, the operatic soprano who became his second wife. It was at Sant'Agata that he not only composed such brilliant operatic master-pieces as *Il trovatore*, *La traviata*, *La forza del destino*, *Don Carlos*, *Aida* and *Falstaff*; it was also where he delighted in the life of a gentleman farmer. He involved himself in the landscaping of the gardens and took great interest in the activities of the extensive estate that he now owned, ensuring that it was well looked-after and above all productive.

Verdi was passionate about the foods and wines of his native land, wrote about them in letters and gave produce from his farm as gifts to friends and colleagues. When he travelled across Europe by carriage, he always ensured that an ample supply of provisions went with him, the wonderful products that today have been acclaimed and granted protected name status: *culatello di Zibello*, *prosciutto di Parma*, *strolghino*, *salame di Felino*, *spalla di San Secondo*, *parmigiano reggiano* cheese, and of course demi-johns of his own-produced wines.

After Maestro Verdi died, the Spigaroli family was able to come to the Antica Corte Pallavicina. For the Spigarolis, this was an upwardly social move that saw the family's lives transformed from being sharecroppers to tenant farmers. Here, by the banks of the fertile and mighty Po, they continued the same mixed activities as before, using the age-old traditional skills and experi-ence that had been passed down through the generations of *mezzadri*: the dif-ference, though, was now they were entrepreneurs and could keep the profit from their activities. The Po was a busy waterway in the early years of the twentieth century. The family caught fish and set up a kiosk along the river-bank to serve to passing boats, and it became a popular and lively venue, especially in the early decades of the century. But when the Po eventually changed course, the family were forced to move on, and the historic Antica Corte Pallavicina fell into ruins.

However, a generation later, in 1990, an opportunity arose for Massimo and Luciano Spigaroli to purchase the Antica Corte Pallavicina. By then, what had once been an important frontier post for the powerful Pallavicino family, protecting river traffic and enabling them to levy duty on goods passing through, had fallen into disuse and was little more than a crumbling ruin. The Spigarolis set to work not only to restore the ancient buildings but also to revive the mixed agricultural activities of the farm, working the land as their forefathers had always done when they had been *mezzadri*. Today, the damp, ancient, humid cellars are once again full of *culatelli di Zibello*—the most prized, profoundly flavoured and precious of all Italian cured pork prod-ucts—while the old cheese-maturing room is stocked with great wheels of *parmigiano reggiano*. The fortified building is now a luxury country house hotel, and Chef Massimo, using the abundance of local produce and products that he is so passionate about, has created a Michelin-star restaurant.

Maestro Verdi loved wine and the exuberance and joy that it could bring to life, something he celebrates in such drinking songs as 'Libiamo ne' lieti calici' in *La traviata*. The opera *Otello* opens in a tavern where the celebrated warrior is being toasted; *Rigoletto* begins in a convivial and happy atmosphere before descending into darkness and tragedy; and in his great comic opera *Falstaff*, the eponymous hero is rarely out of an inn, drink in hand.

Carlo Verdi Rosso is a blend of local grapes cultivated on Maestro Verdi's father Carlo's former holding. It is a wine that makes no claim to greatness. It is fresh, honest and robust and simply an excellent accompaniment to the wonderful cured meats of the Antica Corte Pallavicina estate. It is the sort of wine that you can imagine being enjoyed in the drinking scene of *La traviata*, or else one that Falstaff would knock back prodigiously before breaking into song. It's just the sort of wine that Maestro Verdi would have transported in wicker-covered demi-johns in his horse-drawn carts across Europe to the greatest opera houses of his time, or that his father Carlo might have served in the family's humble *osteria* in Roncole.

11

TOWER POWER

Siena's Piazza del Campo is without doubt one of the most striking public spaces in the world, a shell-shaped, medieval square, created in the thirteenth century, sloping gently down to the Palazzo Pubblico, seat of government for the Republic of Siena. The slender Torre del Mangia keeps guard over this important civic space. I enjoy this view along with a glass of chilled (but not too chilled) Vernaccia di San Gimignano while seated at one of the many bar-restaurants that line the top of the piazza. The wine is deep in colour, yellow tinged with hints of amber, full and forthright, not watery and insipid, made in the old style, fermented on the skins, as such wines were once made here before modern technology stripped them of their soul and local identity.

It is midsummer, and the town is festooned with the colourful flags that indicate the respective contrade *or districts of Siena, neighbourhoods that represent the local identity of the inhabitants of this small city that still thinks of itself as almost an independent republic. There were once fifty-nine* contrade *but, since 1729, when Duchess Violante di Bavaria reorganised them, there have been just seventeen. For the Sienese, even today, when the impracticality of living within the* centro storico *has driven many to move outside, allegiance to one's family* contrada *remains fiercely and vitally important, something far stronger than allegiance to province, region or even to the Italian national state. I swirl my glass, take a long, slow sip, and that flavourful wine penetrates deep into my very bones. For those of us who live in a world of ever greater social mobility, where the certainties of tradition and neighbourhood no longer exist, if they ever did, it is remarkable to consider and to appreciate so many centuries of tradition, continuity, protection, identity and belonging.*

The History

The Italians call it *campanilismo*, and it is one of the enduring—and endearing—features of life here: an abiding allegiance to and pride in the place

119

where each person was born, not just the region, or even the city, but often actually the neighbourhood that one was raised into. The word comes from *campanile* or bell tower, for indeed it is the sound of the bells from one's own local church that resonate in the very soul, the way London's true cockneys can only claim to be so if born within the sound of 'Bow Bells', the bells of St Mary-le-Bow.

Perhaps the most visible expression of *campanilismo* is Siena's twice-yearly Palio, the medieval bareback horse race around the Piazza del Campo whereby horsemen representing ten of the city's seventeen *contrade* compete at breakneck speed around a track laid with volcanic tuff, clay and sand to win the Palio, a silk banner and with it the honour and pride of the whole city. The jockeys are hired mercenaries, some not even born in the city; the horses themselves are determined by the drawing of lots; and bribery, cheating and even the whipping of rival horses is all part of the tradition. With colourful processions of youths in medieval dress, the throwing and catching of flags, music, pageantry and more, it would be easy to believe that this were little more than a spectacle put on to attract tourists and their money to Siena. It's true, tourists do come in the many thousands, and the city undoubtedly benefits economically. But the visceral emotions of rivalry and even hatred that the Palio can engender are but the manifestations of an ancient history of collective joy and sorrow, rights and wrongs, and perceived hurts and insults that date back centuries.

The Republic of Siena was established in 1125, but the growth and influence of Italy's medieval cities dates back much earlier. After the fall of the Roman Empire, the Italian Peninsula was fragmented as order gave way to chaos and waves of invaders descended from the north. By the time Alboin led the Lombards over the Julian Alps in the middle of the sixth century, civility had been disrupted, with town and civilian life in decline, agricultural activity reduced and the countryside ravaged not only by lawlessness and piracy but by a plague that swept through Europe, as detailed vividly by Paul the Deacon in his *Historia Langobardorum*.

The Lombards gradually exerted control and order, installing noble warriors to oversee towns and their supporting countryside, while still leaving them a fair degree of autonomy and independence from the Lombard kings. Was this devolved approach to governance perhaps one factor that led to the localisation of power, as well as the creation of civic identity, certainly an important feature of Italian history throughout the medieval period and persisting even still today? Indeed, from the time of the fall of the Roman Empire until the unification of Italy in 1861, and even well beyond, there was little sense of national political or social unity or even a notion of an 'Italia'. Rather, the history of Italy manifested itself in the form of small and independent civic groupings under the control of strong men who jealously guarded their own fiefdoms. Thus it was that each city, with little central controlling influence, had the possibility to develop and evolve in its own way, militarily, economically, socially, safeguarding its own traditions, customs, language and even food and wine.

Ancient animosities

By the early Middle Ages, a new merchant class was emerging that brought prosperity to the cities. A significant increase in population starting in the eleventh century brought ever more people to live in towns and cities. This made available a ready labour force that allowed merchant capitalism to grow and flourish, with the production of artisan goods, textiles and food to be traded locally as well as internationally. The emergence of new systems of banking and finance helped to facilitate economic growth and expansion. Siena's Monte dei Paschi bank can trace its origin back to 1472, making it possibly the world's oldest bank in continuous operation, but it was actually founded on even earlier financial institutions and statutes that evolved to service and facilitate the growing needs of the new artisan, merchant and entrepreneurial classes.

With no overriding national power, as cities grew in influence, they were able to assert their autonomy, answerable only to themselves, and gaining control over, and the allegiance of, smaller surrounding towns that came under their spheres of influence. Communal government began to evolve, with the most powerful civic conurbations or *comuni* able to assert themselves as independent city-states ruled by the new elite. Whether governed by self-appointed consuls or, later, by a *podestà* selected at first by the nobility, later by citizens (sometimes choosing a stranger to ensure neutrality), Italy's cities grew in power and independence, becoming not just economic powerhouses but also military forces. Wars were waged frequently and sometimes without provocation against their close neighbours. Pisa in perennial conflict with its hated rival Genoa, Florence regularly at loggerheads with Siena, Milan with Pavia: so it was across the entire peninsula, and out of such ancient conflicts, current animosities and resentments, real and imagined, remain even today.

Ever since Charlemagne had been crowned *Imperator Romanorum*—Emperor of the Romans—there was always the potential for an imperial power to rise again that would unite as well as revive the glory of the ancient

Roman Empire. In practice, most emperors, Charlemagne included, were too distracted and busy with struggles elsewhere to try to assert central control over the disparate entities that made up Italy. Frederick I, known as 'Barbarossa' or 'Red Beard', crowned Holy Roman Emperor in 1155, attempted to assert imperial authority over Northern Italy by flexing his not inconsiderable might. However, in a remarkable show of unity, the cities of Northern Italy banded together to form the First Lombard League and were able collectively to take on the might of Barbarossa, defeating his imperial army at the Battle of Legnano in 1176. The Second Lombard League was established in 1226 to counter the powerful ambitions of his son Frederick II, laying the foundation for the Guelph and Ghibelline struggles that dominated Italy through this period, splitting the Italian Peninsula, and even neighbouring towns, cities and city-states, into those affiliated with Guelphs who allied with the papacy and were opposed to imperial authority, and those Ghibellines who sided with the emperor.

Urban fortresses

The concentration of power and wealth in the hands of elite families who were able to control a city naturally led to intense and competitive rivalries that often resulted in bloodshed, simmering feuds, murder. When such violent conflicts increasingly spilled on to the stone-paved streets of medieval towns and municipalities, families began to construct buildings that were to serve as their own personal urban fortresses. Architectural advances enabled the creation of towers that could stretch as high as 90 metres, built on a relatively small footprint but reaching to the skies. Constructing these medieval skyscrapers was no mean feat. A foundation as much as 10 metres deep was needed to support the structure, reinforced with anchor poles pile-driven into the ground. The base of the tower would be made from immense blocks of stone, while the subsequent stories were constructed of ever lighter materials using a technique known as *muratura a sacco*, whereby thin inner and outer walls made from brick were cavity constructed, the interior gap filled with stones and mortar. Building a decent-sized tower might take several years. In addition to serving as safe havens in times of strife, the height of a tower came to be seen as the ultimate status symbol, a monumental phallic symbol to the power and strength of a clan.

Such towers, ever higher and higher, proliferated and were constructed across Italy. By the end of the twelfth century, Florence had about 100. Bologna was another town full of towers, its Torre degli Asinelli, constructed between 1109 and 1119, reaching a vertiginous height of 97.2 metres (while visibly leaning, it can still be climbed today, though to reach the summit requires the ascent of a leg-numbing 498 stairs). The busy wine town of Alba, in Piedmont's Le Langhe, was once known as 'the city of a hundred towers' when it was part of the Lombard League, supporting the papacy against the emperor.

While the tall towers that we associate with San Gimignano and other medieval and Renaissance towns and cities can on the one hand be seen as giant symbols to demonstrate the power and importance of leading families, medieval towers also served important defensive purposes in cities as well as along both the Italian coastline and at strategic positions in the countryside. For example, watchtowers were built in a defensive line along a main route that passes over the Apennine mountains connecting Tuscany with Emilia-Romagna, a route for travel and commerce in peaceful times but a vulnerable flank of potential attack in times of strife.

The town undoubtedly most associated with towers is San Gimignano, located between Florence and Siena directly on the Via Francigena. Like many former Etruscan towns, it is sited on top of a hill at 334 metres above sea level, and the approach, from almost all directions, reveals a startling skyline, a jagged silhouette of medieval skyscrapers that reach to the sky.

When Sigeric, newly appointed archbishop of Canterbury, passed through this way in 990 en route to Rome, San Gimignano was little more than a small village belonging to the bishop of Volterra. By 1200, it had grown in extent, prosperity and influence sufficiently to declare itself a free *comune*, governed first by its own consuls, then by an appointed *podestà*. Its prosperity was based on the considerable traffic that the Via Francigena brought, on the production of its wine that was already famous in the Middle Ages and on the commerce of wool and other trade. The richest families—merchants and money lenders—inevitably vied with each other to build the tallest towers, and in the fourteenth century some seventy-two graced this remarkable town, the most monumental reaching a towering 70 metres. Today, just fourteen remain, still more than sufficient to give an atmospheric impression of life in Central Italy in the Middle Ages. Indeed, the cultural and historic importance of San Gimignano was recognised when UNESCO placed it on the World Cultural Heritage register. Surrounded by the vineyards that produce its famous wine, overcrowded by day when coachloads of visitors descend, it is a place best to enjoy by evening, seated outside at a table along the stone-paved streets, or in a small restaurant or trattoria, enjoying, what else, a goblet of Vernaccia di San Gimignano wine.

The Wines

Montenidoli Tradizionale, Vernaccia di San Gimignano DOCG, Maria Elisabetta Fagiuoli, San Gimignano, Tuscany

In a country that values tradition so highly, it is somewhat startling that Italians embraced such significant changes in taste and style to some of their most historic wines. Modern technology, notably the widescale use of stainless-steel, temperature-controlled fermentation vessels, may have brought huge improvements to many wines, especially lighter and fresher styles of whites, but in some cases, the result has been to strip historic wines of their very soul and identity. Vernaccia di San Gimignano is a case in point. I remember first enjoying this wine in situ in the early 1980s. At that time, many examples were still made in the old way, the white grapes crushed then added to open-topped wooden fermentation vats to ferment on the skins in the same way that red wine is made. The resulting wine would take on some colour from the skin contact, as well as flavour and tannin, making such Vernaccias robust if sometimes rustic whites to enjoy with the local food. With age, such wines might have had the tendency to oxidise, but what these wines most certainly did not lack was character and personality. Modern technology, combined with improvements in the vineyard as well as earlier harvesting to maintain acidity and freshness, has mainly transformed the wines of San Gimignano, as it has done for white wines produced all across Italy. Most examples now encountered are well made, clean and forceful, and some produced in this style are very good indeed. But I'm glad nonetheless that there are still producers who have steadfastly remained true to tradition.

Elisabetta Fagiuoli is one such heroic winemaker. She established the Montenidoli vineyard in 1965, helped the zone to receive recognition with the granting of DOC and later DOCG and has steadfastly produced Vernaccia di San Gimignano Montenidoli Tradizionale in the old style, vinifying the Vernaccia grapes on the skins. Of course, soul and identity in a wine does not just come from its means of production. Grape variety and terroir are also crucial factors. The Vernaccia grape of San Gimignano is cultivated here, only here and nowhere else in Tuscany, an ancient variety that thrives particularly well on the zone's sedimentary soil rich in fossils and marine life from an ancient sea that once covered this territory. This results in a wine that has the potential to be very rich in flavour, and this characteristic is intensified when the grapes are vinified on the skins to draw out some of their natural tannin.

These days, white wines made in this natural and old-style manner, taking on colour and richness, are known as 'orange wines', and we are seeing more and more of them, I'm delighted to say. At Montenidoli, the *tradizionale* is not some new trend but simply the way it has always been done. I adore this wine. It is really a white wine for lovers of red wine, for in addition to its richness it has a touch of tannin as well as tremendous structure, body, length. On the nose, there are hints of wood and herbs, while on the palate there is a mineral-rich intensity with a bitter and slightly salty finish, which makes it such an excellent accompaniment to food. I'd like to think that wines such as this, wines with true soul and identity, slaked the thirst not only of the thousands and maybe millions of pilgrims who passed this way along the Via Francigena but also of those proud and powerful families who brought such prosperity and renown to Tuscany, those men and women who knew where they had come from, those builders of towers that reached up to the sky.

Vernaccia di San Gimignano DOCG Riserva, Tenute Guicciardini Strozzi, San Gimignano, Tuscany

Villa Cusona, the wine estate of the Guicciardini Strozzi family, has been producing wine for over 1,000 years from grapes grown on a vast estate that today spreads across 530 hectares located to the north-west of San Gimignano. Though today the family has other estates elsewhere in Tuscany and across Italy, Villa Cusona remains at the heart of the Guicciardini Strozzi wine operations, the source of wines that are considered historic benchmarks of Vernaccia di San Gimignano and have been enjoyed for centuries. Historical documents indicate that some twenty flasks of Vernaccia were sent from Villa Cusona to Lorenzo de' Medici. Michelangelo said it was a wine that 'kisses, licks, bites, and stings'. Vernaccia di San Gimignano is the only specific wine mentioned in Dante's *Divine Comedy*.

Apart from wine, Guicciardini Strozzi family members played important roles during the Florentine Renaissance, as statesmen, bankers, merchants, mercenaries and *mecenati* (patrons of the arts). It is quite probable that Guicciardinis and Strozzis were among those powerful families vying for supremacy in the tower stakes, for this was an age of conspicuous consumption where money was there to be spent, whether on property or on art. One relative, Lisa Gherardini del Giocondo, was the subject of the famous *La Gioconda* painting by Leonardo da Vinci, making current family members fifteenth generation descendants of the Mona Lisa.

Wine, its production, enjoyment and commerce, has been an activity carried on across generations and centuries. In 1972, Prince Girolamo Strozzi together with other winegrowers founded the Consorzio della Vernaccia to safeguard a historic wine and grape variety, as well as to bring the world's attention to Tuscany's greatest white wine. Vernaccia di San Gimignano is both the name of the grape variety and the name of the wine that is entitled to the Vernaccia di San Gimignano DOCG (there are other grapes named Vernaccia from elsewhere in Italy, but none of them are related genetically).

The Tenute Guicciardini Strozzi Vernaccia di San Gimignano Riserva is a wine produced only in the best years that maintains tradition while making full and intelligent use of modern technology. For example, the tradition of fermenting Vernaccia on the skins here is reinterpreted using cryomaceration. After fermentation, the wine then ages in French oak *barriques*, followed by a year of further ageing in the bottle in the centuries-old cellars of Villa Cusona. This is a rich, full-bodied and -flavoured white wine, the colour deep yellow tending toward golden, with aromas of jasmine and Mediterranean herbs, notes of vanilla and an important structure and persistence in the mouth.

If San Gimignano's famous towers were architectural marvels that provided 'high-profile' opportunities for its leading families to demonstrate their power and importance, this important wine enjoyed since the Renaissance and earlier is a demonstration from one of the zone's most historic families of the enduring excellence of tradition and innovation.

Vigneto Bucerchiale, Chianti Rufina Riserva DOCG, Fattoria di Selvapiana, Rufina, Tuscany

The Selvapiana estate located in the zone of Chianti Rufina to the north-east of Florence lies along a main route that passes over the Apennine mountains connecting Tuscany with Emilia-Romagna. During the medieval era, Selvapiana served as one of a series of watchtowers along the Sieve River that were placed there to protect Florence from attacks or invasion from its north-east flank. Though the property was enhanced and enlarged into a villa during the Renaissance and became a summer residence for noble families and bishops from Florence, the original watchtower is still in place and is depicted on the label of the Selvapiana's Chianti Rufina, testimony to an era of conflict and conquest, when tall watchtowers were vital elements in lines of defence.

Selvapiana was purchased in 1827 by Michele Giuntini, a successful banker and an ancestor of current owner Dr Francesco Giuntini. Since the 1970s,

Dr Giuntini has worked tirelessly to defend the reputation of the Chianti Rufina sub-zone and to demonstrate to world markets that Rufina wines have a unique and distinct personality and identity. Chianti Rufina is the smallest of Tuscany's Chianti sub-zones and takes its name from the small market town of Rufina that lies along the Sieve River. The vineyards lie mainly on the steeper slopes that lead up towards the high peaks of the Apennines, making this the highest of all Chianti sub-zones. The proximity of the mountains influences the micro-climate, which is cooler in summer than in other areas, and with a great diurnal temperature range that gives the wines a fresh acidity, beautiful aromatic compounds and finesse and elegance, with silky tannins that allow the wines of Rufina to age and evolve for long periods.

Giuntini is a visionary and pioneering winemaker. He first produced Selvapiana's Vigneto Bucerchiale Chianti Rufina Riserva, the estate's flagship wine, in 1979, one of the earliest examples of a super-Tuscan before that term was even invented, for it was and continues to be produced from 100 per cent Sangiovese (an innovation at that time) grown in the single cru vineyard Bucerchiale. (Chianti in the '70s and '80s was still mainly a blended wine, and there were few wines from named single vineyards.) Today, Federico Giuntini, Francesco's adopted son, continues to produce Bucerchiale in the best years only when conditions allow. It is a magnificent expression of Chianti Rufina, from grapes grown on this steep balcony of foothills leading to the high mountains: there is a bright freshness to the wine, a concentration of dark and dried fruits, notes of herbs and tobacco, with well-knit tannins that can give a lean and taut finish when young and indicate that this is a wine that will evolve and improve for many years to come. I recently tasted the 1981 vintage, which though more than forty years old still displayed beautifully expansive rich fruit and an explosion of aromas and scents.

From a medieval defensive watchtower along the Sieve River that once served to protect and safeguard the boundaries of Tuscany, Selvapiana today is the source of powerful, long-lived wines that define, defend and safeguard a precious territory: Chianti Rufina.

12

DANTE ALIGHIERI

It had been the most splendid evening, dining in the Foresteria of the Villa Serègo Alighieri, a meal of delicious Veronese specialities—risotto mantecato all'Amarone con scaglie di Monte Veronese, *followed by* filetto di maialino al Possessioni Rosso, *and to finish* delizia al Recioto con fragole candite. *Each dish was accompanied by the acclaimed Valpolicella wines of the estate. Afterwards, we repaired to a drawing room where Professor David Lynn, longstanding editor of the* Kenyon Review, *gave an inspiring lecture about Dante Alighieri and his importance to Italian and world literature. At one point, Conte Pieralvise Serègo Alighieri, a direct descendant of 'Il Sommo Poeta'—the Supreme Poet—slipped into the room to join us. He opened a bottle of his own wine, Casal dei Ronchi Recioto della Valpolicella, and offered us all a glass. The wine had an intense nose of black cherries, complex, gently bittersweet, absolutely luscious, pure and divine in every sense. Professor Lynn asked the count if he would do us the great honour of reciting a few lines from his illustrious ancestor's masterpiece. It still gives me goosebumps when I recall that moment, the count's voice softly mellow and sonorous: 'Nel mezzo del cammin di nostra vita / mi ritrovai per una selva oscura, / che la diritta via era smarrita ...'*

The History

In a medieval era when pride in one's birth city and allegiance even to a neighbourhood gave one a sense of worth and civic identity, the worst punishment that could be imposed—as final, almost, as death itself—was banishment or exile. Such was the fate that befell Dante Alighieri, Italy's greatest poet, when he was expelled from his beloved native Florence in 1302.

Florence at that time, like much of Italy, was riven by a medieval divide that was to shape its history, the constant struggle and conflict between those forces loyal to the papacy and those who favoured the Holy Roman Empire, the former known as Guelphs, the latter Ghibellines. By the thirteenth century, this conflict had grown ever more bitter and brutal. By then, the papacy had become immensely rich as well as ambitious, the pope no longer just a spiritual leader but increasingly a temporal one, as mighty and as greedy for power as any world leader, and able, if he so desired, to live sumptuously in opulence and splendour beyond belief.

Indeed, the pope now had the prerogative to grant ecclesiastical positions to relatives, friends, allies, those who favoured them, the power and the right to bestow influence and privilege. With the political influence of the papacy now extending well beyond the affairs of the Church, it is no wonder that it often found itself at odds with the imperial entity that it had created. Holy Roman emperors, meanwhile, could not help but meddle and get entangled in ecclesiastical matters, wanting to gain influence and control over the powerful Catholic infrastructure that was in place not only throughout Italy but all of Europe. Conflict was inevitable, often martial but also intellectual. Imperial theologians wrote treatises that were damned as heretical by the papacy, while popes issued bulls and edicts that sought to clarify matters of belief while at the same time defining their own sphere of influence and power. Emperors were excommunicated; popes were renounced. These conflicts played themselves out at a civic level especially across Northern and Central Italy, and the stakes were high: cities could be razed to the ground, gruesome penalties imposed on the vanquished and people sent into exile until a time when the pendulum would swing and their faction would be victorious over the hated enemy again, a constant back and forth struggle with seemingly no end.

It was into this turbulent and uncertain world that Dante was born in 1265 in Florence, then the Republic of Florence, a proud city-state. His family were staunch Guelphs, supporters of the papacy. Just before his birth, the Guelphs had been roundly defeated by the Ghibellines in the Battle of Montaperti, their leaders sent into exile. However, by the time Dante was a young man, the papal forces, with the support of the French king, had regained power and managed to expel the Ghibellines forever from Florence. Florentine power and pride were immense, and this proud city-state extended its political influence over territories across Tuscany. Moreover, the city was not just a political force; it was also a centre of intellectual thought and artistic creativity, with some of its most brilliant thinkers ready to serve in the interests of Florence.

DANTE ALIGHIERI

Civic strife

Dante rose to become an important and influential Florentine leader, both artistically and politically. In 1295, he joined the Guild of Physicians and Apothecaries, as membership of a professional guild was a requirement to take part in public life. Yet with the Ghibellines routed and its Guelph supremacy unchallenged, new and bitter factions continued to fester and develop. By 1300, the Florentine Guelphs had begun to fight among themselves, the city divided into Blacks and Whites. While the former continued to support and ally themselves with Pope Boniface VIII, the Whites, the faction to which Dante had chosen to belong, were concerned with the growing influence and territorial ambitions of the papacy and its ever-stronger alliance with the French. The conflict between the White and the Black Guelphs grew ever more bitter. First the Whites were in ascendancy and expelled the Blacks. But Boniface VIII directly involved himself in the conflict, together with the support of French King Philip IV. In 1301, Dante was sent to Rome as a delegate to negotiate a peaceful settlement, and while he was away, Charles of Valois, brother of the French king, entered Florence to side with the Blacks, destroying much of the city and killing many of the opposing side. Trumped-up charges of corruption and financial impropriety were brought against Dante for actions during the time when he had served as a city prior. He was found guilty, ordered to pay a substantial fine, had all his assets seized and was condemned to perpetual exile from his beloved Florence, with death by burning at the stake the punishment should he attempt to return without permission. He was just thirty-seven years old and never set foot in his beloved home city again.

A turbulent period

Thus, Dante began life as a perpetual outsider, dependent on the goodwill and hospitality of those aristocratic families who would accept him. He first brought his family to Verona in 1303, where they were received and given hospitality by Bartolomeo della Scala; he returned to that city in 1312 and stayed there until 1318, this time as the guest of Cangrande della Scala. Dante is therefore still considered very important to the people of Verona: there is a rather severe statue to Italy's greatest poet in the Piazza dei Signori, not far from the Arche Scaligeri where the tombs of the Della Scala family are located. Dante's son, Pietro, clearly came to love this area, for in 1353 he purchased the Casal dei Ronchi estate in Gargagnago, in the heart of the Valpolicella Classica wine hills just to the north of Verona. In addition to

Verona, Dante's wanderings as an exile took him to Liguria, Lucca and finally to Ravenna, where the poet was to live out the rest of his life.

While Dante continued to take part in unsuccessful attempts by the White Guelphs to regain power, political events were taking place that were to change the shape of Europe. The power struggle between the papacy and the Holy Roman Empire was essentially a dispute over who was Christendom's supreme leader over secular and temporal affairs. The ambitious Pope Boniface VIII, who by now had fallen out with King Philip IV and needed to assert papal supremacy, issued a papal bull, *Unam sanctam*, which was an extreme interpretation that declared that every human had to submit to the pope to obtain salvation. Naturally, the French king could not accept this, and when Boniface tried to excommunicate him, Philip sent his troops to the papal residence to rough him up. Boniface was badly beaten and died soon after from his injuries. Clearly, this was a violent era, and competing powers had no hesitation in resorting to any means, fair or foul, to achieve their aims. Following Boniface's death, Philip helped Benedict XI to be elected as the next pope, and he in turn immediately absolved the French king of any involvement in Boniface's untimely demise. Benedict's papacy only lasted eight months before he too died. Once again, the French king had a decisive influence on the election of the next pope, this time selecting a Frenchman, Clement V, who was Philip's personal friend. Clement never had any intention of moving to Rome, so with Philip's assistance the papal seat was moved to Avignon where it was to remain for the next seventy years.

Given the unsettling events of this period, it should be no surprise that Dante, born into a family of Guelphs and hitherto a lifelong supporter of the papacy, underwent something of a damascene conversion. For by now the papacy made little pretence at being anything but a temporal power: it had grown into a political, economic and territorial powerhouse, with untold wealth and immense influence over the Christian lives and souls of its citizens across the Western world. Thus, when the future Holy Roman Emperor Henry VII came to Italy in 1310, Dante saw in him something of a new Charlemagne, that is, an enlightened ruler who could provide balance between the temporal and spiritual and who thus could be a saviour for Italy and the world. These thoughts and beliefs he elucidated in his political treatise *De monarchia*.

La commedia or The Divine Comedy

'Midway through life's journey, I found myself in a dark wood, the right road lost ...', the words that Count Pieralvise had recited to us: so begins one of the greatest works in world literature, Dante's *La commedia* (the 'Divine' was a later honorific addition bestowed by others). Dante himself was midway through his own life's journey when he went into exile, all his certainties, hopes and expectations destroyed by the horrible punishment of permanent exile from his beloved Florence, 'the right road lost'.

The poet began work on his narrative epic poem around 1308, a unique and richly precise vision of a fantastic universe that extended not just to the heavens and beyond but into our own individual and deepest fears and terrors. The poem is divided into three *cantiche*, or parts: *Inferno, Purgatorio* and *Paradiso*, each comprising thirty-three *cantos* written in *terza rima*—three lines of eleven syllables each with the first and third line rhyming, and the second line rhyming with the first and third of the next *canto*. The form gives an ingenious rhythm to the work (while there are outstanding prose translations, Robert Pinsky's brilliant verse translation captures this poetic rhythm quite magnificently) and made it easier for generations of Italians to commit the work, or parts of it, to memory.

In the first part, *Inferno*, Dante vividly, terrifyingly yet often sympathetically depicts the horrible punishment and suffering that sinners—real individuals who had lived, contemporaries, historical figures and characters from classical literature, fallen saints and sinners—had to endure, their positions in Dante's circles of hell based on the level of their wrongdoing, malfeasance or transgressions. So precise is Dante's depiction that it is even possible to envisage hell as if on a map, the nine circles, leading from that dark wood at the beginning, across the Rivers Acheron and Styx, finally to the very heart of darkness, the deepest and most hopeless realm, reserved for those who had committed sins of betrayal. Sins of lust or gluttony are considered milder than those of violence, whether towards others or to self, while sins of fraud are only slightly less heinous than sins of betrayal, whether to family, country or benefactor.

And yet, even in the deepest depths of hell there is always humanity, there is poignancy and longing, there is sympathy and empathy. Dante's protagonist, guided by the Roman poet Virgil, wise and all-seeing, descends into the maelstrom of hell and sees hundreds of individuals who are condemned to suffer for eternity. He pauses to speak to some of them, hearing how they came to be where they are, why they are compelled to suffer as they must. Even when their sins are fully deserved, Dante's language has the power to make us feel their pain and sorrow.

Down through the circles of hell, Dante's protagonist and his guide Virgil travel, meeting gluttons, misers, heretics, those violent towards others, towards themselves, towards God, towards nature, seducers, flatterers, simoniacs, hypocrites, thieves, schismatics, falsifiers, each circle inhabited by those who had committed sins and were condemned forever to suffer punishments that were deemed fitting to the crime.

The great Greek hero Odysseus, lauded by Homer for his wile and craft, and for his trickery to end the Trojan War, is placed by Dante in the eighth circle of hell along with his fighting companion, the hero Diomedes, there to suffer for being false counsellors, deceiving the Trojans, including Virgil's beloved hero Aeneas, the subject of his great work.

Perhaps it is understandable that for Dante the greatest, most unforgiveable sin of all, its practitioners deservedly placed in the deepest and most hopeless circle of hell, is that of betrayal. When Dante's protagonist and guide Virgil finally reach the deepest depths of the ninth circle of hell, it is the most fearful place, for they have reached the icy abode of Lucifer himself, the archangel who had once shone so bright before his spectacular fall from grace. This 'emperor of the realm of grief' is immense, and his head has three faces. The mouth of the central visage is gnawing on a body, its head buried within, its legs flailing: this is Judas Iscariot, who betrayed Christ. The other two faces gnaw on the bodies of Brutus and Cassius, the Romans who betrayed their colleague and friend Julius Caesar. Lucifer's mouths ceaselessly chew on their writhing victims, tearing them to pieces, shredding the skin from them, yet never killing them. This is the eternal punishment reserved for the most heinous betrayers of all.

From the frozen bowels of the deepest and darkest circle of hell, the return journey is made by climbing on the hairy back of Lucifer, up and up towards the light: 'Where we came forth, and once more saw the stars' (*Inferno*, Canto XXXIV, trans. R. Pinsky).

Thus ends the first and most-read part of Dante's great work *La commedia*. Indeed, it is understandable that *Inferno* is what most attracts us rather than *Purgatorio* or *Paradiso*: sin, suffering and torture are infinitely more mesmerising than reading about the good and the worthy, understandably. We therefore associate Dante with his vivid depictions of the horrors of hell, with its eternal flames and infinite pain. However, in the *Inferno* as well as the parts that follow, we see that Dante was truly a visionary prophet of hope, a writer who celebrates humanity and the human condition. While the medieval paradigm of Dante's time was defined by religious scholasticism based on Catholic dogma, Dante's enduring genius went far beyond the depiction of Christian truth as it was perceived in that age. Through the richness of his imagination and the complexity and clarity of a new vernacular that drew not only on Tuscan but also scores of other Italian dialects as well as Latin, he was able to express human emotions—fear, terror, wonder, pain, joy and exultation—as no one had ever done before in an Italian language that was as beautiful as it was terrifying. For this reason, Dante is considered the father of Italian literature and language. The world owes him an enormous debt, and we raise a glass of wine—his own family's wine—to his enduring genius.

The Wines

Possessioni Rosso Valpolicella Classico DOC, Serègo Alighieri, Gargagnago, Veneto

Since Pietro Alighieri, son of Dante, purchased the Casal dei Ronchi estate in the heart of the Valpolicella near Verona in 1353, the estate has remained for twenty-one generations in the hands of the direct descendants of the Supreme Poet. Today, wine continues to be made on the Casal dei Ronchi estate, the Conti Alighieri working together with the forward-thinking leader in Veronese viticulture, Masi Agricola, to produce a range of outstanding and prestigious wines that are fitting heirs to an ancient and noble heritage.

Possessioni Rosso is a wine that pays homage to the Tuscan roots of the family, for it is a blend of Corvina, Rondinella and Molinara, the great grapes of the Valpolicella, with Sangiovese, in memory of the family's Tuscan origins. Possessioni Rosso pays further homage to the family's history in the barrels used for its ageing. In the mid-sixteenth century, the Alighieri family found itself left with only female heirs, one of the most famous and important names in Italian history at risk of dying out. However, when Ginevra Alighieri married Marc'Antonio Serègo, the family ensured its survival, and ever since the descendants have born the double-barrelled family name, Serègo Alighieri. The wedding carriages of Ginevra and Marc'Antonio are still displayed in splendour in the hall of the Villa Serègo Alighieri.

It was Marc'Antonio Serègo, a visionary agronomist and a proponent of agricultural reform, who transformed the estate. As well as concentrating on the growing of grapes and the production of wine, he also made two significant further contributions. He introduced maize, brought over by the Spanish from the New World, to Northern Italy for the first time, a food that in the form of *polenta* quickly became a staple of the diet in the Veneto for rich and poor alike; and he also introduced the plantation of cherry trees into the Valpolicella, still today the region's other most famous crop. Possessioni Rosso, after fermentation, ages in casks made from cherry wood. Wood and fruit rarely confer the same flavours and aromas, yet it seems no coincidence

135

that Possessioni Rosso is a wine with an intense aroma and taste of ripe cherries. Perhaps the bittersweet touch that the wine possesses remains as a constant reminder of the bittersweet memory of Dante's enforced exile from his beloved Florence.

Casal dei Ronchi, Recioto della Valpolicella Classico DOCG, Serègo Alighieri, Gargagnago, Veneto

The Serègo Alighieri family have been one of the most important aristocratic landowners in the Valpolicella for centuries. Indeed, at one point the family owned some 80 per cent of the classic wine country, and they have naturally been leaders in the region's development. But it should be remembered that even on such a prestigious and famous historic estate, the cultivation of grapes here as elsewhere was very much viewed as just another cash crop, just like cherries or corn. The finest, selected grapes, however, especially those destined to undergo the unique Veronese process of *appassimento*, would have always been set aside for the personal production of the estate's two greatest wines, Vaio Armaron and Casal dei Ronchi Recioto. Vaio Armaron is thought by some to be possibly the original vineyard for the production of the wine that has come to be known as Amarone della Valpolicella. Casal dei Ronchi Recioto is a classic *passito* red wine produced from the historic vineyards that surround the villa itself, an intriguing, gently sweet *vino da meditazione*. Like Vaio Armaron, Casal dei Ronchi is produced entirely from grapes that have undergone *appassimento*. In this case, selections from the shoulders of the grape bunches—the name *recioto* in fact comes from the Venetian dialect for *orecchio*, for these 'ears' of the bunches receive more sunshine and are therefore riper—are taken before the main harvest and laid out to dry on the bamboo mats for a period of some months. Once they reach the desired state, the shrivelled grapes are lightly pressed, and the sugar-rich must ferments ever so slowly. So rich in sugar are these semi-dried grapes that even after fermentation, the wine retains an exquisite residual sweetness, an intense aroma of black cherries, spice and just a touch of tannin with a finish that is bittersweet and long. The term *vino da meditazione* is precisely apt for this wine: it is an exquisite rarity to sip slowly and thoughtfully, perhaps while reading or re-reading Dante's *Inferno*.

13

POLITICS AND POWER, ART AND WINE

Artimino is a tiny Etruscan hamlet to the west of Florence, still surrounded by its medieval walls and dominated by the massive Medici Villa 'La Ferdinanda', once the summer home to the grand dukes of Tuscany. We are here to dine at one of our favourite restaurants, Ristorante Da Delfina. When we first visited some decades ago, Signora Delfina was still at the stoves, faithfully preparing the Tuscan classics, often using wild herbs or plants that had been foraged in the surrounding countryside. Returning now, it seems that little has changed in these gorgeous wine hills. Tuscan cooking is timeless, after all. Neither sophisticated nor over-complicated, its classic simplicity relies on the absolute freshest and best seasonal produce available. We enjoy a bowl of ribollita—*a thick vegetable minestrone made with seasonal vegetables, stale, unsalted Tuscan bread and glistening Tuscan extra-virgin olive oil. Then we settle in to enjoy one the great dishes of Italy, indeed the world,* bistecca alla fiorentina—*three fingers thick*—tre dita—*cooked as it should be on the restaurant hearth over the embers of a wood fire. The wine to wash down this classic comes from vineyards that surround the Medici villa in an area where vines have been cultivated since Etruscan times. We're not drinking Tenuta di Artimino's flagship Carmignano DOCG but instead Ser Biagio Barco Reale DOC, named after the private, walled Medici hunting reserve that incorporated this area. Somewhat lighter in body than its aristocratic sibling, it is still a noble accompaniment to the classic Florentine T-bone, cooked pink and seasoned simply with just a pinch of sea salt from Cervia and a good spoonful or two of that wonderful, peppery, grassy-green Tuscan* olio extra-vergine d'oliva. *Here, perhaps more than anywhere else in Italy, in cooking as in life, such sublime simplicity has truly been elevated to a fine art.*

The History

In 1480, at the height of the Florentine Renaissance, the city's great leader and patron Lorenzo de' Medici (known by the honorific 'Il Magnifico'—the

Magnificent) purchased a rustic farm at Poggio a Caiano, in the Carmignano hills west of Florence. There he commissioned the illustrious architect Giuliano da Sangallo to redesign and rebuild it as a splendid country villa in the classical style. Indeed, the Villa di Poggio a Caiano is considered the first Renaissance villa and would presage and inspire the wonderful dwellings that Andrea Palladio would later design and create a half-century later across the Venetian Republic. The Villa di Poggio a Caiano was Lorenzo's only architectural commission, and it appears to have been a labour of love. It became not only Il Magnifico's favourite retreat but also embodied many of the values that he himself brought to the acclaimed lyrical poetry that this Renaissance titan composed, writing not in Latin but in *volgare*, that is, in the Florentine Italian of the 1400s, poems and prose that harked back to a golden, classical age and speak of the bucolic countryside, beauty and love.

The Medici appetite for power as well as beauty was immense. The most important of all Florentine's banking dynasties, they rose to become the mightiest of many illustrious families in Florence, dominating and overseeing this city-state across an extraordinary 300 years (with the exception of only two brief intervals). Not only did the Medici rule over Florence and its dominions, eventually creating the hereditary Grand Duchy of Tuscany, but the family also contributed four popes as well as two queens of France. Across not just Italy but all of Europe, it is hard to imagine a single family that held such power, influence and prestige for so long.

Though we consider the Renaissance an enlightened period, to gain and hold on to power in the 1500s still required ruthlessness and an iron will. When Pope Sixtus IV, not content with granting favours to his innumerable relations and making no fewer than six of his nephews cardinals, plotted with the rival banking family the Pazzi against the Medici, this illustrious dynasty came close to being wiped out. Lorenzo's brother Giuliano, who co-ruled with him, was murdered in the Duomo while a Pazzi cardinal looked on, and Lorenzo only narrowly escaped with his own life, having been stabbed in the neck by two priests. However, the people rallied in support of the Medici, and the revenge on the conspirators was unforgiving and decisive. Jacopo de' Pazzi, the head of the family, was captured, stripped naked and strung from the window of the Palazzo dei Signori alongside the disgraced archbishop of Pisa. Afterwards, his putrid body was dragged through the streets by a mob, thrown into the Arno, fished out again by schoolboys who hung it from a willow tree and flogged it, before disposing of it back in the waters of the Arno. The two priests who had attempted to murder Lorenzo were first castrated then hung by the neck, punishment that would have been entirely apt and fitting for those reserved to reside in the deepest circle of hell for the sin of betrayal in Dante's *Inferno*.

Humanism

Dante lived in an era when the medieval paradigm of the world placed man not at the centre of a Christian universe but rather seemingly adrift and all at sea in a maelstrom where events beyond control could blow an individual this way or that, determining whether they would end up suffering the torments of hell or be lifted into blissful paradise. Little more than a century later, as Italy moved into its golden age, the Renaissance, the power of the individual—the wealthy, privileged individual, it should be qualified—to chart the path of one's own life and to achieve almost anything seemed virtually limitless. A rediscovery of the classical world of ancient Rome and Greece brought new intellectual vigour and cultural insights to those who enjoyed the luxury of being able to study the humanities and the liberal arts: history, philosophy, ethics, rhetoric and of course drama and literature. And it was these same educated, wealthy individuals who not only held power—defending it with the utmost ruthlessness where necessary—but who also had the wherewithal, the sensibility as well as the means to patronise the immense outpouring of art and creativity that we associate with the Italian Renaissance, especially in Florence.

And without doubt the greatest, most powerful humanist patron of all was Lorenzo de' Medici. He was the epitome of the true Renaissance man, talented, sensitive and with a genuine love of and appreciation for art as a means of lifting life beyond the ordinary. An avid collector of ancient texts—his collection of books and manuscripts was later preserved by the Medici Pope Clement VII through the construction of the Laurentian Library, designed by Michelangelo—he was respected in Florence's most prestigious intellectual circles not just as a patron but as a major literary figure and poet in his own right. In this extract from his poem *Triumph of Bacchus and Ariadne*, he harks back to the carpe diem tradition of the Roman poet Horace: 'Quant'é bella giovinezza / Che si fugge tuttavia! / Chi vuol esser lieto, sia: / Di doman non c'è certezza' ('How beautiful youth is / Though fleeting! / Be happy, whoever wants to be: / Of tomorrow, there is no certainty', trans. Marc Millon).

Lorenzo, a country nobleman and curious intellectual, liked nothing more than gathering together groups of friends, artists, writers, musicians and the most brilliant minds of the day to one or other of his country villas for magnificent and overflowing banquets where the food was excellent and the wine flowed freely. As a patron, Lorenzo was generous to the point of lavish in his support for and close friendships with the greatest artists of his age, including Giuliano da Sangallo, Sandro Botticelli, Andrea del Verrocchio, Leonardo da Vinci and, towards the end of Lorenzo's life, the young Michelangelo, whom he brought into his house to encourage and support, raising him almost as a son and allowing him to live and work in his garden at Poggio a Caiano.

Other Medici followed Il Magnifico's example in their patronage of the arts. At the Villa di Poggio a Caiano, for example, two Medici popes continued the embellishment of this grand country estate by commissioning the sixteenth-century early Mannerist painters Pontormo, Andrea del Sarto and Alessandro Allori to adorn the two-storey *salone* with frescoes that depicted the self-glorification of the Medici. It was probably Lorenzo's cousins, Lorenzo di Pierfrancesco and Giovanni de' Medici, who commissioned Botticelli to produce his most famous works, *Primavera* and the *Birth of Venus*, for the Medici Villa di Castello. Grand Duke Francesco I commissioned the architect Bernardo Buontalenti to design theatres in Florence and to design the Villa Demidoff, north of Florence, which he had purchased as a gift to his mistress. Buontalenti also designed the gardens, while Giambologna was commissioned to create the massive *Colosso dell'Appennino* statue of a giant emerging from the stone. Buontalenti was also the architect behind the Villa Artimino 'La Ferdinanda' for Duke Ferdinando I, designed as a grand Medici hunting lodge in that charming Etruscan hilltop hamlet.

Renaissance art and wine

For those with money and position, the Renaissance was clearly a glorious time to be alive. Most affluent families, however they had acquired their prosperity, sought to obtain land in the country not only for their family country villa but also to provide them with a ready supply of food, wine and oil. For this was a time of relative plenty, when the well-off lived, ate and drank in copious abundance.

This was also the best time to be alive if you were a talented artist, architect or sculptor. Not only was there no shortage of wealthy, individual patrons, such as the Medici and other influential families who vied with one another to secure the services of the greatest artists, opportunities also came from civic authorities who wanted to extoll the splendour of their cities, and of course from ecclesiastical patrons including popes. Artists were paid well, treated with respect and honour, often dined with their patrons, and could even specify quantities of wine in their contracts.

POLITICS AND POWER, ART AND WINE

Though Leonardo da Vinci was a Tuscan, he spent much of his time in the service of Ludovico Sforza in Milan. It seems that at some point, he was offered a house that came with a piece of land planted with a vineyard opposite Santa Maria delle Grazie Church, where he had been commissioned to paint *The Last Supper*. He took great interest and pride in this venture, making precise drawings, and giving consideration to the best ways to grow grapes and make wines, even inventing new techniques and equipment to make the best wine he could. In a letter written in 1515, he shared his observations on practices necessary to make good wine: optimising the quality of the grapes by fertilising the vines, advocating the use of fermentation in sealed barrels rather than in open casks and frequent decantation to result in clear not turbid wine. 'Se seguirete i miei insegnamenti berrete un vino eccellente', he wrote—'If you follow my teachings, you will drink an excellent wine.' It seems that with wine, as with so many other subjects, Leonardo was ahead of his times, applying his methodical and curious genius to find and document scientific and rational ways to systematically outline the ways to make the best wine, starting in the vineyard, through fermentation, to ageing and storage. Leonardo loved his vineyard and the wine it produced and even requested that quantities were sent to him in France, where he spent the last years of his life.

Wine, clearly, was an important part of Renaissance life, and during this period wine consumption increased across all classes. Wine also came to be a feature in Renaissance art in a way that it had never quite been depicted before. The Renaissance was in large measure fuelled by a rediscovery and appreciation of classical and pre-Christian subjects that harked back to a long-lost golden age. If medieval art primarily focused on religious subjects, artists were now freer to explore themes and subjects from myths and legends. Witness the depiction of the wine god Bacchus in Renaissance art. In Michelangelo's marble sculpture, commissioned by Cardinal Raffaele Riario, Bacchus is a beautiful, androgenous deity, head tilted at an awkward angle, eyes blank and swaying slightly in inebriation, holding up a chalice of wine as if to offer it to you or me and supported in his unsteadiness by a little satyr nibbling on a bunch of grapes. Considering that in Christian belief, such a beautiful chalice would hold the precious Holy Eucharist containing the blood of Christ, this must have been an iconoclastic depiction indeed.

In Caravaggio's *Bacchus*, painted perhaps a century later, Bacchus also seems to offer us a sip from a chalice of wine, in this case a delicate stemmed wine cup made from Murano glass, a seductive invitation to share wine and, who knows, perhaps something more? A toga is draped over a shoulder, almost falling off, and his bare, hairless chest is smooth yet strong, making us

141

want to reach out and stroke the young deity. He wears a garland made from a grape vine, and before him there is a bowl of fresh and rotting fruit, a bulbous, glistening glass carafe of wine that invites us to pour, to drink. The *carpe diem* sense of rather dissolute and passive sadness this Bacchus exudes is a warning of the fleetingness of life, and the need to drink, to embrace, to love and to be merry while we are still able.

Titian's *Bacchanal of the Andrians* depicts a classical scene of wanton abandonment. A naked, voluptuous female—human or nymph?—lies back in seeming orgasmic bliss; a couple look at each other longingly, soon surely to embark into the woods to enjoy carnal acts of pleasure; wine carafes and cups are held aloft; jugs are being emptied; a little boy urinates in glee; in the distance, a ship sails away. In the centre foreground, there is a musical score with the written lyrics, 'He who drinks and does not drink again does not know what drinking is.' Could there ever have been a more compelling or convincing argument of the power and glory of that most wondrous of all beverages, wine?

The depiction of wine in Renaissance art is apparent not only in classical themes but also in religious works covering such subjects as the Last Supper, the Wedding at Cana and the Drunkenness of Noah. One element that humanism brought to Renaissance art was that such narratives took place often in secular settings with detailed elements that reflect contemporary life. In *The Last Supper*, the fresco painted by da Vinci for the Santa Maria delle Grazie Church in Milan, restoration in the 1990s revealed that the table is laid with dishes, plates, even salt cellars, and the food is shown in remarkable detail, including a platter of grilled eel garnished with orange. Each apostle has a wineglass, and the wine is red. The Last Supper was not only when Christ reveals that he will be betrayed; it is also the moment when, according to the Gospel of St Mark, Jesus 'took a cup, and when he had given thanks, he gave to them: and they all drank of it. And he said unto them, "This is my blood of the covenant, which is poured out for many."' The classic composition of Leonardo's masterpiece shows perspective that came to define the Renaissance, with all the apostles seated on the same side of the table looking out, with Christ centrally seated in a geometric dining hall with a vanishing point that leads to the grey-green countryside in the distance.

Contrast this to the much busier, more riotous representation of the same important moment that Paolo Veronese painted for the Dominican refectory of Santi Giovanni e Paolo in Venice. The painting is immense, displayed today on an entire wall in the Accademia Gallery, showing an almost out-of-control Venetian banquet. There are dozens of people in the painting, not just the apostles but also servants, hangers on, dogs, dwarfs and drunkards. The apostles, clad in velvet and silk, in a luxurious hall with marble floors and Corinthian pillars, hold delicate Murano glass stemware, and there are carafes and silver pitchers on the table. So outrageous was this depiction of such a sacred moment that it was brought to the attention of the Holy Office of the Inquisition, empowered by the Council of Trent to stamp out heresies in response to the Protestant Reformation. This return to religious orthodoxy meant that Veronese was asked to make certain 'corrections' to his composition. He chose instead to ignore the authorities and simply changed the title, calling the painting *The Feast in the House of Levi*.

Granduca Cosimo III de' Medici's Il bando

The Medici were connoisseurs of wine, certainly, but they also appreciated that quality was the route to commercial success, and they worked hard to promote the wines of Tuscany. It is therefore fitting that it was a Medici, Granduca Cosimo III, who is credited in 1716 with the creation of Italy's first legislative example of *denominazione di origine controllata* when he published his *Il bando*, a document that identified the delimited zones for the production of Carmignano, Chianti, Pomino and Valdarno di Sopra wines and stipulated how they were to be produced as well as how they were to be kept unadulterated from other wines to recognise their territorial importance and value.

Wine and art, wine and commerce: the Medici were rulers, patrons, artists, farmers and agronomists. Wine, good Tuscan wine, lubricated their thoughts, actions and lives and brought them pleasure, power and riches.

The Wines

Ser Biagio, Barco Reale di Carmignano DOC, Tenuta di Artimino, Carmignano, Tuscany

The Medici Villa, 'La Ferdinanda', known also as 'the villa of a hundred chimneys', stands in a commanding position dominating the small *borgo* (hamlet) of Artimino and looking out across the surrounding Carmignano wine country. Built for Ferdinando I de' Medici, grand duke of Tuscany, he installed his entire court here in 1594. With Lorenzo Il Magnifico's Villa di Poggio a Caiano and another family hunting lodge at Bacchereto, these wine hills west of Florence were clearly the favoured retreat for the Medici across generations. Indeed, Cosimo I de' Medici, father to Ferdinando I, had already declared a delimited zone in this area to be royal property and constructed some 40 kilometres of stone walls to enclose the so-called Barco Reale as a royal hunting preserve and woodland.

In the gardens and farmland of their country villas, the Medici loved to experiment with agriculture and viticulture. It is probable that they introduced more than one hundred different foreign grape varieties to the zone, including many from France. It is said that Catherine de' Medici, wife to King Henry II of France, first brought Cabernet Sauvignon to the Carmignano wine hills. What is certain is that this favoured French grape variety has long been cultivated here, to be blended alongside Sangiovese for the favoured red wines of Carmignano.

Today, the Tenuta di Artimino owns the Villa 'La Ferdinanda', now a luxury hotel and restaurant. Of the estate's 700 hectares of land, some 70 hectares are given over to viticulture. The flagship wines are its Carmignano DOCG and single-vineyard Carmignano Grumarello Riserva DOCG. Ser Biagio Barco Reale DOC is somewhat lighter, less challenging for a lunchtime beverage, but it is a well-respected wine all the same. Like Carmignano, it is produced from a blend of Sangiovese, the great native grape of Tuscany, and Cabernet Sauvignon together with the addition of just a little Merlot, which adds ripe, juicy fruit. Fermented and aged in stainless-steel not wood, this is a wine to be enjoyed young, while still fresh and exuberant. It is a perfect partner to salty, cured Tuscan *salumi* or to meats such as *bistecca alla fiorentina* (the classic Tuscan T-bone, grilled over a wood fire). Or perhaps it's just one of those deliciously light and delightful wines to drink in copious and joyous quantity, a wine that encourages us to dance, make love and merriment, as in Titian's *Bacchanal of the Andrians*. Could there be anything better?

Villa di Capezzana, Carmignano DOCG, Tenuta Capezzana, Carmignano, Tuscany

Tenuta Capezzana, the flagship estate of the small and prestigious Carmignano wine zone, is one of the oldest wine estates in Italy in continuous production. A parchment document discovered in the Florentine state archives dated 804 CE testifies that vineyards and olive groves were cultivated here in that far-off time, indicating over 1,000 years of activity for the production of wine and olive oil. But this is rich Etruscan country, so it is probable that these same products have been produced here for perhaps as long as 3,000 years. Since 1920, the estate has been in the more than capable hands of the inspirational noble Contini Bonacossi family.

Cosimo III de' Medici's *Il bando* may well have defined Carmignano wine and recognised the value of allowing 'foreign' grape varieties introduced by the Medici into the blend. In fact, it was the Contini Bonacossi family that can be credited with the creation of modern Carmignano, establishing it in the top echelon of Tuscan wines and giving it an important international profile. I recall Conte Ugo explaining to us over a glass of his wine that the introduction of Cabernet Sauvignon into the permitted blend for Carmignano came about because he had been the first to cultivate Cabernet Sauvignon in his vineyard, the vines filched, no less, on a visit to his friend Baron Eric de Rothschild's estate, Château Lafite in Bordeaux.

Villa di Capezzana di Carmignano DOCG is the estate's flagship and part of the very history of the Contini Bonacossi family at Capezzana. There are bottles in the cellar that date back to the 1925 vintage. A blend of 80 per cent Sangiovese and 20 per cent Cabernet Sauvignon, Villa di Capezzana predates the creation of the so-called 'Super Tuscan' wines in the 1970s and demonstrates how successful this blend of the local with the international can be: elegant, refined, with sweet almost spicy aromas, soft in the mouth with a balance of tannin and acidity that allows it to age gracefully and a finish that is long and persistent.

S.to Ippolito, Toscana IGT, Leonardo da Vinci SpA, Vinci, Tuscany

Leonardo da Vinci SpA was created as a union of Italian wineries under the Caviro Group with the goal of promoting history and winemaking excellence through a combination of winemaking projects, culture and oenogastronomy. Its mission is not only to pay homage to Leonardo but also to further rational thought and approaches to winemaking using the knowledge we have today allied with a reinterpretation of the thoughts and observations that Leonardo put down relating to the growing of grapes, the harvest, vinification and ageing of wines. This project is known as the 'Metodo Leonardo', and it is an ongoing scientific research programme.

Meanwhile, Leonardo da Vinci SpA is producing a range of wines inspired by Leonardo and bearing labels that depict his works, wines that are winning prestigious awards. The Villa da Vinci series of wines is produced from grapes grown in the vineyard surrounding the Villa da Vinci where Leonardo spent his childhood. S.to Ippolito Toscana IGT is produced from 40 per cent Sangiovese, 30 per cent Merlot and 30 per cent Syrah fermented in stainless-steel—a closed fermentation vessel, as Leonardo wished, who feared that otherwise the essence of a wine might 'dissipate into the air and all that remains is a flavourless liquid'—then aged in mainly new oak *barriques* for up to eighteen months. The wine that results has a Tuscan character that comes from the Sangiovese, yet the international grapes give a rounder texture and a spicy richness with notes of balsamic herbs, mint, vanilla and spices. Its harmony, elegance and balance epitomise Vitruvian Man, perfectly proportioned, a humanistic blend of art allied with science and technology.

14

MERCHANTS OF VENICE

The gondola may be the symbol of Venice, but equally emblematic is the Venetian water taxi, the long, varnished mahogany craft upholstered elegantly inside, the deep rumble of its powerful diesel engine the epitome of luxury and tradition combined with power. Our driver picks us up near our hotel on the Zattere, and we sit outside at the very back of the craft, smugly enjoying a watery journey that takes us past Santa Maria della Salute, then on to the Grand Canal. San Marco and the Doge's Palace glide by, as do famous hotels like the Gritti Palace and the Danieli, and then we cross through the city by way of the Arsenale, the former shipyard for the most powerful maritime republic in the Mediterranean. Once on the other side, the water taxi speeds up as we follow the channel markers past San Michele and Murano, and so on to our destination, the small and little visited island of Mazzorbo. We are now far from the bustle and the crowds of Venice; here, amid the Venetian lagoon, it is astonishingly quiet and calm.

We have come to this low-lying island to discover a vineyard planted with Dorona grapes, a variety that has quite probably been here since the time of the doges, tenacious, able to survive even inundation from acqua alta, *the regular flooding of brackish seawater. If Venice is a city like no other, Venissa, the wine produced from Dorona, is utterly unique too. Deep gold in colour, at once invigorating and salty at the same time, it is a wine that could only have come from the unique, watery terroir of the Venetian lagoon.*

The History

Venice, say many, is the most romantic city in the world, yet its origins are born from an emotion far more compelling even than love: fear. The legendary foundation of Venice is dated at 421 CE, a time when terrified refugees

147

from the mainland, fleeing barbarian invasions that hastened the fall of the Roman Empire, came to settle on the shifting mudbanks, islets and sandbanks of the shallow Venetian lagoon. As the hordes of Germanic tribes descended over the Alps, those living in the north-east corner of the Italian Peninsula were particularly vulnerable to the rapacious pillaging carried out by the hirsute invaders from the north. Previously, the lagoon had only been the preserve of fisherfolk and salt gatherers who were adept at exploiting the rich natural resources of this watery habitat. But now people felt compelled to leave behind their safe lives on the fertile plains of the Veneto to adapt to a new way of life, simply to survive.

If previously they had returned to their former homes once the danger had passed, gradually and increasingly some chose to stay as conditions on the mainland remained uncertain and dangerous. And besides, it seems many took to this new life on the water, labouring to transform an inhospitable habitat by interweaving osier branches to secure the mud and raise the height of the land so that it could be built on securely, thus constructing their *casoni*—humble huts made of mud and wattle. They reclaimed land on which to grow vegetables and brought livestock to the islands. They planted fruit trees and vineyards, and they made their own wine. Self-sufficiency grew out of necessity, the pressing need for safety and security. But more and more the insular people of the lagoon came to love what this harsh environment could produce and give them in abundance.

If the people of the lagoon became literally insular, turning their backs to the *terraferma* mainland from whence danger had come and still lurked, they learned instead to look seaward, to the east. They dredged the winding channels of the lagoon and constructed boats that could navigate the Adriatic, and they began to trade with their neighbours, profiting from the natural riches of their lagoon habitat, mainly fish and salt.

Theodoric the Ostrogoth had entered Italy ostensibly at the request of Byzantine Emperor Zeno. By the time he was installed at Ravenna in 524 CE, the people of the Venetian lagoon were no longer just cowering there as a place of refuge but were already considered an independent force to be respected. The Roman chronicler and statesman Cassiodorus in a famous letter composed in 537 CE to the *tribuni maritimi* (maritime tribunes) of Venice wrote poetically and approvingly about the unique Venetian way of life:

> You live like birds with your homes dispersed, like the Cyclades, across the surface of the water. The solidity of the earth on which they rest is secured only by osier and wattle. Your people have one great wealth, the fish which

suffices for them all. Be diligent, therefore, to repair your boats—which, like horses, you keep tied up at the doors of your dwellings.

Following Theodoric's death, Emperor Justinian sought to reassert Byzantine authority by restoring the glory of the Western Empire. He sent his great general Belisarius to achieve this end. Belisarius requested the Venetians to assist by making their harbours available for Byzantine ships. Later, the Venetians were asked to help Belisarius's successor, the eunuch Narses, by bringing a troop of mercenaries by sea to Ravenna. Narses, in return, repaid their fealty with the construction of two churches on the island of Rivo Alto. Emperor Longinus paid a visit to the Venetian lagoon, and afterwards Venetian ambassadors accompanied him to Constantinople, returning with the first formal accord between Venice and the Eastern Empire. Thus, even from this early time, Venice's gaze was turned to the east, its fortunes more firmly linked to those of Byzantium than to Rome.

When the Lombards descended into Italy in 568, the island communities of the Venetian lagoon grew once again as they became a refuge for yet more fleeing from the latest set of invaders from the north. The small island of Torcello grew in importance and became the richest, most advanced of all the communities of the lagoon. By 639, a basilica in honour of the Virgin Mary had been erected. Mazzorbo is another island that was one of the earliest settlements in the lagoon, its prosperity predating the settlement of Venice on the island of Rivo Alto. Though but a tiny island, Mazzorbo grew in importance for its religious settlements and eventually supported five monasteries and five parish churches.

Gradually and then more quickly, the people of the Venetian lagoon came together to form a political entity known to its inhabitants by the plural Venetiae. It was at first loosely under the Exarchate of Ravenna, the representative of the Byzantine emperor, who appointed the *dux*—'doge' in Venetian dialect—as a subservient vassal. After the Lombards had been chased out of Italy by the next set of marauders, the Franks, Charlemagne, working his way through the Veneto and into the former Lombard stronghold of Friuli, mounted two failed assaults on Venice, defeated not only by the prowess of the Venetians but also by mosquitoes that spread malaria to his troops. Eventually, the Franks under Charlemagne's son Pepin gave up, in the process leaving Venice excluded from the jurisdiction of the Holy Roman Empire.

The Venetian lagoon, meanwhile, continued to be settled as people moved increasingly from outlying islet communities in greater numbers to Rivo Alto

('Rialto'), which was located in the very centre of the lagoon and was by now the seat of the duchy. Venetian maritime prowess continued to develop not primarily for military reasons—though protection especially from the pirates who roamed the Adriatic was essential—but mainly to develop commerce and trade, for Venice was uniquely poised to serve as a link between East and West, bringing splendours from the former to the markets of the latter.

The Venetians, it turned out, were extraordinary entrepreneurs: over the course of centuries, that loose confederation of island communities, originally made up of fisherfolk and salt gatherers, had transformed itself into a maritime republic and the greatest trading nation in the Mediterranean. Good governance was one factor that enabled this. While other parts of Italy found themselves under the despotic rule of family dynasties or intertwined in struggles such as that between Guelph and Ghibelline, Venice mainly avoided such internecine conflict, preferring instead to get on with its maritime activities, especially commerce, and the serious business of making money.

When enterprising Venetian merchants, landing in Alexandria in the ninth century, somehow contrived to steal the corpse of Saint Mark from its burial place, wrapping the body in pork fat to deter inspection by Muslims, they returned to Venice in triumph, bringing with them a patron saint who could rival even Rome's Saint Peter. The Basilica of Saint Mark, originally meant to be the private chapel of the doge, was constructed to house the remains of the saint, a magnificent building that is considered the greatest of all Italo-Byzantine churches. The lion, emblem of Saint Mark, wise and divine, sometimes with paw on a book or scroll, soon became the symbol of Venice itself, its image and effigy found wherever Venetian power and influence held sway.

This was still an uneasy time, when power and allegiance shifted between the might of the Holy Roman Emperor, the papacy and the Byzantine Empire. Venice's proud independent position was precarious, yet by the early thirteenth century, supreme confidence in its own might and power had grown to such a degree that the Venetians, in charge of transporting Frankish knights to the Fourth Crusade, had the audacity to divert to Constantinople before reaching their destination in Muslim-controlled Jerusalem, ostensibly to assist in the restoration of a deposed emperor. Their forces were led by the septuagenarian Doge Enrico Dandolo himself, who thirty years earlier had endured imprisonment and humiliation under the Byzantines when he went to Constantinople as an emissary on a peace mission after the Byzantines had imprisoned Venetian merchant residents, confiscated their property and possessions, and expelled them from their city. Dandolo's mission then had been an utter failure; now the old war horse, blind though he was (he possibly lost his eyesight at the hands of Byzantines), was determined to get his revenge. The Crusaders under their Venetian ruler shamefully sacked and plundered Constantinople in 1204, a shocking act since the city was under the rule of Christians not the infidel. Now it was the turn of the Venetians to become rapacious plunderers and pillagers, like those invaders from the north from whom they had originally fled to the lagoon. The sack of Constantinople brought untold spoils and riches and consolidated Venetian power and influence.

Monemvasia and the Venetian wine trade

Venetian might, if not absolute, was now paramount across the Eastern Mediterranean, and Venice was no longer just another Italian city-state; it became a colonial power, with holdings that eventually extended from Dalmatia to the Black Sea, including Crete, Corfu, Cyprus, Salonika, Cephalonia and more.

One important holding that came under Venetian rule was Monemvasia, a fortified island just off the Greek Peloponnese. Monemvasia (the name means 'port with one entrance') came to be the source of a strong, sweet and aromatic raisined wine that grew to be hugely popular and hence hugely profitable. Because it was a *passito* wine made from dried grapes not fresh, it was robust enough to be able to withstand transport by sea without spoilage, and so merchants brought it back to Venice to sell there as well as to trade across Italy and all Northern Europe. The first citation for a wine from 'Monemvasios' was in 1214 in a communication with an archbishop from Ephesus, and it was soon referenced in many documents under a variety of names: Monobascia, Monobasià, Malevasie, Malvoisie, Malvasia, Malvagia, Malvaxia, Monavaxia, Malfasia. It became immediately popular, almost as a Venetian brand, and to meet a near insatiable demand they eventually transferred its production to the more productive island of Crete, which they called Candia.

The magic, marketable name of Malvasia, the name that eventually became the most widely used, encouraged other areas to produce their own 'Malvasia' wines, and for that reason there are today any number of Malvasia grape varieties cultivated not only across Italy—from Friuli's Carso in the northeast to Lipari, an Aeolian island off Sicily—but also elsewhere, in France, Spain, Portugal and even on islands off Africa such as Madeira. Indeed, so important did trade in wine—Malvasia and others—come to be that many streets, alleyways, *sottoportegos* (passageways that go under a building) and bridges in Venice were named after Malvasia as well as after wine in general: Sottoportego di Malvasia, Ponte della Malvasia, Calle dell'Uva, Riva del Vin, Riva del Ribolla and so on. Malvasia even had its own harbourside, the Fondaco delle Malvasie, from where Malvasia wines were loaded and unloaded from the great Venetian trading galleys that plied the Mediterranean. I wonder, was it a Malvasia from Venice that Shakespeare had in mind when in his play *Richard III* poor George Plantagenet, duke of Clarence, is drowned in a butt of Malmsey wine?

'What news on the Rialto?'

By the time Marco Polo returned from his sojourn in China in 1299, Venice had grown into the greatest trading nation in Europe. The lagoon settlement of Rivo Alto had now become the main island city, and the Rialto itself was the financial and commercial heart of Venice, a global emporium for the trade of goods from around the known world and a centre for innovative banking and finance. Venetians traded in Constantinople and across North Africa; they travelled overland to trade fairs in Champagne and struck bargains with cloth merchants in the Low Countries; they brought silk from China, wool from England and damask from Syria; and they traded wine, often bartering it in exchange for other goods.

The Venetians thus grew fabulously rich on the proceeds of trade and commerce. Indeed, they were more than happy to deal in any commodity that would bring in profit, and not just wine or exotic spices or beautiful fabrics, silks and damask. It seems that one of the most profitable of all activities was slavery, the human trafficking of not just infidels or people from Africa but even Christians, sold into servitude or prostitution, always at the highest prices.

On these proceeds, Venetian merchants built fabulous *palazzi* of marble and stone, creating some of the most brilliant domestic architecture the world had ever seen. Some were constructed in the Byzantine-Gothic architectural style unique to Venice, while others were built to Renaissance and Neoclassical designs, the latter championed by Venetian architects such as Jacopo Sansovino and Palladio. These palaces were not just status symbols for the wealthy; they were also functional, with ground floors serving as warehouses and sometimes as shops. Above, the private dwellings were magnificently grand, illuminated by the light of Murano glass chandeliers, and with high windows and sometimes loggias that looked down on the most beautiful 'street' in the world, the Grand Canal.

Venice terraferma

By the fifteenth century, the Maritime Republic of Venice, known also as La Serenissima, not only ruled over a maritime empire that extended across the Eastern Mediterranean but had also turned its attentions inland to become a landed state. Thus, the Lion of St Mark exerted a mainly benign influence over an extensive area of North-East Italy, including cities such as Verona, Padua, Vicenza, Udine and Treviso, and across the regions known today as Veneto as well as Friuli–Venezia Giulia.

In 1501, the Portuguese navigator Vasco da Gama, using the lateen sail perfected by Prince Henry the Navigator, managed to sail around the Cape of Good Hope to reach India. Though the Venetians did not know it at the time, this auspicious achievement marked in a sense the beginning of the end, as from then on Venice would begin to lose its near-monopoly on the trade in spices and other precious goods from the east that it had previously been able to command. Furthermore, Venetian maritime prowess and military might was no longer what it once was, and territories were increasingly being lost to the Ottoman Turks. The island of Crete, for example, which had become the main source of Malvasia wine to be traded through Venice, was lost to the Ottomans in 1669.

As Venice gradually lost its control and influence over the Adriatic and the Eastern Mediterranean that its fleet had once commanded and dominated, its inland *terraferma* hinterland became more and more important commercially. The fabled and luscious Malvasia wines that Venetian traders had brought back in laden ships to send across Italy and to Northern Europe needed to be replaced with versions of wines produced from grapes grown in its own territories so that the Venetian brand of 'Malvasia' wines could continue to be marketed across the continent. If the wines were not necessarily made from a common grape variety, they still needed to be created in the Venetian style that consumers had come to value and love, and, importantly, that were robust enough to be able to withstand voyage by either sea or overland. This required the production of sweet wines usually made from raisined grapes that were lightly aromatic and often with a characteristic slightly bitter finish. Such wines came to be produced across the Veneto, for example from Vespaiolo grapes grown around Breganze, as well as from far off places such as the Aeolian island of Lipari, which today continues to be the source of Malvasia delle Lipari, a wine that remains precisely the sort of sweet, robust, navigable wine that the Venetians prized so highly.

Decline and decadence

Despite its efforts, the loss of its influence across the Eastern Mediterranean inevitably caused the sources of Venetian wealth to begin to diminish. Yet still life and art continued to flourish, and Venice managed to eke out something of a golden age of entertainment and pleasure. This was the era, after all, of the Baroque, a style that glorified excess as manifested in florid and complex façades such as that of Santa Maria della Salute, overblown palaces and ostentatious and sentimental statuary. It was a time, too, when wealthy Europeans embarked on their Grand Tours, making their way to Venice to see, discover and experience for themselves what was long reputed to be the most beautiful and alluring of all European cities, the start of a long love–hate affair between Venetians and the tourists. And if Venetian trade and commerce had gone into decline, there were still other ways to make a living for the enterprising: Venice, even then called the city of love, became known for its cultured courtesans, women who were not only the most beautiful in Europe but who were knowledgeable in the arts of poetry, music, literature, love, seduction and passion.

Thus, throughout its long and slow decline, Venice revelled in a golden age. The playwright Carlo Goldoni wrote some of Italy's best-loved theatrical pieces. Antonio Vivaldi, head of music in a girls' orphanage, was a prolific composer, creating an astonishing repertoire of new works that earned him a fortune. The painter Giovanni Antonio Canal, known as Canaletto, made Venice itself, or perhaps the world's idea of Venice, the central subject of his work rather than just the background. The sculptor Antonio Canova produced pieces of polished marble so beautiful and perfect that he became the most celebrated artist of his age. The libertine and writer Giacomo Casanova expressed the life and mores of Venice, the pleasure capital of Europe, in the most vivid and shocking detail in his twelve-volume *Histoire de ma vie* (The Story of my Life).

Eventually, Napoleon Bonaparte put a stop to the endless party that Venice had been hosting for itself. On 12 May 1797, the Great Council met in the Doge's Palace for the last time and voted to surrender to the diminutive Corsican general with 'the object of preserving unharmed the religion, life and property of all those most beloved inhabitants'. Thus, the curtain shut on 1,100 years of proud independence. Napoleon and his troops entered Venice and utterly plundered it of many of its most famous treasures. After Napoleon's demise, the Congress of Vienna saw La Serenissima and its rich *terraferma* hinterland ceded to the Austro-Hungarian Empire under the Habsburgs. But that is another story—and other wines, too.

The Wines

Venissa, Dorona Veneto IGT, Mazzorbo, Veneto

For almost as long as the Venetian lagoon has been inhabited, it is probable that the grapevine has been cultivated here. Viticulture was once extensive on outlying agricultural islands such as Sant'Erasmo, still the source of outstanding vegetables that grow in the sandy, saline soil, giving them a particular taste so beloved by the Venetians. Even in the densely populated islands, such as on Venice itself, vines and other crops historically were grown in the *piazze* of the city, hence the name for many of the squares as *campo* (field). It is even said that there were once vines cultivated in Piazza San Marco itself. But wine production across the Venetian lagoon ceased, as did so much else, on a fateful day, 4 November 1966, when a combination of factors—rain-swollen rivers, a fiercely bitter scirocco wind and a high astronomical spring tide—brought a devastatingly destructive *aqua alta* (an exceptionally high tide) that rose to nearly 2 metres above its normal height. All the islands of the lagoon were plunged under water, a tragic flood that brought untold damage, hardship and loss of livelihood. The destruction of Venetian viticulture, minor as it was, was probably the least of anyone's worries, and at that time, it was deemed not worth replanting vineyards given the cost and the risk, since plentiful wine from the Veneto mainland was widely available at inexpensive prices.

And yet, people remembered and bemoaned the loss of their own local wine, which, like the vegetables and the seafood from the lagoon, had always had its own taste and character. And some dreamed of restoring viticulture to the Venetian lagoon once more. I recall Gianluca Bisol, a visionary winemaker from the classic Veneto heartland of Prosecco Superiore, explaining the Venetian project to me before a single vine had even been planted. He recounted that in 2002, while visiting the island of Torcello, one of the earliest settlements of the lagoon, he noticed an abandoned grape vine. It piqued his curiosity and made him want to explore more. Bisol's research led him to discover that vines had been planted on many of the islands of the lagoon for hundreds and maybe even thousands of years. Even after the great flood of 1966, pockets of vines remained here and there. One such variety that he discovered during his research was Dorona di Venezia, an ancient autochthonous grape that was apparently particularly well adapted to be able to be cultivated in the saline terroir of the lagoon.

Bisol next identified the island of Mazzorbo, adjacent to Burano, as a suitable habitat on which to plant a vineyard. The island, once busy and important, is today barely inhabited, its fields and garden tended by the pensioners

155

who live there. On the site of a medieval monastery, in the shadow of a leaning *campanile* or bell tower, and in a walled close surrounded on three sides by the lagoon, Bisol found less than a hectare of sandy, mineral-rich soil in which to plant a vineyard. The Dorona vines took to this new habitat and indeed proved able to withstand the flooding that happens every two or three years. Eventually yielding a first harvest in 2010, the Dorona grapes were hand-harvested and transported in small crates by boat to the mainland, where they were transformed into wine.

Venissa, the unique and precious white wine that resulted, continues to be made according to Venetian tradition. The white grapes are vinified on the skins in the manner of a red wine. Fermentation is long and slow with the use of a traditional winemaking method known as *follatura* whereby the grape skins that float to the top of a vat are punched down manually with sticks over the course of thirty days, thus helping to extract structure, tannin and flavour. Only 4,880 bottles were produced from that first vintage, but the wine was an immediate success.

Venissa not only connects to the ancient tradition of viticulture in the lagoon, it also celebrates the artisan traditions of Venice. For example, the Berta Battiloro family are the last Venetian *battiloro* who by hand painstakingly hammer gold into fine gold leaf. The Spezzamonte family take these sheets of beaten gold leaf supplied by the Bertas and fuse them on to glass bottles in their Murano furnaces, each pattern of gold leaf serving as a unique 'label' that denotes the different vintages. Every bottle furthermore is hand-engraved with the bottle number. Thus, the Venissa Dorona bottle itself is a beautiful work of art that is a product of Venetian culture and artisanship. It is not surprising that with such precise care of both history and tradition, Venissa immediately became an exclusive and highly sought-after collector's item, prized by lovers of Venetian culture as well as lovers of Italian wine. And Venissa the wine? Quite simply, it is sublime. I have now tasted four vintages, each subtly different yet with an immense character that is unique: deep gold in colour, slightly oxidised on the nose, bone dry, with fresh minerality, notes of dried peel, caramel, butterscotch, toasted almonds and an exceedingly long and persistent saline aftertaste. Venissa is a very special wine to simply sip and wonder, a wine truly fit for a doge, or for salt gatherers, fishermen or hopelessly romantic lovers: Venissa, the golden wine of the Venetian lagoon.

Malvasia delle Lipari DOC passito, Carlo Hauner, Salina, Sicily

When the island of Crete, known as Candia to the Venetians, was lost to the Ottoman Turks in 1669, the Venetians had to turn elsewhere for the production of their beloved and highly profitable Malvasia wine. It appears that around that time a type of Malvasia grape was introduced into the Aeolian island of Salina and came to be used to produce just such a sweet dessert wine made from raisined grapes in order to be able to export it for sale in markets created by the Venetian demand. As the Venetians still controlled this part of the Mediterranean, they were thus able to continue with their trade, bringing the wine to markets in Northern Europe.

In 1963, the late Carlo Hauner, originally from Brescia, moved to the island to paint as well as to grow grapes and make wine. Over time, he restored abandoned vineyards, repaired ancient and abandoned terraces and experimented with both ancient and innovative winemaking techniques. The Malvasia delle Lipari that he began to produce—both *naturale* and *passito* versions—gained national and international acclaim and was soon being hailed as one of the great traditional wines of Italy. Today, the estate is run by Carlo Hauner's son Carlo Jr, wife Cristina and sons Andrea and Michele.

To produce Malvasia delle Lipari *passito*, the Hauners late-harvest Malvasia delle Lipari grapes and then lay them out to dry on cane mats in the sun for fifteen to twenty days. The sugar-rich grape must then ferment with some skin contact in temperature-controlled stainless-steel vessels. The wine that results is a beautiful amber colour, sweet but not cloyingly so, with notes of dried fruits, dates, apricots, honey. This, without doubt, is one of Italy's historic and truly magnificent dessert wines, first created in a time when the merchants of Venice ruled the waves.

Campofiorin, Rosso del Veronese IGT, Masi Agricola, Sant'Ambrogio di Valpolicella, Veneto

When Marco Polo journeyed across Asia, along what came to be known as the Silk Road, he returned with tales of wonder from a far-off and exotic land, China. Marco Polo was one of Venice's great merchants and entrepreneurs, one who was willing to venture into the unknown to discover new cultures, civilisations and markets.

In the decade after the death of Mao Zedong, when China was just emerging from a period of isolation from the rest of the world, Dr Sandro Boscaini, an intrepid Venetian winemaker and trader, saw the opportunity to be one of the first to visit China to bring the wines of his family company, Masi Agricola, to a new and emerging market. The Hotel Kempinski had only recently opened in Beijing, with a restaurant called 'Gondola'. Boscaini proposed that he would transport a real Venetian gondola to the restaurant as a gift provided that the hotel would give him the opportunity to have a week-long festival of Venetian wine and food. This was agreed, and he packed 650 cases of wine into the container that held the gondola. He invited his friend, the rice grower and rice expert Gabriele Ferron of the Antica Riseria Ferron, to join him. Imagine the audacity of this venture, which set out to teach the Chinese how to cook rice—and not any old rice, *vialone nano* grown in the rice paddies of Verona, to be prepared Venetian style as risotto. The week-long festival of Venetian wine and food was a huge success. At first, it was the international visitors who came along. Then, the secretary of the Communist Party and other officials were curious to see this wonder, and as the days went on, increasingly the ordinary people of Beijing, old and young, families, ventured out, ever more curious to see a real gondola and to learn about Venetian wine and food. For indeed the Masi wines were the first from the Veneto to be exported to China. The week was a great success, and Ferron even went on to cook risotto on the Great Wall.

One of the wines that went on that first journey to China was Campofiorin, which has been produced since 1964. It too is a wine that was a pioneer, for its creation led to an entirely new category of wines from Valpolicella—the *ripasso* style. In the 1960s, Valpolicella was still considered mainly a relatively light, easy to drink red wine made from a blend of grapes including Corvina, Molinara, Rondinella and others. Amarone della Valpolicella, by contrast, was made from those same grapes but only after they had undergone a period of *appassimento*. The Venetian genius of Boscaini was to use a by-product that would otherwise have gone to waste—the grape pomace of dried grape residue that was left over after the fermentation of Amarone—to create a new style of wine that has come to be known as *Ripasso*. To produce this, the Amarone grape pomace is used to refresh and enrich the lighter Valpolicella wines by 'repassing' them over this still wine-drenched grape pomace once it had been removed from the Amarone vats. This extra process added the raisiny softness and richness of the dried grapes, as well as an extra degree or so of alcohol, resulting in a wine that was somewhere in between, richer and bigger than straight Valpolicella but not as complex or richly powerful as Amarone. Importantly, too, it could be sold at a price that was interesting and affordable.

Masi and the Boscaini family have constantly evolved Campofiorin over the decades, too. For example, now the process no longer makes use of the used grape pomace left over from Amarone. Rather, after the initial fermentation of fresh Corvina, Molinara and Rondinella grapes, some 30 per cent of whole, semi-dried grapes of those same varieties is used to provoke a double fermentation that extracts greater colour and aroma as well as an increase in alcohol, together with softer and more refined tannins. The result is a beautifully soft and rich red wine with the strong characteristic aroma and flavour of black cherries that is the hallmark of Valpolicella.

Campofiorin is not only a great wine; it is also a fitting tribute to the enduring Venetian spirit of innovation, trade and commercial entrepreneurship that can be traced back to Marco Polo and the intrepid merchants of Venice who brought prosperity and wealth to this uniquely beautiful, watery city.

15

SPANISH ITALY

I'm in the restaurant of Su Gologone, a wayside inn in Sardinia's harsh interior hinterland known as the Barbagia. On the hearth, porceddu allo spiedo—*spit-roasted suckling pig—is revolving over hot embers, the spits expertly turned to cook the succulent meat just right. Elsewhere, women are making* pane carasau, *large, round discs of bread that are as thin and durable as parchment, a flat, crunchy bread that has always served as the staple for the* pastori—*the shepherds—who take it with them into the high slopes where they tend their flocks. A platter of the juicy, succulent, wood-cooked meat is placed before us to enjoy with the crunchy and typical bread. The wine to wash down this meat feast is Cannonau di Sardegna, made from the Garnacha grape first introduced to the island by the Spanish during their centuries-long occupation (or could it, perhaps, have been the other way round, with the variety being introduced from Sardinia to Spain and France?). The wine is vivid, juicy, warm and fleshy, a perfect accompaniment to the fatty, rich meat that we devour greedily with our hands, a little bit of meat juice, a drop or two of red wine maybe dribbling down our chins. But who cares? It is delicious, and the way that food and wine should best be enjoyed.*

The History

Bologna's Piazza Maggiore is one of the most impressive civic spaces in Italy, flanked by the Palazzo d'Accursio, the Palazzo del Podestà, the Fountain of Neptune and the Basilica of San Petronio. Imagine the scene here on 24 February 1530 when the people of Bologna along with the considerable imperial and papal entourages came together for the coronation of Charles V, who was crowned Holy Roman Emperor by Pope Clement VII in San

Petronio, one of the largest churches in all of Christendom. Only three years earlier, Rome had been sacked by Charles's unruly and mutinous troops. Countless works of precious art had been destroyed, and the event is now considered the symbolic end of the Renaissance. It is quite understandable that Charles, wary of retaliation, did not want to go to Rome for his coronation. Bologna was the most important city in the Papal States after the Holy See, a centre of prestige, art and learning, and so was deemed by both parties a fitting venue for such an important imperial event. It was hoped that this momentous occasion would go some way to healing the longstanding religious and political conflict that had divided Italy and Europe for so long.

The preparations went on for months. Music was specially composed by Charles' court composer Nicolas Gombert, and there was much lavish feasting in a city already known as 'Bologna La Grassa'—Bologna the Fat. Charles had a fountain installed in the shape of a black eagle, the symbol of the Habsburgs, and, according to a chronicler, wine flowed freely from it throughout the day. For courtiers and cardinals as for the common man in the street, this was a grand celebration that marked an important moment in history, demonstrating the power, wealth and prestige of both emperor and pope alike.

Charles V was truly a colossus of his age, a man who through the good fortune of his birth had inherited territories that stretched almost over all of Europe. In Italy, he had already taken ownership of the south through the Kingdoms of Naples, Sicily and Sardinia, possessions of the Spanish crown he had inherited as the maternal grandson of Ferdinand and Isabella, the Catholic monarchs of Spain. It was they who had unified their own country, expelled the Moors, conquered the New World and begun the Inquisition. From his paternal grandparents, Maximilian I of the House of Habsburg, himself a Holy Roman Emperor, and Mary of Burgundy, he gained the Austro-Germanic territories of the Habsburgs across Central Europe as well as the Burgundian Lowlands. Two days before his imperial coronation, Charles had also received the Iron Crown of Lombardy, a holy relic of possibly Byzantine construction that was reputedly made from a nail used for the crucifixion of Christ. This honour also brought with it the title king of Italy. Thus, Charles, Spanish on his mother's side, Austrian on his father's, came to rule over much of Italy except for the Papal States and the Grand Duchy of Tuscany. Small but powerfully influential city-states such as the Duchies of Ferrara, Modena, Milan and Mantua all lent their support and mainly remained loyal to the Holy Roman Empire almost until the end. In this way, Spanish and indeed foreign domination over much of Italy was established that was to last for more than three centuries.

Counter Reformation and the Baroque

If the Renaissance had seen the greatest blossoming of the arts, intellectual freedom and liberal thinking since ancient times, the period of Spanish domination is often considered a much darker time. It is true that the Spaniards had initiated a brutal Inquisition in their own country. Following the Council of Trent held between 1545 and 1563 that had been prompted by the Protestant Reformation, they then brought a reign of terror across Italy. Those deemed heretics were pursued by Spanish and Italian prelates with the fervour of the righteous. Intellectuals and free thinkers were persecuted, tortured or burned at the stake and books were banned, including works by Dante, Giovanni Boccaccio, Machiavelli and others. The astronomer Galileo Galilei was imprisoned for his research into the nature of the universe. Jews were rounded up and either expelled or else segregated into ghettos. The substantial numbers of Muslims in Southern Italy and Sicily were subjected to intense efforts to convert them or else were executed or deported. Italy became a much more fearful, restrictive and less open society.

Yet at the same time, Spanish hegemony in Italy, confirmed by the departure of the French who renounced their claim to Milan in 1559, was not all regressive. The latter part of the sixteenth century brought the economic prosperity and growth that comes with peace and stability. Spanish rule in Naples saw the city enter something of a golden age, with the construction of splendid palaces, Baroque churches, a castle and the development of a district known as the Quartieri Spagnoli, or Spanish Quarter. During this period, Naples grew into Europe's second largest city after Paris and became home to such influential artists as Caravaggio and Gian Lorenzo Bernini.

The extreme Catholicism embodied by the Inquisition and deemed necessary as part of the Counter Reformation to combat the threat of Protestantism gave birth to a form of art, music and architecture that came to be known as the Baroque. The Council of Trent had included a discussion on the importance of religious art to instruct and to teach. In contrast to the simpler classicism of the Renaissance, the aim of the Baroque in a religious context was to shock and awe people into believing in the everlasting power and glory of the Catholic Church through an overtly sensorial and emotional appeal that included elements such as rich, dazzling surfaces; curvaceous and twisting features; *trompe d'oeil* painted illusions; gilded statuary and grotesque figures; and contrast between dark and light. The rebuilding of St Peter's in Rome in the Baroque style by the architect Bernini was seen as a means of re-establishing the primacy of the Church to reassert its magnificence and authority, especially for the thousands and millions of pilgrims who came to Rome during Jubilee years.

In lands under direct Spanish rule across Southern Italy and Sicily, a Baroque style evolved that was the most flamboyant of all. Lecce, in the Salentine Peninsula of Apulia, grew to be one of the most important cities in the Kingdom of Naples, and here the Baroque reached outrageous new heights. The soft Lecce stone, quarried from the limestone bedrock that also nourished the vines, was so malleable and workable that fabulous statuary as well as architectural elements could be carved and created. In Sicily's Palermo, an octagonal piazza known as the Quattro Canti was constructed in the heart of the city at the intersection of its two most important avenues. Four great buildings stand on each corner, each with its own fountain and decorated lavishly with statues of the four Spanish kings of Sicily as well as of the city's patron saints, Cristina, Ninfa, Olivia and Agata. Baroque architecture seemed particularly well suited to the Sicilian temperament, and whole cities came to be dominated by the rather repressive and dominating forms of its massive churches and monasteries. Catania, Modica, Noto and Ragusa all have such Baroque monuments that are testament to the Spanish occupation and influence.

The rich opulence of the Baroque was a demonstration of wealth and power, so it is no wonder that the Spanish aristocracy embraced it so fully across the south. Grand Spanish palaces still line the streets of Palermo and Naples today, while in small inland towns and villages there are country estates and villas built in a bombastic style to serve as an example to the peasantry of the might and grandeur of the landed rich, the Spanish nobility. The history of *latifundium* that dates to the era when Roman soldiers and senators alike were granted great tracts of agricultural land, to be worked by peasants in near slave-like conditions for landlords who were usually absent, was further exploited under the Spanish and lasted even until the last century. Indeed, for aristocratic landowners across Southern Italy and Sicily, there was little interest in agricultural reform or enlightenment: the goal was to acquire and maintain as much property and as much wealth as possible, exploiting both the land and its people.

The Spanish Habsburgs ruled Southern Italy, Sicily and Sardinia until 1700, when the last member of the family died without an heir. The War of the Spanish Succession brought a variety of rulers briefly to these areas until they fell into the hands of the Spanish Bourbons, who continued to oversee all Southern Italy and Sicily—unified as the Kingdom of the Two Sicilies in 1816—from 1734 until 1860. Under the Bourbons, the ostentatious display of wealth and power found its greatest expression in the Reggia di Caserta—the Royal Palace—modelled, like other European royal residences, on the Palace of Versailles, only even larger, more opulent and luxurious, the largest royal palace in the world in terms of volume, consisting of 44,000 square metres, 1,200 rooms, thirty-four staircases, over 1,700 windows, an observatory, chapel and miniature theatre based on Naples' Teatro San Carlo. In a country where the ordinary people, apart from the wealthy and the aristocracy, lived lives of poverty and subsistence, it was almost obscene.

The Spanish legacy remains, perhaps most obviously in foods introduced to Italy from Spain's colonies in the New World—the tomato, potato, chilli pepper, sweet pepper, prickly pear and maize. The Spanish left a strong legacy on the wines of Italy too: they introduced grape varieties that are still cultivated today such as Cannonau, the name in Sardinia for Garnacha; Carignano, which is Cariñena in Spain; and Alicante. Tintilia, Molise's most intriguing grape, was introduced by the Spanish Bourbons. The Spanish also left their mark on styles of wine still made in Italy today. The *in perpetuum* dynamic ageing of Marsala, whereby younger wines are blended with older, was introduced under the Spanish and is something similar to the solera system of sherry. Primitivo di Manduria *dolce naturale* and *liquoroso* are wines that are in the same tradition as some of the great *vinos rancios* and *vinos generosos* of Spain—high in alcohol, sometimes fortified and with a degree of oxidation. Vernaccia di Oristano, one of Sardinia's greatest and most characterful wines, matures under a layer of *flor*, a yeast that grows on the surface of the wine in partially filled oak and chestnut casks, similar to wines such as Fino sherry and Montilla.

When Ferdinand IV of the House of Bourbon, who became Ferdinando I as the first king of the Two Sicilies after his restoration in 1816 following the defeat of Napoleon, ordered the creation of his 'Vigna del Ventaglio' at San Leucio, near the famous silk works and the Reggia di Caserta, he chose to cultivate ten different grape varieties that were the most important across the Kingdom of the Two Sicilies. It was by all accounts a beautiful vineyard, a semi-circle divided into ten sections resembling a fan from which it took its name. Each section had its own entrance gateway and was planted with a different species of vine. Two of the ten varieties were native to Campania, Pallagrello Bianco and Pallagrello Rosso. According to a contemporary report: 'The wines of this district are excellent, both white and red, and are the best in the reign for their quality and nature, as well as for the pleasing sensation they leave on the palate.' The Vigna del Ventaglio was not just attractive, it was productive, yielding some eighty barrels of wine each year to go to the royal court, an indication of the importance that the Spanish ruling family attached to the careful cultivation of the grapevine.

The Wines

Mamuthone, Cannonau di Sardegna DOC, Azienda Agricola Giuseppe Sedilesu, Mamoiada, Sardinia

Wine has been made on the island of Sardinia for thousands of years: indeed, evidence of the oldest winemaking press in Western Europe was recently discovered in excavations at prehistoric Nuragic sites. Strategically located in the centre of the Tyrrhenian Sea, Sardinia was long a coveted prize for competing powers: Phoenicians, Romans, Vandals, Goths, Byzantines all fought for control over the island, as did the Republic of Pisa and the Republic of Genoa. The Aragonese conquest of Sardinia took place between 1323 and 1326 and established a Spanish presence that was to last until the island was ceded to the House of Savoy in 1720.

Was the Cannonau grape variety introduced to Sardinia by the Spanish, or did it travel the other way and become known as Garnacha once it reached Spain? Ask a Sardinian, and they will insist that it is the latter, though ampelographers—those who study, identify and classify grape vines—are not entirely convinced, some believing that this prolific and widely grown variety had its origins in Aragon. The grape is certainly at home in Sardinia, for it produces the island's greatest wine, Cannonau di Sardegna. The Barbagia, a harsh inland area mainly in the province of Nuoro, is considered the habitat best adapted to achieve the purest expression of Cannonau. This superb example comes from Giuseppe Sedilesu, a family winery located at Mamoiada. Here the old Cannonau vines, some a century in age, are trained in the *alberello* style as low-lying, freestanding bushes, situated at a dizzying 600 to 800 metres above sea level. At this rarefied height, on harsh, decayed granite soil that is rich in potassium, and on slopes that are sometimes back-breakingly steep, the mountain vines must fight for survival and send roots deep down to gain nourishment. The result is a dense, dark expression of Garnacha, a wine of real power and character, with deep red fruit, firm tannin and a characteristic marked acidity that keeps the wine fresh and vibrant. This is a wine simply to enjoy in quantity while eating simple foods such as spit-roasted *porceddu* or perhaps with a good hunk of *pecorino sardo* cheese, and some freshly baked *pane carasau*.

SPANISH ITALY

Erminia, Fiano di Avellino DOCG, Di Meo, Salza Irpina, Campania

The Spanish under the Bourbons left a strong legacy across all Southern Italy as well as Sicily. Noble aristocratic families held extensive agricultural holdings that underpinned their wealth. The princes of Caracciolo were one of the most distinguished and illustrious feudal families of the Kingdom of Naples under the Spanish Bourbons, and they lived well and abundantly. The chroniclers of the time describe lavish lunches, hunting trips, sonnet readings and succulent breakfasts of cakes, liqueurs, coffee, chocolate and other delicious treats served to the new king Charles III when he visited the Caracciolo family on 5 January 1735. All of this, however, was to end in 1806 when Napoleon conquered the Kingdom of Naples.

Today, a hunting lodge of the Bourbon princes of Carracciolo in Irpinia serves as the headquarters for the Azienda Agricola Di Meo. This grand, classically designed eighteenth-century country house, located in an area still rich in woodland where game animals are hunted, is historic evidence of the lives of the aristocracy in the era under the Bourbons. Did the Caracciolo princes drink and enjoy the wines of Irpinia when they stayed in their lodge? No doubt they did, for this part of inland Campania, about 15 kilometres east of Avellino, has been extolled for the excellence of its wines since antiquity. Certainly, grapes were cultivated here under the Spanish Bourbons, and the best wines, as always, would have found their way to the dining tables of the aristocracy and the ruling classes.

Today, the Di Meos have lovingly restored the hunting lodge, and, in addition to serving as the company base and cellar, it is now a luxurious country residence where corporate and private events are held. The Di Meo estate extends over some 25 hectares, mostly cultivated with Fiano, Greco and Aglianico wines to produce a prestigious range of the classic wines of Irpinia: Fiano di Avellino DOCG, Greco di Tufo DOCG and Taurasi DOCG, all three of which express the strong and distinctive character, personality and terroir of Irpinia.

Erminia Fiano di Avellino Riserva DOCG is an utterly unique and magnificent wine that is a fitting tribute to the richly opulent and glittering splendour of Campania under the Spanish Bourbons. The wine comes from Fiano grapes grown on a single vineyard situated at 550 metres above sea level that surrounds the Salza Irpina estate and hunting lodge. The mature grapes are harvested, softly pressed, then vinified with skin contact at controlled temperature. This is followed by an extraordinary ageing—in the case of the 2004 vintage, for example, of no less than eighteen years before release, of which sixteen years were in stainless-steel tank on the lees followed by a further two years in bottle. It is highly unusual to age a white wine for such a prolonged period prior to bottling, and only a very few white wines would benefit from such a lengthy sojourn.

The Spanish had a long and tenacious sojourn across much of Southern Italy, Sicily and Sardinia of nearly 350 years, bringing splendour, opulence and wealth (at least for the ruling classes). The Di Meo's Erminia demonstrates that Fiano, a grape variety grown in Irpinia since antiquity, has a similar tenacity, an extraordinary capacity to mature and to evolve beautifully, gaining opulent textures, voluptuous tertiary aromas and magnificent complexity through the patient miracle of time.

Judikes, Vernaccia di Oristano DOC Riserva, Cantina della Vernaccia, Oristano, Sardinia

Vernaccia di Oristano is a unique variety that is totally different from other Vernaccia grapes cultivated elsewhere. In Sardinia, it is used to produce one of the great, still mainly undiscovered, white wines of Italy, Vernaccia di Oristano DOC, a wine that is wholly a result of the Spanish habitation of the island. For it was discovered that wines made from Vernaccia di Oristano, like wines made from Palomino in the sherry triangle of Spain's Jerez de la Frontera, or from Pedro Ximénez in Montilla-Moriles, have the unique propensity to grow flor, a thick layer of yeast that settles on the surface of wines placed in oak or chestnut barrels that are not filled completely. In the case of Vernaccia di Oristano, the wines must age for a minimum of three years in the barrel (four for Riserva), with some examples being left for much longer. The flor protects the wine from excessive oxidation, keeping it fresh and exhilarating, while allowing intriguing floral and nutty aromas to develop, with older examples gaining a complexity and concentration that can be quite extraordinary. This cooperative winery, founded in 1954, specialises in the production of Vernaccia di Oristano from its member growers' mainly old vine grapes. This may seem an old-fashioned wine completely at odds with the fresh and exciting modern wines of Sardinia, but it is a unique taste of the island and of its Spanish legacy and deserves to be sought out and enjoyed.

Tintilia del Molise DOP, Di Majo Norante, Campomarino, Molise

Molise is the second smallest region of Italy, located along the Adriatic seaboard between Abruzzo to the north and Apulia to the south-east, with

Latium to the west and Campania to the south. It is a harsh, mountainous land that is one of the country's least populated and visited. Yet Molise too is the source of wines that reflect its history as part of the Kingdom of Naples, under Spanish Habsburg and Bourbon rule until the unification of Italy. In fact, its most interesting and characterful grape variety, Tintilia, was brought to the region by the Spanish Bourbons, widely planted here and virtually nowhere else (the name of the grape, Tintilia, probably comes from 'vino tinto', Spanish for red wine). It was first mentioned in a written document in 1810, and by the 1890s it was identified as the most common grape variety in Molise. However, as happened with many other Italian grape varieties, after the Second World War, it was largely abandoned in favour of more productive alternatives and thus found itself on the verge of extinction. Thankfully, intrepid wine producers realised its value and importance as Molise's most characterful variety, and today it is being cultivated again, albeit on a relatively small scale.

Di Majo Norante, Molise's leading wine producer, makes an outstanding example that is highly regarded. This is a well-structured wine, full in body, with notable tannins, yet still velvety soft and rounded. Wines produced from unknown grape varieties may be difficult to market outside the area, so there is little reason to champion them if they don't offer flavours that are unique and characterful expressions of their land. Tintilia does just that. With its naturally high acidity, it is an ideal accompaniment to the robust cuisine of Molise, a land of herdsmen and peasant farmers, perhaps partnered with *coniglio alla molisana* (stewed rabbit and sausages) or *ragù di agnello* (lamb ragù served over short pasta).

16

NORTH-EAST ITALY

Trieste lives and breathes coffee. As the port of the Austro-Hungarian Empire, it was through Trieste that coffee beans arrived from around the world, to be roasted and dispatched to the great European coffee houses that proliferated in Vienna, Budapest, Prague and elsewhere. It's mid-morning, and I'm in the Antico Caffè Tommaseo, a historic coffee house that has been here since 1830, by the waterfront where important business transactions once took place over a cup of coffee. I order a capo in B *(a small cappuccino served in a glass not a cup) along with a* presnitz, *a typical, snail-shaped pastry created here in the mid-nineteenth century to commemorate the visit of the Austro-Hungarian empress to the city's Miramare castle that overlooks the bay. The atmosphere at Tommaseo is calm, perhaps even nostalgic, and the feel is more middle European than Italian.*

Later, I make my way up to the Antica Trattoria Suban for lunch. Over a bowl of jota, *owner Mario Suban explains to me that his great-grandmother first cooked this rustic soup of beans, fermented cabbage, potatoes and pork 155 years ago—and the exact same recipe is still used today. Throughout this long period of history, during which Trieste had been the port of the Austro-Hungarian Empire, then a part of Italy, then under the control of the Fascists, and then the Nazis, occupied by Tito's partisans, and even made the Free Territory of Trieste before becoming part of the newly formed Republic of Italy only in 1954, during all this long period of change and adaptation, the* jota *served by six generations of the Suban family has changed not one single iota. The wine to accompany this warming taste of Trieste comes from vineyards just above the city, in the Carso, a limestone plateau where native vines such as Vitovska and Terrano benefit from moist breezes from the Adriatic and endure the bitter, fiercely biting cold of the north-easterly* bora *to produce wines that are wholly unique. Indeed, this Vitovska from Benjamin Zidarich, a natural wine fermented on the skins, has immense character, rich in colour and flavour with notes of wild herbs, dried fruit and a tingling minerality on the palate that is a hallmark of wines from the Carso. It is just the wine to stand up to the robust and full flavours of the* jota *at Suban.*

The History

The Triveneto or Tre Venezie are terms used to indicate the north-east corner of Italy that historically links today's regions of Trentino–Alto Adige, Veneto and Friuli–Venezia Giulia. Austria, bordering Italy to the north, had long held sway over these territories. In the eighth century, Bavarians descended into Italy through the Austrian Tyrol via the Brenner Pass to establish themselves in a fertile area below the Alps that is known today as the Südtirol/Alto Adige. They inherited vineyards that had been cultivated by the Romans since the first century BCE. The bishop of Freising, for example, acquired vineyards near Bozen (Bolzano) in 720, and eventually more than forty German bishoprics and monasteries owned vineyards in Südtirol. By the time this area became part of Austria in 1363, the history of viticulture and the appreciation for the wines of this area was well established.

In 1382, the Austrians gained another important foothold in Italy when leading citizens from the port of Trieste petitioned the Habsburg duke of Austria to bring the city under its protection, giving the Austrians their much-coveted window to the Adriatic. Indeed, both Südtirol and Trieste itself, both part of Austria until the country's defeat at the end of the First World War in 1918, should be seen not so much as areas that were occupied by a foreign power over these long centuries but rather territories that considered themselves wholly a part of Austria not Italy. It would only be later, following the creation of the Kingdom of Italy, that irredentism would assert itself and Italian claims to these lands would be fully asserted.

Germanic influence over Italian territories existed from the time of the fall of the Roman Empire. The void after the disintegration of the empire left Italy vulnerable and open to invasion from tribes that descended in waves from the north—Visigoths, Sciri, Ostrogoths, Lombards. Indeed, the latter almost succeeded in bringing all the Italian Peninsula under their rule, except for those territories controlled by the Church and the Byzantines. From the time when the Frankish king Charlemagne was crowned *Imperator Romanorum* (a title that was later to become 'Holy Roman Emperor'), Germanic rulers had continuous claims on Italian territories, city-states and their allegiances. Indeed, the underlying struggle that defined the medieval period often pitted the papacy against the Holy Roman Empire.

The Holy Roman Empire came into the hands of the Austrian Habsburg dynasty for nearly four centuries from 1438 until 1806 (with a brief exception between 1742 and 1745). While the main territories of the Habsburgs stretched across Central Europe and for a time across Iberia as well as into the Burgundian Lowlands, Austrian interest and influence across especially Northern Italy remained constant. On his abdication in 1556, Habsburg Holy Roman Emperor Charles V had ceded his Austrian possessions to his brother Ferdinand I, while his Spanish territories went to his son who was to become Philip II of Spain, including those lands in Italy that extended across not only the whole of the south but also including the important power centre of Milan. When the Spanish Habsburg dynasty expired in 1700 after Charles II died without an heir, the War of the Spanish Succession eventually resulted in the Peace of Utrecht (1713) that passed overall control of much of Italy to the Austrian branch of the Habsburgs.

Skirmishes between the great powers of the day—France, Spain, Savoy, Britain—continued to take place on Italian soil, and lands were bandied about through incessant wars and treaties with little heed whatsoever to the needs or wants of the populace. The French opposed Austrian domination in Italy and allied with Spain. The House of Savoy exchanged Sicily for Sardinia, while Southern Italy including Naples as well as Sicily returned to Spanish hands under the Bourbons. Tuscany, no longer under the Medici, went to the duke of Lorraine in exchange for Lorraine being ceded to France. The Spanish Bourbons defeated Charles Emmanuel and occupied the Duchy of Savoy; Charles Emmanuel, duke of Savoy, was offered Milan and the Kingdom of the Lombards by the French, who wanted to keep it out of Austrian hands. The British took sides whenever it was expedient, using the navy to protect or embargo, allying with Savoy to blockade Nice, helping the Austrians logistically or using their warships to keep the French and Spanish at bay.

It seems that throughout this whole period, there was little awareness of or interest in the concept of an Italian nation. Rather, territories, kingdoms, duchies, cities were fought over, exchanged or bartered as if they were mere pieces in a board game. The middle classes, the merchants and traders, were able to fare reasonably well during the eighteenth century, but in the countryside the peasantry lived lives barely above subsistence level. Agricultural productivity remained below that of other European countries, and there was little commitment to social change or reform.

Yet this was the Age of Enlightenment: intellectual fervour and activity was alive in the cities; the arts, especially music, flourished; and science made notable advancements. Between 1769 and 1773, a young Austrian musical genius, Wolfgang Amadeus Mozart, together with his father Leopold, made extended tours across the most important Italian cities. Not only was Leopold able to demonstrate the talents of his precocious son to an adoring audience but he was also able to encourage his son to continue his musical development by absorbing a unique musical style that had developed in Italy. For at this time, the craft of opera composition was almost solely an Italian art form. Mozart immediately took to the style, breaking with Baroque rigidity and creating his own freer style of opera. Commissions followed, working with the Italian librettist Lorenzo Da Ponte, including *Così fan tutte*, *Don Giovanni* and *The Marriage of Figaro*. Through the beauty and power of his music, his melodies and soaring crescendos, Mozart was able to capture and express emotions and desires that are universal while at the same time depicting something of the essence of the Italian character as seen and interpreted through young Austrian eyes and ears. In *Così*, Mozart's characters, the sisters Fiordiligi and Dorabella, are infinitely more beautiful, interesting and sexually charged than their would-be lovers and changeable fiancés. In *Figaro*, both Figaro, valet to the Count Almaviva, and Susanna, his betrothed and maid to the countess, reveal themselves as members of the servile class to be far more clever, crafty, witty and fun than their aristocratic masters and mistresses. *Don Giovanni* is utterly obsessed with women and sexual conquest (640— *seicentoquaranta*—in Italy alone) and sees wine as one means to get his way. He plans a party and through the aria 'Fin ch'han dal vino' expresses the power of wine to warm the head and seduce women into bed. Would this musical seduction have been as convincing in any other language but Italian? By contrast, when Mozart wanted to create an opera that expressed, as he explained to Habsburg Emperor Joseph II, 'good German values', he wrote *The Magic Flute*, one of the first operas with a libretto in German.

Napoleon in Italy

The rational thought of the Enlightenment gave rise to pan-European ideas about human rights, liberty, equality and freedom from oppression. If the French Revolution toppled a tottering and top-heavy *Ancien Régime*, it also launched a series of conflicts across Europe, including Italy, that would only end with Napoleon's defeat at Waterloo in 1815. France declared war on Austria and Piedmont's House of Savoy in 1792, and French forces invaded Northern Italy. Napoleon speedily conquered Piedmont and swept triumphantly into Milan, Bologna, Verona and across all the Veneto. By 1797, France controlled all Northern Italy apart from the still proud and independent Republic of Venice, which was soon to fall. The Corsican general cared nothing for Venice's long and illustrious history. He permitted his troops to enter the city, and the Venetian army was no match for the French. The last doge, Ludovico Manin, formally abdicated, and the Most Serene Republic of

Venice ceased as an independent state after 1,100 years of existence. Napoleon and his troops plundered and looted Venice of some of its greatest treasures and artworks. Not content with taking over La Serenissima, he negotiated a putative treaty, then ordered his troops to destroy all vestiges of the Republic of Venice across its mainland hinterland, the proud Lion of St Mark, symbol of Venice, removed or defaced in sites across much of the Veneto. Then, rather disdainfully, he ceded Venice to the Austrians, almost like throwing a dog a bone after it had already been gnawed upon, though it would be back under the French from 1805 until 1815.

Nor did Southern Italy escape the ambitions of the French, with Naples being declared the Parthenopean Republic. Ferdinand IV, king of Naples, had to escape ignominiously to Sicily as a stowaway on one of Nelson's ships. Napoleon eventually gained control over almost all areas of the country, naming his brothers and sisters, relatives and trusted friends to oversee satellite 'republics' and in 1805 declared himself king of Italy.

It was a title he dearly loved. By the time things had gone badly wrong for Napoleon and defeat was inevitable, he refused to negotiate with the Austrians to relinquish his claim to the Kingdom of Italy. The Battle of Waterloo, fought on 18 June 1815, saw Wellington roundly trounce the French troops under his command, a defeat that marked the end of the Napoleonic Wars. Napoleon's dream of a grand Italian kingdom was hugely and cruelly diminished through exile to the tiny, volcanic island of St Helena, a thousand miles off the west coast of Africa. The Congress of Vienna met in 1815 to determine the fate of Italy. The Kingdom of Lombardy–Venetia was created and ceded to the Austrians, a vastly important area that encompassed the whole north-east of the country, from Milan and Lombardy across Venice and up through Friuli. Spanish Bourbon rule was restored in the south with the creation of the Kingdom of the Two Sicilies, while the Kingdom of Sardinia under the House of Savoy oversaw much of North West Italy.

Napoleon and the French were only in Italy for a brief period. He had first entered Italy in 1797, and the Kingdom of Italy that he established existed from 1805 to 1815, ruled by his stepson Eugène de Beauharnais. Napoleon's brother Joseph Bonaparte was declared king of Naples in 1806 after the Bourbons had fled and also briefly ruled over Venice. Yet during the short period that the French were in Italy, lasting changes were effected. The Napoleonic campaigns led to the deconsecration of many churches, sometimes disdainfully used as army barracks or stables. Monasteries, those centuries-old repositories of knowledge and wealth, were dissolved and their libraries, treasures, artefacts stolen or destroyed. But there were undoubted benefits, too. He introduced a variation of the Napoleonic Code as a fairer system of law and sought to abolish many ancient feudal rights. The French sought too to introduce agricultural and agrarian reforms. Winegrowers were encouraged to grub up obscure (to the French) local grape varieties and replant with 'superior' French.

The agreements reached at the Congress of Vienna after the fall of Napoleon left the Austro-Hungarian Empire, through its possession of Lombardy–Venetia, now the dominant power on the Italian Peninsula, in charge of the most powerful and vital part of Italy that was its economic powerhouse. Milan had long been either controlled or coveted by the Austrians, easily reached along the corridor that passed by way of the Brenner Pass through Austrian South Tyrol and around Lake Garda. The Free Imperial City of Trieste was Austria's main trading port and shipbuilding centre. From there, goods were imported into Trieste that made their way throughout the Austro-Hungarian Empire, notably coffee beans. Trieste became a centre for the roasting of coffee, and famous and historic coffee houses to rival those of Vienna grew up not just in Trieste but in cities throughout the Veneto, including Venice, Padua, Vicenza and Verona. Venice, meanwhile, now under the Austrians, continued its decline. Austrian power over the north of Italy was consolidated, with the Grand Duchy of Tuscany, the Duchy of Modena and Reggio and the Duchy of Parma (ruled by Napoleon's wife, the much-loved Maria Luigia) retaining a degree of independence while being firmly under Habsburg control. And so, wherever the Austrians were, the wines continued to flow and the music played on.

The Wines

Vitovska, Carso DOC, Azienda Agricola Zidarich, Duino Aurisina, Friuli–Venezia Giulia

Trieste belonged to the Habsburg dynasty from 1382 until 1918. It had its great heyday after Charles VI granted it Freeport status in 1719, making it the vital deep seaport of the Austro-Hungarian Empire. In 1784, Austrian Emperor Joseph II issued a decree that gave the wine producers of a small area above Trieste known as Carso the right to sell their own wine direct without having to pay taxes. Such places came to be called 'osmize', and the tradition remains even today. The name 'osmiza' comes from the Slovenian 'osem', which means eight, the number of consecutive days that they were allowed to open periodically during the year. At such designated times, passers-by could enjoy the simplest of foods—local Tabor cheese, a platter of home-cured *salumi*—together with a selection of the unique, own-produced wines made from indigenous grape varieties cultivated here and nowhere else. Today, though those restrictions no longer remain, some of the Carso's wine producers continue the tradition by offering simple foods to enjoy with their wines.

Carso is one of Italy's best kept vinous secrets, for it is an area that is completely unique. The terrain is so distinctive—sparse limestone rock riddled with deep, natural caves—that it has given its name to karst geological formations wherever in the world they may be found. This is a harsh landscape that underground reveals phantasmagoric systems of caverns shaped by limestone erosion that has taken place over tens of thousands of years. It is not easy to work such sparse and bare stony terrain, and there are only a handful of wine producers left in Carso, but these intrepid winegrowers are able to create wines that are wholly individual and different from those produced anywhere else in Italy.

Vitovska and Malvasia Istriana are used to produce white and orange wines, while Terrano is the indigenous variety for reds. At Azienda Agricola Zidarich, Benjamin Zidarich has dug a wine cellar 20 metres deep into the karst limestone to create a natural environment that provides the perfect conditions for the storage and maturation of wine at an even temperature and humidity that remains constant in summer or winter. His wines are bottled without filtration and are pure and natural expressions of the unique land of the Carso. I am a particular fan of the Zidarich Vitovska, macerated and fermented for a lengthy period on the skins, then aged in a karst stone tank deep in the cellar, before being bottled unfiltered. This is an orange wine that manages to be both delicate and intense at the same time, relatively light in colour given the lengthy skin maceration, with floral and citrus notes, orange peel, sage, good acidity, structure and a rich and long aftertaste. It is just the sort of wine that once would have once been served in the *osmize* of the Carso, those humble places where the winemakers of Trieste were allowed to offer a plate of food, a carafe of wine, to passers-by, including even Austrian emperors.

Linticlarus Gewürztraminer Spätlese, Südtirol / Alto Adige DOC, Weingut Tiefenbrunner-Schlosskellerei Turmhof, Kurtasch, Südtirol

If you travel today to the Südtirol, you could well be forgiven for hardly realising that you are even in Italy. For this autonomous province remains separate and wholly Austrian in every way: linguistically, culturally, architecturally, gastronomically, historically. This territory, located just over the Brenner Pass from Austria's Tyrol, and only a few hours' drive from Munich, has been occupied by German-speaking inhabitants since at least the eighth century and was part of Austria from 1363. The region only became part of Italy at the conclusion of the First World War. Then, during the Second World War, it was occupied by the Germans who had annexed Austria before being restored to Italy after the war, with the guarantee that its citizens would be granted a high degree of self-government. In 1946, a dual region was created to co-join German-speaking Südtirol (Alto Adige) with Italian-speaking Trentino: Trentino–Alto Adige.

Austrian traditions remain strongly intact throughout Südtirol, not least when it comes to winemaking. The Tiefenbrunner family have been producing wines here for five generations, and the winery dates from 1848, before either Italian unification or the later Italian annexation of the region. The family today owns 25 hectares of vineyards in Entiklar, Kurtatsch and Margreid, located at between 250 and 1,000 metres above sea level. A full range of grape varieties is cultivated, including Weissburgunder (Pinot Blanc), Blauburgunder (Pinot Noir), Goldmuskateller (Moscato Giallo), Gewürztraminer, Pinot Grigio, Sauvignon Blanc, Chardonnay, Cabernet Sauvignon, Vernatsch (Schiava) and Lagrein.

I adore the Linticlarus Gewürztraminer Spätlese, not least because it is such a unique example from this region, wholly at odds with Italian wines from just about anywhere else. To produce this wine, the grapes are harvested sometimes as late as December, by which time some of the bunches will have been attacked by *Botrytis cinerea*, the noble rot that concentrates grape sugars and aroma. The sugar-rich grape must then ferments slowly in small wooden barrels for a couple of months, then ages further on its lees for almost another year, followed by more time maturing in the bottle. The wine that eventually emerges has a nose redolent of the exotic—rose petals, quince, dried fruit—and a long, concentrated, lingering, honeyed palate that is simply exquisite. A wine to sip and wonder, and a fitting tribute to the Austrian winemaking traditions of Südtirol.

Chardonnay, Friuli-Colli Orientali DOC, Livio Felluga, Cormòns, Friuli–Venezia Giulia

Grape varieties such as Chardonnay, Merlot and Cabernet do not sound very Italian, and it is easy to consider that these popular so-called international varieties are relatively recent interlopers, especially since, from deepest Sicily all the way up to the Valle d'Aosta, they continue to be introduced and cultivated, often at the expense of native grape varieties. However, the history of these grapes in Italy can be traced directly back to Napoleon and the French armies that swept across the country at the end of the 1700s and the early years of the 1800s. Whether the great general himself commanded that native grape varieties be grubbed up and replaced with 'superior' French, or whether he and his administrators merely encouraged the process, what is without doubt is that Chardonnay, Merlot and the Cabernets were introduced during the French occupation especially throughout North-East Italy, most notably across the regions today known as Veneto and Friuli–Venezia Giulia. They thus have well-established roots that are more than 200 years old, so much so that in a very real and meaningful sense they can and should now be considered wholly Italian native varieties, for they have adapted well to produce wines with their own distinctive character and identity.

Livio Felluga's Chardonnay is an outstanding example. For the *ponca* soil of the Colli Orientali di Friuli consisting of stratified grey marl and sandstone flysch is the perfect habitat for this grape variety to express its full Italian personality. Indeed, this north-eastern corner of Italy is considered the source of some of the country's most exciting and characterful white wines, a reputation achieved in no small measure through the efforts of Felluga and a handful of other pioneering winemakers who transformed the region after the devastation from two world wars.

If Chardonnay has been in this part of Italy since the time of the French, the Livio Felluga style is wholly Italian in character. After destemming, the grapes are left to macerate on the skins for a short period before being softly crushed, followed by fermentation in temperature-controlled stainless-steel. Afterwards, the wine remains on its lees for a few months to increase complexity, resulting in a richly creamy texture and body. This unoaked Chardonnay is a precise wine with an extraordinary purity of fruit—imagine the scent of a ripe and juicy white peach, just plucked from the tree—a gorgeous, fully voluptuous expression of the world's most popular grape, totally at home in this corner of Italy, thanks to Napoleon Bonaparte.

17

RISORGIMENTO AND UNIFICATION

I'm dining in the baglio *of Cantine Florio, just across the road from Marsala's seafront. This immense, low-lying building, with its rough sandy floor of pressed volcanic tuff to regulate natural humidity, contains hundreds of enormous wooden barrels, each about four-fifths filled with Marsala wine. The rich, caramelly, alcoholic fumes that waft over the cathedral-like structure are intoxicating. The atmosphere here is truly heady and extraordinary. Amid the giant barrels, a glass case behind our table displays a collection of short musket-like rifles, the very same weapons that were carried and used by Giuseppe Garibaldi and his 'I Mille' ('the Thousand') when they landed in the port of this small wine town in western Sicily on the night of 11 May 1860. Thus began a march across Sicily and on to the mainland that led to the creation of the modern Italian nation. Garibaldi is celebrated as a hero just about everywhere in Italy but not in Sicily. The point of landing, by Marsala's present-day harbour, near to where we are now sitting, remains virtually unmarked, and the small museum that commemorates the town's pivotal role in Italian history is at best desultory. No matter, at Cantine Florio we dine on history in the shadow of Garibaldi's historic deeds (alongside barrels of wine signed by King Vittorio Emanuele III and the dictator Benito Mussolini), sipping small glasses of exquisitely rich Marsala 'Baglio Florio'.*

A world away and closer to London than to Sicily, I find myself at the other end of the country in Piedmont, in the little wine hamlet of Fontanafredda in the heart of the Barolo zone. Here in a villa built by the first king of Italy for his mistress Rosa Vercellana, I am seated in an upstairs dining room. On the wall, there is a painting of the Contessa Rosa, as she became once she married the king after his wife had died. She is looking down on me somewhat disdainfully, or so it feels. She was reputed to be an incredible beauty, but I find her effigy formidable, even frightening (but then beauty and power have always been fearsome if intimate bedfellows). More to my taste is the Barolo 'Lazzarito', produced on the estate granted by the king to their son, Emanuele, who was to become a visionary winemaker. I savour a bite of agnolotti—*a small, perfectly formed meat-stuffed pasta—and take a sip of the rich and powerful Barolo.*

The History

Visit any Italian city or town and you may find yourself walking down a Corso Vittorio Emanuele II, or along a Via Cavour, or perhaps sitting outdoors at a *caffè* on a Piazza Garibaldi. The names of these three individuals—respectively a courageous and ambitious king, a brilliant and pragmatic statesman, and a remarkable and fearless freedom fighter—are written large and bold across the Italian nation, credited as the fathers of the country. Their story, as always linked to wine, is the story of how out of the chaos of the nineteenth century a new and proud nation was born.

Towards the start of that century, the unification of the Italian Peninsula and its islands was seemingly the last thing on most people's minds. After the downfall of Napoleon, the Congress of Vienna aimed to return Europe mainly to the former conservative status quo. The French, as the losers, had to relinquish any interest and influence they once held in Italy. The Austrians were granted rule over the newly established Kingdom of Lombardy–Venetia and thus became the dominant power on the peninsula. The Spanish Bourbons under Ferdinand were restored in the south, with Sicily now joined to Naples with the newly formed Kingdom of the Two Sicilies. Vittorio Emanuele I of the House of Savoy took charge of a Kingdom of Sardinia that now included not only Piedmont and French Savoie but also extended from Genoa, across Liguria and Provence to Nizza (Nice). The Papal States, meanwhile, remained under the full and strict authority of the pope. The Grand Duchy of Tuscany was under Ferdinand III of Habsburg-Lorraine, while the Duchy of Parma was ruled by Napoleon's wife Marie-Louise (still revered in Parma as the beloved Maria-Luigia) and her Austrian lover, consort and later husband, General Adam Albert von Neipperg. Any hint of an Italian nationalist movement was firmly stamped out by the archly conservative forces, whose collective interest was to preserve the status quo that served them and their powerful interests best.

A reawakening, slowly

Little by little, however, a yearning for change began to be felt, not just in Italy but across all of Europe, a feeling, certainly among some liberal-thinking intellectuals if not yet by the masses, that the time for self-determination would one day be at hand. This slow but insistent reawakening of a national consciousness in Italy is known as Risorgimento, a movement that developed not centrally but in fits and starts over the first half of the century and eventually was to lead to the unification of the country and the formation of the Kingdom of Italy. And yet, this result was far from inevitable, and historians argue that in fact the Italian nation as we know it might not ever even have been created if a few things had gone differently.

After the Congress of Vienna, a residual discontent and dissatisfaction among diverse and varied people across the country led to isolated and local uprisings, in Macerata in 1817, for example, and Naples in 1820. This discontent was to spread to areas as different and as far away as Sicily and Piedmont. In the 1830s, revolts took place in Modena, Parma and Bologna, disrupting peace even in those lands under the strict and reactionary authority of the pope. But there was not yet any cohesiveness to such happenings, and a national consciousness was yet to capture the imagination of the general population. Indeed, for the peasantry, life mainly remained a struggle just to find a way to scratch a living, to eat and to survive.

Gradually, however, intellectuals and progressive thinkers began to suggest the possibility of the foundation of an Italian nation and to conjecture in what form it would best be served. Giuseppe Mazzini, for example, advocated that Italy become a republic and appealed in an open letter to Carlo Alberto, the Piedmontese king of Sardinia, to revolt against the Austrians. Vicenzo Gioberti, a fervent Catholic nationalist, by contrast, believed that a new federal nation would best be served with the pope as head of state. Massimo d'Azeglio, who was later to become prime minister of the Kingdom of Sardinia, argued for Piedmont to take a leading role in any formation of a new nation. A general feeling of unrest and the need for change reflected the revolutionary fervour that at the time was sweeping across Europe and resulted in a series of upheavals across the continent. It seems that after centuries of autocratic rule in one form or another, there was now a collective desire for democracy in some form as well as for the creation of independent nation-states no longer under the yoke of perceived foreign dominations.

Risorgimento and Giuseppe Verdi

In 1848, an uprising against the rule of the Spanish Bourbons took place in Palermo and inspired others to take up arms elsewhere. In Rome, Pope Pius IX was forced to flee, and a Roman Republic was briefly declared. There were revolts in both Milan and Venice against the Austrians. The Venetians were able to hold out for a lengthy period, only submitting after a prolonged siege. Elsewhere, across Europe, people were angry enough to rise and fight: in Prussia, Bavaria and in outposts all across the Austro-Hungarian Empire.

Revolution suddenly was in the air, driven across the continent like a persistent operatic aria by Giuseppe Verdi.

Indeed, the great maestro has long been considered the composer of the Risorgimento. Certainly, he was deeply sympathetic to ideas espoused by Italian nationalists. However, his home in the lowlands of the Po Valley was a part of Austrian Italy, and he was mindful not to upset the authorities as well as his wealthy patrons. Nonetheless, Verdi chose distant references to demonstrate his patriotic commitment to the idea of Italian nationhood. Indeed, through his music, he came to express something of the national mood, even if the average man or woman in the street was hardly yet aware of it. *La Battaglia di Legnano* celebrates the twelfth-century victory of the Lombard League against the Holy Roman Emperor, the German Frederick Barbarossa. In *Nabucco*, the rousing chorus of the exiled Hebrew slaves is seen as a parable for the Italians' yearning for freedom and independence.

The revolts of 1848 allowed Carlo Alberto to seize the opportunity to declare war on Austria, with the aim of taking control over Lombardy and Venice and its hinterland. The Austrians, however, were not yet ready to relinquish power. They defeated his army in a decisive battle at Custoza, near Lake Garda, and the Piedmont king was forced to relinquish all his territorial gains. After a further unsuccessful attempt led to another defeat at the Battle of Novara in 1849, Carlo Alberto abdicated, handing over the Kingdom of Sardinia to his son Vittorio Emanuele II. The Austrians had won, while in the south the Spanish Bourbon King Ferdinand I recaptured Sicily after the uprising that had kicked everything off and exacted a stern retribution. Italian unification at this moment looked further away than ever.

Count Camillo Benso di Cavour

Yet European events elsewhere were to play a part in facilitating the creation of a new nation. An uprising in France led to the abdication of King Louis-Philippe I. Louis Napoleon, nephew of Napoleon I, was elected France's first president and later proclaimed himself Emperor Napoleon III. One result of the 1848 uprisings was that a conservative form of constitutional democracy, at least in name, was granted to some parts of Italy. Piedmont, for example, adopted a two-chamber parliament, with a prime minister overseeing a council of ministers. Massimo d'Azeglio, the first prime minister, had to accept the terms of defeat after the Battle of Novara. Disillusioned, he decided to retire and return to his life as an accomplished painter and artist. His immediate successor, Count Camillo Benso di Cavour, was to prove to be one of

Italy's greatest politicians and diplomats, a staunch supporter of King Vittorio Emanuele II, pragmatic, cunning and flexible enough to allow for the compromises that were required to lead eventually toward the creation of the Kingdom of Italy.

During the Crimean War, Cavour ensured that the Kingdom of Sardinia allied itself with the French, British and Ottoman Empire in their successful campaign against the Russians. This gained some degree of international influence and prestige, even if the Piedmontese military contribution was negligible. Afterwards, Cavour courted Napoleon III and secretly persuaded him to support Piedmont in a war against the Austrians. Their agreed joint plan was to provoke Austria into declaring war, at which moment the French were to be summoned to come to the aid of the Piedmontese. In return, Cavour made a secret deal to grant to France some of the historic lands that the House of Savoy had long held: the Savoie territories across the Alps together with the coastal town of Nizza, which was to become Nice, together with its surrounding county. Thus, it can be argued that the main aim of their joint machinations was not necessarily to unify Italy or create a new nation but rather to rid the Italian Peninsula of the Austrians and to gain and consolidate control across Piedmont, Lombardy and the Veneto at the expense of the loss of Savoie, which would go to the French.

Though the Austrians were reluctant to start yet another war, and for a time, it looked as if Cavour's and Napoleon's plan might fail, they eventually grew concerned at the strength of the Piedmontese army that had been gathered and gave an ultimatum that it be stood down within just three days. When he heard the news, Cavour was ecstatic. At last, the world would perceive the Austrians as the aggressors, the Piedmontese the injured party in need of the international support of the French. His cunning plan was put in place when the French army arrived within just a few days. The battles that resulted at Magenta and Solferino were fiercely contested and bloody, with substantial casualties on both sides. Vittorio Emanuele II himself led the Piedmontese forces, and though the king was later to be celebrated nationally as a heroic ruler-warrior, and though his personal courage was never in doubt, it seems that his military strategies were not always the most astute. Indeed, these brutal battles could not have been won without the valour and skill of the French.

After the Battle of Solferino, it seems that Napoleon III had had enough. After all, it wasn't even his country, and French were dying. He unilaterally called a truce, set up a meeting with Habsburg Emperor Franz Joseph and, without even consulting his Piedmontese partners, agreed on a peace settlement that gave most of Lombardy to the Kingdom of Sardinia while leaving Venice and the Veneto hinterland in the hands of the Austrians. Though Vittorio Emanuele II accepted the terms of the settlement, Cavour was disgusted and enraged, even for a brief time resigning as prime minister. His plans to expand Piedmontese influence not only across Northern Italy but also below the Po Valley and into Tuscany and the centre of the country had been thrown off track. Discussions had already taken place between Cavour and Baron Bettino Ricasoli, a Tuscan aristocrat who from his country estate in the heart of the Chianti came to see the advantage of allying Tuscany with a newly expanded and empowered Piedmont. The patriotic fervour that had been stirred up over the partial defeat of the Austrians could not be extinguished, and there was an appetite for the war to continue.

Giuseppe Garibaldi and 'I Mille'

Meanwhile, during the previous decades of uprising and revolution, a remarkable soldier and freedom fighter had forced himself on the scene. Giuseppe Garibaldi was from Nizza and served originally as a merchant seaman, though he seems to have been born to be a restless guerrilla warrior. Inspired by Mazzini's early ideas about the creation of an Italian nation, he volunteered to fight in an insurrection in Genoa in 1838, his involvement in which earned him condemnation to death. He escaped to South America and became involved in various adventures and misadventures in Brazil and Uruguay, though he never lost his fervour or his intense Italian patriotism. The revolutions and uprising of 1848 inspired him to return to Italy, and he became a parliamentarian deputy in the short-lived Roman Republic. He left Italy again and travelled the world before moving back in 1855. When war between Piedmont and Austria broke out in 1859, he began to gather a group of volunteer soldiers who were to become known as 'I Mille'—'the Thousand'—to fight for the Piedmontese (they and the many volunteers who later joined them also came to be known as the 'Redshirts'). Afterwards, he went to Tuscany, where he planned to continue the struggle for the unification of Italy.

However, when he learned of Cavour's treachery in ceding Nizza, his own home city, and Savoie to the French, he was incensed. Rather than staying to fight for the Piedmontese, he chose instead to take his troops to far-off Sicily to support an insurrection there that had spontaneously erupted against the Spanish Bourbons. The Royal Navy warships *Argus* and *Intrepid* were in Marsala's harbour on the night of 11 May 1860 when Garibaldi and the

Thousand came to land, but the British turned an apparent blind eye to their arrival, while the Bourbon troops hesitated to fire on Garibaldi's ships as they came in, possibly for fear of hitting the British and thus provoking an international incident. Was it in the British interest to allow Garibaldi to land and thus encourage unrest in Sicily and so facilitate the fall of the Spanish ruling class? Or was their presence in the harbour that night to protect the British Marsala wine empires that had already been established, as well as British interest in Sicily's vitally important sulphur mines? Or maybe the British sensed that, as was happening elsewhere in Europe, an old order was crumbling, and it was not their role to interfere?

Certainly, across Sicily as much as anywhere on the Italian mainland, there was a feeling that change was inevitable, something that could no longer be halted. In *The Leopard*, the brilliant novel by Giuseppe Tomasi di Lampedusa that details Sicily from the moment of Garibaldi's arrival, Tancredi, the opportunistic nephew to the prince of Salina, explains to his aristocratic uncle why he himself, an aristocrat, has chosen to fight with Garibaldi's Redshirts. He asserts simply, 'Everything must change for everything to stay the same.'

Garibaldi was clearly a brilliant military strategist and a general who could inspire his troops as well as attract others to join and support his cause. Though at times the Neapolitan troops loyal to the Spanish king greatly outnumbered his men, he and his band of freedom fighters found a way to defeat a much larger and better organised and equipped foe. Today, across Sicily, in every town where Garibaldi and his men stopped, there is a plaque on an exterior wall commemorating that the great man had been there, perhaps to address the local population from a first-floor balcony or window, or maybe just to sleep. For the middle-class Sicilians as well as for workers and the disenfranchised, he was inspirational, and the local population increasingly rose up to fight alongside his Redshirts.

Perhaps for this reason, in Sicily today Garibaldi is considered something of a traitor by many. For in helping to replace a distant Spanish king with an even more distant and disinterested king from Piedmont, it turned out that his actions, stirring though they were, did not actually result in the improvement of people's lives all that much, if at all. Indeed, for many Sicilians, the unification of Italy has come to be perceived as just another riff on a centuries-old succession of rule by foreign powers that they have had to endure since the times of the Greeks, the Phoenicians, the Romans, Byzantines, Arabs, Normans, Angevins, Spanish Habsburgs and Spanish Bourbons. Maybe, as Lampedusa suggests, it was pre-ordained: that everything had to change for things to remain the same. For aristocrats like the old Leopard himself, the maintenance of the status quo for the privileged few was certainly more desirable than the righting of centuries and millennia of social inequality.

Willed on by those who believed in him, or who saw opportunity for profit, Garibaldi's progress through Sicily was remarkably swift and decisive. Just sixteen days after landing in Marsala, Garibaldi and his Redshirt army had entered Palermo, which fell on 6 June. A decisive battle took place at Milazzo on 20 July. The fighting was fierce, but with the support of the local population Garibaldi eventually won the day, allowing him to progress on to Messina. There he made the bold decision, entirely against Cavour's wishes, to cross the Straits of Messina to the Italian mainland and continue the struggle to subdue and remove some three and a half centuries of Spanish rule. By the end of August, Garibaldi's Redshirts had taken Calabria and continued through Campania to Naples, which was entered on 7 September. Garibaldi next set his troops on the road to Rome. Another series of battles against the Neapolitan troops took place at Volturno at the end of September into October. Though Garibaldi eventually won the day, the skirmish, after such an intense and unrelenting campaign, took its toll on his exhausted troops and he was forced to pause. A further advance to Rome, in any case, was halted by Cavour, as the French were by then giving protection and support to the pope.

Although the country was not yet fully unified, what had already been achieved was truly remarkable: almost by the force of Garibaldi's will and personality alone, in just a little more than five months, he and his volunteer force of Redshirts together with local volunteers had taken on the full might of the Spanish Bourbons' Neapolitan army and roundly thrashed them. On 8 November 1860, Garibaldi humbly and formally presented Southern Italy to King Vittorio Emanuele II, refusing honour or reward, then departed to his island home on Caprera (not surprisingly, he didn't stay there for long, later involving himself in further skirmishes and battles as well as serving in the newly formed Italian parliament). The Papal States, except for Rome and its surrounds, were next secured by the Piedmontese army. The Kingdom of Italy was formally proclaimed on 17 March 1861, with Vittorio Emanuele II declared king of Italy and the capital of the new nation initially set to be in Turin.

Having seen Italy mainly unified, Camillo Benso, count of Cavour, Italy's first prime minister, was suddenly taken ill and died on 6 June 1861. He was only fifty years old. The great statesman, agronomist and lover of wine was replaced by a completely different character, a Tuscan aristocrat, Baron Bettino Ricasoli. Baron Bettino, known as 'the Iron Baron', may not have possessed the brilliant political skills of his predecessor, but during his two terms he was nonetheless unyielding in his effort to bring Rome into the new nation, adapting the slogan 'Roma o morte'—'Rome or death.' The problem was that Rome, which of course would have been the obvious capital of the new nation, and the papacy remained under the protection of the French and Napoleon III. Turin, it was generally agreed, was not really suited to be the capital of the newly formed Kingdom of Italy, and Ricasoli, a proud Tuscan, certainly did not want his own nation or indeed the rest of the country to be seen as merely an annexation of Piedmont. So, with Rome unavailable at the time, it was agreed that Florence would become the capital of Italy, a position it held from 1865 until 1870.

The pope, naturally, was vehemently against the foundation of this new secular state, and the Austrians were determined to hang on to what was left of their Italian territories. But Venice and the Veneto were eventually delivered to the new nation in 1866, and Rome was taken on 20 September 1870, with the pope retaining only the Vatican City together with his summer residence at Castel Gandolfo.

'Italy has been made', as Massimo d'Azeglio was so famously to assert, 'Now we must make the Italians.'

The Wines

'Baglio Florio' Marsala DOC, Cantine Florio, Marsala, Sicily

When Garibaldi returned triumphantly to Marsala in July 1862, he visited Cantine Florio, already at that time one of the leading wine producers in Sicily. The Florio family were ever keen to seize a marketing opportunity, and so they created a special Marsala wine named in the great man's honour. Garibaldi for his part donated some of the guns used by his men during their successful expedition across the island, including one of his own. These are on display in the Cantine Florio *baglio* today, in a glass case set among the towering wooden barrels of ageing Marsala wine, yet another direct link between the story of Italy and the story of Italian wine.

Marsala is an amber-coloured, rich, fortified dessert wine developed not as a drink for the local people but as a product that was stable enough to be exported by ship to markets in Britain, the Low Countries and Northern Europe. Sicily is hot and arid, too hot and dry, one might imagine, to produce fine wine. But here on the western coast of the island, Spanish influence since the sixteenth century had encouraged the production of a unique, oxidised style that utilised the solera system of dynamic ageing, as perfected in Jerez de la Frontera for sherry. In Marsala, this was known as *in perpetuum*, whereby casks were fractionally blended with wines from previous vintages. The barrels were left only four-fifths full, and thus the heat and humidity caused the wines to oxidise. Each year, a portion of each barrel would be drawn out and that barrel refreshed with wines from the new vintage.

When an Englishman, John Woodhouse, a merchant from Liverpool, found himself stormbound in Marsala, he sampled the local 'Perpetuum' wine and found it to his liking. More to the point, he noted that since it was a wine not dissimilar to sherry there was an opportunity to import it to England. However, to ensure its stability on the lengthy sea voyage, he added some grape brandy to fortify the wine to make it more robust. Thus, in 1773, Marsala wine was born. The wine was an immediate success, and its popularity was confirmed when Lord Nelson ordered a large consignment for the Royal Navy. After the Battle of Trafalgar, the wine was bestowed with the title 'Marsala Victory Wine'.

Marsala today has sadly gone out of fashion, more often used as a cooking wine than enjoyed and celebrated as one of Italy's great historic wines. Now is the time to rediscover it. Marsala 'Baglio Florio' is one of the company's flagships, produced entirely from Grillo grapes cultivated on seaside vineyards north of Marsala, pressed and vinified, then matured for upwards of at least ten years in wooden cask. The result is quite magnificent, almost bone dry, best served lightly chilled, an intensely concentrated amber wine with notes of toasted hazelnuts, walnuts and dried fruit. It is a reminder of how great the traditional fortified wines of Marsala can be—most definitely not a wine for cooking with or to use to make *zabaglione*—but a gloriously nutty, caramelly, complex elixir, a thoughtful wine to sip and to consider how great individuals and historic acts can lead to consequences not always entirely foreseen.

Enoteca Regionale di Grinzane Cavour, Grinzane Cavour, Piedmont

The Castle of Grinzane Cavour is located just 5 kilometres from Alba and stands in a commanding position overlooking the majestic Barolo wine country, its lofty position looking across to similar castle-topped eyries such as those that stand atop the towns of Barolo itself, Castiglione Falletto, Serralunga d'Alba and Monforte d'Alba, names that are all rallying cries for lovers of Barolo. Today, the vine-carpeted hills of Barolo indicate that this is single-minded wine country, but it was not always so.

The Castle of Grinzane Cavour is so named because it was the home to Camillo Benso, count of Cavour, who resided here from 1830 until 1849. As a wealthy, aristocratic landowner, and mayor of Grinzane, he sought to bring an empirical and rational approach to viticulture and winemaking. His travels in France had enabled him to learn about and appreciate that country's great wines, notably the *grands crus* of Burgundy. The wines from his own area, by contrast, were at the time considered anything but noble. Indeed, the Nebbiolo grape, a notoriously late ripener, was only able to produce wines that were light in colour and slightly sweet (due to the cold temperatures at harvest time, sometimes as late as November, fermentation would proceed only in fits and starts, leaving behind unfermented residual sugar in the wine). Cavour had studied the research of General Paolo Francesco Staglieno, who believed that Piedmont had the potential to produce a different style of wine: dry, full-bodied and capable of ageing. Cavour wanted to put these ideas into practice, and so he engaged the services of a French oenologist, Louis Oudart from Reims, to put in place some of the ideas that Staglieno had advocated in relation to both viticulture and winemaking: pruning more severely to limit yield and increase quality, and favouring long, slow fermentation in closed containers to more fully extract tannin and structure, followed by lengthy ageing in wooden barrels. Thus, a new and potent style of wine was born that was to prove fit both for a king and for a new nation, and that wine was Barolo.

Today, the Castle of Grinzane Cavour is a UNESCO World Heritage Site, recognised as 'an emblematic name both in the development of vineyards and in Italian history'. There is a small museum that includes Cavour's modest living quarter, as well as an extensive enoteca or wine library that displays some of the best producers of Barolo, Barbaresco and other wines of the area, as well as a notable selection of grappa. The wines are available for tasting and purchase, so this is a great place to visit and learn more not only about Italy's first prime minister but also about the great wines of this area. The Italian nation owes Cavour a great debt for his vital role in the unification of the country; wine lovers similarly are indebted to him for the work he did to help to create modern Barolo, one of Italy's, indeed the world's, greatest wines.

Barolo 'Lazzarito' DOCG, Casa E. di Mirafiore, Serralunga d'Alba, Piedmont

Most statues of Vittorio Emanuele II depict him heroically astride a powerful horse, sword in hand. Italy's first king was indeed a courageous warrior who personally led his troops into battles and who was ultimately victorious in unifying the Italian nation. Massimo d'Azeglio referred to him as 'il re galantuomo' ('the gentleman king'), and he is revered across the nation. Almost certainly, his marriage to Adelaide of Austria, his first cousin, was one of convenience, an opportunity to ally the House of Savoy more closely with the House of Habsburg. There must have been some passion, for she bore him eight children, including their son Umberto who was to become the second king of Italy. He also had numerous mistresses with whom he fathered several illegitimate offspring. The great love of his life, however, was Rosa Vercellana, born in Nizza (today Nice), the daughter of a standard bearer in the Napoleonic Guard. It became something of a scandal when he installed her in a villa in a small wine hamlet in the Langhe hills of Barolo, especially after he was crowned king of Sardinia in 1849 when his father Carlo Alberto abdicated the throne following defeat to the Austrians in the upheavals of 1848. When his wife Adelaide, duchess of Savoy and queen of Sardinia, died in 1855, Vittorio Emanuele was free to co-habit with the love of his life, 'La Bela Rosin', as she came to be popularly known. They spent much time in what was to become a royal villa. Indeed, so fond were the couple of this place that in 1858 the king bestowed it to his mistress by royal decree, granting her the title countess of Mirafiori and Fontanafredda, recognising their two children and granting them a new surname, Guerrieri. They did not marry until 1869 and only because the then king of Italy as he had now become had fallen gravely ill. She never became queen, and their children had no rights to the throne.

Their second son Emanuele Alberto Guerrieri nevertheless inherited the title count of Mirafiori and Fontanafredda together with the extensive estate and proved to be a visionary farmer-entrepreneur. He founded Casa E. di Mirafiore to oversee the estates in Barolo and Fontanafredda, dedicated himself to wine and was committed to the creation of a powerful and prestigious modern style of Barolo. At the same time, he constructed a model village for the estate's employees, including farmhouses, stables, a church and even a recreational club. By 1890, the wines of the estate had earned international awards and were being exported all over the world.

After Emanuele's death, his son Gastone took over the business. At first all went well, and the wines continued to be produced and sold internationally. But this started to change in the 1920s. With phylloxera ravaging the vineyards of Europe and a global economic depression, the company went bankrupt, and this historic estate was all but forgotten. However, in 2008, Mirafiore returned to the heart of the Fontanafredda estate, the modern winery located in the village just by the royal villa where it all began with that love affair between the king of Italy and his mistress La Bela Rosin.

The rebirth of Casa E. di Mirafiore thus remains rooted in the history of the Fontanafredda estate as well as in the history of Italy. The wines are still produced in strict observance of the Piedmontese tradition of winemaking, respecting above all the vineyards, which are now being cultivated entirely organically. The aim is to produce wines that express precision, balance and elegance. The cru Barolo Lazzarito is a great example of a traditional Barolo produced from Nebbiolo grapes cultivated in front of the medieval Castle of Serralunga at 340 to 380 metres above sea level. Barolo is never a simple, easy wine, nor should it be. Barolo Lazzarito will certainly mature and evolve with lengthy ageing, yet younger vintages are also approachable and enjoyable, with a ripe and sumptuous bouquet of plums, earthy undertones of woodland, truffle and mushroom, well-knit tannins and a warm and long finish. The best place to sample this and other wines from the Casa E. di Mirafiori estate is in the royal villa itself that today is the home to a magnificent traditional restaurant, Guido Ristorante.

Bettino-Ricasoli Chianti Classico DOCG, Barone Ricasoli SpA, Gaiole-in-Chianti, Tuscany

Baron Bettino Ricasoli, Italy's second prime minister, came from a noble family that could trace its origins back to the time of Charlemagne. The family's great feudal estate was—and still is—centred on the Castello di Brolio, an imposing medieval fortress in the heart of the Chianti region, in the hands of the Ricasolis since 1141, where grapes and olives have always been cultivated. Documents show that by the late 1600s, wines from Brolio were already being exported to Amsterdam and London.

Like Cavour, Baron Bettino was intimately involved with the management of his own wine estate and was equally devoted to trying to improve the wines of the whole area in order to bring economic benefits and improvements to the lives of those who worked the land. Indeed, the Iron Baron himself is credited with the invention of a 'recipe' for Chianti wine that defined it for more than 100 years: 'From Sangioveto the wine takes the main component of its bouquet as well as its vigorous quality; Canaiolo softens the tone of the first without taking anything away from its bouquet; and Malvasia, which could be omitted for those wines intended for ageing, tends to slightly dilute the product resulting from the first two, making it lighter and suitable for everyday drinking', wrote the baron in a letter in 1874.

The key is that last sentence, the creation of a wine 'suitable for everyday drinking'. Under Baron Bettino's formula, Chianti was never envisaged to be

193

a great wine destined for lengthy ageing. The inclusion of white grapes in the blend (later Trebbiano as well as Malvasia) meant that the wine would always be lighter in body than if produced exclusively from red grapes. The baron furthermore advocated a winemaking technique that became known as *governo all'uso toscano* whereby partially dried grapes were added to the wine after its first fermentation. This gave a grapey freshness, a touch more alcohol, as well as a bit of lively effervescence that kept the wine vivacious, the perfect style to be bottled in the classic Chianti *fiasco*, that charmingly bulbous straw-covered bottle that many of us remember fondly.

Chianti Classico—wines from the heartland between Florence and Siena in which Castello di Brolio is located—have changed character greatly. Indeed, the potential for truly great red wines to be produced here utilising primarily Sangiovese, sometimes with the addition of international grape varieties such as Merlot or Cabernet Sauvignon, vinified to extract tannin and structure, and often aged in French oak *barriques* has resulted in a range of top-quality wines that rightly rank among Italy's finest.

At Castello di Brolio today, the current Baron Francesco Ricasoli produces a wine that is a fitting tribute to his illustrious ancestor: Brolio-Bettino Chianti Classico. The wine is produced from 90 per cent Sangiovese with the addition of 10 per cent Abrusco, a local variety not often encountered. Unfiltered, aged in large oak casks for at least eighteen months, the result is powerful yet harmonious, an elegant if unyielding wine that is a fitting tribute to the Iron Baron, Italy's second prime minister.

18

NATION-BUILDING THROUGH THE STOMACH

I am in the small town of Forlimpopoli taking part in a cooking class at Casa Artusi, Italy's first centre of gastronomic culture devoted entirely to Italian home cooking. My 'Marietta' gently takes the mattarello *from me and begins to work the* sfoglia, *the sheet of pasta made from just flour and eggs. She wraps the now smooth dough around the long, wooden rolling pin, rolls up the sheet, working quickly with her hands moving from the centre out, gently stretching as she presses down and smooths, working hard with her stout forearms, rolling and stretching, stretching and rolling. She gives the sheet a quarter turn, hands me back the rolling pin and gestures for me to do the same. Try as I might, my efforts are clearly fumbling and unsatisfactory. She resists for as long as she can, then takes over again, rolling and stretching, stretching and rolling, slapping the sheet of pasta down and half-turning, until at last the* sfoglia *has become huge and so thin that it is smooth and almost translucent.* Bravo, *she says to me, though we both know in truth that I have done very little.* Bravissima, *I respond humbly.*

The masterclass has whetted my appetite. Fortunately, a wonderful lunch is at hand. First a selection of antipasti typical of Romagna: cured salumi *of course—*prosciutto crudo, coppa, salami, mortadella; *piadina* flatbread; gnocco fritto, *a sort of fried pasta dough;* squacquerone *cheese, young, fresh and sweet;* formaggio di fossa, *intense in flavour and aroma, aged anaerobically in sealed stone pits; fresh vegetables to dip in* olio extra-vergine d'oliva *from Brisighella. To follow, the pasta that we have handmade ourselves (with the assistance of our 'Mariettas'):* tortellini *served with a light tomato sauce, and* tagliatelle al ragù—*the fine, hand-rolled egg noodles bathed in the traditional meat* ragù *of Bologna. The* ragù *is perfectly paired with a deep and rich red Sangiovese di Romagna. Suitably replete from this simple repast, smugly proud of our culinary expertise, we relax afterwards with a small glass of Albana di Romagna* passito. *The wine is sweet, complex, exquisite, and we raise a toast to Pellegrino Artusi, the father of Italian home cooking, and one of the unlikely fathers of the Italian nation.* Salute, maestro e bravo!

195

ITALY IN A WINEGLASS

The History

If neither Vittorio Emanuele II nor the ambitious but pragmatic Count Camillo Benso di Cavour initially set out with the unification of Italy as the primary goal in their political machinations with France against the occupying Austrians, the result of their actions, together with the considerable assistance of Garibaldi and his 'Thousand', was to achieve just that, almost to the surprise of all. With the eventual addition of Venice and the Veneto in 1866 followed by Rome and its surrounds in 1870, a new nation had been born out of what had previously been a disparate collection of separate states and client states: the Spanish in Southern Italy and Sicily; the Austrians across the north-east from Venice to Milan; the Kingdom of Sardinia ruled by the House of Savoy overseeing North West Italy and across the Alps into France; the Papal States stretching from Rome over the Apennines to the Adriatic Coast and up into Emilia-Romagna; and client state duchies in Tuscany, Parma, Modena and elsewhere that owed their allegiances to the nations that kept them in power.

Yet, when a Spanish king was overthrown in Naples and replaced with the new king of Italy who came from Piedmont, could that in any way have served to unite those living in the Kingdom of the Two Sicilies with people from Northern Italy? Could Venetians even understand the language of those who came from Naples or Brindisi or vice versa? Did Italy's first king spare even a thought for his subjects living in abject poverty in Lucania or Calabria? A long history of neighbouring cities and city-states at war with one another— a legacy of the Lombards and after them of internecine conflicts such as those between Guelphs and Ghibellines—meant that deep-seated enmities remained between towns and cities, as well as between the disparate former countries and regions.

There were great differences in food traditions, ingredients and produce too, as well as methods of cooking and eating across the new nation. Class undoubtedly played a part. The working classes and country folk survived on a crafty subsistence diet based on whatever ingredients were in season or available wherever they lived, the so-called *cucina povera* that we celebrate today. Noble families and the wealthy often had French cooks and enjoyed meals at formal banquets that consisted of dishes with French names cooked in the French style. So culturally, linguistically and gastronomically, it seemed in the immediate years after unification that the varied peoples across the Italian Peninsula sometimes had very little in common with each other, if anything at all.

Pellegrino Artusi might seem to be an unlikely protagonist to assist in the lofty process of helping a new nation to come together. A bourgeois middle-class businessman from Forlimpopoli, with flamboyant mutton-chop whiskers that were out of date even in his own time, Artusi had made his career and his fortune as a salesman travelling throughout the Italian Peninsula in the years before the creation of the Kingdom of Italy. Staying in inns and *osterie*, or sometimes in people's homes, he thus had the opportunity to sample and enjoy the varied cuisines that he encountered along the way, from the Spanish Kingdom of the Two Sicilies up to Austria's Kingdom of Lombardy and from the Piedmontese Kingdom of Sardinia across the broad and fertile Po Valley across Emilia into Romagna and the Papal States. He visited and ate in Venice, Naples, Rome, Padua, Ancona, Milan, Turin and Trieste, amongst many other places. As a native of Romagna and a resident of Florence for most of his adult life, he was already acquainted with the cuisines of those important areas. Not only did he travel and eat, but he also took copious notes and seems to have had an extraordinary memory for the tastes of the foods that he had encountered and enjoyed along the way.

Artusi came from a wealthy family with landed interests in the Romagna countryside and went on to amass a fortune as a businessman and astute investor. On retiring, he found himself with both the time and money to be able to devote himself to his intellectual interests, writing two non-fiction books that even he appears not to have found overly stimulating: as he modestly wrote in the introduction to his work on Giuseppe Giusti, an Italian poet and writer, 'May God save you from yawns.'

By the 1880s, Artusi had moved to the elegant Piazza d'Azeglio in the centre of Florence, a beautiful square named after Massimo d'Azeglio, the great statesman who had dreamed of the creation of the Italian nation and who had helped to see that dream come true. It was from here that Artusi began to write his greatest work, *La scienza in cucina e l'arte di mangier bene* (Science in the Kitchen and the Art of Eating Well). Perhaps it might seem a little presumptuous for someone who had no apparent interest in cooking himself, and who had probably never lifted a saucepan or wielded a *mattarello* (rolling pin) in anger in his life, to set out to teach a new nation how to cook. But that is precisely what he did. Based on his notes and recollections, he instructed his faithful cook Marietta Sabbatini (hence the 'Marietta' who helped me to learn to handmake pasta) and housekeeper Francesco Ruffilli to test and prepare the recipes that he described to them while he wrote down the resulting recipes, together with wry asides, comments, observations and notes.

On completion of his masterpiece, a substantial book containing no fewer than 475 recipes, Artusi set about finding a willing publisher. Like many aspiring authors, he had to suffer the disappointment of rejection. Finally, in 1891, at the age of seventy-one, he decided simply to pay to produce, print and publish the book himself. He had 1,000 copies printed and worked tirelessly to promote the book, taking out newspaper advertisements and promoting it through women's societies. He was involved in the direct sale of the book and even signed each copy personally before sending it off. Thus, he managed to sell out that first print run.

Soon, a curious thing happened: readers began to write to him to tell him how much they enjoyed his book but noted that he had missed out this or that important recipe or that their version of a recipe he had included was done differently in their home or area. They sent him their own recipes or versions of recipes, and when he reprinted the book he included them in each new edition, the book thus growing organically to become a true and of-the-moment snapshot of how people were cooking and eating across the Kingdom of Italy. There were recipes linked to places throughout the new country: *tortellini alla bolognese*; *riso e luganighe* as enjoyed in the Veneto; *cuscussù*, a dish linked to the Arab occupation of Sicily; the saffron-tinted *risotto alla milanese*; *maccheroni alla napoletana*; *maccheroni con le sarde* as still enjoyed in Palermo today; *saltimbocca alla romana*—Roman of course; *stracotto di vitella* from Florence; and much more. Not every single one of Italy's twenty regions of today is covered—it seems unlikely Artusi ever travelled to Sardinia—but the book's comprehensive scope remains impressive even now.

Science in the Kitchen and the Art of Eating Well thus grew to become an important and vital work that reflected a young and new nation as it came to define itself through its varied cuisines. Like Cavour before him who believed in science to improve viticulture in his native Barolo region, Artusi believed that a scientific approach to cooking was the key to teaching his readers 'the art of eating well'. As he says in the opening pages,

> Cooking is a troublesome sprite. Often it may drive you to despair. Yet it is also very rewarding, for when you do succeed, or overcome a difficulty in doing so, you feel the satisfaction of a great triumph. ... The best teacher is experience, under an adept's watchful eye. Yet even lacking this, with a guide such as mine, and devotion to your labours, you should be able, I hope, to put something decent together. (trans. Murtha Baca and Stephen Sartarelli)

Artusi's self-deprecating and avuncular tone endeared him to his readers and to generations of Italians who even today reach up for a battered copy, perhaps handed down over generations, to consult *L'Artusi*. By including an increasing number of recipes supplied by the readers themselves, he cleverly made older editions obsolete, and by crediting his contributors by name, he gave them a piece of ownership of the work. Fourteen editions were published, and more than 50,000 copies sold before Pellegrino passed away at ninety years of age, presumably a happy, well-fed and very rich man. He rewarded his silent co-authors, Marietta Sabbatini and Francesco Ruffilli, by bequeathing them significant sums 'free of inheritance tax'. He furthermore acknowledged Marietta's contributions by naming recipe 604 after her: *Panettone Marietta*, saying that 'she was a good cook, and such a good-hearted, honest woman that she deserves to have this cake named after her, especially since she taught me how to make it'.

Artusi was an astute businessman, and he knew his market well. *Science in the Kitchen* was directed to an affluent female readership, or those who had socially upward aspirations to upper-middle class airs. Literacy at the turn of the century was still linked to class and gender, as well as to geography, with the south lagging far behind the north. For many women, Artusi's tome would have been one of the first books they themselves had ever owned.

Artusi's genius was to speak directly to his readers with a gentle voice and in a language they could understand. It must be remembered that Artusi wrote at the end of the nineteenth century, a time when there was neither a codified Italian national cuisine nor yet a codified national language: there were scores of different languages and dialects spoken not just from region to region but sometimes even from village to village, as can still be the case even today. Though originally from Romagna, he chose to write in Tuscan Italian, the language of Dante, and the language that would come to be accepted as the preferred form for written Italian. He is happy to acknowledge that language differs from place to place and to point out curious terms or names used in certain areas (in the headnote for recipe 294 he states, 'What a strange language they speak in learned Bologna!').

He is contemptuous of the use of foreign terms, especially when used to sound grandiose. As he states for recipe 38, *Zuppa sul sugo di carne* (soup with meat sauce):

> Certain cooks, to give themselves airs, mangle the phrases of our less than benevolent neighbours, using names that resound mightily and say nothing. According to them, this soup should be called *mitonnée*. But for the sake of our national dignity, I have made every effort to use our own beautiful and harmonious language, and so it pleases me to call the soup by its simple and natural name.

For recipe 277, *Piccioni all'inglese* ('Squab English style'), he comments:

> I would like to make it clear once and for all that names do not mean much in
> my kitchen, and that I give no importance to high-sounding titles. If an
> Englishman should tell me that I have not made this dish according to the
> customs of his country, I do not care a fig. All I care is that it be judged tasty,
> and that is the end of the matter.

Curious and antiquated though the book may seem today, *Science in the Kitchen
and the Art of Eating Well* is of more than mere historical interest. Written over
130 years ago, it has stood the test of time remarkably well. In extolling and
explaining in plain language a cuisine that embraced virtually the whole country, in celebrating the national over the foreign and in defining what has come
to be seen as a quintessential element of the Italian character ('the art of eating
well'), wherever in the country one comes from, Artusi's great work undeni-
ably helped to shape the newly emerging Italian nation and bring its people
together.

Home cooking today in Italy remains firmly rooted to region, territory,
city, neighbourhood, or just to the way things have always been done in each
person's individual household, as handed down from their *nonna* or *bisnonna*.
Food undoubtedly and intrinsically is linked to each Italian's very personal
identity. Yet in bringing such delicious diversity together in the pages of a
single book, Artusi achieved what d'Azeglio longed for: he created a common
bond for all peoples across the Italian Peninsula and its islands through the
common love of and interest in food—its careful and scientific preparation,
and the pleasure of its consumption.

The Wines

*Trapunta, Romagna Albana DOCG Secco Macerato, Giovanna Madonia, Bertinoro,
Emilia-Romagna*

'I love the good and the beautiful wherever I find them', wrote Artusi in the
preface to the fourteenth edition of *Science in the Kitchen and the Art of Eating
Well*, 'and hate to see anyone squander, as they say, God's bounty. Amen.'
Though this now classic work was first published in 1891, this elderly Italian's
views on food, wine and living and eating well seem remarkably modern and
in keeping with our concerns today. Wine features in *Science in the Kitchen*,
but it should be remembered that in that era it was not an exalted product as

it is today, nor was the culture of wine drinking particularly well developed or sophisticated. Nonetheless, from letters and correspondence on display in Casa Artusi, the foundation dedicated to Italian home cookery in the town of Artusi's birth, there are indications that he always retained a fondness for wine from his native Romagna, and in particular wine from Bertinoro, where the Artusi family had landholdings.

Giovanna Madonia in Bertinoro is an entirely artisanal winery that produces wines *come una volta*. Once the grapes—the two principal native varieties of Romagna, Albana and Sangiovese—are harvested, fermentation takes place using the natural indigenous yeasts present on the bloom of the grapes, with no recourse to temperature control or filtration and using a minimal amount of sulphites. Long maceration for red as well as white is an important feature of these wines, and afterwards there is lengthy ageing in an underground cellar that dates to the 1700s.

Romagna Albana or Albana di Romagna was the first white wine in Italy to be granted select DOCG status in 1987. The grape variety, Albana, was extolled in antiquity and rightly so, for its virtues are the strong phenolic character that comes from the skins allied to an elevated acidity that keeps the wine fresh. Giovanna Madonia's Trabunta is what we would today call an orange wine, that is, a white wine made like a red wine through fermentation on the skins. Albana grapes, cultivated on calcareous-clay soil at an altitude of around 300 to 350 metres above sea level, are harvested, crushed and allowed to ferment spontaneously, the fermenting must remaining on the skins of the grapes for about seven months, with a further five months of ageing on the lees. This is how white wines used to be made in Italy, and the result is extraordinary: a burnished gold colour, complex aromas of bitter peel, aromatic herbs, tropical and exotic fruits, with a little bite of tannin, and a richness and fullness in the mouth. Orange wines today are considered new and exciting, but in fact this is a wholly traditional wine produced in a style that Artusi would most certainly himself have recognised and fully enjoyed, in moderation of course.

Scaccomatto Albana di Romagna passito DOCG, Fattoria Zerbina, Faenza, Emilia-Romagna

The link between diet and health was something that Artusi was already aware of. In a chapter titled 'A Few Health Guidelines', he notes that 'some health experts' advise against drinking wine during meals. However, he adds, 'You may try this if you have the nerve for it; to me it seems a bit too much to ask.'

I'm sure that Artusi would certainly have considered a glass of Albana di Romagna *passito* to be an ideal post-prandial tipple to aid the digestion. Fattoria Zerbina produces one of the best examples, an exquisite dessert wine made from Albana grapes that have been affected by *muffa nobile* or noble rot, the beneficial fungus *Botrytis cinerea* that attacks grapes when conditions are just right—usually damp or foggy mornings followed by dry, well-ventilated and sunny afternoons—to drive out moisture, concentrate grape sugars and lend aromas and textures that are quite extraordinary and magnificent. At Fattoria Zerbina, Albana grapes are late-harvested, usually in several passes, so that only those bunches affected by the *muffa nobile* are collected. In those years when conditions do not allow, then the wine simply is not made. The grapes are fermented either in small stainless-steel vats or in used French oak *barriques* followed by a further period of ageing in stainless-steel and in the bottle. This extraordinary wine has a tremendous capacity to age and is considered among the great dessert *passito* wines of Italy.

19

IDEALS, ECONOMICS AND HEROIC WINES

The Cinque Terre is without doubt one of the most beautiful and magical of all Italy's many beautiful wine lands. It is also one of the harshest, most inaccessible and labour intensive. Here on the Ligurian seaboard, the steep cliffs have been carved out of shifting, inhospitable, sedimentary terrain of flint and slate into a wave-like pattern of vine-covered terraces held in place by centuries-old small, dry-stone walls. I recall walking through this harshly beautiful vinescape many years ago when our son Guy was just two years old. As we struggled uphill from Manarola towards Groppo, we met an elderly barefoot woman, emerging from the vineyards, her head wrapped in a scarf to protect from the fierce midday sun. She stopped to admire our little boy.

We talked about life in the Cinque Terre and the work in the vineyards. 'Yes, it is very hard', she said. 'The only people you see working in the fields are the old ones like me, no? The young today don't want to do it. In twenty years, all these vineyards will be gone, turned back to scrubland and woods.'

In fact, that was now more than thirty years ago, and the vineyards today are thriving more than ever, thanks in no small part to the efforts of a visionary and far-reaching cooperative winery that has found a way to ease the backbreaking workload in these vertiginous slopes and to champion and safeguard a remarkable wine and way of life that would otherwise have been lost. It is bakingly hot, thirst-inducing in the sunshine, and we finally reach the Cantina Cinque Terre. Here we pause in the shade to enjoy a glass of chilled Cinque Terre bianco, fresh, quenching, clean and fragrant, with a slightly salty aftertaste. This is a heroic wine, in absolute perfect harmony with the land that gives it birth, and with the simple maritime cuisine that it best accompanies.

The History

A recurring reality across the history of Italy is that the rural population has long endured hardship, sometimes to the greatest and most brutal degree.

From the slavery that existed during the times of the ancients, serfdom in the Middle Ages and the somewhat more enlightened *mezzadria* that—in theory if not always in practice—gave tenants at least ownership over half of what they produced, to the many millions of landless labourers who worked at less than subsistence level for generations with no hope of escaping their misery, the rural poor, upon whom the well-being of the country's economy depended, undoubtedly carried the heaviest and most onerous burden.

By the nineteenth century, however, spurred on by reforms and revolutions that had rocked Europe, new ideas were being brought to the fore to improve social conditions and the lot of the working classes, both in country and city alike. The cooperative movement was one such idea that took root in Italy by the middle of the century, encouraged by liberal thinkers such as Giuseppe Mazzini, the progressive nationalist politician and activist who had advocated the creation of an Italian republic. The first cooperative in Italy in fact was established in 1854 in Turin, before Italy was even yet a nation.

After the Kingdom of Italy was created, changes in land tenure did take place. Certain feudal rights were abolished, large rural estates were broken up and large tracts of land owned by the Church were sold off at state auction. The landless peasantry had little or no opportunity to purchase land for themselves, not even a scrap or a tiny parcel. How could they when they had absolutely no surplus money or any means of borrowing? Nonetheless, change did happen as a new class of small landowners emerged together with tenant farmers who at least had the right to profit from the sweat of their own efforts. It was mainly to them that the new form of cooperative venture was most appealing.

The basic ideal behind these early cooperatives was to find a way to create businesses or organisations that were owned and run jointly by their members for their mutual benefit rather than for the profit of landowners or shareholders. But beyond this simple ideal lay a multiplicity of motivations. As socialism and later communism rose in prominence, some cooperatives were formed to promote the abolition of private property. At the other end of the spectrum, a Catholic urge to promote social improvement was inspired by Pope Leo XIII's encyclical on capital and labour, *Rerum novarum*, which in 1891 affirmed the worth of the working classes and exhorted rich and poor to work together for the common good. Thus, these two main wings—socialism and the Catholic Church—offered competing foundations based on different values upon which the early cooperatives were created towards the end of the nineteenth and the early years of the twentieth centuries. From its origins, the cooperative movement in Italy has thus always been connected to political ideals.

By 1910, Italy had some 7,400 cooperatives with over a million members; a decade later, the Italian Ministry of Labour reported that this had grown to over 19,500 cooperatives across the country. The cooperative model was highly adaptable, able to be applied to any number of activities and businesses, urban and rural, for the benefit of worker and consumer, as well as to provide essential services such as transport and banking. From a food and drink point of view, not only did the cooperative model work particularly well for wine-making cooperatives but there were also cooperative dairies for processing and transforming fresh milk into butter and cheese, cooperative mills for processing grain into flour, cooperative olive oil mills, as well as cooperative fishermen's societies, among others.

Not even Fascism was able to completely undermine the cooperative ideal. Mussolini himself, in a declaration delivered on 13 November 1922, professed his admiration for cooperative enterprises that served as a defence against greed and speculation. But the truth was that Fascist opposition to socialism in any form meant that any socialist-leaning cooperatives that were allowed to continue could only do so after completely reorganising their structure, with the appointment of new directors and managers who were members of the Fascist Party. Nonetheless, at the beginning of 1937, there were still 179 officially sanctioned winemaking cooperatives with a membership of 16,500 that collectively produced some 200 million litres of wine, a considerable amount by any calculation.

Some of Italy's most important cooperative wineries still making wine today can trace their history back to the earliest days of the cooperative movement. The Kellerei/Cantina Terlan was founded in 1893, Kellerei/Cantina Tramin in 1898 (both are in Südtirol/Alto Adige, which at the time of foundation was part of Austria–Hungary), while the La Versa cooperative in Lombardy's Oltrepò Pavese dates to 1905. In those early years, cooperatives were formed from winegrowers who banded together to pool their resources to help each other. Small farmers would not have had the resources to invest in a winery nor the skills necessary to market the resulting wine. What the cooperative could offer was to buy grapes from its members at a fair price, and the grapes would be transformed into wine that could be sold in whatever way seemed best at that time, whether *sfuso*—'loose' or in bulk—or, usually much later, in bottle. *Soci* or members would have their say in how a cooperative was to be run, though there would always be a president or management committee to make the ultimate decisions. In this way, small grape growers, including tenant farmers and even sharecroppers, were guaranteed to receive a fair market price for their grapes. Any profit made from selling the resulting wine was invested back into the cooperative, with a certain percentage shared with its respective umbrella organisation.

The reconstruction that followed the Second World War saw an expansion of cooperatives. Article 45 of the new Italian Constitution expressly acknowledged the importance of cooperation: 'The Republic acknowledges the social function of cooperation as a form of mutual aid devoid of all private speculative intent. The law promotes and encourages the expansion of cooperation by the most suitable means.' The two main umbrella strands of cooperative endeavour were reorganised as Legacoop (the left-leaning socialist-communist arm) and Confcooperative (the Catholic arm, closely linked to the Christian Democratic Party). Some of the country's most important wine cooperatives across the country were founded in this post-war period: Cavit in Trentino in 1950, Cantine Settesoli in Sicily in 1958, Cantina Tollo in Abruzzo in 1960, Cantine Leonardo da Vinci in Tuscany in 1961, Cantine San Marzano in Apulia in 1962, Cantina Produttori Cormòns in Friuli in 1968, among many others.

In this post-war period, when the concept of modern Italian fine wine had not yet been defined or fully articulated, the wines that many cooperatives produced did not aspire to greatness or even to high quality. That wasn't ever their goal or even intention. Usually, from the smallest member to the director or president of a wine cooperative, they were first and foremost a collection of grape growers. The cooperative's role was therefore to provide an outlet through which to process their produce, transforming grapes into a commodity that could be sold. Since payment was by weight, growers sought to reach the highest yields they could manage. There was little or no incentive, nor perhaps even the knowledge, to encourage growers to reduce yields in order to produce higher-quality wines. Moreover, in a sun-drenched country like Italy, grapes grown particularly in southern vineyards would have reached high levels of sugar that transformed into correspondingly high levels of potential alcohol, too high to ever produce wines of delicacy and finesse. No wonder that much of the wine produced was for local consumption only, or to be used to 'boost'—that is, to add colour and alcohol to—lighter and more insipid wines from northern climes, to be used in fortified wines such as Vermouth or else to be distilled into grape alcohol.

However, by the 1970s, as wine technology improved, most notably through the introduction of stainless-steel vessels in which fermentation temperature could be controlled, the best cooperatives saw the opportunity to produce sound, clean table wines that could be bottled and sold locally, nationally and even internationally. Not only did they need to invest in modern equipment, replacing concrete fermentation vats with stainless-steel and continuous wine presses with softer pneumatic ones, but they also needed to change the mentality of their grape growing members. Quality wine begins in the vineyard, and growers had to be convinced to reduce yields and to harvest at optimum times as well as to take note of specific sites historically noted for their excellence; for such superior grapes, the best cooperatives paid their growers a considerable premium to encourage their efforts.

In some cases, cooperative wineries were created not only to safeguard historic vineyards but also ways of life. In those areas where the cultivation of the grapevine is carried out at the extreme limits of its viability and where small grape growers would otherwise find it difficult to carry on and make a living, cooperative wineries have enabled such activities to continue where otherwise they would have been lost. The Cantina Cinque Terre in Liguria has helped to maintain viticulture in one of the harshest, most demanding and labour-intensive yet stunningly beautiful stretches of wine country. Meanwhile, high up in the Alps, just under the towering Mont Blanc glacier, a cooperative winery, the Cave Mont Blanc, helps to support grape growers working some of the highest vineyards in Europe, located at a vertiginous 1,300 metres above sea level. Here, in this rarefied mountain atmosphere, the vines are trained on low-lying pergolas to enable them to benefit from the full heat of the alpine sun to produce ethereal, light mountain wines that are absolutely unique. These examples represent more than just the production of wines: the extreme effort necessary to continue viticulture in such conditions makes the resulting products nothing short of heroic.

Today, there are at least 500 cooperative wineries across the country accounting for a staggering 60 per cent of Italian wine production as well as a high proportion of the Italian wines that are exported abroad. Some cooperative wineries are as technologically advanced as any in the private sector, and the best offer support to grower members in the vineyard, helping with vineyard management, pest control, identifying the best parcels of land, advising on the best grape varieties to cultivate and specifying the optimum moment to harvest.

Because wine cooperatives represent the interests of their grape-growing *soci*, there is a built-in awareness of the need to be environmentally responsible, respecting the very land that nourishes their vines. Cooperative wineries have also helped to safeguard Italy's unique vinous biodiversity. Rather than encouraging members to grub up local varieties in favour of international, cooperatives have continued to support the cultivation of local and autochthonous grape varieties, safe in the knowledge that these varieties have been cultivated for generations and that the wines produced will at least always find a local market. Increasingly, this very biodiversity has become a marketing strength as intrepid wine drinkers are seeking new flavours and wines to discover.

Social awareness and responsibility have also been part of the cooperative ideal from its onset. In 1991, social cooperatives—organisations that exist to serve the general interests of the community—were legally recognised. In Sicily, the Libera Terra cooperative makes wines from grapes grown on lands confiscated from the Mafia. In Tuscany, the San Patrignano cooperative provides a community as well as work for young, recovering addicts.

Is the spirit of cooperation, of working together for the common good part of the Italian character? Italian cooperatives were born out of idealism in the mid-nineteenth century, and ideals, ethics and economics are still very much at the heart of the best of such endeavours. The cooperative model is sometimes considered old-fashioned or out of synch with today's modern economy that celebrates the individual and private enterprise. Yet, on the contrary, cooperatives have proved to be particularly deft at adapting to today's challenging economic and climatic conditions. In fact, Italy today is one of the most cooperative countries in the world: the overall movement oversees some 60,000 cooperative enterprises providing employment for more than a million workers. The ongoing success of cooperative wineries across the country is proof that, through cooperation, ideals and economics can come together to preserve livelihoods, support traditional agriculture, promote biodiversity, combat climate change and yield a wealth of exciting wines that are expressions of their territory, the land and the people from which they are born.

The Wines

Cinque Terre bianco DOC, Cantina Cinque Terre, Groppo, Liguria

Italy's Cinque Terre is made up of five stunningly beautiful, colourful villages that cling tenaciously to the steep cliffs of the Ligurian coastline below Levanto: Monterosso, Vernazza, Corniglia, Manarola and Riomaggiore. Traditionally, this was an area where people lived by fishing along the rocky coast and by tending vineyards planted on historic dry-stone terraces carved out of the steep, shifting sedimentary terrain of flint and slate. The vineyards, planted in low *pergola* fashion to protect the grapes from the strong sea winds that blow up in the mornings, are back-breakingly difficult to tend, and such is their steepness and inaccessibility that they are among the most labour intensive in the world.

In order to collectively ease the workload and make tending grapes economically viable, the winegrowers of this area banded together in 1973 to form a cooperative winery that has enabled them to safeguard not only a historic wine that might otherwise have been lost but also to protect an ancient way of life. Today, there are 220 cooperative members tending collaboratively just 46 hectares of vineyards. The cooperative has made considerable investment to ease the workload in the vineyards as well as to preserve the biodiversity of a unique vineyard: for example, both funiculars and *monorotaie*—mini-monorails—have been installed throughout the vineyards for the transport of workers' tools, materials and grapes at harvest time from one steep slope to the next or to the road for ease of collection. The centuries-old dry-stone walls are kept intact and collectively maintained to keep soil integrity in place as well as the uniquely beautiful shape of the vinescape. Helicopters are used to spray treatments across the vineyards in those areas that would otherwise be inaccessible. These are luxuries that a small winegrower working on their own would never be able to afford.

The wine that results, Cinque Terre *bianco*, is rarely encountered outside of this beautiful and popular region, not least because it finds a ready market with the millions of tourists who make their way here each year to walk along the coastal footpath and to visit and stay in the five charming villages along the coast. Dry, with a hint of herbs on the palate, a flinty, mineral finish and a somewhat salty aftertaste, rarely will you find wine in better harmony with its surrounding and with the local cuisine that it accompanies: platters of *antipasti di mare*, *penne ai scampi* or locally landed fish simply cooked over charcoal. Cinque Terre *bianco* is a heroic wine not because it makes claims to greatness but precisely because it does not. The intrepid winegrowers of the Cinque Terre deserve to make great wine as a reward for their considerable efforts. It is to their immense credit that they continue to grow grapes and make wine at all, seemingly against all odds, thanks to the efforts of this visionary cooperative winery.

Terlaner I Grand Cuvée, Alto Adige DOC, Kellerei Cantina Terlan, Terlan, Südtirol

When twenty-four small winegrowers decided in 1893 to band together to form the Kellerei Terlan, it was a daring departure, for at that time, under the Austrians, most of South Tyrol was in the hands of large and powerful landowners. This was—and remains today—historic and favoured wine country, with evidence of grape growing dating back to pre-Roman times. Though at the end of the nineteenth century, this area was noted mainly for its red wines, Terlan was already famous for the quality of its white wines. The Terlan cooperative decided from the outset therefore to concentrate on the production of quality white wines, and this is still the focus of its activities. Today, 143 growers work 190 hectares of vineyards, bringing their grapes to the modern winemaking facility to be transformed into an outstanding and award-winning range of wines.

The quality of the fruit grown in these steep, well-exposed alpine vineyards is the key to the success of the cooperative. The vineyards lie between 250 and 900 metres above sea level, planted on complex terrain that ranges from light, sandy loam to quartz porphyry of volcanic origin. The mountains protect the vineyards from cold northerly winds, and the microclimate is at times almost Mediterranean in feel with a marked contrast between day and night temperatures throughout the growing season.

The white wines that result—70 per cent of production—have remarkable complexity as well as an extraordinary ability to mature and evolve with age. Kellerei Cantina Terlan has almost uniquely invested in the infrastructure necessary to age its white wines for very lengthy periods, in the case of the Rarities range for upwards of decades, something very unusual for producers of white wines. Such wines are uniquely produced by a process known as the Stocker method named after the cooperative's former winemaker, Sebastian Stocker. By this method and only in the best years, selected white wines are vinified and matured for twelve months in oak barrels before being placed in small, sealed stainless-steel tanks where they are left to age on their lees for between ten and thirty years. During this lengthy sojourn, they develop a complex structure and a wealth of aromas while maintaining a remarkable youthful freshness. Only when the winemaker feels that they have attained perfect harmony will a Rarity vintage be released, always an important and long-awaited moment.

The most typical wine of Kellerei Cantina Terlan is Terlaner, a historic blend of Pinot Bianco, Chardonnay and Sauvignon that has been produced since the foundation of the cooperative. While the Rarity is undoubtedly the pride and pinnacle of the cooperative's wines, another special *cuvée* is produced that is said to be 'the innermost expression of Kellerei Cantina Terlan': Terlaner I Grand Cuvée. This special wine is produced from a blend of 65 per cent Pinot Bianco, 32 per cent Chardonnay and 3 per cent Sauvignon. After gentle, whole cluster pressing, the must ferments slowly in large oak barrels, spending time on the lees for about a year, with periodic *bâtonnage*. The wine that results is extraordinary in depth of flavour, rich and complex on the nose with a powerful structure and multi-layered texture in the mouth, and an intense and lingering concentrated finish that leaves the tastebuds tingling from the minerality that is a true expression of its terroir.

Chaudelune vin de glace, Valle d'Aosta DOC, Cave Mont Blanc, Morgex, Valle d'Aosta

Valle d'Aosta is the smallest of Italy's twenty regions, an autonomous mountainous area that nestles amid the Alps that lead via passes and tunnels to and from France and Switzerland. This is an ancient corridor that has served to link Italy to the rest of Europe for millennia. It is also an ancient and historic wine land where vineyards have been cultivated since at least the time when Augustus founded the region's capital, Aosta. Here in the high and starkly beautiful mountains, surrounded by snow-covered peaks that dominate in all directions, somewhat amazingly and unexpectedly, vines are cultivated at the highest limit of their viability, up to a dizzying 1,300 metres above sea level, making them the highest vineyards in Europe.

This is not nor ever will be a major wine-producing region by any means, and growing grapes is rarely a full-time activity. Rather, those who live and work here often have a small patch of land, maybe handed down over the generations, where vines are trained on the low-lying *pergole basse* to fan out to expose them to every minute of fleeting but fierce alpine sun in an atmosphere that is clean and rarefied. Here, one local, indigenous grape variety reigns supreme: Prié Blanc.

As in Cinque Terre, working such historic vineyards is backbreaking. In the past, individual wine growers—who might also have a herd of cows to tend—would cultivate their vines, harvest and make the wines themselves, usually in tiny quantity. Then they would try to sell their efforts, something that was not always easy. In 1971, a visionary parish priest from Morgex, Don Bougeat, felt that such efforts, admirable as they were, were not doing justice to the historic tradition and to the sheer effort required to make this special alpine wine. He set in motion the idea for the creation of a cooperative winery that would recognise and reward its winegrowing members in a more just and fitting way. Thus, the Cave Mont Blanc de Morgex et La Salle was born in 1983. The cooperative received regional assistance to invest in the creation of a modern winery that would serve the interests of its part-time grape growing *soci*. Today, there are eighty *soci* who produce around 140,000 bottles of wine, entirely from the unique, autochthonous Prié Blanc.

Blanc de Morgex et de la Salle, the still version, is one of the most unique and ethereal of all of Italy's varied expressions of the fermented grape, so light, so delicate that its alpine floral aromas and taste seemingly linger for but a moment then are gone. An excellent range of sparkling wines is also produced through secondary fermentation in the bottle. The fruity acidity of Prié Blanc cultivated at high altitude results in wines that are light, delicate and elegant.

However, the most remarkable wine produced by this cooperative winery must be Chaudelune, a *vin de glace* or ice wine made only in those years when conditions allow for the Prié Blanc to be left on the vine well into late November or December when the first frost and snows arrive. Only once the individual grapes have frozen are they harvested, transported quickly back to the winery and immediately pressed so that the sugar-rich must is separated from the ice that is left behind. This concentrated grape must goes into small oak casks where fermentation takes place very slowly. In this way, a unique wine results that manages to link two traditions: the *eiswein* of Germanic tradition with the more traditional oxidised style of dessert wines that in Italy are more usually made from grapes that have been harvested and then laid out to semi-dry to raisins. Chaudelune is an astonishing creation, born in the snowy, glacial heights of Mont Blanc from grapes ripened in the warm, alpine Italian sunshine. It is an exquisite *vino da meditazione* to sip in front of a fire after a day spent outdoors walking or skiing, reflecting on the majesty, beauty and power of the mountains, all contained within one small, glistening glass.

Montepulciano d'Abruzzo 'biologico' DOP, Cantina Tollo, Tollo, Abruzzo

Cantina Tollo produces in quantity powerful, straightforward wines that are an expression of Abruzzo, an isolated mountainous region in the south of Italy. Its red Montepulciano d'Abruzzo and whites Trebbiano d'Abruzzo and Pecorino Terre di Chieti are the sort that you might encounter in your local wine shop, supermarket or served in an Italian 'tratt' or pizzeria anywhere in the world. You've probably already tasted them yourself. They are fairly priced, great value and are wonderful to enjoy with simple foods. They are also wines that have brought prosperity to an impoverished land, helped local people to remain rather than emigrate and given vital employment to many.

A sad reality in Italy is that its people, primarily from the Mezzogiorno, the south, historically had to leave their beloved home localities in search of a better life, whether that meant transferring to the industrial north where they could find employment in factories, or else leaving to start a new life in other parts of Europe, America, South America or Australia. Driven out by poverty, by generations of subsistence living and sometimes even by hunger, millions of Italians were on the move at the end of the nineteenth century and early years of the twentieth, and this trend continued steadily through the years following the end of the Second World War.

Such was the situation in Abruzzo, an isolated mountainous region, particularly in the small wine communes like Tollo, located in the foothills of the Apennines overlooking the Adriatic Sea to the east. Thus, in 1960, a handful of small winegrowers took the brave decision that, rather than leave their homeland for a new life elsewhere, as many of their country folk had done and were doing, they would instead stay and band together to form a cooperative winery to concentrate exclusively on making wines from the region's indigenous grape varieties, most notably Montepulciano and Trebbiano. The success of this venture over the past sixty years has been considerable: today, Cantina Tollo oversees some 2,700 hectares of vineyards and has become a major source of both sound and outstanding wines that have helped to put Abruzzo on the wine map of Italy and the world while helping people in the region to remain in their homeland and earn a good livelihood from their efforts.

Cantina Tollo is particularly proud of its line of wines that are certified organic, meaning that no chemical herbicides and pesticides are used in their production, the use of sulphur dioxide is kept to the absolute minimum and non-animal products are used to fine, or clarify, the wine, making them suitable for vegans. Montepulciano d'Abruzzo *biologico* is an outstanding example. The beauty of the organically cultivated fruit of the Montepulciano grape is allowed to shine through purely and vividly in this full-bodied, well-balanced and clean red wine. It is produced ecologically and ethically by those conscious of the need to work in a sustainable manner that causes no harm to the majestic and beautiful land from which it is born.

Grillo, Sicilia DOC, Cantine Settesoli, Menfi, Sicily

Wine cooperatives can be totally transformative. Western Sicily in the 1950s was known for only one wine, Marsala, produced from bush-trained, high-yielding primarily Catarratto, Inzolia and Grillo grapes that were grown to be used to produce the fortified and oxidised wine that had been created in the eighteenth century primarily for export markets. It was thus a bold and determined vision when sixty-eight winegrowers banded together in 1958 to create the Cantine Settesoli cooperative with the aim of cultivating grapes to produce quality table wines. One of the main drivers behind the cooperative was Diego Planeta, who served as president of Settesoli from 1973 to 2011. Planeta is considered one of the giants of modern winemaking in Sicily. Through his efforts and under his guidance, Settesoli succeeded in both improving the quality and significantly enhancing the awareness and reputation of Sicily's wines. Cantine Settesoli today has some 2,000 winegrowing *soci* or members working 6,000 hectares of vineyards and producing an extensive range of wines from the everyday to premium, wines that have won prestigious awards and that feature in the best guides to Italian wines.

Cantine Settesoli was a pioneering wine cooperative in so many ways. At a time when many wine cooperatives particularly in Sicily and Southern Italy were still selling wines in bulk, Cantine Settesoli under Planeta carried out important research in collaboration with institutions such as the Istituto Regionale della Vite e del Vino and with universities. From such studies, the first plantation in Sicily of international grape varieties began in the 1980s. Careful analysis of different terroirs, viticultural zoning and clonal selection further gave winegrowers the opportunity to cultivate the varieties best suited to their vineyard sites, and the cooperative rewarded them for concentrating on quality rather than quantity. In 2010, the company introduced the first nocturnal, mechanical grape harvester, enabling grapes to be harvested when temperatures are cool, thus best preserving the grapes' aromatic qualities and freshness. From traceability and sustainability to a commitment to social responsibility, Settesoli has been and continues to be a leader in the wine sector, winning numerous awards and accolades.

Cantine Settesoli has wines that are more prestigious than this basic Grillo Sicilia DOC, but for me it represents something of the soul and origins of the cooperative. Grillo was unknown as a varietal named on the label until relatively recently, in no small measure through the efforts of Cantine Settesoli. Originally cultivated in western Sicily primarily to produce Marsala, today Grillo has emerged as one of Sicily's most characterful and reliable white grape varieties. This inexpensive Settesoli example always satisfies, for it embodies the warmth and sunshine of Sicily in a wine with the scent of citrus blossom and honey and a lingering, rich-in-the-mouth stony finish, an ideal accompaniment to the fish and seafood of western Sicily, such as *cous cous di pesce alla trapanese*.

20

WARS AND WINE

The vineyard that surrounds Cantina Produttori Cormòns looks nothing out of the ordinary, yet it is a remarkable testament of hope and goodwill born out of a land torn with war. Friuli–Venezia Giulia, located in the far north-eastern corner of Italy, as we have seen, has suffered since time immemorial. Invasions have always come from the north—the Visigoths, Huns, Lombards and Franks all crossed the Julian Alps to conquer this beautiful land. The Venetians vied with the Austrians to control this corner of the country. Napoleon briefly established French rule before ceding territory to Austria. In the last century, the region was the scene of the fiercest fighting in the First World War when it found itself on the front line against the might of the Austro-Hungarian Empire, while in the Second World War North-East Italy, like much of the country, was occupied by the Nazis.

Out of strife and turmoil, post-war renewal and reconstruction saw vineyards replanted and prosperity return to this coveted and fertile land. To mark the terrible events that had happened, the grower-members of a forward-thinking cooperative winery decided to gather a collection of different vine varieties from all five grape-growing continents. Thus, in 1983 the Vigna del Mondo—Vineyard of the World—began to take root, planted with 530 different varieties (today there are more than 800), including twelve vines taken from the slopes of Mount Ararat, where, according to the Bible, Noah's ark came to rest, as well as from where the Prophet Muhammad gave his final sermon. A selection of fruits from this wholly singular world vineyard are harvested and vinified to result in a unique wine, Vino della Pace—a touching gesture of human solidarity, peace and brotherhood, this wine produced from grapes grown on former killing fields.

The History

The Great War

By the first decade of the twentieth century, a restless nationalism had begun to spread across Europe as old orders and certainties came under threat. The

First Russian Revolution took place in 1905, provoked by social and political unrest across the vast Russian Empire. The Austro-Hungarian Empire felt similar tremors across its territories, too, especially in the Balkans, where peoples and nations were desperate to shed the yoke of imperialism. In Italy, a nation but four decades old, writers such as Gabriele D'Annunzio extolled an ultra-nationalism that sought to 'reclaim' from Austria–Hungary those parts of its empire that they thought belonged to Italy historically and culturally, most notably South Tyrol, Trieste and parts of the Slovenian and Dalmatian coast.

In 1909, Filippo Tommaso Marinetti published the *Manifesto of Futurism*, a declaration of intent that rejected Italy's past:

> It is from Italy that we launch through the world this violently upsetting incendiary manifesto of ours. With it, today, we establish Futurism, because we want to free this land from its smelly gangrene of professors, archaeologists, ciceroni and antiquarians. For too long has Italy been a dealer in second-hand clothes. We mean to free her from the numberless museums that cover her like so many graveyards. (trans. R.W. Flint)

The Futurists celebrated youth, speed, the power of mechanical machines and the beauty of war.

When, on 28 June 1914, Archduke Franz Ferdinand, heir to the Austro-Hungarian throne, and his wife Sophie, duchess of Hohenberg, were assassinated in Sarajevo by Yugoslav nationalist Gavrilo Princip, a Bosnian Serb, it was said to be 'the shot heard round the world'. For indeed, that act of rebellion against a great power was to precipitate the start of what came to be called the Great War. In Italy, there was already an agitated sentiment across parties, especially among those living in the north and including the young and vociferous Benito Mussolini, that Italy needed to be able to find its own destiny and even pursue Italian imperial ambitions in Africa.

At the time that war broke out, Italy was part of the Triple Alliance with Germany and Austria–Hungary. However, as this accord was defensive by nature, the still-youthful nation was allowed to remain neutral without having to offer material support to its allies. Behind the scenes, however, political machinations and the perceived opportunity that the war presented brought the government of the day in early 1915 to negotiate a secret Treaty of London in which Italy agreed to enter the war on the side of the Triple Entente (Britain, France and Russia) in return for the promise of substantial gains in territory should their efforts be successful. Italy thus resigned from the Triple Alliance and subsequently declared war against Austria–Hungary in May 1915.

Yet sadly, Italy was almost totally unprepared militarily to support the ambitions of its politicians. The Italian army numbered fewer than 300,000 men at the time that war was declared, and while conscription saw the army eventually mobilise some 5 million men, the mainly peasant conscripts were poorly led and poorly equipped almost throughout the entire war. Many of the soldiers were from the south, from far-off places such as Apulia, and had no natural desire or motive to fight for distant territorial gains that would not affect or improve their lives one single bit.

The north-eastern corner of Italy became a major battlefield, the frontline against Austria–Hungary. If the Somme was the main front in the Great War in France, it was the Isonzo, the Carso, the Bainsizza that came to be Italy's killing fields. The First Battle of the Isonzo, a broad river that flows from the Julian Alps to the Adriatic, took place in June 1915; by September 1917, that very same front was to see a further ten significant battles, with attempts to gain territories in the naturally fortified rocky terrain of the Carso and Bainsizza, a to-and-fro struggle that saw immense loss of life on both sides and that demonstrated the utter futility and folly of this tragic war.

The poet Giuseppe Ungaretti, stationed here as a soldier, captured the horror of the Italian frontline:

San Martino del Carso
Valloncelle dell'Albero Isolato 27 August 1916

Of these houses
nothing remains
but a few
fragments of wall

Of so many
who were like me
nothing remains
not even that much

But in the heart
no cross is missing

My heart
is the most lacerated country.
(trans. Marc Millon)

Despite the shortcomings in preparation, equipment, even food, the Italian army fought bravely on the Isonzo, in the Adige and on the *altopiano* of Asiago, managing to hold out against far superior forces as well as to make significant advances. In fact, the Eleventh Battle of the Isonzo was the largest ever Italian offensive, involving more than a million men and supported by massive artillery and mortars. Gains were made in the Bainsizza, so difficult to take and to hold, and the Austro-Hungarians were driven significantly backwards. However, at this point, the Germans, relieved of their burden to fight on the Russian front, came to the aid of their most important ally. Able now to concentrate on the Italian front, they inflicted on the Italians the most mighty and humiliating defeat at Caporetto, wiping out all the gains that had been made. Some 40,000 Italians were killed or wounded, and more than 280,000 were taken as prisoners.

The Piave is a broad and important river, rising in the Alps and descending for some 220 kilometres to enter the Adriatic just above Venice. It has historically been a watershed, a frontier upon which battles have been fought. Napoleon's troops took on the Austrians there in 1809, a decisive battle that saw the French briefly retake control of these lands. When the Italians retreated to the Piave after the debacle of Caporetto, they regrouped under new military leadership and put up a spirited defence until the eventual arrival of Allied forces to aid them. The Battle of the Piave took place in June 1918 and was to prove decisive, leading to the end of the Austro-Hungarian Empire. By the autumn of 1918, the Austrians and their allies the Germans were in full retreat as Italian and Allied forces drove north, eventually leading to the signing of an armistice on 4 November.

At the conclusion of the Great War, Italy found itself on the winning side. Yet the war had been a complete disaster for the country, as it was for almost every other nation that was involved. More than half a million Italians had lost their lives and more than two and a half million were wounded in the conflict. The civilian population suffered greatly, too, and the economy of the country was left in tatters. The battlefields of the north, especially across important wine lands in Friuli, Veneto, Trentino and South Tyrol, had been utterly destroyed.

In return, the vast territorial gains promised by the secret Treaty of London were not honoured, and the Treaty of Versailles proved to be a massive disappointment. Though Italy was granted Trentino and South Tyrol (the latter to the discontent of the region's German-speaking population), as well as Trieste and parts of Venezia–Giulia up to Gorizia, promised gains along the Dalmatian coast, and even including Adriatic islands and parts of the old Ottoman Empire, were not honoured; nor was the dream of an imperial Italy even close to being realised.

The rise of fascism

The humiliating post-war settlement gave fuel to right-wing extremists such as the poet D'Annunzio, who had served and distinguished himself in the Italian army during the war. His anger at what he and others saw as a wholesale betrayal led him, together with other ultra-nationalist fanatics, to seize and occupy the city of Fiume—today Rijeka in Croatia. Fiume was self-declared an independent state, the Regency of Carnaro, led by D'Annunzio himself under a precursor fascist regime that was to foreshadow what was soon to follow across Italy.

Though Fiume was ultimately surrendered to the newly formed Kingdom of Yugoslavia, its loss was more than symbolic. Combined with the worsening economic situation, food shortages and rising unemployment, it contributed to the eventual collapse of the liberal state and fuelled the unrelenting rise of right-wing extremism. Though Mussolini came from working-class origins in Romagna, and though he was originally a leading member of the Socialist Party, his political transition to the extreme right helped his newly formed Fascist Party to attract supporters from the middle and upper classes, especially landowners, all eager to protect their own vested interests in the face of left-wing disruption such as general strikes called by the trade unions, or social agitation drummed up by the communists. By 1922, Mussolini and the Fascist Party had gained virtually total control of the government through the active or tacit support of the establishment, including the king of Italy. The Catholic Church was brought into the fold when in 1929 Pope Pius XI and Mussolini negotiated the Lateran Agreements that saw the creation of the Vatican City, the world's smallest sovereign state, as well as enshrining Catholicism as the state religion and other guarantees, in return for papal recognition of the Italian state.

Once it had established total control over government, the Fascist Party was able to impose authoritarian rule over the Italian people in a way that impacted all aspects of life. Freedoms of the press and of speech were curtailed. Elected local officials were expected to be members of the Fascist Party, and indeed membership of the party came to be necessary across nearly all professional walks of life for those who wanted to improve themselves. Opposition was met increasingly with force and violence, including political assassinations. Fascism and Fascist thought and beliefs gradually came to permeate all aspects of society, impacting on the personal freedoms and the actions of individuals. Those who opposed Fascism, like the writer Carlo Levi, were exiled abroad or else to remote parts of Italy.

Fascism, food and wine

Mussolini self-styled himself as a man of action, too busy to waste time on the frivolous act of enjoying a meal around the table. He promoted a frugal, abstemious and sober lifestyle and encouraged his Blackshirts to follow his example. Indeed, they were often depicted eating while on the march, standing up to hastily consume their rations. At the same time, the Fascist 'Battle for Grain' sought to make Italy self-sufficient and not dependent on foreign wheat imports. To this end, he supported the Futurists' disdain for that most Italian of foodstuffs, pasta. Marinetti stated in *The Futurist Cookbook*, first published in 1932, 'We believe necessary the abolition of *pastasciutta*, an absurd Italian gastronomic religion.' Marinetti believed its consumption resulted in the Italians' 'lassitude, pessimism, nostalgic inactivity, and neutralism'. To support the home rice industry, people were encouraged to eat risotto rather than pasta, even southerners who were less familiar with rice as a staple.

Mussolini himself was supposedly teetotal. A Fascist slogan stated: 'L'abuso del vino e dei liquori non deve più oltre corrompere e degenerare la razza italiana' ('The abuse of wine and spirits should not be allowed to corrupt and degenerate the Italian race'). In this sentiment, he was in accord with the strong temperance movement that had become widespread in Italy, as well as in other countries (Prohibition in the United States was in force from 1920 to 1933). The longstanding Federazione Antialcoolista Italiana worked tirelessly to eradicate the 'social plague' of alcoholism through targeting especially those working-class venues—*osterie, taverne, bettole*—where alcohol was consumed. Posters, placards, informational leaflets, campaigns in newspapers and on broadcast media emphasised the harm that drinking wine could bring—'the tavern is the bedchamber of the hospital', was another one of their slogans.

Though Mussolini was initially sympathetic to the temperance movement, even passing legislation to combat alcoholism by increasing sales tax on wine and limiting the number of establishments selling wine in any given town or municipality, Fascist attitudes towards wine consumption eventually had to change, not least because of the immense importance of wine production to the national economy. A subtle campaign began to distinguish between the consumption of wine 'come bevanda di famiglia'—a beverage to be enjoyed in the home with family meals—as opposed to stronger alcohol such as grappa. Doctors who were in the pro-wine camp were enlisted to advocate the health-giving qualities of moderate wine consumption. Mussolini himself declared: *Chi non beve mai vino è un agnello.* 'Chi non beve mai vino è un agnello. Chi beve giusto è un leone. Chi ne beve troppo è un suino' ('He who never drinks wine is a lamb; he who drinks moderately is a lion; he who drinks too much is a swine').

The Fascist government introduced legislation to encourage the production of *vini tipici*—wines that were representative of their region or territory, a recognition of the importance of terroir as a determinant of both quality and individuality. Consortiums were formed to defend the interests of named wines such as Soave, Chianti, Barolo and Barbaresco, among others, laying down rules of production such as permitted grape varieties, yield and minimum alcohol levels to ensure a consistency of style as well as to discourage the fraudulent use of famous wine names. Such an approach was the precursor to the system of *denominazione di origine controllata* or DOC that would eventually be introduced in 1963 to safeguard the production of Italy's best wines.

One way to promote Italian wines was the creation of the Mostra-Mercato dei Vini Tipici d'Italia—an 'Exhibition Market of Italy's Typical Wines', which took place in 1933 in the imposing Medici fortress in Siena. Gathered within this vast and austere space were typical wines from throughout all of Italy, where they could be viewed, learned about, enjoyed together with simple foods. This initiative, begun during the Fascist era, continues today in the same space as the Enoteca Italiana di Promozione del Vino Italiano, or National Institute for the Promotion of Italian Wine.

Civil war

The Second World War proved to be even more destructive and devastating for Italy than the Great War. Fascism at its heart was aggressive and militaristic, and war was glorified. In the years leading up to the onset of global conflict, Italy subdued Libya, and this was followed by the invasion of Abyssinia in 1935 in a misguided attempt by Mussolini to create a new Italian empire. In 1939, Italy invaded Albania and signed the Pact of Steel in support of Germany, which had already declared war against Britain and France. The easy early victories that the Nazis had inflicted on France, combined with the prospect of gaining more power in the Balkans and Adriatic, led Mussolini to declare war in June 1940.

It was to prove to be a disaster almost from the onset. Though Mussolini saw himself as a leader on the same level as Adolf Hitler, Italy was always only ever a junior partner to Nazi Germany. When Italy attacked Greece of its own accord, it was defeated ignominiously, with the Germans having to send troops to its aid. When Italian troops, badly prepared and equipped, were sent to the Russian front to support the Germans, they were either massacred by the Russians or perished from the bitter Russian cold. Italian troops were defeated in North Africa by Allied troops mainly led by the British.

As in Germany, a shameful policy of antisemitism was brought in under the Fascist government. Jews had lived in Italy for more than 2,000 years and by the 1930s were almost completely integrated into Italian society, with little overt antisemitism in the community. From the beginning of 1938, legislation was passed that removed Jews from government jobs, banned marriage between Jews and non-Jews, dismissed Jews from the military and removed them from positions in the mass media, among other measures. Internment camps were created where Jews of foreign nationality were held. This was utterly against the sentiment of most of the Italian people. Though mercifully such laws were not always fully enforced, and though there was resistance when the Germans demanded the deportation of Jews, nonetheless the economic and psychological damage caused by this policy saw many Jews emigrate, primarily to the Americas.

By 1942, it was clear that the war was going badly. It had never been popular with the Italian people, who saw it more as a Fascist campaign than an Italian one. Italian troops were losing their lives, being wounded or finding themselves captured and held as prisoners of war. At home, the social consequences of war were food rationing, rampant inflation, increased taxation, conscription of men and prohibitions on many aspects of live that made living worthwhile, including the banning of motor vehicles and even dancing. Civilian morale was increasingly badly affected by Allied bombing. Meanwhile, an anti-Fascist movement gained in strength, whether underground or led by dissidents who had moved abroad.

The Allied landing in Sicily in July 1943 precipitated a crisis of confidence in the Fascist government. Mussolini's own Fascist Grand Council met and issued a vote of no-confidence in 'Il Duce'. This humiliating decision was used by King Vittorio Emanuele III to order Mussolini's arrest. An armistice was agreed with the Allies in September 1943, and an entirely new government was created, led by Marshall Pietro Badoglio. The Germans immediately moved in to attempt to seize most of Italy. The new government had to flee Rome to Brindisi and from there declared war on Germany in October 1943. Mussolini was rescued by the Germans, who set him up as the head of a puppet government, La Repubblica Sociale Italiana based in Salò, a small town on the shores of Lake Garda. From there, he undertook reprisals against those who had dared to vote against him, including his own son-in-law, Galeazzo Ciano, who was executed in January 1944.

With those Italian troops that stayed loyal to the Fascist cause, Mussolini continued the war alongside the Germans. But by now the Italian regular army was broadly in disarray, anxious to avoid meeting the Germans who might either kill them or deport them to German and Polish internment camps where they would have to endure forced labour. Some troops in the regular army remained loyal to the king, others simply deserted. Many chose to join the partisans—groups from all backgrounds, political parties and beliefs—who then fought underground and became the main focus of the Resistance.

From October 1943, the Nazis began to round up and deport Jews in Rome. Many were murdered, and several thousand were sent to perish in extermination camps. The role of the Catholic Church during this terrible period is not entirely clear, nor is there consensus among historians. The Lateran Pacts that had been agreed between the Vatican and the Italian government in 1929 had led the conservative Church to give support to the Fascist government while Mussolini was in power. But after Mussolini had fled, when the Nazis moved in to begin to deport Jews, did Pope Pius XII seek to help Jews by granting 'non-Aryans' sanctuary to be hidden in Church institutions, as has been claimed? Or did in fact the pope and the Catholic Church turn a blind eye as the Jews were rounded up to be put on trains to be sent to Auschwitz, where so many perished in the gas chambers? This dark period of Italian history remains deeply disturbing.

Meanwhile, the Fascist troops loyal to Mussolini continued the fight against their fellow countrymen. This was a terrible time for Italians, when the country had to endure the tragedy of civil war, with brother pitted against brother and where Italians found themselves in the position of having to kill one another.

Following the Allies' landing at Salerno, American and British forces moved up the Italian Peninsula with the Germans in retreat, leaving mayhem and destruction in their wake. An important and decisive battle took place at Montecassino, resulting in the complete destruction of the monastery founded by St Benedict in 529. The war in Italy was hard-fought, and the British and Americans had to resort to a heavy and brutal campaign of bombing, destroying not only the country's industrial base but also the spirit of the people in cities such as Milan, Turin, Naples, Rome and Genoa. Other cities and towns found themselves on the frontline of the fighting as the Germans retreated.

The war continued into 1945, when, with Allied help, the Italian Resistance was able to liberate cities and areas across Piedmont, Lombardy and Veneto. The bravery of the partisans and their enduring spirit has become part of Italian lore, immortalised in the writings of Beppe Fenoglio and Cesare Pavese, among others.

On 28 April 1945, Mussolini, disguised as a German soldier, was apprehended trying to flee into Austria together with his mistress Claretta Petacci. The partisans shot and killed them both and took their bodies to Milan, where they were hung heads down in Piazzale Loreto to the jubilation of huge crowds. The war in Italy was effectively over, and democracy was restored after more than two decades of dictatorship. Now it was time, with so much of the country, including much of its precious wine lands, utterly destroyed, for the long and laborious process of reconciliation, healing and economic recovery to begin.

The Wines

Vino della Pace, Cantina Produttori di Cormòns, Cormòns, Friuli–Venezia Giulia

Cormòns, a small wine town in the heart of Collio, one of Friuli–Venezia Giulia's most prestigious wine zones, today lies just a few kilometres from the frontier with Slovenia. Its fortified castle was built by the patriarch of Aquileia in the eleventh century. In the thirteenth century, it came under the rule of the Ghibelline counts of Gorizia until 1497, when it was ceded to the Austrians. The Venetians and the Austrians continued to fight over it until it became part of the Austro-Hungarian Empire in 1521. During the First World War, its strategic location made it the scene of some of the fiercest fighting. Cormòns finally became part of Italy after the post-war settlement of 1918 but then saw itself occupied by the Nazis during the Second World War.

The reconstruction of this war-torn land began with the replantation of its wine hills, traditionally the source of outstanding white wines—including some of the best in Italy—as well as notable reds. The Cantina Produttori Cormòns was begun in 1968 by local winegrowers who came together with the aim of creating a cooperative winery that remained true to ancient tradition yet which made use of the most modern technologies. Today, the Cantina represents 120 winegrowing families and has a reputation for the quality and typicity of its wines, fitting representatives of the prestigious Collio vineyard. In order to commemorate the fact that today's vineyards are cultivated on former battlefields, one of its earliest initiatives was to gather grapevines from five different continents and to plant them all around the cooperative winery itself in what has come to be known as the Vigna del

Mondo—the Vineyard of the World. The first harvest took place in 1985, a joyous occasion and an event that was applauded and recognised around the world of wine.

Around 80 per cent of the grapes cultivated in the Vineyard of the World were and still are white varieties; the rest are red and are vinified off the skins to produce a single white wine. The Vino della Pace—the Wine of Peace—was thus born and first released in 1986, with special labels created by celebrated contemporary artists such as Arnaldo Pomodoro, Enrico Baj and Zoran Music. Much of Baj's acclaimed work revealed an obsession with nuclear war, while Music, a Slovenian artist whose father had served in the Austrian army in the First World War, painted not only beautiful land-scapes but also horror scenes from the Dachau concentration camp. The artists were therefore fitting choices to decorate the bottles of this wine with a special message of hope and brotherhood.

As for the wine itself? It would be fanciful to think that such a random and hodgepodge collection of grape varieties would result in the production of a great wine. The greatness of this unique wine is symbolic, a message of good-will and fraternity between fellow men and women. Yet it is also a wine to drink and enjoy. Recent bottles tasted have revealed a wine that is gently sweet, soft, not in the least bellicose, a wine perhaps to enjoy with a typical pastry such as *gubana*, in the shape of a snail, filled with nuts, raisins and lemon zest that is enjoyed throughout the region.

Refosco dal Peduncolo Rosso, Friuli Isonzo DOC, I Feudi di Romans, San Canzian d'Isonzo, Friuli–Venezia Giulia

After the devastation that had taken place across North-East Italy, post-war reconstruction saw the replantation of its wine lands with both native grape varieties and international: Friulano, Malvasia Istriana, Pinot Grigio, Verduzzo Friulano, Moscato, Pinot Bianco, Chardonnay, Sauvignon, Traminer, Riesling, Pignolo, Refosco dal Peduncolo Rosso, Schioppettino, Pinot Nero, Cabernet Franc, Cabernet Sauvignon and Merlot. Wines from these grapes are primarily vinified *in purezza*, that is, as single varietals that are expressions of a gravelly, alluvial terroir that extends along the gentle hills that rise from both banks of the Isonzo from the Slovenian border below Gorizia to form the important DOC wine zone Friuli Isonzo, or Isonzo del Friuli.

This is a generous and abundant wine land, well ventilated by the cool and dry Bora wind coming from the north-east as well as with the moister warm breezes from the Adriatic. The sunny, relatively dry weather and good diurnal temperature variations between night and day results in a harvest of well-ripened grapes that have flavour and aroma to produce both everyday and outstanding red and white wines, as well as superb sparkling wines.

Refosco dal Peduncolo Rosso is a less well-known native variety that is popular in the region and deserves to be better known. A good example is produced by the Lorenzon family at the I Feudi di Romans wine estate. I love this grape because it makes wine that has a somewhat savage character, even when tamed in wooden barrels. Ruby red tinged with purple, rich in colour, tannin and alcohol, it is not what I would call a super-refined wine but rather a powerful one with scents of undergrowth, herbs and red fruits and a characteristic bitter finish.

Aglianico del Vulture DOC, Casa Vinicola D'Angelo, Rionero del Vulture, Basilicata

Mussolini sought to impose full authoritarian rule over people's lives, even their thoughts and beliefs. Those who opposed Fascism could be sent away to exile. This was the fate imposed on the painter, writer and activist Carlo Levi, who, at the start of the Abyssinian War in 1935, was banished to deepest Lucania, a remote province of Southern Italy. For an educated Italian from Northern Italy, it was almost like being banished to a primitive foreign country. Indeed, even to the people living there, Lucania was considered a pagan land, a land even beyond Christianity and the modern world. Wrote Levi, "'We are not Christians,'" they say. "Christ stopped short of here, at Eboli.'" In Lucania, he learned to live among the poorest peasants, exiled, he said, 'from time ... and thus able to be truly contemporary'. A medical doctor by training, he immersed himself in this extraordinary and almost surreal and timeless world. From that enforced experience, he wrote a beautiful book, *Cristo si è fermato ad Eboli*—'Christ stopped at Eboli'—to describe his experience and to give dignity and grandeur to the lives of the simple people he lived among and came to love.

Today, Lucania is known as Basilicata, and it is still one of Italy's most impoverished and little visited regions. Though post-war land reform improved the situation somewhat for subsistence farmers, as in other parts of the south, many chose to emigrate or else had to move north in search of employment. Wine production, though relatively small, was, and now more than ever is, an important means of bringing wealth to the region. For indeed, the majestic, bare slopes of Monte Vulture have proven to be the source of one of the great wines of Italy, and one of the greatest expressions of the mighty Aglianico grape.

Monte Vulture is not a land of single-minded monoculture. On Vulture, patches of vines are cultivated here and there, sometimes just tiny squares of ancient, gnarled vines planted amid groves of olives, fields of wheat or tobacco. The vines are traditionally trained either free-standing or in the *a capanna* style, up three posts tied together to form a sort of 'teepee'. Aglianico grapes—one of the great native red wine grapes of Italy—ripen on rich, mineral volcanic soil to produce intense and energetic Aglianico del Vulture wine, as in this outstanding example from Casa Vinicola D'Angelo. This is a wine that is full of fruit, acid, tannin, alcohol, powerful and exciting. It is a wine born from poverty yet majestic and aristocratic in every way, and a truly fitting tribute to the hardworking and long-suffering people that Levi wrote lovingly and unblinkingly about and who have been the backbone of the region from time immemorial.

Five Roses rosato, Salento IGT, Leone De Castris, Salice Salentino, Apulia

After the Allies had landed in Italy, it was a great logistical task to keep the troops fed and watered. General Charles Poletti oversaw procurements for the American forces stationed throughout Italy. At the time, procuring wine was not always easy as so much of the wine country had either been destroyed or else the retreating Germans had vandalised stocks that they couldn't take with them. Furthermore, the wine country's men had mainly been away at war, so the work in vineyard and cellar had not been undertaken. The Leone De Castris winery in deepest Apulia, on the heel of the Italian boot on the Salentine Peninsula, had managed, against almost all odds, to keep making wine, including an aged *rosato* known as Rosato Stravecchio del Salento. General Poletti liked the wine and purchased a huge provision of it. In fact, he was so fond of it that he suggested that after the war it could sell well in America, if it was given a suitable English name. As the farm that it was produced on was called Cinque Rose, the wine was called 'Five Roses'. It was the first Italian rosé bottled and sold abroad, and it was an immediate success, helping to rebuild Italy's broken and shattered economy after the devastation of the war.

Today, Five Roses is still considered one of the best of all Italian *rosato* wines, produced from 90 per cent Negroamaro and 10 per cent Malvasia. Though modern tastes mean that it is no longer aged for lengthy periods as it was originally, it remains a wine of considerable stature that can stand up to the most robustly flavoured foods.

ITALY IN A WINEGLASS

Barbera d'Alba DOC 'BG', Cascina Fontana, Perno, Piedmont

The partisans have become part of the lore of Italian history, and books have been written about them. One insider account is by one of Piedmont's greatest writers, Beppe Fenoglio, who was from Alba, today the centre of the Barolo, Barbaresco and Roero wine zones. Without romanticising the partisans, he writes eloquently, honestly and sometimes humorously about events that happened based on his own experience as a partisan. In the short story *The Twenty-Three Days of the City of Alba*, he writes about when the partisans managed to rout the Germans out of his hometown and of a brief moment—just twenty-three days—when the people helped by the partisans were able to hold out against the might of the German and Fascist forces:

> There was nothing more to be seen in Via Maestra: having reached the end of it, the partisans turned the corner. A crowd of them, which increased in size at every intersection, ran to the city's two whorehouses, followed by a swarm of little boys, who fortunately stopped at the door and waited patiently for whichever partisan whose uniform or weapon had impressed them most to emerge. There were eight professionals in those two houses, and they worked so hard that day and the days that followed as to deserve a medal for valor. Even the madams were valiant and succeeded in collecting most of what was owing, and that was a miracle with men like the partisans, accustomed to getting everything for free. ... The afternoon was declared a holiday, and people filled the cafés and bought drinks for the partisans. (trans. John Shepley)

Whether *badogliani*, those who gave their allegiance to Marshal Badoglio and the king, or *garibaldini*, those who were mainly left-wing or communists—my hunch is that that they all would have been drinking in vast quantity as much Barbera wine as they could get their hands on.

Barbera d'Alba Superiore 'BG', produced by Mario Fontana, is just the sort of authentic Barbera that would have been loved by all, then as it is now. Barbera has a naturally high acidity, one reason it accompanies food so well, and Mario's main production of Barbera d'Alba spends some time in used *barriques* to temper this just a bit. The 'BG', however, is put into 'botti grandi'—the large Slavonian oak casks that are the traditional wine vessels in Le Langhe. This keeps the acidity a touch higher while leaving those rough edges just as they are, sharply angular. As a result, the wine is more rustic in character, more *genuino*. I love it, and I'm sure the partisans who took Alba and held it for those brief but glorious twenty-three days would have, too.

21

THE 'ECONOMIC MIRACLE'

Memories of our favourite Italian restaurant in England, thirty, maybe even forty years ago: there are red-and-white checked tablecloths, green, red and white paper serviettes, and on each table there is a bulbous, straw-covered bottle with a candle in it. The candle is lit, the wax begins to soften and drip, and each table is enclosed within its own gentle glow.

To go with our spaghetti alla bolognese, lasagna, or pollo alla milanese, we'd order that same Chianti in the straw fiasco, not least because the bottle always made us happy. Or else maybe it would be a waisted anfora bottle of Verdicchio dei Castelli di Jesi, with a little paper scroll tied around the neck. Or a squat, clear-glass bottle of Frascati, or a bottle of Soave, a fresh, clean wine that never disappointed. These were the wines that represented Italy in restaurants around the world, immediately recognisable from their distinctive bottles alone. They were satisfying, quaffable and never expensive, of their time and typical of what we all thought Italian wine should taste like. In those days, we didn't ask for anything more: just simple, good times in a bottle. Now, just seeing these characteristically shaped bottles once again, even after all these years, always brings back memories of the happy, simple times that wine, Italian wine, brought then and continues to bring now.

The History

Italy was left utterly devastated by the Second World War. Both city and country alike had suffered considerable damage and destruction, the former destroyed by the unrelenting air raids of the Allied bombers, the latter by battlefields, retreating armies and neglect as crops went unharvested with the men of the country at war or serving as part of the Resistance. Much of the

229

country's industrial infrastructure had been almost obliterated. Italy's overseas possessions had all been lost. There was a bitter territorial dispute over Trieste, which communist Yugoslavia wanted to seize. Vineyards up and down the Italian Peninsula were either neglected or destroyed and thus almost completely unproductive. The country was left divided between the anti-Fascist opposition, including Resistance fighters and the parties to the left; right-wing conservative forces and the Church; and unrepentant Fascists, of whom there were many.

In 1946, Italy voted narrowly in a referendum to become a republic, forcing the House of Savoy and the incumbent King Umberto II into exile. A nation less than a century old not only had to rebuild itself from ruin but at the same time had to find a new identity and purpose. Italy was at a crossroads as political struggles see-sawed between the centre-right and the left. There was a real fear in the West that Italy could choose the path to communism and even ally itself with the communist bloc that had formed across Eastern Europe after the war.

The post-war film industry portrayed the grim conditions that Italians had endured both during the war and in its aftermath. By choosing mainly to use non-professionals as actors, directors created a new form of cinematic neo-realism that depicted the hopelessness of the situation Italy found itself in. Vittorio De Sica's *I ladri di biciclette* (The Bicycle Thieves, 1948), brought cinema to the streets, depicting poverty, squalor, and the desperation of men to find work. By using working-class people as the actors in the film rather than the well-known stars of the time, De Sica and other directors of neo-realist films made viewers—Italian middle-class cinema-goers—confront the terrible situation that so many of their countrymen were having to live through and endure.

If the poor, the downtrodden were portrayed as heroic in Italian films, many of which won acclaim and international awards for their directors, in reality little was being done to make the lives of the working classes, as well as the impoverished peasants scratching a bare living off the land, much better at all. Opportunities remained few and far between, and people from the south had to look elsewhere in search of a better life. Thousands of Italians chose to move abroad, both overseas and to other parts of Western Europe.

With the newly formed Christian Democratic Party in power, the most pressing need across the country was economic reconstruction. This was facilitated with the support of the United States and its European Recovery Program, which came to be known as the Marshall Plan. Italy was the programme's third largest recipient, receiving some $12 billion between 1948 and 1952. The aid went towards financing the reconstruction of cities that had been destroyed, as well as infrastructure and industries that had been heavily damaged. This was not only a means of helping America's key allies as well as its former enemies in Western Europe; it was also a means to stop the spread of communism on the European continent as the Soviet grip on power grew ever stronger.

Italy's post-war recovery was quicker than perhaps anybody could have hoped for. With state aid, industrialists and trade unions alike got behind a reconstruction programme that saw pre-war industrial production levels regained by 1948. Italy joined NATO as a founder member in 1949. The onset of the Korean War (1950–3), and the demand for military hardware that it brought, provided further stimulus to the economy. Italy entered into a virtuous circle of newfound prosperity, a period that has been called *il miracolo economico*—'the economic miracle'—and saw an annual rate of economic growth of nearly 6 per cent from 1951 all the way through to 1968. In the process, using advanced technology and mechanisation, Italy had managed to transform itself from a mainly rural into a manufacturing nation, becoming a global producer of automobiles, washing machines, televisions, typewriters, textiles and much more.

The changes to society and culture were considerable, too. The agrarian reforms that had been promised in the south never materialised, or whatever small gains had been achieved had not filtered down to the landless peasant farmers. Whereas in the past, such impoverished Italians would have had to look abroad in search of a better life, opportunities for 'emigration' away from the bare subsistence fields of the Mezzogiorno now came from the bustling new factories located mainly in the north-west of the country. The internal movements of Italians primarily from south to north during this period were both considerable and transformational. Whole families from Campania, Apulia, Abruzzo, Basilicata, Calabria and Sicily moved north in search of work. They brought with them their strange accents and languages, their foods, their traditions, their ways of living. The northerners were mainly glad to accept their labour, especially for manual jobs that they didn't want to do themselves, but undoubtedly there was a lot of barely disguised racism, a shameful North–South divide that still exists today and has given rise to far-right political parties such as the Lega.

Italy's food industries

If Italy's manufacturing sector was transformed after the war, another area of great success was the industrialisation of Italy's traditional food patrimony.

The generous fertility of the country had always been appreciated since antiquity, but now there was also a realisation that Italian foodstuffs and traditions could be produced on a much larger scale using new technologies so as not only to be able to feed the Italian nation but also to produce products that could be exported around the world.

Many Italians who had been forced to emigrate had opened Italian restaurants, and they were in need of the foods that were and are the cornerstone of Italian cuisine. Dried pasta, for long a staple of the Italian diet, even if Mussolini had tried unsuccessfully to ban it, could now be created on an industrial scale, making this a food that all could enjoy. As a dried product, it did not spoil and thus could be transported and sold all around the world. The origins of Barilla go back to 1877 when Pietro Barilla opened a bread and pasta shop in Parma. After the Second World War, brothers Gianni and Pietro Barilla looked to the United States for new techniques for packaging, distribution and marketing. By 1969, the company could boast the largest pasta production plant in the world, built just outside Parma with more than 120 metres of production line, capable of producing 1,000 tons of pasta per day.

And what was that pasta seasoned with? Under a hot Italian sun, vegetables such as the tomato, only brought over to these shores by the Spanish after the discovery of the New World, could reach an optimum degree of ripeness. But such ripeness is highly perishable. The challenge was how to preserve this seasonal bounty. As long ago as 1856, even before the creation of the Italian state, a young man named Francesco Cirio, from Nizza Monferrato, in the Asti wine hills, sought to find a way to preserve that natural bounty of produce from his native region so that it could last through winter months and even be exported to other countries. Through research into the so-called 'appertisation' process developed by Frenchman Nicolas Apperti, Cirio developed innovative ways to preserve the outstanding fruits and vegetables of this fertile agricultural area through heat treatment to kill bacteria followed by storage in sealed tin cans. By the time of his death, the Cirio tinning industry had grown to be one of the largest and most prestigious food manufacturers in all of Europe. Today, the company is part of Gruppo Cooperativo Conserve Italia, a European leader in the food preservation industry.

Emilia-Romagna benefits from its extensive expanse of arable land located along the broad and fertile Po Valley. Because the stretch of valley is more suitable for larger-scale farming than other areas, the region became the home of some of the country's most successful food industries for the production of such iconic products as *parmigiano reggiano*, *prosciutto di Parma*, *mortadella di Bologna*, *aceto balsamico di Modena* and much else. Indeed, it seems that the genius of the region has been not just in the creation of such wondrous and delicious foods but in finding a way to produce them on a near industrial scale to enable them to be exported throughout the country and the world.

Industrialisation of Italian wine

If Italy's food industries prospered during the period known as the economic miracle, so too did its wine industry. Under the Fascist government, there had been an attempt to give structure to Italy's wonderfully chaotic wine patrimony by placing emphasis on regional wines: Chianti from Tuscany, Soave and Valpolicella from Veneto, Frascati from Rome, for example. In post-war Italy, this trend was maintained, especially as technological advances in winemaking came to permit the process of transforming grapes into wine on a consistent industrial scale and in quantity.

Case vinicole—private wineries—emerged, eager to purchase grapes from scores of small growers in return for cash. As during the period of the *mezzadria*, in those days there was little incentive for quality: rather the aim of the small grower was simply to produce as high a yield as possible, while the aim of the producer was to transform an abundance of grapes into quantities of clean, sound wine that could be bottled and sold.

Through the years of Italy's economic miracle, a wealth of Italian wines came on to the market that became known and much loved throughout the world. Verdicchio dei Castelli di Jesi from Le Marche is a good example, marketed in an 'amphora' bottle that implied that this was never supposed to be a serious wine, rather a fun one to go with lighter foods—fish or chicken— or else a wine just to drink and enjoy. Chianti came in its distinctive *fiasco* bottle, covered in straw. If the wine was indifferent, no matter: the bottle itself was charming and made a nice candle holder once the wine had been drunk. Jug wines came from Verona, such as Soave and Valpolicella, in large *bottiglioni*—2-litres closed by screw caps (long before screw caps became an acceptable or valued form of closure). And Frascati, from the Castelli Romani above Rome, where grapes had been cultivated since antiquity, was another alternative in Italian *ristoranti* and *trattorie* throughout Italy and the world, usually found in a squat, clear-glass bottle.

As with its food industries, technology lay at the heart of this post-war industrialisation and commercialisation. For centuries, Italian white grapes were processed much the same as red, that is, crushed and vinified at least for a brief time on the skin, adding a little colour, even a bite of tannin to the finished wine. Such wines, however, often had the tendency to oxidise

233

quickly, that is, turn brownish and gain flat, stale flavours, wines, it was said, that 'didn't travel'. The advent of the use of cylindrical presses to allow the juice to be cleanly and gently separated from the skins and drawn off into fermentation vessels revolutionised the process, while the introduction of stainless-steel fermentation vats helped to make cleaner, fresher wines less prone to oxidation. Oenologists introduced scientific analyses to create wines of requisite strength, acidity and balance (sometimes through the use of permitted additives), while high-speed bottling and labelling lines, and the development of national and international networks of transport and distribution, allowed such wines to reach vast new markets in Italy and beyond.

Italy's economic miracle lasted from the 1950s well into the 1960s. Society was transformed as the material standard of living was elevated considerably. During this time, Italy had become the largest producer of wine in the world—a position, depending on the vagaries of each vintage, that it often still holds today—while the country was also among the largest consumers of wine per capita. Wine had long been a normal feature on the everyday Italian table, across all classes, since the time of the Romans. But, for many, such wines in the past had often been anonymous beverages, purchased *sfuso*—loose, by the 54-litre demi-john, to be bottled at home, perhaps sealed with just a layer of *olio enologico*, oenological oil, a small amount added to open bottles to protect from oxidation. Now, however, wine had become something to purchase by the bottle, perhaps at the supermarket, choosing by name, provenance, bottle shape. The enjoyment of wine with every meal was—and still is—very much at the heart of daily Italian life, but the concept of fine wine, and even of designer wine, was yet to come, for indeed the renaissance of modern Italian wine still lay just around the corner.

The Wines

Titulus anfora, Verdicchio dei Castelli di Jesi DOC, Fazi Battaglia, Castelplanio, Le Marche

If Verdicchio is a wine that came to be known and loved throughout the world, much of the credit must go to Fazi Battaglia, the company that more than any helped to create the 'brand' of Verdicchio in its famous amphora bottle with the little scroll hand-tied around the neck. The company began in 1949 out of a small *cantina* in Cupramontana, in the very heart of the Castelli di Jesi. It wasn't until 1953 that Francesco Angelini, who later went on to found the still very important Angelini Pharma group, came up with the idea of creating an amphora-shaped bottle to draw connection to the ancient vinous patrimony of the region. Ancona had been a Greek colony, and the Etruscans had also settled here, so grapes have almost certainly been grown and wines made in these beautiful hills for more than 2,500 years. Verdicchio in the 1950s was not yet a grape variety widely known throughout Italy, nor would it have been a familiar name on international markets. Yet, in its distinctive curvy bottle, it soon conquered the world and placed Le Marche on the world wine map.

The early success of Fazi Battaglia *anfora* has allowed the company gradually to acquire some 130 hectares of vineyard holdings in the best zones and sub-zones of the Castelli di Jesi, in Maiolati Spontini, Cupramontana, Montecarotto, Mergo and Castelplanio. Titulus is the flagship, a proud representative of the company's heritage and success. Whereas other producers have now eschewed the amphora bottle, considering it not suitable for serious wines, Fazi Battaglia continues with its use, as the bottle itself is still widely considered very much a beloved Italian style icon. The wine itself has evolved over the decades and today is produced exclusively from the company's own Verdicchio grapes grown on these beautiful wine hills. After cold maceration in the press to extract more flavour and aroma, followed by fermentation in stainless-steel at 14–16 degrees, the wine further ages on the lees to add a richness and tangy minerality.

Titulus represents part of the very history of modern Italian wine. I love the Fazi Battaglia amphora bottle—it gives me immense pleasure whenever I see it with its little scroll, still tied by hand to each one of the more than a million bottles produced every year. While undoubtedly representing a post-war era when Italian wines came to conquer the world, this is nonetheless a wine of character and personality, made from one of Italy's greatest white grape varieties, and very much an expression of a proud and beautiful territory.

Castelgreve Fiasco, Chianti Classico DOCG, Castelli del Grevepesa, San Casciano Val di Pesa, Tuscany

The bulbous, straw-covered Chianti *fiasco* of old was one of the most charming wine bottles ever manufactured. What a shame, then, that producers of Chianti, whether in the elite Chianti Classico or in any of the other Chianti sub-zones, now mainly shun its use, a reminder of the days when Chianti was a simple wine whose only ambition was to give simple pleasure. Chianti is now in the Serie A of Italian wines, rightly considered one of Italy's great-

235

est and most serious red wines, and so for many if not most producers, it just wouldn't do to bottle such a wine in anything as frivolous or unserious as the *fiasco*.

Fortunately, not all producers agree. The Castelli del Grevepesa cooperative winery was founded in 1965, initially with just seventeen winegrowing members, and one of its best-selling wines in those early days was its Chianti *fiasco*. Today, the cooperative has about 120 winegrowing members, making this quality cooperative one of the largest producers of Chianti Classico in the region. Its members have vineyards across some of the best and most highly regarded zones, and thus Castelli del Grevepesa can produce a range of Chianti wines, including examples from the highest level of the Chianti Classico quality pyramid: Gran Selezione wines as well as cru wines from the newly approved UGAs (*unità geografica aggiuntiva*, or communal designations) Lamole and Panzano. Yet at the same time, it is not ashamed of the historic past upon which the success of Chianti was based. Thus, Castelgreve *fiasco* is a wine that celebrates the Chianti tradition of the charming, bulbous bottle, covered with natural straw. This excellent example celebrates that past while at the same time expressing the majesty of the region's greatest grape variety, Sangiovese (95 per cent), aged for twelve months in large Slavonian *botti*. While still a wine that is meant to be consumed relatively young, it is most definitely a proud Chianti Classico, bright ruby red, with hints of violets and red fruit on the nose, and gently soft tannins and a backbone of acidity that makes it a good partner to foods such as salty Tuscan *salumi* or a plate of pasta.

Luna Mater Riserva, Frascati Superiore DOC, Fontana Candida, Latium

The Colli Albani are a series of gentle volcanic hills that lie to the south of Rome. Cato the Censor, who wrote a treatise on winemaking, *De agricultura*, was from Tusculum, near Frascati; the great orator Cicero had a villa here, too. Pliny the Elder considered the wine, Albanum, one of the 'great growths' of the ancient world.

And yet, in post-war Italy, even well into the 1960s and '70s, winemaking here had progressed very little. Perhaps the ready and easy market that the wines enjoyed in Rome gave little incentive for small winegrowers to up their game. For the wine already found an easy market sold by the carafe in wine dens in the Colli Albani as well as in restaurants and *osterie* in Rome alike, golden in colour, simple and, when fresh, a delightful accompaniment to the full-flavoured foods of the Eternal City, but, when less than fresh, sometimes brown and flat.

The advent of industrial winemaking technology brought new opportunities. Fontana Candida seized the chance to work with the small winegrowers of the Colli Albani to produce a new style of Frascati that was clean, sound, almost colourless and able to be produced in vast quantity. It was a simple, fresh style of wine instantly recognisable in its squat, clear-glass bottle, an easy-drinking white that could be knocked back not only in *osterie* and *trattorie* in nearby Rome but also in Italian *trattorie* around the world. Indeed, this popular Italian white, together with Verdicchio and Soave, revolutionised the world's perception of Italian white wines, and the sales soared as a result.

Today, Fontana Candida works with around 180 winegrowers in the Colli Albani and continues to produce vast oceans of wines. However, the best selection of grapes goes into superior offerings that demonstrate why Romans—from antiquity through popes to today—have always rated the wines from this complex ridge of volcanic hills so highly.

Frascati Superiore Luna Mater Riserva has a concentration and richness in flavour and body. Produced from old vine Malvasia Bianco di Candia and the superior Malvasia Puntinata with a little Bombino and Greco, there is complexity that comes from a terroir rich in potassium, calcium, magnesium, iron. You feel the weight and structure in your mouth, and there is a long and persistent aftertaste that lingers and tickles.

Lambrusco Reggiano DOC, Cantine Reggio Emilia-Emilia, Emilia-Romagna

It is perhaps ironic that a cooperative winery with socialist origins from a region once considered a centre of Italian communism had the entrepreneurial nous to create a market for a wine that became a runaway bestseller in the largest free market in the world, bringing prosperity to its members. Cantine Cooperative Riunite was founded in 1950 in Reggio Emilia by just nine winegrowers to transform their autochthonous grape varieties—Lambrusco Grasparossa, Lambrusco di Sorbara, Lambrusco Salamino, Lambrusco Maestri and Lambrusco Marani—into a range of traditional Lambrusco wines that had long been much loved in the region, wines that went so well with another product for which Emilia was so famous, the cured-pork *salumi* of which there was such an outstanding variety and tradition. The Lambruscos are one of Italy's oldest families of native grape varieties, cultivated in the Po Valley for hundreds of years to produce light, quaffable and usually slightly sparkling wines high in acid, traditionally dry, off-dry and also sometimes sweet. The genius was that these same grapes and this same style of wine could be transformed industrially into a stable, manufactured sweet, sparkling red wine that could be exported internationally.

The wine found almost immediate success in the American market in no small measure through the brilliant marketing acumen of the Mariani brothers, John and Harry, who through Banfi Vintners became the exclusive importer of Riunite wines into the United States. Lambrusco Amabile was marketed on television and radio, an industrial product that was like a sweetly alcoholic soda pop, reaching American consumers who had in many cases never even tasted wine before. Americans were yet to develop a sophisticated palate for dry wines, and Lambrusco was able to capitalise on this. The bottles were closed by screwcap, so a corkscrew wasn't even necessary, and the wine could be put in the refrigerator to be chilled, just like soda pop, or else you could even pour the wine over ice, as suggested by one successful advertising campaign—'Riunite on ice, that's nice.' Sales were simply phenomenal: Riunite Lambrusco soon became the number one imported wine in the United States, a position it held for a quarter of a century, with, at its peak, sales topping nearly 12 million cases a year.

Those glory days may be mainly gone, but Lambrusco Amabile still has a strong following stateside, while new markets have developed elsewhere around the world. What of Riunite's wines today? The Riunite winery is still going strong, still producing vast oceans of wine each year while giving its cooperative grape-growing members a fair return for their efforts. The wines have an important presence in the Italian as well as international market today, and there is a full range of Lambruscos on offer of every style, from ancestral method *amabile* to bone dry and fizzy. Reggiano Lambrusco is the latter, produced mainly from Lambrusco Marani, a variety that is fruity and naturally high in acidity. This is the true wine of the Reggio Emilia country: deep purple in colour with delicate aromas of black cherry and plums mixed with the more delicate scent of violets. High in acid, raspingly dry, with just a touch of tannin, and relatively low in alcohol, it is a chunky, fizzy red that goes excellently with the cured meats of Emilia such as *prosciutto di Parma*, *culatello di Zibello* and *mortadella di Bologna*, the sharpness of the bubbles helping to 'pulire la bocca'—clean the mouth.

Soave DOC, Bolla, Pedemonte, Veneto

Another iconic Italian white wine that came to dominate export markets was Soave, and in particular, Soave produced by the Bolla family. Abele Bolla was an innkeeper in the small medieval town of Soave to the south-east of Verona at the end of the nineteenth century. He began to gain a reputation for the wine he served in the inn. Later generations of the family continued his dedication to the production of wine, but it was not until after the Second World War and Italy's economic miracle that the company really took off. By sourcing Garganega and Trebbiano di Soave grapes, as well as the lesser Trebbiano Toscano, planted on the flat and fertile *pianura* rather than just in the low-yielding but higher-quality hill vineyards of the Soave Classico zone, the Bollas were able to create a lightly soft—'soave' coincidentally means 'soft'—clean and neutral wine that was easy to drink as well as inexpensive. Like Fazi Battaglia's Verdicchio dei Castelli di Jesi and Fontana Candida's Frascati, Bolla Soave found immense success across Italy as well as internationally, most notably in the United States. Stainless-steel technology ensured clean consistency, and if the highly productive vines from the flatter plains gave grapes that were insipid and lacking in character, who really cared too much when the wine was selling so well?

Today, Soave Classico, produced from the volcanic and limestone dry-stone terraced vineyards of the classic heartland, is considered one of the great white wines of Italy, with the best examples displaying extraordinary complexity and depth of flavour. Such wines sometimes from single cru vineyards sited on the volcanic hill vineyards of the Soave Classico are rightly considered among Italy's greatest white wines with prices to match. On the other hand, there is still a place and a market for the simple, the inexpensive, clean and fresh, and that is precisely where Soave Bolla still seeks to position itself, a wine with enduring appeal and popularity.

22

'MADE IN ITALY'

I remember tasting it for the very first time, probably in the late 1970s or early 1980s, a wine that had already become legendary, a so-called super vino da tavola, *that is, classified as just a 'table wine'—Italy's most humble category of classification—but one that had already become a global sensation. What was immediately apparent when we tasted it was that there was nothing humble about this wine at all, no matter what the denomination said on the label. The colour was deeper than we expected, and on the nose there was the unfamiliar scent of new oak, something that was simply not encountered in Italian wines at that time. The wine was astonishing: the familiar taste of Sangiovese, one of the greatest native red grapes of Italy, but also something unmistakably different, the equally familiar scent and taste of Cabernet Sauvignon, the great grape of Bordeaux. It was seductive and exhilarating, the tannins sweet and velvety with the sleek smoothness that comes from ageing in new French oak. We had never tasted an Italian red wine like this. This was Tignanello, and it changed the trajectory of Italian wine.*

The History

'Made in Italy' is a term that emerged in the 1980s and has come to be applied to products across traditional industries that collectively share a uniquely Italian sense of utility allied with the highest quality combined with an unmistakable Italian style, design and flair. Whether relating to fashion, engineering (including automobiles), food and wine, beauty and wellness products, domestic appliances, furniture and house furnishings or just about anything, 'Made in Italy' products go beyond the merely functional and demonstrate the ability and capacity for Italians to make things that the whole world desires. Today, the Italian Trade Agency in offices around the world serves to promote, highlight and strengthen the image of 'Made in Italy' products across all sectors.

Beautiful and shiny

Witness Italy's astonishing success in the automotive field. Giovanni Agnelli founded his first Fabbrica Italiana Automobili Torino (Fiat) factory in Turin in 1899. From its headquarters at Lingotto, outside of Turin, with its famous test track on the roof of the factory, Fiat established itself as the manufacturer of some of the bestselling cars in Europe. One of its early successful models was the Fiat 509, which was incredibly popular, selling some 90,000 units.

During both the First and Second World Wars, automobile companies had to turn their attention to the production of military vehicles. Mussolini wanted a people's car and urged Agnelli to develop an inexpensive model that ordinary people could afford. Thus the Fiat 500, known affectionately as 'Topolino', was born. The post-war economic boom saw the 'Topolino' replaced in 1957 by the Fiat 500 'Nuova', an inexpensive, practical, small model that appealed to the masses and helped to fuel Italy's economic miracle.

But the mass production of functional vehicles, though an undoubted boost to the economy, was not a reflection of that inherent Italian genius to create the extraordinary. Indeed, from the earliest days of the motor vehicle, there were those who looked beyond the practicality of creating a vehicle that could merely transport the nation. The beauty of speed had been glorified by the Futurists, and almost as soon as the motor car was invented, there was something of a national obsession for creating vehicles that could as go fast as possible and that were also beautiful objects of desire. Indeed, it seems almost inevitable that the Italian creative genius came to be applied to the production of cars that combined not merely mass-produced functionality but also the highest sports performance allied with Italian design, flair and style.

Iconic Italian car manufacturers became known for hand-crafting cars in limited editions that for decades became the benchmark for motoring enthusiasts not just in Italy but around the world. Such classic cars include the Ferrari 212 Touring Barchetta, produced from 1951 to 1953, the aerodynamic contours of which made for fast driving. Only four models of the Maserati A6GCS Berlinetta were ever produced, designed by the famous Pininfarina SpA, and it became an immediate classic. The Lamborghini Miura, built in the 1960s, could be said to be one of the world's first supercars, with its sleek design that must have seemed amazingly futuristic at the time. Or what about Alfa Romeo's sleek and sexy 33 Stradale? If James Bond didn't drive a British-built Aston Martin, surely his first choice for a motor vehicle would have been a hand-built Italian one.

Today, cars built by Ferrari, Maserati, Alfa Romeo, Lamborghini and other Italian marques are still among the most sought after, prestigious and desired, not only for their speed and top-end engineering performance but above all for their sometimes radical and always cutting-edge designs and simply for their sheer beauty.

Textiles and fashion

Italians have long had a passion—indeed almost a national obsession—for fabrics and textiles, their feel and touch and beauty. Roman sculptures depict flowing gowns and togas, the creases and pleats almost billowing in imagined wind, despite being carved from hard stone. In Italian art across the ages, the depiction of sumptuously draped fabric garments has been a challenging subject that has been magnificently conveyed, giving us a tactile sense of splendour and grandeur, elevating the personages adorned in such magnificence, whether the ecclesiastical samite robe with threads of gold worn by the priest in Giovanni Bellini's *The Circumcision*; the crimson dress and deep blue mantle of the Virgin Mary as she ascends in astonishment into heaven in Titian's *Assumption of the Virgin*; or the fine, muted fabrics in autumnal colours of the dress worn by the Mona Lisa in Leonardo da Vinci's most famous painting.

Certainly, by the Renaissance, luxurious fabrics made from silk, wool and velvet were precious commodities, to be crafted into the most beautiful garments worn by wealthy private individuals, those in positions of political power and for ecclesiastical vestments, the rare and expensive fabrics themselves an expression of power, wealth, authority, as well as of-the-moment fashion.

From 1400 to 1600, Italian weavers mastered the expertise to produce the most sumptuous and sought-after fabric of all: velvet. Crafted from an intricate process of weaving silk, velvet was a fabric with the greatest depth of colour, a beautiful sheen and a soft and dense pile, while the addition of glittering threads of gold brought it to its highest and most prized refinement. Creativity and innovation in fabric design gave employment to thousands. Venice, Florence and Genoa grew to be the most important centres for the production of velvet. In Venice in 1600 there were an estimated 6,000 looms in the city, while the production of velvet further fuelled other associated industries, such as the cultivation of silkworms, the spinning of the thread from the silk filaments extracted from the cocoons, dyeing and the creation of dyes, the preparation of gold and silver strips to wind around the threads, the weaving itself and the production of garments from the finished cloth by skilled tailors, dressmakers and ecclesiastical vestment specialists.

True industrialisation of Italy's textiles industry came after the Second World War when the 'economic miracle', financed in large measure by the Marshall Plan, brought the most modern machines as well as a marketing mentality that allowed producers to sell their wares worldwide. Italian firms built their reputation on the excellence of their fabrics, setting store on design and appearance, lightness and texture, and employing the most modern and sophisticated production processes, often from small factories that were artisan in scale. With such cutting-edge technologies, the opening of international markets, allied with the creative design that had been a feature of Italian textile production down the ages, the stage was set for Italy's greatest fashion designers to flourish and conquer the world: Missoni, Versace, Armani, Dolce e Gabbana, Gucci and more.

The renaissance of modern Italian wine

Italy's post-war economic miracle was a boon to Italian wine producers who were able to create wines that became global brands that were also known and loved all around the world. But no one claimed that these wines were the greatest in the world, far from it: they were simple wines that brought simple, happy times. And therein lay the rub. Creative Italians with ambition, scope, vision and entrepreneurial skills wanted to create the very best, just as they had done in other industries: they yearned to be able to handcraft wines of the highest quality and personality that really could stand alongside the very greatest in the world—and sell for prices to match the very best.

This could only happen at a time when there was an evolving social and cultural aesthetic as Italian consumers came to view wine no longer as merely an everyday food commodity—*bianco o rosso* to accompany meals—but as a product of real artistic worth and indeed intrinsic beauty and value. Post-war Italy had seen an utter transformation of society. Technology had changed and brought improvements to life in many ways, as it had across Europe. People found themselves with leisure time, perhaps for the first time in generations, and many, too, now found themselves with sufficient income to enjoy some of the luxuries in life.

One of Italy's most important wine pioneers who saw this potential for change was Marchese Piero Antinori, the twenty-fifth head of the Antinori family who have been wine producers in Tuscany since 1385. Marchese Piero understood that for the wines of Chianti to be taken seriously, to stand on the world stage alongside the very best, they had to be reinvented almost entirely, a return to a past that was once illustrious but that had somewhere along the way been lost. In effect, what was needed not only in Tuscany but also elsewhere was a renaissance of modern Italian wine. This was a brave and also an incredibly exciting moment in the long and illustrious history of Italian wine, for although Italy had—and has—a vinous patrimony that is unrivalled and dates back to antiquity, in a sense Marchese Piero had the extraordinary vision to see his country anew, as if through entirely fresh eyes, envisaging a potential for greatness that had not yet been realised and that could not be realised under the existing wine regulations.

He therefore set out to break the rules and start afresh. The new wine that he created was produced from Sangiovese grapes cultivated on the family's best vineyard, Tignanello, rich in calcareous soil with *albarese* marl limestone, blended together with a small proportion of Cabernet Sauvignon and Cabernet Franc, 'foreign' varieties not permitted in the Chianti blend. Furthermore, he decided to age the wine not in the traditional large chestnut *botti* of Tuscany but in small 225 litre *barriques* made from new French oak. These innovations were radical to say the least in an industry that had always prided itself on tradition, on doing things the way they always had been done. Indeed, it was deemed that Marchese Piero had gone too far, by producing a wine outside the regulatory discipline of Chianti, using French grapes in place of those laid down in the 'recipe' for Chianti by Baron Bettino Ricasoli in the nineteenth century. The resulting wine was therefore harshly demoted to Italy's lowest-quality category, a mere *vino rosso da tavola*, a red table wine entitled to no quality or geographic designation.

Yet Tignanello was an immediate sensation, a wine that astonished and delighted Italian wine experts, critics and foreign journalists and wine lovers alike. This simple 'table wine' was clearly an aristocrat in disguise! It became an immediate style icon and almost instantly spawned an entire new category of Italian wine: the super *vini da tavola* or Super Tuscan, a term that refers to wines that are hand-crafted, and whether produced from native or international grape varieties, works of art and beauty.

Naturally, other growers followed suit, some utilising Sangiovese *in purezza*, others choosing instead to concentrate on French varieties including Cabernet Sauvignon, Cabernet Franc, Merlot and Syrah. Eventually, the authorities saw sense and realised that Chianti Classico would never reach its potential without changes to its discipline. White grapes are no longer permitted in the blend, and indeed Chianti Classico can now be made entirely from Sangiovese if desired, or with the addition of permitted international grape varieties. As for the Super Tuscans, the so-called 'super *vini da tavola*', Italy's authorities had to concede the utter nonsense of designating some of the country's undoubted greatest—and most high-value—wines with its lowliest quality classification. Many are now marketed as IGT (*indicazione geografica tipica*), a category of quality that allows for a much freer and less rigid set of regulations.

Tignanello, Sassicaia, Le Pergole Torte, Solaia, Ornellaia, Cepparello, Flaccianello delle Pieve and many others were truly iconoclastic ground breakers, wines that stunned the world and that continue today to bring immense pleasure. Of the highest quality and pedigree, they are expressions of Italian artistic creativity, individuality and a tenacious genius and cultural aesthetic that could only be 'Made in Italy'.

The Wines

Sassicaia, Bolgheri Sassicaia DOC, Tenuta San Guido, Bolgheri, Tuscany

It is fascinating that the story of the renaissance of modern Italian wine begins on the estate of Tenuta San Guido, a property that has long belonged to one of Tuscany's oldest families, the Della Gherardesca. The Della Gherardesca can trace their origins back to the Lombards and rose to become one of the most powerful and prominent families in the Republic of Pisa, their Germanic origins ensuring that they remained staunch Ghibelline supporters of the Holy Roman Emperor. It was the Della Gherardesca who first brought viticulture to Bolgheri, possibly at the end of the seventeenth century. Guidalberto Della Gherardesca rationalised the estate, renovated older vineyards and planted the famous Viale dei Cipressi that connect Bolgheri with San Guido, a vista of towering cypresses made famous by Giosuè Carducci in his poem *Davanti San Guido*.

The transformation of Bolgheri into one of Italy's most exciting wine regions came much later, when Marchese Mario Incisa Della Rocchetta married Contessa Clarice Della Gherardesca in 1930. Marchese Mario's greatest passion was breeding thoroughbred racehorses. He also reorganised the farming side of Tenuta San Guido, replanting the vineyard in the early 1940s not with Tuscan varieties but with cuttings of Cabernet Sauvignon that he had taken from the vineyard of his friends, the noble Salviati family of

Migliarino, both because he liked their Bordeaux style of wine and because he found a similarity in the stony terroir of San Guido with the Graves area of Bordeaux. From 1948 to 1967, the wine produced was only consumed by the family, as well as offered to guests. It was Marchese Mario's nephew, Marchese Piero Antinori, who recognised the commercial possibility of marketing the wine, now named Sassicaia after the stony nature of the vineyard terroir. Antinori's acclaimed oenologist Giacomo Tachis, together with French wine guru Émile Peynaud, who had already revolutionised winemaking in Bordeaux, supervised the harvest and the winemaking. Sassicaia almost immediately gained critical acclaim. By 1978, in a tasting of top Cabernet Sauvignon wines organised by *Decanter Magazine*, Sassicaia 1972 came out on top, emerging victorious against thirty-three top Bordeaux blends from around the world, including the greatest Bordeaux *premiers grands crus classés*, a massive shock to the world of fine wine and especially to the Bordelais themselves. Renowned wine critic Robert Parker further brought the world's attention to this remarkable wine in 1985 when he gave it the extraordinary perfect score of 100/100.

Sassicaia continued to make Italian wine history when in 2013 it gained its own exclusive Bolgheri Sassicaia DOC, an appellation that can only be used by Tenuta San Guido, the first and at present only single vineyard wine to have its own *denominazione di origine controllata*. In 2018, the *Wine Spectator* awarded Sassicaia 2015 97/100 points and declared it 'the best wine in the world'.

Just over forty years ago, in the early 1980s, Bolgheri was not even mentioned as a quality wine region. Today, spurred by the success and high profile of Tenuta San Guido's iconic Sassicaia, there are now scores of other high-profile estates producing outstanding wines from both French varieties such as the Cabernets, Merlot and Syrah, and from traditional Tuscan varieties such as Sangiovese. But it is vital to recognise that Italy's modern wine renaissance began right here.

The wine itself? Though on a level with the finest Cabernet-based wines in the world, Sassicaia is completely different from *premiers grands crus classés* of Bordeaux's Médoc and Graves. Here in the warmer terroir of Tuscany's seaboard, on the rocky limestone marl of the Sassicaia vineyard, the result is most always a ripe, concentrated and full explosion of fruit on the palate with the sweetly smooth vanilla and cedar tannins of new French oak. This makes it more immediately approachable than many other top Cabernet blends that can be more initially closed, yet, like the greatest wines in the world, Sassicaia only fully reveals its majesty and complexity with age.

Tignanello, Toscana IGT, Marchese Antinori, San Casciano Val di Pesa, Tuscany

When Marchese Piero Antinori took over his ancient family estate in the heart of the Chianti Classico in 1966, he immediately began to think of ways to improve the wines. It was a moment of profound change as landowners had to adapt to a different reality following the abolition of the *mezzadria* by taking direct management of their own lands for themselves for the first time in centuries. The potential to produce world-class wines with appeal to international as well as Italian markets had been demonstrated by the success of his uncle Marchese Mario Incisa della Rocchetta with Sassicaia. This convinced Marchese Piero that there were other ways to make wine than simply by following the Chianti 'recipe' that had been in place for more than the past 100 years.

Thus, Tignanello was born, an altogether new wine for a new age, and it needed to have a label that signified this significant moment while maintaining ties with a historic past. Antinori turned to the artist Silvio Coppola to design the label for the release of Tignanello 1971. Noted for his minimalist approach to home furnishings and lighting as well as for his striking book cover designs for the publisher Feltrinelli, Coppola was just the person to design the label for this special new wine that was quite simply different from anything that had previously been produced. The result was contemporary yet also classic, with a stylised circular pattern that suggests peering down into a shimmering glass of garnet wine, and with the family *Te Duce Proficio* crest of arms that dates to 1385 as well as the signature of Marchese Piero's father.

Tignanello, such a modern and even shocking and innovative wine when it was launched in 1971, is now more than half a century old, and the wine today remains just as exciting as ever: elegant, with firm tannins and high acidity that comes from Sangiovese cultivated on its *albarese* terroir, with intensely bright and deep colour from the Cabernet and a gentle roundness and grippy tannins that come from time spent in new French oak *barriques*. Even after the passing of years and decades, Tignanello stands alone, a modern classic, an icon and a demonstration of 'Made in Italy' excellence in every sense.

Barbaresco DOCG, Gaja, Barbaresco, Piedmont

By the late 1970s, Italian wine may have begun to be recognised as good, indeed very good, increasingly appreciated and enjoyed by knowledgeable connoisseurs and wine lovers not only in Italy but around the world. But there was still a problem: the very best wines could not yet command prices as high as those reached by wines that had for centuries been acknowledged as the greatest in the world, most notably those from Bordeaux and Burgundy. It took a precise and creative winemaker and entrepreneurial genius from one of Italy's most traditional wine regions, Le Langhe, to break this mould. The influence and impact of Angelo Gaja, who joined his family business in the early 1960s, on the wines of his homeland Le Langhe as well as on Italian wines as a whole cannot be overestimated. He began by first working in the vineyards of Barbaresco to gain an intimate understanding of the primary material, Nebbiolo grapes, then in the wine cellar to gain a deep knowledge of how those grapes are best transformed to make great wine. Working with his wine-maker Guido Rivella, he quite simply set out determined to handcraft wines with the utmost precision and care that would come to be considered among the very best in the world—and that could command prices accordingly.

Gaja was the first to introduce the use of French oak *barriques* in a wine zone where the big red wines of Barbaresco and Barolo had previously always endured lengthy ageing in large Slavonian oak *botti*. The use of *barriques* in the 1960s and 1970s was at the time considered almost a heresy in this most traditional of wine regions, but Gaja believed that it was necessary to allow the power and depth of Nebbiolo grapes grown in the most privileged and well-exposed sites to reveal their unique blend of elegance, depth and char-acter and complexity while at the same time smoothing out the underlying tannic structure that is so important for wines destined for lengthy ageing and investment.

Gaja was a modernist in an area that had long been strictly traditional and the source of traditional wines. It was therefore on his shoulders to find new markets for this new style of wine. Thus, the wines of Gaja—the family name prominently displayed on the label—came to be sold relentlessly on his trav-els around the world, wines that were soon being extolled by wine experts, wine lovers and collectors, earning countless awards and gaining the highest ratings in the most important and prestigious wine guides. Equally important, the wines of Gaja were now able to be sold at prices that matched the greatest wines in the world.

Not simply content with creating a new image for the wines of Barbaresco and Barolo, and in the process elevating both wine regions to the huge ben-efit of other producers, Gaja decided to go one step further. He had the audacity and courage to grub up prized Nebbiolo vineyards and replant with international grapes such as Cabernet Sauvignon (imagine if a producer in Burgundy chose to grub up Pinot Noir and replace with Cabernet Sauvignon or Nebbiolo—it just couldn't, wouldn't happen). Gaja's father, aghast at this decision, was said to have simply commented, 'Darmagi'—which apparently translates as 'What a pity' in Piedmontese. So Darmagi was the name that Angelo gave to the wine that resulted when it was first released in 1985, wholly and unashamedly modern in outlook, gazing towards the future, not the past.

While Gaja has long been a champion of single vineyard wines, most notably the Barbaresco *crus* Costa Russi, Sorì Tildin and Sorì San Lorenzo, the straight Gaja Barbaresco that is produced from a blend of Nebbiolo grapes from across the family's fourteen vineyards is a magnificent wine that demonstrates some of the classic Gaja hallmark characteristics, combining incredible depth, elegance and a certain silky, satiny texture or mouthfeel to the tannins that are almost sweet though notable nonetheless and that give the wine its architectural structure.

Palazzo Lana Extrême, Franciacorta Riserva DOCG, Berlucchi, Borgonato, Lombardy

The story of Palazzo Lana Extrême is the story of the invention of an entirely new wine and a new wine zone: Franciacorta.

The wine zone is located around beautiful Lake Iseo in Lombardy, between Brescia and Bergamo. Today, manicured vineyards extend across the southern flank of the lake on an amphitheatre of gentle moraine hills shaped by the advance and retreat of glaciers thousands of years ago. The word 'Franciacorta' has not only come to define this territory but also signifies a precise production method that follows specific rules and disciplines, as well as the bottle-fermented sparkling wine itself. Indeed, though 'bollicine'—sparkling wines—are made across Italy today, Franciacorta has become Italy's answer to Champagne, a sparkling wine not only of great elegance and finesse but also with an image of the highest exclusivity, prestige and glamour, at least for Italians if not yet for the rest of the world.

It was in Palazzo Lana, a sixteenth-century stately country house, that Count Guido Berlucchi first met a young and innovative winemaker, Franco Ziliani, in 1955. Indeed, it was literally through conversations around the kitchen table of Palazzo Lana that the idea to create a new sparkling wine was born. Count Guido already had extensive landholdings in the area south of Lake Iseo. However, he was having some technical difficulties and therefore sought the advice of Ziliani, a young winemaker who had recently graduated from the School of Oenology in Alba. It was Ziliani's idea to produce traditional bottle-fermented sparkling wine, explained Cristina, his daughter, who now oversees the company together with her two brothers Arturo and Paolo. The conditions and the terrain were favourable, Ziliani had conjectured, with moraine soil ideal for the cultivation of the classic grape varieties of Champagne: Chardonnay and Pinot Noir. The climate was also favourable for sparkling wines, influenced by both the Alps and the proximity to Lake Iseo, with a high diurnal range between day and night temperatures to keep the wines fresh and vibrant. It was an idea worth pursuing, the two agreed, and after a few fits and starts, the first bottle was released in 1961, labelled Pinot di Franciacorta.

The rest is wine history. In an era of pride in 'Made in Italy', a wine of this quality that could be compared with Champagne and yet that was wholly Italian in every way soon caught the imagination of the Italian public. Others came to the area to begin projects. Anna Maria Clementi Zanella purchased a little house in chestnut woods in Erbusco in the mid-1960s. She planted a small vineyard around her *ca' del bosc'* and from such tiny viticultural beginnings a dream was born and realised by her son Maurizio, who had begun to believe in the creation of a prestige wine estate when he was only fifteen years old. Thus began Ca' del Bosco. In 1977, businessman Vittorio Moretti transformed a small wine farm on the Bellavista hill into a full-fledged sparkling wine estate with a beautifully designed cellar where production methods remain strictly traditional. Investment in the region has been considerable, and the countryside has literally been transformed. Sparkling wine production requires the most advanced technologies and equipment, as well as the liquid capital to be able to allow wines to age patiently until they can be released. Even still, small winegrowers, too, have followed suit, deciding to produce their own Franciacorta traditional method sparkling wines themselves, rather like the small-grower *récoltants-manipulants* of Champagne.

Palazzo Lana Extrême is a magnificent wine that truly demonstrates that great Franciacorta has a character and personality entirely its own. Produced from 100 per cent Pinot Nero cultivated on two single vineyard plots, Quindicipiò and Brolo, both within sight of Palazzo Lana, the grapes are harvested and only the free-run must is used after the lightest pressing. Fermentation is in stainless-steel, with the finest lots further ageing for six months in barrel on the lees. The *assemblage* takes place in the spring following the harvest, and the wine is bottled and left to undergo a secondary fermentation on the lees for a minimum of ten years before disgorging. The wine that results from this lengthy ageing process is truly extraordinary. Though at least eleven years old, the mousse is lively and persistent, with aromas of stone fruit, candied peel, pastries and bread crust, absolutely bone dry and with a richness and complexity on the palate, fresh acidity and a saline, tingling minerality that is long and persistent.

23

CRIME AND WINE

My plane from London touches down at Aeroporto Falcone e Borsellino, formerly called Aeroporto Punta Raisi, located some 19 kilometres north-west from Palermo city centre. The airport was renamed after the two courageous anti-Mafia magistrates who were viciously murdered by Cosa Nostra in separate massacres in 1992. A large plaque featuring their portraits is prominently displayed by the airport entrance, bearing the inscription: Giovanni Falcone—Paolo Borsellino—Gli Altri—L'Orgoglio della Nuova Sicilia *('Giovanni Falcone, Paolo Borsellino, the others: the pride of the new Sicily'). On the taxi ride into Palermo, it is impossible to miss the monument that marks the so-called* Strage di Capaci, *the exact spot where a half a tonne of explosives had been planted under the motorway. The massive bomb was detonated by Mafioso Giovanni Brusca, calmly watching from his position on a hillside situated above the motorway (that exact position is also marked with a sign). The explosion killed Falcone, his wife and three policemen travelling in the cavalcade with them, a heinous murder that shocked not only Sicily but the whole world.*

Are those days gone? The Mafia is still as powerful today as ever, but at least there are organisations fighting back, organisations that give people hope. I check in to my hotel, Palazzo Centrale, on Via Vittorio Emanuele II, just down from the Quattro Canti, the 'four corners' at the heart of old Palermo, where baroque cornices, balconies and statues of four kings from Spain look down from the lofty pedestals to the pedestrian crowds below. It's been a long day of travel, and in my room, I find a bottle of Centopassi Argille di Tagghia Via from the Libera Terra cooperative. I open it, pour myself a glass and admire the deep purple liquid produced from organic Nero d'Avola grapes cultivated on the high uplands of San Giuseppe Jato. I take a sip and roll it around my mouth, enjoying its bright freshness, vivid, crunchy fruit and flavours that are refreshingly frank and totally honest.

The History

On the morning of 29 June 2004, the people of the city of Palermo awoke to a brave new world. Overnight, an anonymous group had distributed hundreds of paper notices all around the city bearing a simple and direct message: 'Un intero popolo che paga il pizzo è un popolo senza dignità'—'An entire people who pay protection money is a people without dignity.' The Mafia, who have dominated life in Palermo and across Sicily and much of Italy for more than 150 years, have long exerted control over whole communities as well as individuals by demanding the regular payment of protection money—*pizzo*. After decades of murder on the streets and in the country; after the high-profile Maxi Trial that lasted from 1986 to 1992 and saw some 475 Mafiosi indicted and convicted for a variety of blood-curdling criminal activities; after the brutal assassinations of magistrates Giovanni Falcone and Paolo Borsellino that followed; after further revelations of the extent to which the Mafia's iron grip extended across not just Sicilian but also national Italian politics even to the very top, it seems that on a sunny day in June one year, the weary people of Palermo had finally had enough, and some were willing to bravely stand up and say so.

From its earliest origins, the Mafia found ways to infiltrate almost every aspect of Sicilian society. Extortion on both a micro and macro scale has long been one of its principal weapons to achieve dominance and control over the people. The payment of *pizzo* at all levels—whether by small individual market traders and shopkeepers or by some of Sicily's and Italy's largest corporations—had become so prevalent that it came almost to be considered a legitimate business expense.

The launch of the Addiopizzo movement on that June morning in 2004 was therefore a brave watershed event in Sicilian society, a moment when collectively the people of Palermo stood up to say, *Basta*, enough is enough, the fightback to reclaim our dignity has begun. I recall in 2009, just five years after the movement had been launched, strolling along Corso Vittorio Emanuele II in the heart of the *centro storico* and coming across a small shop called 'Punto Pizzo Free'. Inside there was hotchpotch of merchandise and products—textiles, artwork, clothing, ceramics and scores of quality food and drink products including pistachios from Bronte, chocolate from Modica, jams, *biscotti*, artisan pasta, fruit juices, Sicilian *olio extra-vergine d'oliva*, pestos, pâtés, cheeses, cured meats and of course table wines, fortified wines and liqueurs from throughout Sicily. What united all these products was simply that they were all from businesses and individuals who proclaimed their allegiance to the Addiopizzo movement, businesses, in short, that refused to pay protection money and were not afraid to declare it.

The Mafia is a vast global empire that profits from the misery it inflicts on others. Its income is so vast that in 2014 Italy's Foreign Ministry claimed that it had a budget—an estimated 200 billion euros—that even exceeded the total European Union spend—140 billion euros. Lucrative criminal activities include extortion on a mammoth scale, racketeering, procurement of lucrative government contracts for its own benefit, gambling, bribery, embezzlement, tax fraud and above all the wholesale domination of the international drugs trade.

Yet the very origins of the Mafia, murky though they may be, seem to have long been firmly rooted in the very fertile agricultural soil of Sicily. Exploitation of the land and of those who have always been compelled to work it has sadly had a painful and long history across the largest island in the Mediterranean going back millennia at least to the time of the Greek tyrants. For control over land has long been the primary source of wealth, with vast profits to be made from the sweat, toil and suffering of the island's people, with immense estates owned by feudal lords and vassals who owed allegiance to whatever foreign power was currently in charge.

Citrus groves had first been introduced to Sicily during the Arab occupation in the ninth and tenth centuries CE, complete with sophisticated systems of irrigation to keep them well watered. This agricultural industry proved to be the source not only of delectable fruit but also of incredible wealth, especially after Sicilian citrus growers landed first a contract with the British Navy to help safeguard sailors against scurvy and then began the lucrative trade of shipping both lemons and sweet oranges across the Atlantic to America. This tantalising, moneymaking activity presented great opportunities for the newly emerging class of entrepreneurial Mafiosi. In the Conca d'Oro, the 'shell' of verdant land that once extended out from Palermo and that was almost entirely carpeted with citrus groves, they were already the richest landowners. Now they found themselves able to control and exploit all aspects of citrus production and commerce, from growing the fruit to supplying water at exorbitant prices to those without a source of their own, to setting wholesale fruit prices and even to controlling the transport to take the fruit to the ports to be loaded on to the boats. At every stage along the way, there was pizzo to be paid; should someone refuse, the consequences were sinister, severe and often terminal. Tales of death and slaughter among the orange groves of the Conca d'Oro are part of Sicilian legend and history.

Even today, the rural roots from which the Mafia emerged continue to extend deeply into the fertile soil of Sicily. Increasingly, the Mafia along with its counterparts in other organised criminal syndicates that originate across the Straits of Messina in Calabria, Campania and Apulia are finding that huge illicit profits can be harvested richly from the country's agricultural countryside. Intimidation, torture, threats and murder are all means by which the Mafia has been able to infiltrate Sicily and Italy's lucrative food industry. It was estimated in 2018 that organised crime was able to generate a turnover of more than 22 billion euros from Italy's food industries, a 30 per cent increase on previous years. One lucrative means of exploiting agricultural land has been simply to threaten owners to give over their property and then to apply for and receive EU subsidies. In many instances, the land is not ever even farmed. Why bother when a mob clan is able to claim around 1 million euros in EU subsidies on a 1,000-hectare patch of land that it had managed to acquire for a pittance? This exact scenario took place repeatedly in the Nebrodi National Park, a protected area in the north-east of Sicily above Etna, though controls have more recently been put in place to try to stop this criminal activity.

The so-called 'Agro-Mafia' business extends far beyond just the illegal acqui-sition and exploitation of land to virtually every aspect of the food and drink chain, including cultivation of crops; the raising, butchering and curing of live-stock; transport and distribution; production and packaging; markets, whole-sale and retail outlets; restaurants and catering; supermarkets; wine production, and more. These are all highly profitable outlets that furthermore provide means to launder profits gained through more obviously nefarious criminal activity. Literally from field to fork, organised crime is soiling one of 'il Bel Paese''s most beautiful, evocative and economically powerful industries.

The counterfeiting of genuine produce and goods, especially those granted exclusive and prestigious DOP (*denominazione di origine protetta*—protected designation of origin) and IGP status (*indicazione geografica protetta*—protected geographical indication) is one way for criminals to make huge profits. It is estimated that as much as half of all extra-virgin olive oil sold in Italy has been tampered with, adulterated with cheap, poor-quality oil that doesn't even necessarily come from Italy. *Parmigiano reggiano*, *mozzarella di bufala* or *pro-sciutto di Parma*, all products that have earned valuable DOPs as well as national and global reputations for quality, can be counterfeited with fake, cheaply produced lookalikes.

Wine is another area where the possibility for fraud is legion: by simply labelling an inferior, cheap red wine as Brunello di Montalcino DOCG or Barolo DOCG, the profit margin can be increased exponentially if illegally. In 2020, Italian police seized more than 4,000 bottles of counterfeit Sassicaia, the fabled original produced by Tenuta San Guido in Bolgheri, one of Italy's greatest and most prestigious Super Tuscan wines that can fetch prices of up to 360 euros per bottle or more. The fake operation originated in Sicily and was sophisticated, with bottles, labels, capsules, corks, wooden cases all fabricated to replicate the genuine, and the bottles themselves filled with a far inferior and cheaper vintage. Orders for the wine at 70 per cent less than the price of the original had, according to investigators, been placed by potential customers in China, Russia, Korea and elsewhere. Other high-value and iconic 'Made in Italy' products have been similarly targeted.

Fraudsters in Italy have not only confined themselves to counterfeiting famous Italian wines; in 2009, French customs officials intercepted a consignment of 2,000 fake Champagne bottles that had been crafted in a factory in Turin and were part of a consignment of around 300,000 bottles that had found their way around France and Europe, including Britain. The trade—and the profits—from counterfeit wine is literally in the billions per annum. These are not just examples of rogue products being substituted for the genuine. In other cases, fraudulent adulteration can cause serious public health scandals. In 1986, there was an instance where red wines from Piedmont were laced with methanol, a poisonous substance more usually used as a component in antifreeze, resulting in the death of twenty-four people. The damage this rogue operation caused to the reputation of Italian wine was considerable and took many years to repair.

Of course, not all wine fraud is necessarily the result of Mafia activity or the acts of organised criminals. As long as man has made wine, there have been opportunities to deceive and profit. There are countless instances where wine producers and bottling companies are under investigation or have been convicted for fraudulently passing off cheaper wines as more expensive and prestigious bottles. In other instances, unscrupulous producers have attempted to 'improve' their wines by blending them with cheaper wines usually from Italy's south, wines that may have more colour, alcohol and body but that come from outside the permitted region or zone of production of the original. So it has probably always been. Indeed, that sign/price list in a bar in Pompeii advertising Falernum was almost certainly an attempt to hoodwink its customers, for surely a wine of such prestige and scarcity as genuine Falernum was in antiquity would certainly have cost far more than merely quadruple the price of ordinary plonk.

Libera Terra

The fight against fraud in the wine and other agricultural industries and against the organised 'Agro-Mafia' is a never-ending one that requires constant vigilance. The problem is widespread: Coldiretti, Italy's largest agricultural confederation of farmers and agricultural entrepreneurs, has found criminal agricultural activity in ninety-eight of Italy's 102 provinces. This has long been a serious problem that governments have tried to deal with. As long ago as 1982, an important Italian law known as Rognoni-La Torre was passed that sought to define the Mafia and other criminal organisations and to weaken their economic base by allowing the state to seize assets, land and property that the convicted criminals owned. However, once the lands and property had been confiscated, Rognoni-La Torre did not provide any way for them to be used constructively. Thus, in 1995 the Associazione Libera was born when Don Luigi Ciotti, a Catholic priest, led a campaign that raised a million signatures for a petition for the adoption of a law that would allow the social use of lands confiscated from the Mafia and other organised crime syndicates. The number who supported this anti-Mafia initiative demonstrated a groundswell of desire to make something constructive and of benefit to society out of the misery caused by these criminal organisations. This led in 1996 to the passing of Law 109 that allows the state to enable these confiscated lands and property to be leased to anti-Mafia cooperatives, social enterprises and regional authorities provided that the initiatives will benefit the community.

Thus, Libera Terra was created—the name means 'Free Land'—to oversee that use of state-owned land for free under renewable leases to not-for-profit organisations and cooperatives for socially beneficial projects. The first such Libera Terra enterprise was the Cooperativa Placido Rizzotto, named after an activist from Corleone who was kidnapped and murdered by the Mafia. This cooperative is in San Giuseppe Jato, just a few miles from Corleone, a Mafia stronghold that had been the home of the late Salvatore 'Totò' Riina, who, among countless other capital crimes, had ordered the assassinations of the magistrates Falcone and Borsellino (and afterwards celebrated their demise by toasting the event with French Champagne, presumably real not fake). Riina was on the run from the authorities for decades, yet he was eventually captured at his villa in the heart of Palermo where he had been living all along. His capture and subsequent conviction could only have ever happened in part through the assistance of the so-called *pentiti*—former Mafiosi criminals who finally were willing to testify against their former bosses in return for reduced sentences and/or state protection from the almost certain retribution that they would have otherwise received.

Today, there are ten Libera Terra cooperatives all using lands confiscated from criminal organisations in Sicily, Calabria, Campania and Apulia. Collectively, they manage some 1,400 hectares of land cultivated organically and yielding an extensive range of produce: grapes certainly for wines in Sicily and Apulia, and grain, fruit, vegetables, nuts, olives and much more. This produce is then transformed by Libera Terra cooperatives into organic high-quality products that are sold by Libera Terra Mediterraneo through its online shop, its own shop in Palermo, as well as in gourmet boutiques and delis around Italy and even abroad.

The Mafia and other powerful criminal organisations in Italy are not going away, even if there have been notable if still sporadic successes in bringing them to justice. The Libera Terra project, though miniscule in comparison to the vast sums and profits that crime organisations continue to harvest, is significant nonetheless and in more than merely a symbolic way. The reuse of confiscated lands shows that good can come from bad, a tangible demonstration to those living where these activities are located who have suffered for decades and generations under fear that they need no longer do so. Those who choose to purchase Libera Terra's products know that they are not only buying high-quality food and drink; they are also making a conscious statement against the Mafia, helping the fight against organised crime and supporting the honest employment that the Libera Terra cooperatives bring.

The Wines

Centopassi Argille di Tagghia Via, Nero d'Avola biologico, Sicilia DOC, Cooperativa Placido Rizzotto, San Giuseppe Jato, Sicily

Each of the Centopassi wines produced by the Cooperativa Placido Rizzotto is dedicated to someone murdered by the Mafia. It is fitting that this flagship wine is dedicated to Peppino Impastato, the young political activist who campaigned tirelessly against the Mafia, including members of his own family, by ridiculing them over a pirate radio station. Eventually, Impastato's uncle Don Tano Badalamenti had enough and ordered his assassination in 1978. The killing shocked Sicily and all of Italy. Impastato's ideals and bravery inspired others to stand up against the Mafia and to fight for freedom from the stranglehold they exerted over the island. *Centopassi* (100 Steps) is an award-winning film directed by Marco Tullio Giordana that tells the story of this brave young activist. The name of the film has been taken as the name of the wines produced to represent the winemaking soul of Libera Terra as interpreted and produced by the Cooperativa Placido Rizzotto.

Centopassi Argille di Tagghia Via, Nero d'Avola *biologico* is one of the cooperative's flagship cru wines, expressing the highland territory of the Upper Belice Corleonese, a breath-taking and majestic landscape. Here Nero d'Avola grapes are cultivated organically at an altitude of 550 metres above sea level on predominantly sandy-clay soil from the Tagliavia vineyard that was confiscated from the Grizzaffi, the mob boss Totò Riina's own clan. The grapes are harvested manually in small boxes, transported to the winery where they are vinified in stainless-steel with a lengthy maceration on the skins to give structure and body, followed by ageing in part stainless-steel vats and part in large oak barrels. The wine is direct, pure and clean, deep in colour and expressing the dense fruit of Nero d'Avola, combining both power and elegance, the complete antidote to crass brutality.

Centopassi Terre Rosse di Giabbascio, Catarratto DOC Sicilia, Cooperativa Placido Rizzotto, San Giuseppe Jato, Sicily

Catarratto is normally considered something of a workhorse white grape variety, planted extensively on lowland vineyards especially across the west of Sicily where it has traditionally been allowed to ripen to a high degree to be used as part of the base wine for the production of fortified Marsala. Here it is cultivated organically on the iron-rich, red clay terroir of the Giambascio vineyard at 300 metres above sea level. The grapes are harvested by hand and fermented in stainless-steel then aged on the lees in part in clayver ceramic wine vats, resulting in a wine that demonstrates richness, a saline minerality and real character.

The Giambascio vineyard on which the Catarratto vines are planted was confiscated from the Brusca clan. It was Giovanni Brusca, a self-confessed multiple murderer, who detonated the bomb that killed magistrate Giovanni Falcone and his wife in 1992. Brusca's direct involvement came to light when Santino Di Matteo was captured and became one of the first of Falcone's killers to become a *pentito*, explaining to his captors in detail how the act had been committed. In retaliation, Brusca had Di Matteo's eleven-year-old son Giuseppe kidnapped and held in captivity for 779 days before the child was strangled and his body dissolved in a vat of acid. Brusca was captured in 1996 and turned state witness himself, having derided, tortured and murdered others who had done so. His sentence was reduced to a mere twenty-six years in prison, and in 2021 the assassin of Giovanni Falcone was released to his freedom.

Terre Rosse di Giabbascio Catarratto is 'dedicated to Pio La Torre and to his never-ending struggle for peace and justice'. Pio La Torre was an inspirational politician and the leader of the Italian Communist Party who was murdered by the Mafia in 1982 after he helped to draft the Rognoni-La Torre Law, the very same law that enabled the state to confiscate property, land and assets from convicted Mafia criminals and that eventually led to the creation of the Libera Terra cooperatives. It seems fitting to me that this wine, produced from Catarratto, an often-overlooked grape variety, through careful cultivation and winemaking on land that had once been owned by a notorious criminal clan, has been elevated to reveal a character that is at once understated yet forceful and strong. In a way, it pays homage to all the ordinary, uncelebrated people who were in fact each unique and exceptional in their own ways and whose lives had been blighted or wiped out by the Mafia.

Negroamaro Rosato Salento IGT, Hisotelaray, Torchiarolo, Apulia

Hisotelaray is the winemaking division of Libera Terra Puglia, a cooperative winery in the Alto Salento, the far-southern 'heel' of the Italian boot, in the province of Brindisi. Here the cooperative works 27 hectares of land confiscated from Apulian organised crime syndicates such as Sacra Corona Unita. Two grape varieties reign supreme in Salento, Negroamaro and Primitivo, and the cooperative cultivates and transforms both into a range of wines, powerful and beefy reds as well as some of Italy's very best *rosato* or rosé wines, most notably from Negroamaro. The Salento *rosatos* are a world away from pink tipples found elsewhere. Hisotelaray's Negroamaro Rosato Salento has a relatively deep hue of pink that comes from Negroamaro grapes left to macerate on the skins for some hours followed by gentle pressing and fermentation in stainless-steel. The wine that results is forceful, bone dry and with enough backbone to accompany the outstanding full-flavoured cuisine of Apulia. Indeed, it is the ideal wine to enjoy with a plate of *orecchiette con cima di rape*—little handmade ears of pasta served with a sauce of turnip tops stewed in garlic, Puglian extra-virgin olive oil and plenty of *peperoncino*, or in summer with some baby octopus—*polpetti*—from Bari, either stewed or grilled over charcoal.

The cooperative is poignantly named after Hiso Telaray, a young Albanian who had crossed the Adriatic to seek work and a better life in Italy only to find himself exploited under the practice known as *caporalato*, an insidious form of semi-servitude whereby migrants are compelled to borrow extortionate sums of money from organised gangs of criminals to secure employment. They are then forced to work long hours and live in encampments that

261

are little better than prisons. Hiso refused to succumb to the threats of the *caporali* and was therefore murdered at the age of only twenty-two. The citation for this wine made in his honour reads, 'This wine is dedicated to Hiso and to the people who do not bow their heads in front of the Mafia arrogance.' It is fitting that the Hisotelaray cooperative is located on land and property confiscated from Cosimo Antonio Screti, who was the *cassiere* or treasurer for Sacra Corona Unita, the criminal organisation that oversees much of the *caporalato* practices. Out of hopelessness and despair, the cooperative that bears Hiso's name can now give honest employment to young people including migrants and to produce wines that are a true reflection of the Salento territory.

Falco Peregrino, Terre Siciliane IGT, Bosco Falconeria, Partinico, Sicily

The fight against the Mafia is carried out on many levels. From a grassroots point of view, Addiopizzo is one of the most important, for it is a movement that has given voice and support to individuals and mainly small businesses who refuse to be forced to pay protection money to the thugs who have long considered it their right to demand it. When the movement was launched in 2004, the Mafia was still—and remains today—a powerful force, ever present across society especially in Sicily. The decision for individuals and businesses to adhere to the Addiopizzo movement and to proclaim this publicly took bravery, especially for those living and working in the Mafia's traditional heartland of western Sicily.

Partinico, home of the notorious Vitale clan, has long been a Mafia stronghold. Bosco Falconeria, the family farm of Antonio Simeti and Mary Taylor Simeti, lies just outside Partinico, about 40 kilometres from Palermo. Mary is a well-known American food historian, writer and the author of numerous books about food and culture in Sicily. Bosco Falconeria is her husband Antonio's family farm, now overseen by their daughter Natalia.

Mary recalls joining Addiopizzo almost right from its start:

> We joined the Addiopizzo Association shortly after it was founded, and participated in the protest marches and the fairs, because we felt that a pledge to denounce any attempt at extortion by the Mafia exemplified the way in which we wanted to live and produce in Sicily, free from coercion and compromise. Some five years later the Association introduced the 'Prodotto PizzoFree' brand, and we happily added its logo to our wine and oil labels as a way of spreading the message to a wider audience. In the past twenty years the number of businesses adhering to the movement has gone from just over a hundred

to over a thousand scattered across the island, and membership appears to be a successful deterrent to would-be extortionists.

Bosco Falconeria has been a pioneer of organic farming, growing grapes on hillsides that lie about 230 metres above sea level in red, calcareous light clay soil. The vines are trained either on trellises or in the so-called *all'alberello alcamese* fashion. Wild plants and legumes are planted between the rows for green fertiliser. Says Natalia:

> My father Antonio has cultivated these vines for twenty-five years according to the principles of organic agriculture. Taking a step back, learning to exercise restraint, to respect the natural equilibrium and to intervene as little as possible. Together, my father and I are learning to do the same with the wine. Year after year, wine after wine, learning from others, exploring, and experimenting, attempting in this as well to be ourselves.

Falco Peregrino, named after peregrine falcons, birds of prey that often circle the farm, is a very pure, natural wine produced from Catarratto grapes fermented on the skins using the indigenous yeasts, with no added sulphites, then aged in stainless-steel tank for about nine months. I love this wine for its bite, its perfume of orange peel and wildflowers, the touch of tannin that comes from skin maceration and a finish that is always slightly bitter. It is the perfect wine to accompany the simple, honest and genuine foods of Sicily, such as those that Mary writes about so beautifully.

Gorgona, Costa Toscana IGT, Frescobaldi, Tuscany

Can wine become a positive means of rehabilitation even for hardened criminals? Gorgona is the northernmost island in the Tuscan archipelago, located some 18 nautical miles from Livorno, an isolated haven rich in wildlife, most notably marine birds. Its very isolation attracted religious communities, and there was a large monastery on the island in the Middle Ages. Today, Gorgona is Italy's only remaining island penitentiary. To reach it takes an hour and a half by boat across open sea; when weather is inclement or stormy, it can be cut off entirely for days or even weeks. Gorgona has been a penal colony since 1869 and currently holds some of Italy's longest-serving criminals, many of whom have been handed down life sentences for violent crimes. However, Gorgona gives hope for a new beginning, for all the inmates here are in the final period of their detention, working on the prison farm and living freely by day, immersed in work and nature in the hope of eventual release to freedom and the start of a new life.

The Gorgona project is an important step in this rehabilitation process. A collaboration between the Frescobaldi family, who have been making fine wines in Tuscany for more than 700 years, and the Gorgona Penal Institute, it involves inmates working on the island vineyard, cultivated with Vermentino and Ansonica vines, as well as learning winemaking skills under the supervision of Frescobaldi's winemakers. The project began in 2012 utilising an already existing island vineyard that had been abandoned until 2008. The wine cellar needed to be equipped with vinification equipment and ageing vessels, and with all the tools necessary to produce quality wine. Inmates who work on the project are paid a salary at fair rates and learn skills that can be put to good use on their eventual release. The aim, the dream, for many of the inmates, should they be released, is to continue to work in wine, ideally for the Frescobaldi on their numerous wine estates, a dream that has been realised by some.

Gorgona is a wine story that has captured the imagination of the world. The first bottle, a magnum of Gorgona 2012, was presented by Marchese Lamberto Frescobaldi to Giorgio Napolitano, president of Italy. Andrea Bocelli, the great Italian tenor whose home is on the Tuscan seaboard, created the text and signed the label of the 2013 vintage. Giorgio Pinchiorri, owner of the three-star Michelin Enoteca Pinchiorri in Florence, supports the project by promoting the wine in his world-renowned restaurant. Simonetta Doni of Studio Doni & Associati, an internationally known wine-label agency, donates her time and talent each year for the label graphics.

What, then, of the wine? Limited production and the expense of producing the wine under such challenging circumstances mean that this is a premium product that has become something of a collector's item, with only limited allocations released to export markets. The bottle capsule is wax, and the label is sealed with wax, to be peeled and read from the other side, the 2021 vintage revealing a 'newsletter' that tells the story of Gorgona and the project. Produced from a blend of Vermentino and Ansonica grown in this unique island environment, the wine is a beautiful expression that encapsulates the hope that the project brings: yellow-golden in colour like sunshine, fresh like a salty sea breeze, with aromas of apricot, mango, honey and bitter island herbs and a beautiful, creamy, sumptuous texture. Coming from this small, untouched and fertile island far from anywhere else, it is a luscious wine that reveals an explosion of flavours that are waiting to be released, so eager are they to escape from the bottle. Gorgona is a gorgeous, special and unique wine that is also deeply symbolic: a demonstration that through manual labour in the purifying sunshine of this beautiful and faraway island, a wine results that brings the hope of redemption, liberation, perhaps even salvation.

24

DONNE E VINO

A visit to the wine cellar at Casato Prime Donne is a beautiful and unique experience. This is perhaps the only winery in Italy entirely staffed by women and has become a flagship in an industry that had formerly been almost exclusively the domain of men. Perhaps not surprisingly, the cellar itself, far from being just a functional and utilitarian place, as working cellars often are, is beautiful, the walls decorated with frescoes that tell the history of Montalcino together with fascinating legends such as the miracle that saved the city during the sixteenth century. In the vineyard surrounding the winery, there is a hiking trail that is enriched by contemporary works of art as well as with extracts from writing by the female winners of the Casato Prime Donne Award. Donatella Cinelli Colombini, the proprietor of Casato Prime Donne, is also a founder and president of Le Donne del Vino, an important movement that serves to connect women in the world of wine.

Donatella eases the cork out of a bottle of the wine that she is perhaps most proud of, Brunello di Montalcino Prime Donne. When she first produced this wine in 1993, in recognition of the importance of women in wine, she assembled Prime Donne from selected parcels of Brunello grapes that had been vinified separately, blended in consultation with four expert female tasters, and this collaborative process continues today.

Brunello di Montalcino is one of Italy's most famous wines, noted for its power, structure and longevity. How would Donatella's example be an expression of the women who helped craft it? In the glass, Brunello di Montalcino Prime Donne is a wine that absolutely transcends gender, forcefully powerful with a persistence balanced by a harmonious elegance that is complex, intriguing and simply beautiful. I salute Donatella and all the many talented women working in wine across Italy.

The History

Italy is a country of strong, independent, productive and creative women. Throughout the ages, women have made significant contributions to society, intellectually, politically, commercially and in the arts and sciences. That they have been able to do so in a society and culture rooted from antiquity to Silvio Berlusconi and beyond in sexism and misogyny, in which women were often treated as second-class citizens, makes their achievements even more remarkable.

For the story of Italy, like the story of its wine, has long been a narrative controlled and dominated by men. Yet women have played their part, too, and have sometimes been able to rise above their station and their time. Born in 1046, Matilda of Tuscany became one of the most powerful rulers of her age, overseeing a vast territory across Tuscany, Lombardy and Emilia-Romagna, and involving herself in some of the great historic moments of her era such as when Holy Roman Emperor Henry IV had to prostrate himself for three days in a blizzard outside her castle at Canossa seeking forgiveness and absolution from Pope Gregory VII, a defining moment of the Middle Ages.

Christine de Pizan, born in Venice in 1364, was a writer who became one of the most respected literary figures in the courts of medieval Europe. Living and working in France where her father was court physician and astrologer to Charles V, she wrote *Le livre de la cité des dames* (The Book of the City of Ladies). In a sense, this pioneering work that extolls the qualities of women in a spirited defence of her sex could be called one of the earliest examples of feminist writing. She confronts the ingrained misogyny of her era by envisaging a city defined by the female virtues of reason, rectitude and justice and inhabited by women of virtue. 'My ladies', she exhorts at the conclusion of the book, 'see how these men assail you on all sides and accuse of every vice imaginable. Prove them all wrong by showing how principled you are and refute the criticisms they make of you by behaving morally' (trans. Rosalind Brown-Grant).

Some, confronted with the misogyny that was the order of the day, found other ways to express themselves. Artemisia Gentileschi was considered one of the most talented and accomplished painters of the seventeenth century. The daughter of a Tuscan artist, she learned her craft from an early age and was celebrated for her expressive and naturalistic paintings that were dramatically powerful. In her early career, she had been raped by the artist Agostino

Tassi, a friend and collaborator of her father, and this horrific act was to shape her life and work. Her father, betrayed by his friend and colleague, pressed charges, the case went to court and Artemisia was tortured with thumbscrews to verify her testimony. Tassi was convicted, though the sentence was never carried out. Despite her traumatic ordeal, she established herself as a successful and independent artist, becoming an early female member of the prestigious Accademia del Disegno in 1616. Even so, the incident had an enduring impact on her work. In her celebrated painting *Salome with the Head of St John the Baptist*, the Mannerist depiction with which Salome inspects the head presented to her on a plate leaves us with a sense of her revulsion and satisfaction in equal measure.

But these and other women were exceptions. Generally, the role of women in Italian society required subservience to men, as was the case elsewhere throughout Europe. The nineteenth century, Risorgimento and the creation of the Kingdom of Italy was an opportunity for reform of Italian society in any number of ways, including the emancipation of women. Women, after all, had played an active role in the struggle to be free from the yoke of the Spanish, the Austrians and the French, yet the new nation's new Civil Code left many women feeling disenfranchised. Anna Maria Mozzoni, born in 1837 in Milan, is considered by many to be the founder of the Italian women's movement for the treatise she wrote, *La donna e i suoi suoi rapporti sociali … in occasione della revisione del codice civile italiano* (Woman and her Social Relationships on the Occasion of the Revision of the Italian Civil Code). She focused on legal reforms, most notably of family law, and campaigned for suffrage for women. She also represented Italy at the International Congress on Women's Rights that took place in Paris in 1878. She was not alone in her campaigning writings: the first women's magazine, *La Donna*, was founded by Adelaide Beccari in 1860.

Little by little, it seems, some progress was made. Women were admitted to Italian universities in 1876. By 1877, women could serve as witnesses to legal acts. The first national Feminist Congress was organised by Per La Donna in 1911, and speakers began to campaign for reform to divorce laws.

Fascism and post-war Italy

If the late nineteenth century and early twentieth had seen the incipient development of a politically active women's movement composed of both elements from the left and a socially aware, liberal, middle class, the rise of Mussolini and Fascism was a major setback to women's rights. The Fascist government consolidated power in part through gaining the support of the Catholic Church when they signed the Lateran Treaty guaranteeing the sovereignty of the Vatican City to the Holy See. The conservative influence of the Catholic Church and Pope Pius XI lent support to the Fascist ideal of paternal authority in the family. By extension, Fascist ideology dictated that a woman's greatest contribution and indeed duty to society was to have as many children as possible, with population growth seen as an indicator of national virility as well as a motive for imperialistic expansion.

This message was conveyed through propaganda using media such as film as well as posters with strong graphics and typography for slogans urging maternity and fertility. The ideal Fascist woman was portrayed as strong, ruddy, with large breasts and broad child-bearing hips. Indeed, for Mussolini, the 'battle of the births' to repopulate Italy with the blood of pure Italians was almost as important as the armed conflict, for it was through procreation that the Fascist dream of a new Italian nation would be reached. Women were excluded from political life, and their rights in the workplace were severely diminished. A tax was imposed on 'unjustified celibacy', and women were encouraged not to seek jobs but to raise large families. In 1938, a law was passed that restricted female employment in private and state enterprises to 10 per cent of the workforce (though in practice it was not possible to impose this).

After the fall of Mussolini, the bombings by and the advance of the Allies, followed by the retreat of the Germans, post-war Italy lay in ruins, like much of Europe. Italian society was similarly left in fragments, divided into opponents of Fascism, ex-Fascists, accomplices, partisans from the right and the left, Catholics and communists alike. Women finally gained full suffrage in 1945, yet the Italian government's agenda gave little heed to women's rights. The Christian Democrat Party, which was to rule for fifty years, remained heavily dependent on the support of the Catholic Church, thus the sanctity of marriage was confirmed and abortion and adultery were considered crimes as well as sins.

This grim, post-war period was documented well in the genre of cinema known as neo-realism. The liberation from Fascist ideas and ideals gave directors a new cinematic opportunity to portray female characters that were far from Mussolini's propagandist role models. In Roberto Rossellini's *Roma, città aperta* (Rome, Open City, 1945), the character of Pina (Anna Magnani) is a woman who is liberated sexually, tough, natural in appearance and demeanour and politically motivated. De Sica's *L'oro di Napoli* (The Gold of Naples, 1950) presents several short vignettes. In 'Pizze a credito', a young, beautiful Sophia Loren is the wife, Sofia, to a short, dumpy fried-pizza street seller, Rosario. She herself sells contraband cigarettes on the black market. Purportedly a devout churchgoer, she is in fact resourcefully using the time when she should be in church to visit her lover. For this independent woman, life is all a bit of a rush, and on one instance she happens to leave her wedding ring by her lover's bedside. When her husband notices it is missing, she says it must have fallen into the pizza dough, and thus begins a comic series of visits to everyone who had purchased a *pizza fritta* that morning. The character of Sofia is streetwise, hard-working, desirable and beautiful—a woman who is quite free and confident to seek pleasure for herself, not anyone else. *Riso amaro* (Bitter Rice, or Bitter Laughter, 1949), a film directed by Giuseppe De Santis, portrays the hard life of women with more brutal realism. The film gives a harsh depiction of the *mondine*—the itinerant women compelled to work in the mosquito-ridden rice paddies of Piedmont to help to produce the rice that Mussolini wanted Italians to eat in lieu of pasta. We experience this through the eyes of Silvana (played by Silvana Mangano), desperate to be free of a life of rural drudgery and misery. Not content with accepting her lot, she becomes involved in a plot that leads to love, betrayal and murder. Federico Fellini's *La strada* (The Road, 1954) is a dream-like mythic portrayal of the sad life of Gelsomina (Giulietta Masina), sold by her mother for just 10,000 lire to Zampanò (Anthony Quinn), a strongman who shows off his might and muscle by performing feats of strength while Gelsomina passes around a hat. He treats her brutishly, and when she attempts to escape, he beats her. Yet there is a strange and tender fondness between them, perhaps Fellini's allegory of the unequal relations between man and woman?

The feminist movement in the 1970s

Italy's 'economic miracle' during the 1960s gave new opportunities to women in the burgeoning industries that were prospering. Television, too, along with cinema, brought new worldviews directly into people's homes. As Italy recovered from the war and prosperity came, so did the fight for women's rights gain new strength and momentum. The issues of divorce, abortion and reform of family law were the catalyst for more radical action. Feminist groups were started such as Rivolta Femminile, which published its manifesto in July 1970. 'Women must not be defined in relation to man. This awareness is the foundation of both our struggle and our liberty' is the first guiding principle of this new creed, which sought to emphasise the differences between the sexes rather than simply to strive for equality, a fundamental change of direction. 'Liberation for woman does not mean accepting the life man leads, because it is unlivable; on the contrary, it means expressing her own sense of existence.'

In *Melmaridè*, a documentary directed by Elisa Bozzarelli and Alice Daneluzzo in 2018, we meet a group of women from Piacenza who were activists during the 1970s and relive that time through recollections of the excitement of that era: the huge public rallies (20,000 women gathering in the Campo de' Fiori in Rome to demand freedom to control their own bodies, freedom to pursue relationships with people of whatever gender) and the struggle to achieve the passing of legislation for women to have the right to an abortion. Feminist publications such as *Effe* appeared that gave voice to women; the Teatro della Maddalena was founded in 1973, a theatre exclusively run by women. The Piacenza group started a clinic in the city that was self-organised and financed to give support and information to women about birth control and to help with abortion as an extreme solution (women in Italy at that time were compelled to travel abroad for an abortion).

Many important victories were achieved during these years. The right to divorce was enacted in 1970. In 1975, family law was reformed, removing adultery as a crime, establishing gender equality within a marriage, as well as removing discrimination against children who were not born in wedlock. Conjugal rape was made a crime in 1976. Equal treatment in the workplace for men and women was established in 1977. The right of abortion was enshrined in law in 1978. The right to mitigation of punishment in cases of 'honour killings' was repealed in 1981.

If something of the excitement and high-profile energy of the women's movement in the 1970s diminished in subsequent years, legislative progress has continued to be made that has positively changed the lives of women including laws against stalking and sexual violence (2009, 2013), and laws to further strengthen equality in the workplace (2010), while new legislation has recently been proposed (2023) that will enable the effective enforcement of equal pay between women and men.

That said, it should be noted that the various years of government under Berlusconi, who controlled much of the Italian media, including television and print media, only helped to entrench the perception of Italy as a nation deeply rooted in sexism and misogyny. During his periods as prime minister (1994–5, 2001–6, 2008–11), he did few favours for the progress of women, with his crude sexist comments made on the international stage, the infamous 'bunga-bunga' sex orgies and his alliances with far-right and neo-fascist parties such as Lega Nord and the National Alliance, arch-conservatives on issues such as abortion and same-sex marriage. As of 2023, Italy's government is led by a woman, Giorgia Meloni, the first female to hold this position. She is the leader of Brothers of Italy (Fratelli d'Italia), a far-right populist party with neo-fascist links that opposes abortion, is anti-LGBTQ+ and supports the 'traditional' family unit. Hard-earned women's rights have already begun to be overturned, and even the right to abortion as enshrined by Law 194 is perceived to be under threat. Her government has already ordered local authorities to stop registering same-sex couples as parents, leading to the removal of some from their children's birth certificates. As much of the world has lurched to the populist right, experiences elsewhere—the overturning of Roe vs Wade by the United States Supreme Court—demonstrate that women's rights must never be taken for granted. Meanwhile, women continue to shake up Italy's male-dominated political scene. In 2023, the centre-left Democratic Party, which is the main opposition to Brothers of Italy, elected Elly Schlein as its leader, a progressive who is queer and a strong supporter of LGBTQ+ rights.

Le Donne del Vino

The context of this brief feminist overview is important in the world of wine, which has historically been an industry mainly dominated by men. Of course, women as well as men have long toiled in the fields, working vineyards alongside many other agricultural tasks since time immemorial. But it was relatively rare for women to oversee or run a winery, and indeed, it was only in 1978 that the first Italian woman was qualified to be an oenologist or winemaker. The world of wine—making it, selling it, even drinking it—was mainly the domain of men. Relatively few women were in positions where they could make the major decisions in a wine business, nor were they yet actively involved in sales and marketing.

In part to address this, the Associazione Nazionale Le Donne del Vino—the Association of Women in Wine—was founded in 1988 as a non-profit association. There were only around twenty founder members. Recalls Donatella Cinelli Colombini, the current president of the association:

> When the association was born in 1988 in Florence, men laughed because women were almost absent in the management of the cellars. Today they no longer laugh. The agricultural area of businesses run by women is 21 per cent of the total but produces 28 per cent of Italian agricultural income. This shows that female performance is better than male performance. Some of the most important and famous wines in Italy are made by female winemakers (Sassicaia,

Masseto). Some of the most influential wine critics are women. The largest Italian wine group (GIV) has a female CEO.

Le Donne del Vino now has close to 1,000 members including wine producers, restaurateurs, wine shop owners, sommeliers and writers and journalists. The association was born out of the desire to promote an understanding and culture of wine based on the experience and knowledge of women working in wine across all these complementary sectors. This was considered a highly innovative idea for its time.

Today, the aims of the association are to develop the culture of wine and responsible consumption; to promote the role of Le Donne del Vino in society and in the workplace; to bring the association's members together, encouraging shared initiatives as well as learning and educational trips; to take the voice of Le Donne del Vino to Italian and foreign institutions and wine organisations. Communication lies very much at the heart of the association, the need to be able to spread knowledge of wine within a broader cultural context than merely from an agricultural or commercial point of view. Currently, over 80 per cent of those involved in the marketing and communication of wineries are women. The association is furthermore a valuable conduit for communication among members, creating a vital network that allows women to share experiences, problems and challenges.

If Le Donne del Vino was not born directly out of the women's and feminist movements that laid the ground for improved conditions for women in the workplace and home, the association is nonetheless sensitive to the role of women in the wine workplace and the challenges they face. In 2016, an important survey, 'Indagine sulle Donne del Vino', was undertaken to discover the experiences of women working in wine across all sectors, including women who are owners or co-owners of wineries, wine shop workers, sommeliers, restaurateurs, PR and marketing people, journalists and wine experts and consultants. Even among those who owned or co-owned wineries, a third thought that women still did not receive the same salary as men for doing the same job; in other sectors, the percentage was considerably higher. For those working in journalism and PR as well as marketing, nearly two-thirds believed or were certain that male colleagues were paid more. Sexism, discrimination and sexual abuse or harassment were problems that they had to defend themselves against both in the workplace and at events such as wine fairs. A further point that emerged from the survey is that many women have had difficulty reconciling their professional commitments to family commitments, and many have only been able to start families at a relatively late age.

The full result of this study indicates that there is still much work to be done. Concludes Cinelli Colombini: 'Some points were confirmed, some were surprises, especially regarding more sexism than we expected. The role of women in the world of wine is improving, but it is still not great, and there is still a lot to be done to reach real gender equality.'

Gender and the language of wine

As women at last have the opportunity to take leading roles across all sectors of wine, it is important for wine writers to be aware that antiquated notions of gender in wine should no longer have a place. Writing about taste is always a highly subjective exercise, and wine writers use metaphor to help to describe and pinpoint primary and tertiary aromas and bouquet as well as flavours and textures that can be ethereal, fleeting and difficult to elucidate precisely. But in trying to do so, gendered descriptions may hinder more than help. Big, powerful, well-structured and tannic reds have long been described as 'muscular', or even 'manly'; velvety, softer styles of wines are considered 'feminine'. By such reckoning, Taurasi, with its chewy tannins and rich acidity, would seem to be a wine for men, while softer and sometimes lightly sweet Prosecco would be a tipple for women. Is that indeed the case? I know many women who adore big, powerful, beefy reds, while Proseccos, especially from the classic heartlands of Valdobbiadene and Conegliano, are glorious expressions of the Glera grape, loved equally by one and all. Similarly, Barolo has long been considered more 'masculine' than Barbaresco, which has a shorter ageing discipline, less concentration and tannins that are sometimes less to the fore, ergo a more 'feminine' expression of the mighty Nebbiolo grape. Implicit in such descriptions is an implied patriarchal hierarchy of quality, that wines suitable for men are the best.

Wine writers of a certain age—male wine writers usually (and I hold my hand up)—have long been guilty of falling into such sloppy tropes, and I hope this book offends no one. To be clear, wine should no more be described in gendered binary terms than sexuality should be. Wine writers need to find an acceptable language that respects all humans.

The Wines

Brunello di Montalcino 'Prime Donne', Casato Prime Donne, Montalcino, Tuscany

The Progetto Prime Donne began in 1998 at a time when women in wineries were very rare. Donatella Cinelli Colombini had departed from her family

273

winery, which had been bequeathed to her brother, to start a new activity, transforming Fattoria del Colle, another family farm at Trequanda, as well as creating a new Brunello di Montalcino winery. First, she had to find a wine-maker, so she made enquiries at Siena's School of Oenology only to be told that there were no good young winemakers who were available. However, when she asked if there were any female winemakers, it turned out there certainly were because most wineries didn't even consider employing a woman winemaker. 'At that moment', she recalls, 'I saw discrimination that was so ancient and widespread that it had become almost invisible. I decided to demonstrate that women can produce great wines just like men and there-fore I set out to create the first Italian winery with an all-female team.' Thus, Casato Prime Donne was born.

Brunello di Montalcino 'Prime Donne', the estate's top wine, is therefore a flagship for the feminine world of wine. It is produced only in the best years and to a strictly limited yield of about 6,000 bottles destined to be sold to high-quality restaurants and wine stores around the world. The wine is not only produced by the all-female staff at Casato Prime Donne; in addition, a panel of four international female tasters help to create the final blend, includ-ing a wine store owner (Astrid Schwarz), a sommelier (Daniela Scrobogna) and two Masters of Wine (Rosemary George MW and Madeleine Stenwreth MW). It is their task to help select the wines from different vinified parcels of Brunello and to decide the type of oak barrels for the ageing, as well as to make the final blend from the different barrels.

Brunello di Montalcino is a wine destined for lengthy ageing and important occasions. In fact, says Donatella, the wine was inspired not by women but by her grandfather Giovanni Colombini. It is a return to a more natural method of farming and winemaking that he championed:

> My grandfather taught me that the earth must be kept alive to produce great wines. He taught me that we need to have a dialogue with the final consumer of our wines. These ideas are accepted by everyone today but forty years ago they were the opposite of the general accepted beliefs. At that time everyone had faith in chemistry and industry.

This special wine is a classic Brunello di Montalcino: complex, richly tex-tured, age worthy, displaying scents of red fruits and sensual spices, harmoni-ously balanced with silky tannins that stretch out to a long and persistent finish, beautiful, elegant and perfectly balanced.

Vigna Monticchio Rubesco Riserva DOCG, Cantine Lungarotti, Torgiano, Umbria

Teresa Severini Lungarotti of Cantine Lungarotti in Umbria was a pioneer when she became Italy's first female oenologist after gaining qualification from the University of Perugia in 1978:

> No other woman had chosen to study oenology before me, even though there were women who were running or managing farms. The world of wine was very different then and women mainly worked in secretarial roles or else in public relations. It certainly wasn't open for women to work in areas that required technical expertise. Despite this, as a woman I encountered no resistance in my studies at either Perugia or later when I went to Bordeaux to take more specialised courses. However, when I returned to Cantine Lungarotti and began working, introducing new techniques from France such as low-temperature fermentation, I initially encountered resistance from the cellar workers. I could certainly understand why: they had years of experience under their belts and now a young woman was there putting them all to the test by bringing in new innovations in the production processes.

Teresa worked with her stepfather Giorgio Lungarotti, himself a pioneer who had brought specialised viticulture and modern winemaking practices to Torgiano, an area of Umbria that before his arrival had been unheard of as a quality wine-producing area. Today it is considered one of the most exciting wine regions in Umbria, with the Lungarotti winery regularly winning top national and international awards and accolades for its extensive range of wines, many of which Teresa herself developed, from Brezza, light and fresh as a summer breeze, a wine that she created in the 1980s, and Aurente, a full-bodied, barrel-fermented Chardonnay, to new interpretations of the Lungarotti classics.

Vigna Monticchio Rubesco Riserva is a wine that Teresa feels particularly attached to:

> This wine, first produced by Giorgio in 1964, will always have a piece of my heart not just because of what it represents for our family heritage but also for what it represents for our region and for our country, a Sangiovese based on politeness and finesse that is able to win the battle with time and last for several years and decades. The 2005 vintage of this wine can be considered the first vintage of the second Lungarotti generation, a vintage I will never forget.

The wine is produced entirely from Sangiovese grapes grown on the Monticchio single vineyard: it has a deep ruby colour, primary bouquet of sour cherries, blackberries and balsamic herbs, and some wood notes that evolve with age into warm, spicy tones of black pepper, coffee, cocoa, beautifully balanced with a powerful structure, round tannins and a finish that is long and persistent.

Today, Teresa dedicates herself to furthering the work of the Lungarotti Foundation, which was started by her mother Maria Grazia who created and curated the Lungarotti Museums of Wine and Olive Oil in Torgiano. The foundation today remains dedicated to promoting connections between culture, art and wine and oil, from antiquity to today. 'Women', she says, 'are able to take a more holistic approach than men, and this is important for the work of the foundation.'

Guido Cocci Grifoni, Offida DOCG, Tenuta Cocci Grifoni, Ripatransone, Le Marche

'Mother Nature is the main partner of the winegrower', says Marilena Cocci Grifoni, the head of her family business Tenuta Cocci Grifoni, which she runs with her two daughters, Camilla and Marta:

> She is a woman and we women have a high sensibility to working with Nature cooperatively. It is still challenging to be a woman working in the world of wine. We must continue to strive to guarantee inclusivity, to give the same opportunities to women as men, to consider viticulture as activity where both women as well as men can make contributions. We need to learn how to share ideas, share experiences, and we need to ensure that we give fair wages to women. In this respect, the work of Le Donne del Vino has been vital above all to create a network between women where ideas, strategies, problems, and experiences can be discussed openly among female colleagues who all share a deep connection with rural culture.

Marilena grew up on the family farm in the southern part of Le Marche in the province of Ascoli Piceno. She studied economics and qualified as an accountant and lawyer. It was only after her father Guido Cocci Grifoni passed that she became more fully involved, quitting her previous profession to dedicate herself to develop the export market. Now, working with her daughters, they have continued to develop the estate and its wines, as well as creating the Relais Cocci Grifoni, which offers a beautiful wine hospitality experience. Tenuta Cocci Grifoni has now achieved B Corp certification demonstrating its deep commitment to sustainability and an inclusive, regenerative approach to agriculture and the environment. 'This is very important', says Marilena,

> with climate change, we have had to learn to be very flexible and manage in a pragmatic way. There is still not enough known about how to manage the

impact of this important variable in our viticulture. However, I think that my daughters have the education and the youthful energy and enthusiasm to confront the challenges that lie ahead.

Guido Cocci Grifoni Offida DOCG is a wine that Marilena crafted in remembrance of her father, who was a pioneer of Italian viticulture and championed tirelessly to improve and promote the wines of Ascoli Piceno. His greatest contribution was the rediscovery of the Pecorino grape variety, which had become virtually extinct. He found the last remaining vines high in the Sibillini mountains, propagated them and planted the original Pecorino Mother Vineyard. 'My father taught me always to be serious, honest, and fair with everybody, to respect the people we work with, and above all to respect Mother Nature. This wine is my homage to him.'

The Pecorino grapes used to produce Guido Cocci Grifoni Offida DOCG come entirely from that original Mother Vineyard. 'I wanted to say to my father, "Thanks for this legacy".' Only the best bunches are harvested. They are fermented then left on the lees for one year, with *bâtonnage* once a week. The result is a concentrated expression of Pecorino, with a nose of wild herbs, yellow flowers, a beautiful creamy texture and a steely backbone of acidity, intense in the mouth with a mineral and persistent finish. It is a wine of immense finesse and precision made lovingly by a daughter in homage to her father.

Loretello Verdicchio dei Castelli di Jesi DOC, Cantine Politi, Arcevia, Le Marche

Growing up in Jesi, in the heart of the beautiful hinterland of Le Marche, Giuditta Politi used to love going out into the countryside to accompany her father on regular visits to the family farm at Arcevia that he oversaw, together with the other men in the family, her uncles. Though they were not full-time farmers and worked in other sectors, they had had the great foresight in 1962 to plant 11 hectares of Verdicchio vineyards, the first specialised vineyard in the area. Despite her passion for the countryside and the desire to work in agriculture, however, Giuditta was discouraged from entering a wine world that was not considered suitable for women. So instead, after gaining a PhD in genetics, she became a scientist and carried out research work in developmental genetics at the Centre of Genetic Evolution at the Sapienza Università di Roma. It was only after her father had passed in 1996, along with some of her uncles in the same year, that the family found themselves at a crossroads: they either had to sell the farm or else find a way to keep it going as a family concern.

Giuditta was thus suddenly presented with the opportunity to change career and life completely, to leave behind the artificial lights of the laboratory, where the careful analyses of the variables of each experiment followed precise guidelines, for the open-air laboratory where variables such as drought, hail, excessive rain and more would be completely out of her control:

I very soon learned that you can't improvise. Passion is not enough; it takes preparation that only learning can give, so I completed a masters degree in oenology where I learned the theoretical bases of viticulture and winemaking. Certainly, my scientific background and the fact that I had long worked with yeasts helped me a lot. Then, armed with new knowledge, my passion, commitment, and enthusiasm did the rest.

It was not easy in those early years. Our workforce was made up of men of a certain age who did not look favourably on being told what to do by a young woman. At this time, in our area of Arcevia there were no other women running wine estates. In my territory, the challenges that a woman winemaker must face, I think are mainly due to the historical prejudice deriving from the sharecropping world of the *mezzadria* that long characterised Le Marche territories. For example, a prominent figure in the Le Marche trade union world, originally from Arcevia, is still convinced that our company and above all the wine is the kingdom of my husband, the man of the house, even though he works in a completely different sector outside the region. It is not possible, according to this 'enlightened gentleman' that a woman can have the skills to do so much work. Fortunately, nowadays the world of wine looks with different eyes at women working in agriculture and more and more often the company directed by a woman has, in the common perception, an added value.

Certainly, the wines that Giuditta crafts at Cantine Politi demonstrate the precision and vision of a scientist turned skilful winemaker who knows exactly the sort of wine that she seeks to create. Loretello Verdicchio dei Castelli di Jesi is a brilliant expression of one of Italy's most characterful and interesting native white grape varieties. It has a rich fullness in the mouth that comes in part from two harvests of the Verdicchio grapes, the first early to retain freshness and aroma, the second only once the grapes are slightly over-ripe to lend a fullness and richness to the wine. After a soft pressing, the must ferments at low temperature to allow the yeasts to bring out the full expressiveness of the Verdicchio. This is followed by ageing on the lees until April to give the wine its intense creamy character and structure. 'I am very proud of Loretello', says Giuditta:

278

Every year, when I go to taste the results of so much work and commitment, just before the ageing phase when the wine is still youthful and not fully evolved, I intuitively sense that what at first taste seems to be an ugly duckling has all the potential to become my most beautiful swan. And I am happy!

Sceg Aglianico del Vulture DOC, Azienda Agricola Elena Fucci, Barile, Basilicata

Elena Fucci's story is inspiring. Basilicata is one of Italy's most impoverished regions, historically and still today: in 2020, it was estimated that more than 20 per cent of the population exist below the poverty line. People have long felt compelled to leave the region to travel across the world in search of a better life. Elena explains that her great-grandfather Nicola Salvatore and grandfather Generoso grew up working under the age-old system of *latifundium*. Life was hard, and Nonno Generoso saw no other option but to leave his home, taking his family, including Elena's father, to South America, where he settled and worked in Venezuela, saving as much money as he could. Only once he had acquired sufficient funds was he able to return to Italy. With his life savings, he managed to purchase the same plot of land that he and his family had previously worked in Barile, on the flanks of the ancient, extinct volcano of Monte Vulture. It comprised a vineyard and olive groves as well as the Torre Titolo, the yellow house where Elena herself was born. The vines of the vineyard were gnarled, ancient and, growing at altitude, produced small yields but of extraordinarily high-quality fruit. The grapes were therefore always in demand to be sold not as wine but as a cash crop either to the *cantina cooperativa* or to wine buyers in the region, in Campania or even up to the wine lands of Le Langhe.

Monte Vulture is a fascinating if remote wine land. With vineyards located at altitude (up to 800 metres above sea level), the climate can be hellishly hot in summer, bitterly harsh during the long, endless winters. Majestic, bare hills ripple down from the slopes of the ancient volcano, not exclusively covered with vines but a patchwork still of subsistence farming, people growing a bit of this, a bit of that, scratching a living however they can.

For youthful Elena, at only nineteen years of age, like many of her generation, she had dreams of moving elsewhere, doing other things. However, when her parents, who were both teachers, and her grandparents told her that they were going to sell Torre Titolo, the family home she had been born in together with its surrounding land, she suddenly realised that this was her home, and she could imagine being nowhere else. Thus, rather than moving away, she decided to study oenology and create a new winery at her family home. What was perhaps most significant was that as a young person, a young woman, instead of feeling the need to leave Basilicata in search of a better life, Elena found a way to stay in the land that she loved and to champion the region and its wines, which she felt so deeply about. In this respect, she has proved to be a role model for a new generation of women and men alike who are finding ways to be able to remain in the lands they call home.

The Elena Fucci winery was created in 2000, and fortune clearly favours the brave. For the fruit from this ancient wine land, from vines with an average age of more than half a century, has indeed proved to be exceptional, combined with Elena's own winemaking skills. The flagship wine, Titolo Aglianico del Vulture DOCG, consistently wins top awards in all the most important guides and competitions.

Elena is proud to be a woman who has succeeded in what has been an industry mainly dominated by men:

> I think we are on a *strada buona*—a good path. The work of pioneering women such as Donatella Cinelli Colombini combined with the work of Le Donne del Vino has changed the face of this industry. Here in Basilicata, there are now many family wineries that are run by women, and women are no longer relegated to secondary roles. Without taking anything away from our male colleagues, I believe that women bring a greater sensitivity, humanity, and refinement to the world of Italian wine. In whatever field they are working, women can grasp details and facets and nuances that men often overlook.

Elena's wine Sceg is a fascinating expression of Aglianico del Vulture, a wine that comes from a 1.5-hectare single vineyard with very old vines (an average age of over seventy years). This vineyard had previously been tended by friends of her grandfather's, now old men who could no longer carry out the hard, manual toil. This invaluable patrimony of old vines, grown on clay and lava soil, would have been lost if Elena had not taken the vineyard over. The name comes from the Lucanian word for pomegranate, symbol of fertility and abundance, and indeed it is fitting. For this is a wine that comes from grapes grown on ancient, gnarled Aglianico vines previously tended by old men, now transformed by this dynamic female winemaker into a wine with freshness, beautiful fruit, combined with herbal, tarry flavours of the volcano and tannins that are velvety soft, a wine that embodies the beauty and confidence of youth.

BACK TO THE FUTURE

In 2021, Etna erupted more than sixty-five times, sending clouds of volcanic ash, pumice and lapilli high into the stratosphere, then raining down a covering of black grit that settles on to everything and that eventually enriches the soil with its extraordinary minerality. Today, Nerello Mascalese, Nerello Cappuccio and Carricante vines are cultivated on lava fields formed from eruptions that took place hundreds of years ago, or thousands, or tens of thousands, while the more recent flows of yesterday and yesteryear will harden into solid rivers of black rock that over time will eventually erode and break down into lava-rich soil that can be cultivated fruitfully.

Yet if this is an entirely natural process that takes centuries, millennia or more, today's climatic changes to our planet are happening frighteningly more quickly, posing immense challenges to us all, and not least to Italy's winegrowers. Meanwhile, the pandemic that struck the world in 2020 reminds us of the fragility of our human condition, that we must take care of ourselves and of our earth if we are to survive for future generations. It is a wholly sobering moment in the history of mankind, yet wine gives us solace. I open a bottle of Salvo Foti's Etna Rosso, made from grapes grown on the same volcanic slopes where, according to Homer, the Cyclops Polyphemus cultivated his vines. Wine, good honest, Italian wine, connects us to the past ... and gives us hope for the future.

The Present

History will one day teach that the start of the third millennium was a restless time once again. As happened 3,000 years ago with movements of people across the Mediterranean, or after the fall of the Roman Empire when Germanic tribes descended in waves into the Italian Peninsula, it will be remembered as an age when people were on the move. Driven to escape wars or by hunger, poverty or economic hardship, boatloads of desperate migrants are risking their lives to make their way to Italy, landing in places like the tiny island of Lampedusa, not far off the coast of Tunisia, or entering Italy by land across former frontiers that no longer present barriers. Meanwhile, the age-old divide between Christian and Muslim worlds has grown into a seemingly unbridgeable chasm, bringing mistrust, religious hatred and intolerance to levels not seen since the time of the Crusades. In Italy, the dark forces of extreme nationalism have grown stronger with the rise of ultra-right parties such as Brothers of Italy and Lega.

Historians will note, too, that in early 2020 Italy became the first country in Western Europe to be struck down by a virus called COVID-19. Cases appeared at first in just a few towns in Lombardy and Veneto, which had to be put into isolation. By early March, the entire country was under lockdown, with severe restrictions placed on what people were allowed to do. The world watched in horror as Italy's health service was overrun, with terrible images of patients in corridors or on ventilators broadcast around the world, and corpses overwhelming the country's morgues. Movement between towns or regions was forbidden, people were only allowed to leave their homes once a day, restaurants and bars were closed and a strict curfew was put in place. Soon the entire world was experiencing this same terrible plague.

Reading about the past teaches us about the present—and gives hope for the future. Paul the Deacon's *Historia Langobardorum*, written in the late eighth century, describes a terrible pestilence that passed through Northern Italy during that time: 'Everywhere there was grief and everywhere tears.' In 1347, Italy became the first country in Western Europe to be visited by the Bubonic Plague, a pandemic that originated in the east and came to be known as the Black Death. To stop the spread of the disease, inhabitants had to keep to their houses, the wealthy fled to country estates and strict hygienic regulations were brought in (restrictions not at all dissimilar to what the Italians and indeed much of the world put in place to attempt to stop the spread of COVID-19).

Giovanni Boccaccio's great work *Decameron* relates what happened during this terrible time. Written in the vernacular Italian, he described in graphic detail some of the horrors of the plague when Florence was ravaged by the disease in 1348:

> A great number departed this life without anyone at all to witness their going.
> … Many dropped dead in the open streets, both by day and by night, whilst a
> great many others, though dying in their own houses, drew their neighbours'

attention more by the smell of their rotting corpses than by any other means. … Ah, how great a number of splendid palaces, fine houses, and noble dwellings, once filled with retainers, with lords and with ladies, were bereft of all who had lived there, down to the tiniest child! (trans. G. H. McWilliams)

In *Decameron*, to escape such horrors, seven young ladies and three young men decide to leave Florence to seek refuge in the country. There, in an ample and comfortable villa, over the course of ten days they entertain each other by telling stories and singing songs, exploring themes of fortune, virtue, lust and love, ten stories told daily by each in turn, 100 stories in all. Naturally, wine is an ever-present feature to console, entertain, inspire and help them fill their days and nights, for the villa has a well-stocked cellar of good wine 'more suited to the palates of connoisseurs than to sedate and respectable ladies'.

The dark days of COVID-19 that Italians—and indeed the whole world— had to endure were at times surreal, nightmarish, unbelievable. As in times past, wine, it seems, has been able to bring solace, comfort and pleasure. In a survey 'Italians and Wine' carried out by the Vinitaly-Nomisma Wine Monitor Observatory and presented in Rome in anticipation of Vinitaly 2022, figures showed that consumption of wine in Italy increased during the pandemic, especially among young people. During the dark days of lockdown, 89 per cent of Italians drank wine, with Generation Z and millennials increasing their consumption considerably from 84 per cent to 90 per cent.

Climate change

Meanwhile, as we recover from the pandemic and its aftermath, the world, it seems, is on fire. In Sicily, the record for the highest temperature in European history—48.8 degrees C (120 degrees Fahrenheit)—was recorded on 11 August 2021. In 2022, sixteen Italian cities were issued red extreme heat alerts, and firefighters battled up and down the country to extinguish wildfire blazes. In the European heatwave summer of 2023, the number of cities in Italy added to the red alert list rose to twenty-three, from Turin and Trieste in the north to Bari, Naples, Palermo and Cagliari in the south and islands. Temperatures exceeding 40 degrees were not uncommon across the country as Italy sizzled.

When considering the effects of our changing climate on viticulture, there are further factors that are equally as significant as elevated temperatures. We are now regularly seeing and experiencing changes to patterns of temperature in summer and winter alike, including extreme cold; the likelihood of drought or excessive rainfall; the paucity of snowfall in winter; the prevalence of severe wildfires; unexpected and violent hail storms that can destroy vineyards in minutes; rains that fall not evenly and regularly but come down like explosive water bombs, the huge amounts of water too excessive to be absorbed by the ground. All of these factors and the sheer unpredictability of the weather are having a profound effect on winegrowers across Italy and indeed across the globe.

It is not possible to be a wine lover and a denier of climate change: the effects are clearly evident in our wineglasses. As sugar levels in grapes rise under unrelenting sunshine and heat, wines inevitably are reaching higher and higher levels of alcohol. Wines that previously had moderate levels, say 11.5 per cent for whites or 12 per cent for reds, now routinely weigh in 13.5 per cent and 14.5 per cent respectively, a considerable increase. Furthermore, it is not just a question of overall alcoholic level; when sugar levels rise precociously, it may mean that grapes must sometimes be harvested before they have reached full phenolic ripeness. There is an important distinction between sugar ripeness, which refers to the accumulation of fermentable sugar that occurs with the lessening of malic acidity, and phenolic ripeness, which refers to alterations in the tannins that occur naturally in grape skins, seeds and stems. Grapes that have reached desired levels of sugar ripeness but not yet phenolic ripeness when fermented may result in wines that are high in alcohol but that have excessive, harsh, green tannins.

In Italy, winegrowers are seeking ways to adapt to what seems to be an irreversible climatic trend. Harvests have come forward considerably across the country. Nebbiolo grapes for the production of Barolo in Piedmont's Le Langhe, for example, sometimes used to be harvested as late as early November and the season of mists and fog. That rarely happens now; more likely is that the grapes will have all been brought in by mid-October or earlier. In Sicily, meanwhile, some vineyards are now being harvested as early as mid-July.

Sites previously considered unsuitable for viticulture are being discovered or rediscovered. North-facing sites, previously shunned in many wine zones, are now being cultivated to provide shelter from the unremitting sun, while vineyards sited at higher and higher altitudes are also demonstrating that they too can now produce great wines. Wines from Etna are a prime example, with vineyards planted with both Nerello Mascalese for red and Carricante for white now being sited at altitudes of higher than 1,000 metres above sea level. Elsewhere, producers are re-evaluating ancient grape varieties that had been overlooked or disregarded. In Franciacorta, Italy's premier wine zone

for the production of traditional method sparkling wines, warmer temperatures have meant that the Chardonnay, Pinot Noir and Pinot Bianco varieties
traditionally used to produce the cuvée have been at risk of lacking acidity and
freshness. Therefore, an ancient and mainly unheard of variety, Erbamat,
which had long been rejected as inferior by winegrowers, is making a spectacular comeback. This late-ripening, thick-skinned indigenous white grape
variety is neutral in character with a naturally high acidity. It is also relatively
resistant to disease. Since 2017, the Franciacorta DOCG discipline has been
changed to allow for up to 10 per cent of Erbamat in the finished blend.

One of Italy's greatest vinous strengths is its immense biodiversity that
comes from a wealth of native grape varieties that have mainly been steadfastly clung to across the centuries. Now, however, in some cases winegrowers may need to look for alternatives, even—heretical though the thought
may be to traditionalists—to the introduction of hybrid varieties, that is,
grape varieties that are the product of the crossing of two or more *Vitis* species. Hybrid varieties are normally crosses between the European *Vitis vinifera*
and another species such as *Vitis labrusca* or *Vitis riparia*. Such hybrid varieties
seek to combine qualities from each, for example organoleptic quality with
disease resistance. PIWI has become an established brand to indicate hybrid
varieties that are fungal resistant and enable a significant reduction in the use
of pesticides.

There is admittedly a huge and longstanding resistance to the introduction
of such grape varieties in European vineyards and in Italy. Professor Attilio
Scienza, Italy's leading vine geneticist, argues that this deep-seated and
ingrained prejudice against any vines that are not pure European *Vitis vinifera*
is wholly misguided and based on fake science. In his book *Vine and Prejudice*,
he maintains that as increased heat and humidity bring conditions that impact
on the growing of *Vitis vinifera* across Italy, any such prejudices should be
abandoned as the need to turn to hybrid varieties could become increasingly
more urgent, their grapes either to be used in blends or even to produce
varietal wines in their own right.

The gen(i)e in the bottle

Studies into sequencing the grape genome, meanwhile, are ongoing and continuing at pace, motivated in great measure by the threats to European viticulture posed by fungal diseases such as powdery and downy mildew, which
if not controlled could become both commercial and environmental disasters.
Proponents of what is called Techniche di Evoluzione Assistita (TEA or

Assisted Evolution Techniques) argue that the ability to edit the genome of existing varietals, for example to create a vine that is more disease resistant, is a vital scientific advance that must be explored if not embraced. Climate change is making many wine zones more humid and thus more prone to these mildew diseases than ever before. If the grape genome can be genetically improved in such a manner that leaves the grape's aromatic and polyphenolic profiles unchanged, through procedures that effect such changes as if they had occurred through natural mutation or mutagenesis, then this process can help to produce more sustainable grape varieties that bring economic, social and environmental benefits for producers, consumers and the planet alike.

According to Professor Scienza, such cisgenic gene editing is not the same as genetic modification, for it seeks to insert exact copies of genetic material from related species that already exist in the gene pool. Transgenic gene editing, by contrast, would seek to introduce foreign DNA from unrelated species or even artificial genes or artificial combinations of genes. Cisgenic gene editing using TEA procedures results in slight genetic changes that could have arisen naturally through conventional selective propagation in the vine nursery. That unassisted process in the nursery, however, would have taken at least five or six cycles and normally around fifteen to twenty years before it could yield results that could be put into practice. Cisgenic genome editing can thus speed up the process considerably and bring results far more quickly. With climate change happening so frighteningly quickly, it is not hard to understand the scientific urgency.

This remains a complex and controversial subject. Because cisgenic plants are similar to traditionally bred plants since the transferred genes come from the same gene pool, it is argued that they are as safe as traditionally bred plants and should not be considered as genetically modified organisms. The green light has now been granted in Italy for field trials of resistant grapevines bred using TEA techniques. This will allow scientists, geneticists and winegrowers to verify responses to vine diseases as well as whether the procedures have altered the quality of the wines. If successful, TEA techniques could allow for the creation of fully disease-resistant vines that are more resilient to climate change and that will minimise the need to use chemicals in the vineyard.

The potential benefits are without doubt considerable. And yet, many winegrowers as well as consumers remain wary if not downright fearful of the introduction of any type of genetically modified vines into European vineyards. In 2010, activists in France destroyed a vineyard in Alsace planted with vines that had been modified to resist a particular vine malady. Public opinion polls have indicated increasing concern about any genetically modified crops and foods, including wine grapes. Yet should consumers and winegrowers be wary, given the scientific evidence as well as the huge potential benefits as weighed against the looming catastrophe that climate change is fast bringing to Italian and indeed global vineyards?

The argument to introduce TEA procedures to produce disease-resistant vines is compelling. One valid concern is that without rigorous safeguards in place there might be nothing to stop these same or similar procedures from being used for other motives, perhaps to modify taste and aroma profiles, or the colour of wine, or to manufacture new 'products' that don't yet exist or have not yet even been thought of. Would it matter if this were to occur? I think it would. We like to believe that despite all the interventions that man has made over the centuries and millennia to produce wine, it is overall a natural product that is a beautiful expression of grape variety, terroir, culture, history and climate. Furthermore, there must be concern, too, that research into the development of disease-resistant vines will only be carried out on those grape varieties that are most commercially viable. Yet one of Italy's greatest strengths is its incredible vine biodiversity. Would TEA procedures be utilised on all those obscure grape varieties that continue to be cultivated for no other reason except that they always have been, or would a large element of Italy's magnificent but little heard of vinous patrimony be left to eventually wither away and die on the vine? That certainly would be an immense pity.

Science uses rational thought and argument to seek objective truths to make advances that bring benefits to humanity. Yet wine also is, should be and I hope always will be a natural product that we approach subjectively and emotionally. I of course respect the views and opinions of leading scientists such as Professor Scienza, and I also appreciate the extreme urgency to act quickly. Yet I am also mindful of the arguments and opinions of individuals, organisations and activists that I respect, such as friends at Slow Food, a global, grassroots organisation that works to prevent the disappearance of local food cultures and traditions and to promote biodiversity. I can't help but be fearful that once the genetically modified genie-in-the-bottle has been uncorked, procedures and technologies developed genuinely with the best will in the world could inevitably pass into the hands of multinational agri-food-drink conglomerates whose only motive is profit, and who knows then what the results could be? That said, I believe the urgency and the speed of climate change and its detrimental effects on viticulture (and other crops) makes it imperative to act.

Sustainability

'Sustainability' has become a buzzword in recent years, and so it needs to be. The pressing challenge to protect our planet and indeed all of mankind has become an imperative that none of us can ignore. Overall, Italian wine producers have embraced the concept of sustainability with a gusto sometimes bordering on zeal. Producers are nowadays almost as eager to boast their 'green' credentials as they are to explain their wines.

As recently as the early 2000s, organic wine in Italy was something of a curiosity—or an irrelevance. Certification was complicated and costly, and only the most committed saw the benefits in farming in such a sustainable way. Biodynamic wine was even rarer, considered by many to be the kookiest of all farming methods, with its dependence on the lunar calendar and its potions made by mixing cow manure in a cow's horn and burying it underground. It was easy to poke fun at those who carried out such practices or who worked according to the phases of the moon and the positioning of the planets, but no one is laughing now. Organic and biodynamic viticulture and winemaking have become mainstream across Italy, and the results are now being seen in both better soil fertility and in better and better wines. Indeed, wines produced by such methods and systems are now regularly winning top accolades and awards. It seems that producing wines without chemical fertilisers, herbicides or pesticides, minimising the use of sulphites and fermenting using the indigenous native yeasts present on the grape skins rather than yeasts created in a laboratory are all factors that can lead to outstanding results.

At the annual 5-Star Wines competition held every year before Vinitaly, the Wines Without Walls section is now dedicated entirely to organic, biodynamic and sustainable wines and wineries, and the wines that win such awards are truly stunning. In the annual Gambero Rosso *I Vini d'Italia* guidebook, which awards *bicchieri*, or wine glasses, to Italy's best and greatest wines, with Tre Bicchieri the top accolade, there is now an entire section dedicated to Tre Bicchieri Verdi, recognising excellence in wines that are made through certified organic or biodynamic management. In the 2023 edition, there were 154 wines that earned the Tre Bicchieri Verdi accolade, a full 33 per cent of the Tre Bicchieri wines awarded.

So mainstream has sustainable viticulture now become that a wine zone as important and acclaimed as Chianti Classico can proudly boast that half of the 400 wine estates that belong to the Consorzio Chianti Classico are now farming organically. It is accepted that sustainability goes hand in hand with the ability to express greater territoriality as well as to result in higher-quality wines. Furthermore, if in the past, winegrowers thought that to maintain quality it was necessary to replant vineyards every thirty years or so, the value of old vines, in some cases up to a century in age, is now widely recognised. Such old vines may not only yield higher quality and more concentrated fruit (at the expense of quantity) but also seem able to withstand the excess vagaries of temperature and weather that climate change is bringing.

Sustainability in a winery also means finding ways to be as carbon neutral as possible. Systems for recycling wastewater are being put in place, photovoltaics installed, new cellars are being designed and excavated to produce wine *cantine* that are at once energy-efficient and stunningly beautiful.

Companies are also looking at ways to reduce their carbon footprint in terms of packaging, even going so far as to design and manufacture more sustainable bottles. Alternatives to glass bottles are also finding their way to the marketplace: wines in bag-in-boxes, paper and plastic bottles and wine in tins or cans are all now available. Globally, the screwcap has now widely replaced the natural cork as a means of stoppage—though not yet with most quality Italian wines—and consumers have adapted remarkably quickly, so it seems likely that alternative forms of packaging will also increasingly become more available and accepted. Certainly for millennial and Generation Z wine drinkers, such alternative forms may even come to be preferable, both for the benefits to the environment and for ease, convenience and even style: a heavy glass bottle stoppered with a natural cork that requires a separate instrument to open it might come to be seen as an incredibly inefficient and antiquated method of delivering wine, one that only their parents or grandparents would choose.

Back to the future

Space. The final frontier. If humanity is one day to colonise the moon or Mars, then, if Italians are involved, there is a good chance that wine will be needed to sustain them. In a project created by the Italian Space Agency and the Italian Sommelier Foundation, three iconic Italian wines are to be launched on a rocket that will take them to the International Space Station, where they will age for about a year at zero-gravity while orbiting the earth at some 28,000 kilometres per hour. Furthermore, cuttings of vines from the same grapes used to produce the wines will also spend time in space to see whether they can survive in such conditions. The chosen wines to take part in this space-age experiment are Biondi-Santi Brunello di Montalcino Riserva, Gaja Barolo Sperss and Feudi di San Gregorio Taurasi Riserva Piano di

Montevergine, wines made respectively from Italy's trio of greatest and most noble red grape varieties: Sangiovese, Nebbiolo and Aglianico.

Meanwhile, back here on planet earth it seems that things may be moving in quite the opposite direction. While technology has always been a vital and essential part of winemaking since humankind first mastered the art of creating clay vessels capable of holding liquid, it seems that for many today there is a desire to move away from the glistening and shiny stainless-steel technologies that transformed the Italian wine world as recently as the 1970s, a transformation that some say stripped wines of their identity, their very souls.

The so-called 'natural' wine movement continues to gain attention and relevance, particularly with a new generation of wine drinkers. It seems that millennials and Generation Z wine drinkers are less impressed by brand names or famous reputations and are seeking instead to find wines that are being produced as simply and as naturally as possible, wines that are unique and utterly different from those produced by conventional methods. There is no precise or official definition for a natural wine. In the broadest sense, it indicates a low-intervention approach whereby grapes are grown as simply and as naturally as possible, perhaps following organic or biodynamic principles—without necessarily needing certification to prove it—and then doing as little in the winemaking process as possible. Natural indigenous yeasts are always preferred for fermentation, the use of sulphites is kept to a bare minimum, wines might be racked or bottled according to the phases of the moon, and wines are often unfiltered, meaning that there is a bottle sediment that can make them cloudy. Certain styles of wine have become associated with the natural approach. 'Pét nat' (from 'pétillant naturel') indicates a wine made by the ancestral method of making sparkling wines in the bottle with no recourse to trying to clarify the wine by removing the sediment that is a by-product of secondary fermentation. 'Orange wines' indicate white wines made like red wines, that is, white grapes macerated and fermented on the skin (most white wines are fermented from just the grape must that has been drawn off the skin), resulting in richer and more complex flavours, aromas and textures.

If computer-controlled stainless-steel is eschewed as a vessel for fermentation, what, then, is the alternative? Terracotta vessels, often imported from Georgia where the art of making earthenware fermentation vessels known as *qvevri* was never lost, have become ever more popular in wine cellars across Italy. Called 'amphora'—though in fact nothing like the far smaller Roman amphorae in which wine, olive oil and garam were stored and shipped all around the Roman Empire—they are usually buried underground to maintain a stable temperature. Whole bunches of grapes might be crushed and added, stems and all, or just the juice and skins, to macerate and ferment slowly in cave-cool conditions: wine being made today as it was made literally centuries and millennia ago. The future it seems may well be found in the past.

But hasn't it been ever so in Italy? Across the centuries; in restless times and in settled; over high alpine mountain passes, on the slopes of smoking volcanoes, or on the *pianura* plains, too; from Dark Age brilliance to the Renaissance; across cultures and languages and influences that came from afar; enduring what we call 'history' that has brought occupations, invasions and wars; in times of desperate want and in times of prosperity, one constant has remained: since almost the beginning of time, Italians have found a way to cultivate the grapevine, harvest fruit grown in a fertile, mineral-rich land watered by rain and melting snow and ripened under a baking sun, and to make wine, good Italian wine, by age-old traditional or by space-age modern methods alike, wine that nourishes the soul and brings comfort and joy to all our lives, wherever we may be, whatever history—our own histories—may bring our way.

The Wines

I Vigneri, Etna Rosso DOC, I Vigneri di Salvo Foti, Milo, Sicily

If the future of Italian wine is to be found in the past, then we need look no further than to Mount Etna, where this book began and where viticulture has been carried out virtually since the beginning of time. If Homer's Cyclops grew grapes on the lava-encrusted slopes of Europe's most active volcano, so that activity has continued over the centuries. Certainly in the nineteenth and early twentieth centuries, the wines of Etna enjoyed a heady reputation, produced in rudimentary, stone, mountain-side *palmenti* or press-houses, the finished wines sent down in demi-johns or casks to the port of Riposto from where these strong, navigable wines, stable and robust enough to withstand transport by sea, were sent north to be blended with more insipid vintages or to serve as a substitute for those wine markets that had lost their local tipples following the devastation of phylloxera.

Yet somewhere along the way, a great, millennia-old vinous tradition was almost completely lost as the vineyards of Etna were abandoned, its historic wines replaced with industrially produced wines made from grapes grown on easier-to-tend and far less dangerous vineyards elsewhere. By the 1980s when we first visited Mount Etna, the historic traditions of grape-growing on the volcano had been almost completely abandoned, its great wines mainly a distant memory, with little left than hideous lava-encrusted bottles peddled to gullible tourists.

It is only since the 1990s that Etna has seen an incredible renaissance, an ancient land that is now being hailed as the source of some of Italy's, and the world's, greatest and most exciting wines. In large measure, the credit for this must go to Salvo Foti and his I Vigneri project, which has been about so much more than just creating great wine. Rather, in seeking to revalue the wisdom of the past, to restore his stone *palmento* above Milo on the eastern flank of the volcano, to utilise traditional systems of viticulture such as the *albarello etneo* (a system of training whereby the vines cling to a single pole) and to make wines that fully express the unique biodiversity and terroirs of Etna, Foti has been an inspiration to others, brought life back to the abandoned mountain and demonstrated that wine is not just a liquid in a glass but an entire world of historic and cultural experiences and memories.

Salvo Foti's I Vigneri Etna Rosso, then, is an iconic wine that represents both the past and the future, a wine that is pure, ancient and genuine. The wine recalls a tradition when the owners of the Etna vineyards gave an allocation of grapes each year to the workers for them to make wines themselves in their own rudimentary stone *palmenti*. This was a form of payment that was once standard on Etna, says Salvo. Today, up high in his own stone Palmento Caselle, wine is being made today as it was in the past. There is no de-stemming of the traditional Etna grape varieties Nerello Mascalese (90 per cent) and Nerello Cappuccio (10 per cent). The first crush is carried out by naked foot followed by maceration with the skins and stalks for eight days with fermentation occurring through the action of the indigenous yeasts on the grapes. The wine then rests in amphorae buried underground. It is thus fermented as naturally as possible, with racking and bottling carried out according to the phases of the moon. I Vigneri Etna Rosso is not particularly deep in colour, but it is certainly not light in flavour or character. On the nose, it reveals fragrant, brambly fruit, richly complex in the mouth, with well-knit and grippy tannins that will allow it to age gracefully for many years. This is a gorgeous wine that contains within it both the beauty and the power of the volcano together with the energy, the commitment and the passion of Salvo Foti and his sons Simone and Andrea. It is a wine that gives utmost respect to the ancient past while at the same time looking to the future.

Fresco di Masi Bianco, Verona IGT, Masi, Gargagnago di Valpolicella, Veneto

COVID-19 and the lockdown that resulted gave winegrowers precious time to consider new ideas, and new wines emerged from this enforced period of introspection. Raffaele Boscaini, the seventh generation of the Masi winery, explained:

> During lockdown, people rediscovered that they had time to cook, to be together, to share everyday wines with meals like we used to do in the past before life got too busy. With the Fresco di Masi project, we wanted to return to making simple, genuine wines, *come una volta* but as good as we expect them to be today.

Fresco di Masi wines—both *bianco* and *rosso*—were thus born during lockdown's gestation, wines created with a total commitment to sustainability and minimising man's intervention, a process, as it were, of subtraction, eliminating any steps in the grape-growing or winemaking process that were deemed unnecessary. For the Fresco di Masi Bianco, organic Garganega, Chardonnay and Pinot Grigio grapes are hand-harvested early morning when temperatures are cool, then fermented using only indigenous wild yeasts to produce an unfiltered wine with a moderate level of alcohol that retains above all the freshness and vivacity of the grapes. 'We sought to have the shortest route from the vine to the glass', explains Boscaini.

The packaging of Fresco wines is equally important. An entirely new bottle was created for the project, designed by Piero Lissoni, the internationally acclaimed architect and designer. His brief was to create a wine bottle that was not only aesthetically pleasing and in keeping with Masi's traditions but that can also be produced with a considerably lesser quantity of glass, thus reducing the energy required during manufacture, transport and movement. Indeed, the Masi bottle weighs 33 per cent less than most average wine bottles, yet it retains its strength and aesthetic appeal. The label is printed on recycled paper, and the bottle is closed with a natural cork and recyclable capsule.

Masi produce some of Italy's greatest and most complex wines, most notably its Amarones made from grapes that have undergone a period of *appassimento*. Such iconic wines, magnificent though they are, are not for the everyday. The Fresco di Masi wines are quite the opposite, fresh, vibrant and for a young, modern taste. If the aim has been to produce wines as if they have been made from grapes that have been squeezed in your bare hands then simply fermented and bottled, then the result is very successful. Fresco di Masi Bianco is just this sort of wine, bright, fresh, with bags of clean, deliciously juicy fruit—pears, white peaches, white flowers—and a totally clean and fresh finish. It is a wine for today. A wine for every day.

ITALY IN A WINEGLASS

El Masut, Terre di Ger, Pordenone, Veneto

As climate change brings both hotter and more unpredictable weather patterns to Italy's wine country, the risk posed by fungal maladies such as downy and powdery mildew is increasing and poses a real threat to viticulture. The 2023 vintage was a salient warning of things to come: excessive heat and humidity led to devastating outbreaks of downy mildew across the country, with some areas seeing a reduction in as much as 70 per cent of the expected crop. Winegrowers are therefore desperately looking to find solutions.

One such solution is to encourage the cultivation of hybrid grape varieties that have been bred to be resistant to these maladies. Indeed, since phylloxera first struck European vineyards at the end of the nineteenth century, winegrowers have experimented with crossing the European *Vitis vinifera* with species from North America and Asia. Organoleptically, however, the results were disappointing, with the resulting wines often having what was deemed to be a 'foxy' character that was unpleasant. Even still, in parts of Veneto, a nostalgic taste remains for wines made from grapes such as 'Clinton' and 'Fragola' (varieties that were considered illegal, only adding to their appeal).

Immense research, most notably in Germany and France, however, has led to the creation of a new breed of resistant varieties that can produce fine wines in their own right. PIWI is a collective name given to wines produced from such hybrid grape varieties with resistant properties. They allow for a significant reduction in the use of pesticides, and therefore wines can be made with a lower environmental impact. It is important to note that PIWI vines have not been created in the laboratory but in the nursery, without genetic engineering. They are the result of work that has been ongoing for years and decades by dedicated vine breeders.

Terre di Ger is one Italian vineyard already making a range of wines from resistant PIWI varieties. El Musat is an example, produced from Cabernet Eidos (Cabernet Sauvignon crossed with Bianca), Merlot Kanthus (Merlot crossed with Kozma 20–3) and Merlot Khorus (Merlot crossed with Kozma 20–3 in different proportion). All three of these PIWI varieties were developed in a vine nursery in the Pordenone province of Veneto. The result is a medium body red wine with ruby colour, red fruit and violet aromas, and soft tannins, to enjoy perhaps with grilled meats or with a platter of cheese, the pleasure that comes from drinking this wine enhanced by the knowledge that its cultivation and production has made a lower environmental impact and thus is helping to safeguard our planet. Is this the future of Italian wine? Climate change can most definitely not be ignored, so wines made from disease-resistant PIWI varieties may most certainly have an important part to play in future years to come.

'Piano di Montevergine', Taurasi Riserva DOCG, Feudi di San Gregorio, Sorbo Serpico, Campania

The initiative to send Italian wines into space demonstrates the importance of wine, its culture, history and tradition as human civilisation moves into the future.

There is a scientific rationale behind the project: to see how wines age in zero gravity as well as to ascertain whether vines can be grown in outer space. The Italian Space Agency's Analysis Laboratory will examine the bottles before the trip, while the same wines will be kept at the Italian Sommelier Foundation for comparison with the bottles after they return to earth.

Antonio Capaldo, president of Feudi di San Gregorio, one of three chosen wine estates who are working with the Italian Space Agency, commented:

Feudi di San Gregorio was born to introduce the beauty of Irpinia and its wines to distant lands, but I never thought they would travel this far. To see Aglianico selected from among the great Italian red grape varieties—and our Piano di Montevergine vineyard along with two extraordinary wines that have made the history of our country—is a source of great pride.

Taurasi Riserva 'Piano di Montevergine' is an extraordinary wine. In ancient times, the greatest wines were 'navigable'—powerful and stable enough to withstand voyages by sea and so able to be transported without spoilage to reach new markets. 'Piano di Montevergine' can clearly travel, too, even to outer space: it is concentrated, dark ruby in colour, with deep notes of black-berry, plum, mushrooms, woodland undergrowth, yet with a freshness that comes from a streak of acidity, with beautiful, well-balanced tannins.

The Taurasi wine zone in inland Campania is an area where vines were cultivated in the time of the Romans and possibly earlier. If in the past the Romans carried the grapevine with them to give the gift of wine to the lands they conquered as a mark of Roman civilisation, it seems entirely fitting that humankind may one day carry the grapevine, perhaps this ancient Aglianico grapevine, to give as the gift of wine, the mark of human civilisation, brought to who knows what faraway and brave new worlds?

Ribolla Gialla, Venezia Giulia IGT, Gravner, Oslavia, Friuli–Venezia Giulia

We end our wine journey where we began: with a wine made as wine was made some 5,000 or 6,000 years ago. Josko Gravner is considered one of the giants of the Italian wine world, a producer who had the vision and the courage to turn his back on all the advances that had been made to improve Italian wine over the past decades, and to see instead that the future for him really is rooted firmly in the past.

Ribolla Gialla is a native grape variety of Friuli–Venezia Giulia that has been grown in the vineyards of Collio for probably at least 1,000 years, where it thrives on the mineral-rich *ponca* terroir. Gravner's vineyards above Oslavia, cultivated with immense hand-care to biodynamic principles, yields fruit that is of exceptional quality, high in acidity, rich in minerality and concentrated in flavour. These grapes can reach their highest expression when they are allowed to be transformed as simply and naturally as possible. In 2000, Gravner was convinced that the best way to achieve this would be through fermentation in terracotta amphora. He thus eliminated all his stainless-steel fermentation vessels, the refrigeration equipment, filters and other winemaking tools, and instead installed the most basic: terracotta *qvevri* from Georgia, simply buried underground. It is in these vessels that since 2001 all the Gravner wines ferment.

Gravner produces Ribolla Gialla as simply and naturally as possible: the grapes are destemmed, lightly crushed and then transferred to the *qvevri* and left to ferment and to macerate on the skin slowly for upwards of seven or eight months, an exceptionally long period of time. This slow maceration on the skin extracts all the flavours and all the goodness out of the grapes. Afterwards, the wine is racked and blended with the press wine, then it ages for a further five months or so back in amphora before being transferred to large old oak barrels where the maturation continues for another six years. For Gravner, this extraordinarily lengthy sojourn in terracotta and old wood results in a wine of exceptional purity, as if one were returning directly to the source, to the very essence of the grape and the wine.

Our journey through the story of Italy and its wines has been a long and I hope enjoyable one. This truly legendary and iconic wine is a fitting one to finish on. Indeed, Gravner's Ribolla Gialla is exceptional, burnished amber in colour, with aromas of dried and candied fruit, resin, balsamic herbs, an intense scent and mouthfeel of beeswax, complex in texture, extraordinarily rich in flavours that continue to evolve and develop with each sip. It demonstrates the sheer beauty and magnificence of wine at its purest, its power to transport us across centuries and connect us with cultures and civilisations. This is not a wine to drink with joyous abandon: it is a wine to sip and savour, remembering the past—our own pasts—as we look to our futures.

GLOSSARY

amphora	In modern Italian winemaking, this does not usually refer to Roman-type amphorae that were used to transport wine and usually contained between 40 and 80 litres. Today, the term 'amphora' refers to an earthenware vessel in which primary fermentation and sometimes subsequent ageing takes place. In some cases, the vessels are large egg-shaped *qvevri* that come from Georgia, buried in the ground. In other cases, they may be smaller *orci* similar to vessels that have traditionally been used for storage of olive oil. The important feature is that the amphora is made of terracotta.
appassimento	The process of drying freshly harvested grapes either by laying bunches out on cane mats or hanging them vertically in airy attics or lofts for a period of months, or else, particularly in Southern Italy, laying out the grapes to dry to a semi-raisined state outdoors in direct sun for a period of ten to twenty days.
barrique	The French term is used to indicate an oak barrel containing 225 litres. Often the oak comes from France, and cellars will have a mix of new and used *barriques* to balance the amount of flavour, aroma and texture that they wish to have in the finished wine.
bâtonnage	A process of stirring lees either in the *barrique* or tank in order to increase the contact of the solid matter with the wine, thus imparting richness and complexity.
biodynamic	A system of organic farming based on the ideas and precepts of Rudolf Steiner that not only follows prescribed steps in the vineyard and the wine cellar but that also has ideals that are metaphysical and spiritual.

botte	A large traditional wooden barrel, often made from Slavonian oak.
cryomaceration	A process of chilling freshly harvested grapes to a very low temperature prior to pressing and the start of fermentation, carried out by some wineries to improve the extraction of colour, flavour, tannin.
DOC, DOCG, DOP	Italy's system of wine classification. DOC stands for *denominazione di origine controllata* and lays down requirements relating to a number of matters including permitted vineyard area, grape variety or varieties, yield per hectare, minimum alcohol, ageing requirements and more. DOCG adds an additional *garantita* with even stricter requirements. Such wines must furthermore undergo technical analysis as well as tasting. DOP complies with European Union quality regulations that are similar to DOC, and some producers are choosing to use this designation.
IGT, IGP	In theory, IGT—*indicazione geografica protetta*—and IGP—the EU equivalent—are lower tiers on the Italian wine quality pyramid. However, many producers choose these designations over DOC or DOCG even for their top wines because they allow more latitude and creativity.
in perpetuum	A term applied to the production of Marsala wine to note a system of dynamic ageing similar to the solera system in Spain's sherry zone. The finished wines are not the product of a single vintage or year but rather are a mix of older and younger through fractional blending whereby older barrels that have wine drawn out are then topped up with wines from the next oldest barrel, and so on.
lees, lees ageing	Lees are the sediment that is left in barrel or bottle after fermentation, consisting of the residue of dead yeast cells and other solid matter. Ageing on the lees in barrel or, in the case of traditional method sparkling wines, in the bottle, adds flavours, aromas and textures to result in more complex wines. In the case of barrel- and tank-aged wines, this can be enhanced by lees stirring or *bâtonnage*.
natural wine	The term has no official definition but has come to refer

to wines made as naturally as possible and without additives, taking care in the vineyard to eliminate the use of chemical fertilisers, pesticides and herbicides. Fermentation takes place using the natural indigenous yeast present on the grape's bloom. The goal is often to use no or minimal sulphites. Stabilisation is done naturally, sometimes by chilling and gravity. Such so-called 'natural' methods of winemaking are becoming increasingly mainstream.

oenology · The science and study of wine and winemaking.

orange 'Orange' wine is a term that has come to be used to indicate white wine fermented on the skin, a process that extracts varying degrees of colour, tannin, texture and aroma. It is normally used in reference to natural wines.

organic Organic viticulture is on the increase in Italy, linked to the move towards natural wines made with minimal use of chemicals and additives. To be officially organic, wines must be certified by an approved body. Many producers follow organic precepts but don't bother with certification.

passito Wine that is made from semi-dried grapes that have undergone *appassimento*.

phylloxera A vineyard pest (a type of aphid originally native to North America) that destroyed almost all the vineyards of Europe. The eventual solution was to graft European vines (*Vitis vinifera*) on to North American rootstock, a procedure that still must take place today. In some rare instances, pre-phylloxera vines are cultivated in soils or terrains where the insect could not survive, such as on the volcanic lava slopes of Mount Etna. Such ungrafted vines are often referred to as *piede franco*.

rimontaggio A process for making red wine whereby the fermenting must is pumped back over the grape skins and other solid matter that has risen to the top of the fermentation vessel. *Rimontaggio*, which is usually carried out once or twice a day during fermentation, serves to extract colour, tannin and other polyphenols more gently than other methods.

ripasso A method of wine production mainly from the Valpolicella whereby wine made from fresh grapes is 'repassed' over either semi-dried grapes or semi-dried grape pomace after the grapes have been fermented (to produce Amarone for example). This method maintains the bright and lighter character of the wine made from fresh grapes, combined with the raisiny richness and soft tannins that come from the semi-dried fruit.

Super Tuscan, super *vini da tavola*

Once an important term to indicate an exceptional wine made from grape varieties and/or methods of production that were outside the bounds and regulations for DOC and DOCG. The resulting wines, at first mainly from Tuscany, were therefore demoted to Italy's lowliest classification, *vino da tavola*. Yet such wines, often made from grape varieties such as Cabernet Sauvignon, Merlot or Sangiovese, aged in new French *barriques*, were some of the most exciting—and expensive—wines in the country. Today, that anomaly has mainly been rectified with such wines now entitled to bear IGT or IGP quality designations.

ACKNOWLEDGEMENTS

I began writing this book almost at the start of lockdown in the UK in March 2020, a strangely quiet and productive period of our lives. However, the gestation of this project began more than thirty years ago when Kim and I travelled to every single one of Italy's twenty regions while researching, writing and photographing *The Wine Roads of Italy*, which was published in 1991. Over the course of nearly two years, we lived in Italy and met so many people who shared their stories and who inevitably brought together links between today and the past—whether the ancient past or more recent happenings—revealing to me how intimately the story of Italy is linked to the story of its wines. Extensive research travels for *The Food Lover's Companion Italy* (1996) and *Oz Clarke's Wine Companion Tuscany* (1997) gave us further opportunities to meet and learn more about the story of Italy through its wines, foods and culture. Many of the wine producers we met over the course of these and other research trips feature in this book.

Writing a book is one thing; finding the right publisher is quite another. As an author, I have been fortunate for this book to have not just one brilliant agent but two. Philippa Sitters at David Godwin Associates, London, has believed in this project since I first brought it to her (it helps that she loves wine almost as much as I do!). Andrea Somberg of Harvey Klinger Inc. has been equally enthusiastic and supportive, offering wise advice in helping me to make important decisions on finding the best home for this book. I am deeply grateful to them both.

I am proud that this book is being published by two outstanding independent publishing houses, Hurst Publishers in the UK and Melville House in the United States. My grateful thanks to Michael Dwyer at Hurst for commissioning the book, and to Alice Clarke, with whom I have worked closely and who edited the manuscript, made suggestions and improvements. Carl Bromley at Melville House commissioned as well as personally edited the manuscript, for which I am deeply appreciative. In an Internet age when content can be published instantly at the click of a mouse, it seems sometimes

ACKNOWLEDGEMENTS

that traditional publishing skills such as copy-editing can be overlooked. I was fortunate to work with a brilliant copy-editor, Tim Page, who was meticulous, curious, careful and considerate. This book is much better because of his efforts and skills. I would also like to thank Hurst's and Melville House's respective design, production and marketing teams. I love both book covers, which are completely different and beautiful in their own ways. For the UK edition, Rob Pinney's illustration captures just the right feel of Italy past and present in the shade of a wine garden. I also love Melville House's composite image created by Art Director Beste Miray Doğan based on Kim Millon's wineglass photograph taken by the Rialto in Venice combined with a detail from a painting by Lorenzo Pecheux that depicts a cherub pouring wine into a young Bacchus's mouth.

I would like to thank the team at Martin Randall Travel (MRT) for giving me the opportunity to research, help develop and lead gastronomic cultural tours in Italy, a task I have been enjoyably undertaking since 2012. The six gastronomic cultural tours in Italy I helped to develop and have been leading over the past many years have given me vital opportunities to get to know in more depth many aspects of Italy, Italian culture, history and gastronomy. I have worked closely and enjoyably with Lizzie Watson for many years. Anna Cahill, Alberto Spairani and Charlotte Howlett-Jones are inspirational tour managers whom I have been privileged to work with. I have also greatly enjoyed co-hosting MRT tours with art historians Roberto Cobianchi and Tom-Leo True.

I would like to acknowledge a huge debt of gratitude to Stevie Kim and the Vinitaly International Academy. As managing director of Vinitaly International, Stevie has worked tirelessly to promote Italian wines around the world. To further this aim, she has created an educational programme that grants a highly respected professional qualification to those who pass the rigorous and dauntingly difficult exam to become a certified VIA Italian Wine Ambassador. Lecturers Sarah Heller MW and Henry Davar are keys to this learning process through their brilliant and up-to-date overviews of Italian wines in all their magnificent diversity, as well as through teaching the VIA method of wine tasting and evaluation through practical tutored tastings of hundreds of wines. We are privileged, too, that world-renowned Professor Attilio Scienza is VIA's chief scientist, lending his prodigious knowledge and expertise on vine genetics and more as well as his always trenchant and pressing thoughts on the future of viticulture in Italy, especially in the face of climate change. I am proud to be a VIA Italian Wine Ambassador and count many other IWAs as close personal friends—too many to name all, but you know who you are!

ACKNOWLEDGEMENTS

Stevie's mission to spread the gospel of Italian wine has resulted, further-more, in a range of communication and publishing ventures under the Mamma Jumbo Shrimp publishing and YouTube video imprint, as well as through the creation of the Italian Wine Podcast channel, which has grown to become one of the most popular wine podcasts in the world. I am proud to have my own weekly show on this channel, 'Wine, Food and Travel with Marc Millon', which has given me the opportunity to interview more than 130 wine producers, many of whom feature in this book. I would like to thank former producer Joy Livingstone, whom I worked closely with for two years, and also the fabulous current Italian Wine Podcast team, especially Lyka Caparas, Elena Voloshina and Geovanna Nuñez.

Wine has been a professional interest for more than forty years (since we wrote and photographed our first book *The Wine and Food of Europe*, published in 1982). But much more than that, it is a passion and a source of immense pleasure, especially when enjoyed around the table with family and friends. I have shared countless good and sometimes great bottles with Dr David Lynn, longstanding former editor of *The Kenyon Review*. In 1996, we travelled to Italy together to co-host a wine and literature tour that we organised for alumni of Kenyon College, our alma mater. My deep friendship with Michael Caines MBE, two-star Michelin chef and the creator of Lympstone Manor, was born out of our shared love of wine and food, not just consuming it but also talking about it over the past twenty-five years. Mention must be made of our dear mutual friend, Nello Ghezzo, whom we remember and honour in the annual Nello Century Cycle Challenge that we began in his name in 2000. Mario and Luisa Fontana of Cascina Fontana, award-winning wine producers in Barolo, are a close part of this story, too, and we remember these special friendships every time we open a bottle of their wonderful wines, which I try to do as often as possible. Other dear, much-missed friends who shared a love of wine with me over the past four decades are Geoff Bowen, founder of Pebblebed Vineyards, and our dear red-wine-loving friend Jilly Phillips. This book would not be what it is without the many rich con-versations with these and other much-loved friends over many glasses and bottles of wine shared across the last four decades.

As a patron of the Oxford Cultural Collective (OCC), I have taken groups of students to Italy on learning trips. OCC has also given me the opportunity to participate in numerous conferences, festivals and educational events where the importance of placing gastronomy—wine and food—within a cultural context has been fundamental to our aims. I thank Donald Sloan, the founder of OCC, for his vision and leadership, our deep friendship fuelled by fascinating and thoughtful conversations over many glasses of wine.

303

ACKNOWLEDGEMENTS

For the past twenty years or more, I have been studying Italian with Valentina Todino, who has also created the Italian Cultural Association in Exeter. Valentina has taught me much more than just the Italian language— she has given me insights into Italian culture, history, current events, cinema, literature, food and more. We have had some great evenings together, too, especially with fellow Italophiles Hester, Chris, Claire and Anna, and I look forward to more such evenings in the future.

I would like to thank Antonietta Kelly and Claudio Povero of the Italian Trade Agency in London who have given me numerous opportunities to attend wine tastings as well as help in support of travel to Italy to attend important events and occasions.

I would like to express deep gratitude to friends who perused or carefully read the finished manuscript, offered advice, corrections, encouragement: Dr David Lynn, Donald Sloan, Cynthia Chaplin IWA and Charlotte Howlett-Jones. Their input has been invaluable, and the book is infinitely better for their insights and astute observations. Any and all errors that remain are entirely my own.

My mother Lorina Kim had a deep love for Italy and Italian culture, and especially for Venice. Coming from Hawaii, she felt completely at home in that strange and unique watery city where she lived for many years. It was always very special to visit her frequently in Dorsoduro and of course to share wine and food, usually with Puccini on in the background, as loudly as possible. Mom was an inspiration, my biggest fan, and she was also an accomplished professional editor and writer who helped in the copy preparation of our early books. It was a tragedy when she died at far too young an age, and she is still deeply missed by me and my family, as well as by my sister Michele, brother David and his family.

During lockdown, we were incredibly fortunate that our son Guy and his partner Hannah were living next door to us, and our daughter Bella and her now husband Michael were able to move from London to live above them. We could thus enjoy something of a normal life during this far from normal period, so it was in many ways a very close and special period of our lives that we will always remember. Throughout this time, I was working diligently, sometimes obsessively, on this book, and I thank them all for their support, patience and love.

Extra special gratitude goes of course and as always to Kim, my beautiful, strong, patient and wholly supportive wife of more than forty-five years who is behind everything I have ever done and achieved. While Kim has been the photographer for most of our previous books, she is also a diligent editor and proof-reader. She furthermore kept me going with delicious meals and plentiful glasses of good Italian wines while I was madly working to meet my copy deadline. I could not have completed this book without her. It is very special for us both that we can now share this book with our first grandchild, Sol.

INDEX OF WINES BY REGION

INDEX OF WINES BY REGION

INDEX OF WINES BY REGION

DIRECTORY OF WINE PRODUCERS

Chapter 1

Azienda Agricola COS
www.cosvittoria.it
Azienda Agricola San Salvatore 19.88
www.sansalvatore1988.it
Azienda Agricola Sciara
www.sciaraetna.com
Cantine Vincenzo Ippolito
www.ippolito1845.it
Donnafugata
www.donnafugata.it

Chapter 2

Barberani
www.barberani.com
Marchesi Antinori SpA
www.antinori.it
Tenuta Decugnano dei Barbi
www.decugnanodeibarbi.com

Chapter 3

Roberto Lucarelli
www.roberto-lucarelli.com
Tenuta Whitaker
www.tascadalmerita.it

Chapter 4

Arrighi Vini
www.arrighivini.it
Cantine degli Astroni
www.cantineastroni.com

Mastroberardino SA
www.mastroberardino.com
Villa Matilde Avallone
www.villamatilde.it

Chapter 5

Casa Vinicola Garofoli
www.garofoli.it/en
Casale della Ioria
www.casaledellaioria.com
Masi Agricola
www.masi.it/en
Pomilia-Calamia Vini Srl
www.pomiliacalamiavini.it
Principe Pallavicini
www.principepallavicini.com

Chapter 6

Azienda Agricola Dorigo
www.dorigowines.com
Azienda Agricola Lamoretti
www.lamoretti.eu
Cantina Fratelli Pardi
www.cantinapardi.it

Chapter 7

Azienda Agricola Abbazia di Monte Oliveto Maggiore
www.agricolamonteoliveto.com
Badia a Coltibuono
www.coltibuono.com
Kloster Neustift/Abbazia di Novacella
www.kloster-neustift.it

Chapter 8

Azienda Agricola Giampaolo Tabarrini
www.tabarrini.com
Azienda Vinicola Rivera SpA
www.rivera.it

Chapter 9

Les Crêtes
www.lescretes.it/en

Famiglia Cotarella
www.famigliacotarella.it
Tenuta Caparzo
https://caparzo.it/index-eng.html

Chapter 10

Antica Corte Pallavicina
www.anticacortepallavicinarelais.com
Castello Pomino
www.frescobaldi.com

Chapter 11

Fattoria di Selvapiana
www.selvapiana.it
Montenidoli di Maria Elisabetta Fagiuoli
www.montenidoli.com
Tenute Guicciardini Strozzi
www.guicciardinistrozzi.it

Chapter 12

Serègo Alighieri
www.seregoalighieri.it

Chapter 13

Leonardo da Vinci SpA
www.leonardodavinci.it/en
Tenuta di Artimino
www.tenutadiartimino.com
Tenuta Capezzana
www.capezzana.it

Chapter 14

Azienda Agricola Carlo Hauner
www.hauner.it
Masi Agricola
www.masi.it/en
Venissa
www.venissa.it

Chapter 15

Azienda Agricola Giuseppe Sedilesu
www.giuseppesedilesu.com

Cantina Sociale Cooperativa della Vernaccia
www.vinovernaccia.com
Di Majo Norante
www.dimajonorante.com
Di Meo
www.dimeo.it/index_en.html

Chapter 16

Azienda Agricola Zidarich
www.zidarich.it
Livio Felluga
www.liviofelluga.it
Tiefenbrunner Srl
www.tiefenbrunner.com

Chapter 17

Barone Ricasoli SpA
www.ricasoli.com/en
Cantine Florio
www.duca.it/en/florio
Casa E. di Mirafiore
www.mirafiore.it/en
Castello e Enoteca Regionale Piemontese Cavour
www.castellogrinzane.com

Chapter 18

Casa Artusi Foundation
www.casartusi.it/en
Fattoria Zerbina
www.zerbina.com
Giovanna Madonia
www.giovannamadonia.it

Chapter 19

Cantina Cinque Terre
www.cantinacinqueterre.com/en
Cantina Tollo
www.cantinatollo.it
Cantine Settesoli
www.cantinesettesoli.it
Cave Mont Blanc de Morgex et La Salle
www.cavemontblanc.com

DIRECTORY OF WINE PRODUCERS

Kellerei Cantina Terlan
www.cantina-terlano.com/en

Chapter 20

Antica Azienda Agricola Leone De Castris
www.leonedecastris.com/en
Cantina Produttori Cormòns
www.cormons.com/en
Casa Vinicola D'Angelo
www.dangelowine.com/en
Cascina Fontana
www.cascinafontana.com
I Feudi di Romans
www.ifeudidiromans.it/en

Chapter 21

Cantine Bolla
www.gruppoitalianovini.it/index.cfm/en/brand/bolla
Cantine Riunite
www.riunite.it/en
Castelli del Grevepesa
www.castellidelgrevepesa.it/en
Fazi Battaglia
www.fazibattaglia.com/en
Fontana Candida
www.gruppoitalianovini.it/index.cfm/it/brand/fontana-candida

Chapter 22

Gaja
www.gaja.com
Guido Berlucchi & C. SpA
www.berlucchi.it/en
Marchese Antinori
www.antinori.it/en
Tenuta San Guido
www.tenutasanguido.com

Chapter 23

Azienda Biologico Bosco Falconeria
www.boscofalconeria.it
Cooperative Libera Terra
www.liberaterra.it
www.centopassisicilia.it

DIRECTORY OF WINE PRODUCERS

Frescobaldi
www.frescobaldi.com
Terre di Puglia—Libera Terra
www.hisotelaray.com

Chapter 24

Azienda Agricola Elena Fucci
www.elenafuccivini.com
Cantine Lungarotti
www.lungarotti.it
Cantine Politi
www.cantinepoliti.it
Casato Prime Donne
www.cinellicolombini.it/en/wineries-and-wines/casato-prime-donne/
Tenuta Cocci Grifoni
www.tenutacoccigrifoni.it

Chapter 25

Azienda Agricola Gravner
www.gravner.it
Feudi di San Gregorio
www.feudi.it
Masi Agricola
www.masi.it/en
Terre di Ger
www.terrediger.it
I Vigneri di Salvo Foti
www.ivigneri.it

BIBLIOGRAPHY

Alighieri, Dante (trans. Robert Pinsky), *The Inferno*, London: J. M. Dent, 1996.

Anderson, Burton, *Vino*, London: Macmillan, 1982.

Artusi, Pellegrino (trans. Murtha Baca and Stephen Sartarelli), *Science in the Kitchen and the Art of Eating Well*, Toronto: University of Toronto Press, 2003.

Atlee, Helena, *The Land Where Lemons Grow*, London: Penguin Books, 2015.

Barzini, Luigi, *The Italians*, London: Penguin Books, 1968.

Beard, Mary, *Pompeii*, London: Profile Books, 2010.

———— *SPQR*, London: Profile Books, 2015.

Beccalli, Bianca, *The Modern Women's Movement in Italy*, https://newleftreview.org/issues/i204/articles/1756

Biggers, Jeff, *In Sardinia: An Unexpected Journey in Italy*, New York: Melville House, 2023.

Black, Jeremy, *A Brief History of Italy*, London: Robinson, 2018.

Boardman, John, Jasper Griffin and Oswyn Murray (eds), *The Oxford History of the Classical World*, Oxford: Oxford University Press, 1986.

Boccaccio, Giovanni (trans. G. H. McWilliam), *The Decameron*, London: Penguin Books, 1995.

Booms, Dirk and Peter Higgs, *Sicily: Culture and Conquest*, London: British Museum Press, 2016.

Boscaini, Sandro, *Amarone and Beyond*, Milan: Bocconi University Press, 2022.

Bozzarelli, Elisa and Alice Daneluzzo (dirs), *Melmaridè*, 2018.

Breccola, Giancarlo, *Montefiascone e il suo vino*, Montefiascone: Comune di Montefiascone Assessorato al Turismo, 2009.

Brown, Dale (ed.), *Etruscans: Italy's Lovers of Life*, Alexandria, VA: Time-Life Books, 1995.

Capalbo, Carla, *The Food and Wine Guide to Naples and Campania*, London: Pallas Athene, 2005.

———— *Collio, Fine Wines and Foods from Italy's North-east*, London: Pallas Athene, 2009.

Caparas, Lyka, Jacopo Fanciulli, Rebecca Lawrence and Lan Liu, *Jumbo Shrimp Guide to Italian Wine*, Verona: Positive Press, 2020.

Cernilli, Daniele, *The Essential Guide to Italian Wine 2022*, Rome: DoctorWine, 2021.

Cevola, Alfonso, 'On the Wine Trail in Italy', https://acevola.blogspot.com/

Charters, Steve (ed.), *Wine and Society*, Oxford: Butterworth-Heinemann, 2006.

BIBLIOGRAPHY

Cibarium of Friuli Venezia Giulia, Udine: Agenzia Regionale per lo Sviluppo Rurale, 2015.

Clarke, Oz, *Oz Clarke on Wine—your global wine companion*, London: Academie du Vin Library, 2021.

Clemente, Pietro, *Enigmatica mezzadria: Una testimonianza*, Ancona: Università Politecnica delle Marche, 2013.

Da Mosto, Francesco, *Francesco's Venice*, London: BBC Books, 2004.

De Sica, Vittorio (dir.), *L'oro di Napoli*, 1954.

Dickie, John, *Cosa Nostra*, London: Hodder Headline, 2007.

———— *Delizia!*, New York: Free Press, 2008.

Diritti, Giorgio (dir.), *L'uomo che verrà*, 2009.

Edwards, John (ed. and trans.), *The Roman Cookery of Apicius*, London: Random Century, 1984.

Eskins, Julia, 'Ancient Wines Are Having a Moment in Italy: Here's Why', *National Geographic*, 7 July 2021, www.nationalgeographic.co.uk/history-and-civilisation/2021/07/ancient-wines-are-having-a-moment-in-italy-heres-why

Euripides (trans. James Morwood), *Bacchae and Other Plays*, Oxford: Oxford University Press, 2008.

Fanciulli, Jacopo, Rebecca Lawrence and Attilio Scienza, *Jumbo Shrimp Guide to International Grape Varieties in Italy*, Verona: Positive Press, 2021.

Farrell, Joseph, *Sicily: A Cultural History*, Oxford: Signal Books, 2012.

Ficari, Quinto, 'La leggenda di Montefiascone', dissertation, 2015, www.academia.edu/38588458/LA_LEGGENDA_DI_MONTEFIASCONE_EST_EST_EST

Filiputti, Walter (ed.), *The Modern History of Italian Wine*, Milan: Skira, 2016.

Freedman, Paul (ed.), *Food: The History of Taste*, London: Thames & Hudson, 2007.

Gennai, Paolo, *Carmignano, il vino dei Medici e dei Lorena*, San Miniato: Editori dell'Acero, 2018.

Gilmour, David, *The Pursuit of Italy: A History of a Land, Its Regions and Their Peoples*, London: Penguin Books, 2012.

Giordano, Marco Tullio (dir.), *Centopassi*, 2000.

Gordon, Susan H., 'What You Should Know about Italy's Cooperative Wines', *Forbes*, 19 December 2018, www.forbes.com/sites/susangordon/2018/12/19/what-you-should-know-about-italys-cooperative-wines

Griffith, Brian, '"Chi ne beve giusto è un leone": anti-alcoolismo, vitivinicoltura, e la realizzazione di una bevanda nazionale nell'Italia fascista', *La vigna news* 9, no. 35 (2016).

Hales, Dianne, *La bella lingua*, New York: Broadway Books, 2009.

Harris, Robert, *Pompeii, a Novel*, London: Hutchinson, 2003.

Hesiod (trans. Evelyn White), *Homeric Hymns, Epic Cycle, Homerica*, H. G. Loeb Classical Library 57, London: William Heinemann, 1914.

Hibbert, Christopher, *The Rise and Fall of the House of Medici*, London: Penguin Books, 1979.

BIBLIOGRAPHY

Holmes, George, *The Oxford Illustrated History of Italy*, Oxford: Oxford University Press, 1997.

Homer (trans. E.V. Rieu), *The Odyssey*, London: Penguin Books, 1946.

Hooper, John, *The Italians*, London: Allen Lane, 2015.

Hough, Richard (ed.), *Wine Democracy*, Verona: Mamma Jumbo Shrimp, 2022.

Inno, Elisa Flaminia (dir.), *I Pagani*, 2016.

Johnson, Hugh, *The Story of Wine*, London: Mandarin, 1991.

The Life and Wines of Hugh Johnson, London: Academie du Vin Library, 2022.

Kim, Stevie (ed.), *Italian Wine Unplugged 2.0*, Verona: Mamma Jumbo Shrimp, 2023.

Kurlansky, Mark, *Salt, a World History*, London: Jonathan Cape, 2002.

Lawrence, D. H., *Etruscan Places*, London: Tauris Parke Paperbacks, 2011.

Levi, Carlo (trans. Frances Frenaye), *Christ Stopped at Eboli*, Harmondsworth: Penguin Books, 1982.

———— *Cristo si è fermato a Eboli*, Turin: Einaudi editore, 1990.

Lintner, Valerio, *A Traveller's History of Italy*, Moreton-in-Marsh: Windrush Press, 1989.

Lonzi, Carla, *Manifesto di Rivolta Femminile*, Milan: Rivolta Femminile, 1970.

Mack Smith, Dennis, *Cavour*, London: Weidenfeld & Nicolson, 1985.

Malagreca, Miguel, 'Lottiamo Ancora: Reviewing One Hundred and Fifty Years of Italian Feminism', *Journal of International Women's Studies* 7, no. 4 (May 2006).

Marinetti, Filippo Tommaso (trans. Suzanne Brill), *The Futurist Cookbook*, London: Penguin Classics, 2014.

McGovern, Patrick E., *Ancient Wine*, Princeton: Princeton University Press, 2003.

———— *Uncorking the Past*, Berkeley: University of California Press, 2009.

Millon, Marc, *Oz Clarke's Wine Companion Tuscany*, London: Websters International Publishers, 1997.

———— *Wine, a Global History*, London: Reaktion Books, 2013.

———— 'Wine, Food and Travel with Marc Millon', Weekly podcast on Italian Wine Podcast Channel.

Millon, Marc and Kim Millon, *The Wine & Food of Europe*, Exeter: Webb & Bower, 1982.

———— *The Wine Roads of Europe*, London: Robert Nicholson, 1983.

———— *The Wine Roads of Italy*, London: HarperCollins, 1991.

———— *The Food Lover's Companion to Italy*, London: Little, Brown & Co., 1996.

Morris, James, *Venice*, London: Faber & Faber, 1978.

Morris, Jan, *Trieste and the Meaning of Nowhere*, London: Faber & Faber, 2001.

Norwich, John Julius, *A History of Venice*, London: Penguin Books, 2003.

———— *Sicily: A Short History, from the Greeks to Cosa Nostra*, London: John Murray, 2015.

Parzen, Jeremy, 'Do Bianchi', https://dobianchi.com

Paul the Deacon (trans. William Dudley Foulke), *History of the Langobards*, Kindle edn, Logia, 2012 [Department of History, University of Pennsylvania, Philadelphia, 1907].

Pavese, Cesare (trans. R. W. Flint), *The Selected Works of Cesare Pavese*, New York: New York Review of Books, 1996.

BIBLIOGRAPHY

Piccini, Gabriella, *L'Italia contadina, in Il Medioevo. Dalla dipendenza personale al lavoro contratatto, a cura di Franco Franceschi (Storia del lavoro in Italia, a cura di Fabio Fabbri, vol. II)*, Rome: Castelvecchi, 2017.

Plato (trans. Christopher Gill and Desmond Lee), *The Symposium*, London: Penguin Books, 1999.

Pliny the Elder (trans. John Healey), *Natural History*, London: Penguin Books, 1991.

Raju, Alison, *The Via Francigena: Canterbury to Rome*, part 2, *The Great St Bernard Pass to Rome*, Kendal: Cicerone, 2014.

Riall, Lucy, *The Italian Risorgimento*, London: Routledge, 1994.

Riley, Gillian, *The Oxford Companion to Italian Food*, Oxford: Oxford University Press, 2007.

La riscoperta del Pecorino: Storia di un vitigno e di un vino, Milan: Techniche Nuove, 2009.

Robb, Peter, *Midnight in Sicily: On Art, Food, History, Travel & La Cosa Nostra*, London: Harvill Press, 1999.

Roberts, Paul, *Last Supper in Pompeii*, Oxford: Ashmolean Museum, University of Oxford Press, 2019.

Robinson, Jancis (ed.), *Vines, Grapes & Wines*, London: Mitchell Beazley, 1986.

———— *The Oxford Companion to Wine*, 3rd edn, Oxford: Oxford University Press, 2006.

Rohrwacher, Alice (dir.), *Lazzaro Felice*, 2018.

Rosi, Gianfranco (dir.), *Fuocoammare*, 2016.

Rosselini, Roberto (dir.), *Roma città aperta*, 1945.

Sabellico, Marco, Gianni Fabrizio and Giuseppe Carrus (eds), *I vini d'Italia 2023*, Rome: Gambero Rosso, 2022.

Sarda, Pietro, *Il discorso del Vino*, Milan: Associazione Cultural 'Zero in Condotta', 2013.

Sciascia, Leonardo (trans. Avril Bardoni), *The Wine-Dark Sea*, London: Granta Books, 2001.

Scienza, Attilio, *Vine and Prejudice: Fake Science and the Search for the Perfect Grape*, Verona: Mamma Jumbo Shrimp, 2022.

Scienza, Attilio and Serena Imazio, *Sangiovese, Lambrusco and Other Vine Stories*, Verona: Positive Press, 2019.

Simeti, Mary Taylor, *On Persephone's Island: A Sicilian Journal*, New York: Alfred A. Knopf, 1986.

Simeti, Mary Taylor and Maria Grammatico, *Bitter Almonds: Reflections and Recipes from a Sicilian Girlhood*, New York: William Morrow and Company, 1994.

Spivey, Nigel, *The Ancient Olympics*, Oxford: Oxford University Press, 2004.

Suchet, John, *Verdi: The Man Revealed*, London: Elliott and Thompson, 2017.

Tanasi, Davide, 'Prehistoric Wine Discovered in Inaccessible Caves Forces a Rethink of Ancient Sicilian Culture', The Conversation, 13 February 2018, https://theconversation.com/prehistoric-wine-discovered-in-inaccessible-caves-forces-a-rethink-of-ancient-sicilian-culture-89116

Tereshtenko, Valery J., 'The Cooperative Movement in Italy', reprinted from the *Rochdale Cooperator* 13, nos. 8–9 (August–September 1944).

BIBLIOGRAPHY

Tomasi di Lampedusa, Giuseppe (trans. Archibald Colquhoun), *The Leopard*, London: Harvill Secker 2010.

Travis, John, 'Uncorking the Grape Genome', *Science* 320 (25 April 2008).

Ungaretti, Giuseppe, *Vita d'un uomo: 106 poesie 1914–1960*, Milan: Arnoldo Mondadori, 1966.

Van Cleve, Thomas Curtis, *The Emperor Frederick II of Hohenstaufen*, Oxford: Oxford University Press, 1972.

Varriano, John, *Wine: A Cultural History*, London: Reaktion Books, 2010.

Ventrella, Francesco and Giovanna Zapperi, *Feminism and Art in Postwar Italy: The Legacy of Carla Lonzi*, London: Bloomsbury, 2021.

'Via Francigena: The Road to Rome', www.viefrancigene.org/en

Wennerholm, Josephine, Frascati Cooking That's Amore, https://frascaticookingthatsamore.wordpress.com/

Younger, William, *Gods, Men, and Wine*, London: Wine and Food Society, 1966.

INDEX

INDEX

INDEX

INDEX

INDEX